# SQL SERVER 7

## Data Warehousing

# SQL SERVER 7

## Data Warehousing

MICHAEL **COREY**,
MICHAEL **ABBEY**,
IAN **ABRAMSON**,
LARRY **BARNES**,
BENJAMIN **TAUB**,
AND RAJAN **VENKITACHALAM**

Osborne/**McGraw-Hill**

Berkeley   New York   St. Louis   San Francisco
Auckland   Bogotá   Hamburg   London   Madrid
Mexico City   Milan   Montreal   New Delhi   Panama City
Paris   São Paulo   Singapore   Sydney
Tokyo   Toronto

Osborne/**McGraw-Hill**
2600 Tenth Street
Berkeley, California 94710
U.S.A.

For information on translations or book distributors outside the U.S.A., or to arrange bulk purchase discounts for sales promotions, premiums, or fund-raisers, please contact Osborne/**McGraw-Hill** at the above address.

**SQL Server 7 Data Warehousing**

1234567890 AGM AGM 90198765432109

ISBN 0-07-211921-7

**Publisher**
  Brandon A. Nordin
**Editor-in-Chief**
  Scott Rogers
**Contributing Authors**
  Evan Ross
  Jeremy Fitzgerald
**Acquisitions Editor**
  Wendy Rinaldi
**Project Editor**
  Cynthia Douglas
**Editorial Assistant**
  Debbie Escobedo
**Copy Editor**
  Dennis Weaver

**Proofreader**
  Stefany Otis
**Indexer**
  Rebecca Plunkett
**Computer Designer**
  Jani Beckwith
  Ann Sellers
**Illustrator**
  Brian Wells
  Beth Young
**Series Design**
  Peter Hancik

Microsoft is a registered trademark of Microsoft Corporation. SQL Server is a trademark of Microsoft Corporation.

This book is dedicated
to the information technology professionals
who live and breathe relational and decision support databases.
We love them; we hate them;
can't live with them; can't live without them!

# ABOUT THE AUTHORS...

Michael Corey is the Chief Operating Officer of Database Technologies, Inc., a wholly owned subsidiary of PKS Systems Integration, LLC. Database Technologies, Inc., based in Wellesley, Mass, in the United States, is one of the first and most experienced relational database, data warehousing, and Internet solutions providers. Database Technologies is also a Microsoft Solutions Partner. A technical and business expert on deploying relational database and data warehousing solutions, Mike can easily be reached at mcorey@dbtinc.com.

Michael Abbey lives and works in the Ottawa, Ontario area, having worked exclusively in the relational database technology arena for the past 12 years. He presents at technical conferences in Canada, the USA, and Europe, and can be reached via email at masint@istar.ca..

Ian Abramson is the President of IAS, Inc. based in Toronto, Ontario. His expertise with databases has been gathered over a 12-year period in Canada, the United States, and England. He has co-authored two other books about databases and data warehousing. Ian specializes in data warehousing, system development, and database administration. He is also a regular presenter at conferences on databases and data warehousing. He can be reached by email at ias@magi.com.

Larry Barnes is an Architectural Engineer for the Microsoft New England District. Larry has more than 20 years of experience in the industry, with a focus on client/server database development and data warehousing. Larry was a founding member of the ODBC standards committee, has presented at Tech-Ed, and is a Microsoft Certified Systems Engineer, Solutions Developer, and Trainer. Larry is one half of the "Bob and Larry Development Series," a popular seminar series that focuses on building scalable Web applications.

Benjamin Taub is the founder and CEO of Dataspace, Incorporated, one of the Midwest's largest data warehouse consultancies (offices located in Ann Arbor, Chicago, and Kansas City—www.dspace.com). He has served as the data warehousing focus area manager for the International Oracle User Group-Americas (IOUG-A) conference committee. He is also a co-author of Oracle8 Data Warehousing, published by McGraw-Hill as part of their Oracle Press series. During his career, Mr. Taub has held information technology positions with both Andersen Consulting and MicroStrategy, Incorporated.  Mr. Taub, a certified public accountant (CPA), holds a Bachelor of Science degree from Lehigh University and a Master of Business Administration degree from the University of Michigan. He can be reached via email at btaub@dspace.com.

Rajan Venkitachalam is a Director at Database Technologies, Inc. a wholly owned subsidiary of PKS Systems Integration, LLC. Database Technologies, Inc. based in Wellesley, Massachusetts, is one of the first and most experienced relational database, data warehousing and Internet solutions providers. Rajan currently resides in Acton, Massachusetts and can easily be reached at rajanv@dbtinc.com.

# AT A GLANCE

# CONTENTS

# FOREWORD

was delighted when Michael Corey contacted me about his intent to team up with his longtime partner, Michael Abbey, on this SQL Server data warehousing book. I was delighted for two reasons. First, Michael and Michael are two of the pre-eminent authors in the industry and have teamed up together on six previous database publications. They both have a great understanding of databases and data warehousing and can communicate these concepts with great clarity and depth.

Second, this is their first book on SQL Server, which indicates that with SQL Server 7's Fall Comdex 1998 release, the pre-eminent authors of databases now consider SQL Server an enterprise database. Augment Michael and Michael's vast experience with Larry Barnes, a 20-year veteran of the database industry and a well-respected SQL Server authority within Microsoft, and what you get is a publication for which I am proud to write the foreword.

This release of SQL Server 7 is a defining moment for the industry, for Microsoft, and for me personally. At a personal level, I have been working for more than four years to make SQL Server 7 a reality. SQL Server 7 holds special significance for me because I've been personally associated with the SQL Server product since SQL Server Version 1.1, running on OS/2. The product has made great strides over the years. SQL Server has set the standard for ease of use and management in relational database technology, and we've scaled SQL Server to levels where we can now support thousands of users and Terabyte-sized databases. The Microsoft Terraserver web site, http://www.terraserver.com is a great example of this.

This is also a defining moment for Microsoft. The SQL Server 7 release is really the culmination of the combined effort of many of the best database minds in the industry. About five years ago, Microsoft recognized that in order to truly become an enterprise database player, it needed to build a solid foundation moving forward into the 21$^{st}$ century. This solid foundation starts with a great team. Microsoft recruited some of the best minds in the industry: Jim Gray, one of the visionaries behind scalable transactional processing systems, whose resume includes IBM DB2, Tandem and Digital's Rdb; Goetz Graffe, one of the pre-eminent figures in query processors for the last 25+ years; Hal Berenson and Peter Spiro, 20+ year veterans of the industry who were, respectively, the team leader and architect for Digital's Rdb database; Casey Kiernan, a veteran of Ingres, and the architect for SQL Server management tools; Bill Baker, a 20+ year veteran of the OLAP industry, and former principal of IRI Software; and Amir Netz, the development lead for MS OLAP Services. The list goes on.

This team has been focused on one objective during the last five years: SQL Server 7. One of the prime focuses of SQL Server 7 was data warehousing. SQL Server 7 provides an integrated solution that not only includes a great easy-to-use, scalable relational database with a state-of-the-art fully parallel query processor, but also a state-of-the-art OLAP server for multi-dimensional analysis, data transformation services, a powerful and flexible extraction and load tool, a repository that drives the design and management of the warehouse, profiler and index analysis tools for capturing and replaying workloads, and—optimizing performance—a natural language query interface. All of this technology is available to customers in a single, integrated product.

Finally, SQL Server 7 will have a profound impact on the industry as a whole and data warehouse industry in particular. SQL Server 7's breadth of features, ease of use, and low cost of ownership signal a shift in the market. The business benefits of data warehousing and Online Analytical Processing (OLAP) , which have traditionally been restricted to a select club of companies who could afford it, are now available to a broad range of businesses.

Integral to the success of any effort—data warehouses included—is the availability of resources and guides that describe how to successfully deploy solutions, ideally with specific information on your intended deployment platform. You not only need information about a specific product, you also need information about the successful process and team required to make a data warehouse project a success. You need this information from people who have been in the trenches, who have implemented successful data warehouses, and who can speak from experience, not theory. This book provides you with the best of both worlds.

So sit back, enjoy this book from cover to cover and as a reference guide, and let your data warehouse help you understand where you been, where you are, but most importantly, where you want to go.

Doug Leland
Group Product Manager
SQL Server Marketing
Microsoft Corporation

# ACKNOWLEDGMENTS

Well, this is now my seventh book. As I look back at what it took to make this a reality, I realize I have a lot of people to thank. First and foremost, my family. It is they who suffer most throughout this effort. I want to thank my wife Julie, and my children John, Annmarie and Michael for their continued love, understanding and support during the writing of this book. To my good friend and co-author of seven books, thank you Michael Abbey for always being there. The biggest gift these many books have given me is your friendship. To Ian Abramson, what can I say but YATFG. Thank you for your friendship and support in the writing of this book and the many others. I don't know how we ever wrote a book til you came along. To Larry "Mr. Microsoft" Barnes, the newest member of the team: Thank you for all your behind-the-scenes efforts, like getting us the latest versions of SQL Server to work with. You constantly impressed me with your deep knowledge of the SQL Server database. To my other co-authors Rajan, Evan, Jeremy, Ben: Thanks for all your efforts. We could not have done it without you. To Stev Shelgrin from the Boston office of Microsoft: You are a class act; I can never begin to say thanks enough for all your efforts. To Doug Leland, Steve Murchie, Thomas Gruver, Jim Ewel: Thank you very much for all your behind-the-scenes efforts to make this book possible. We needed your help, and you were all there. To Scott Rogers and Wendy Rinaldi at Osborne/McGraw-Hill, thank you for all your efforts. I know working with a team of authors like us can stretch one's patience at times. To the many people I don't have room to mention: Hey, thanks.

Michael J. Corey

I would like to thank Mike Corey, Ian Abramson, Ben Taub, Larry Barnes, Evan Ross, Rajan Venkitachalam, and Jeremy Fitzgerald for the work they have done to bring this book to completion. Thanks as well to the gang at Osborne—especially Scott, Wendy, Mark, Cynthia, and Dennis. Yossi Amor has been a big help in my whole IT career, especially with his knowledge of SQL Server.

Michael Abbey

I would like to thank my father, Joe. He has always encouraged me to achieve my fullest potential. So, Dad, how am I doing? To Susan, Baila, and Jillian, you are my inspiration and my anchor. To Michael Abbey, thanks for getting me into this gig, YATFG. Evan Ross, it was a pleasure to write with someone as good as you. Mike Corey, you are a big man with a bigger heart. Thanks. To the rest of the team: Ben, Larry, Rajan, and Jeremy Fitzgerald, thanks for getting this great book together. This was one team I am proud to say I have played for.

Ian Abramson

I would like to thank Stev Shelgren, Rick Green, Mike Kosek, and Dianne Gregg for supporting me in this effort, and my seminar partner, Bob Familiar, an extraordinarily creative individual. Most importantly, I want to thank my wife, Linda, for tolerating my all-consuming obsession with the computer industry.

Larry Barnes

I would like to acknowledge the support I received from everyone at Dataspace Incorporated, the most talented group of data warehousing professionals I've ever worked with. In addition, the support of David Gregory has been invaluable during this process. Also, I'd like to thank all my co-authors, new and old, for yet another opportunity to work with them—thanks, guys, it's always fun!

Benjamin Taub

I would like to thank my wife, Ritika, and son, Daniel, for their patience and sacrifice. Many thanks also to the rest of my family. I would never have had this opportunity to write were it not for Mike C. I would also like to recognize my cohorts in this effort, Michael A., Ian, Ben, Larry, Evan, and Jeremy, without whom this book would not be a reality.

Rajan Venkitachalam

# INTRODUCTION

To say there is an explosion in decision support solutions may be an understatement. What with the daily advances in technology, this phenomenon is perhaps closer to a reality than ever before. A database theory book we ran across in college claimed that if there had been as many advances in the automobile industry in the last 20 years as there have been in the computer business, one would now be able to buy a Rolls Royce that would last 25 years for 10 quid!

Data warehousing, you say! A new kid on the block? Perhaps… we think the term is simply a different way of saying something we have all been doing for many, many years—using a hodge-podge of data derived from a number of sources to make decisions. Remember Lotus 1-2-3 in the early days of the micro-computer (or perhaps the T-Rex of PCs—8088 with the whopping clock speed of 7 Mhz!)? We would gleefully proceed to cell C84 and change the number of its contents from 32000 to 40000 and then watch the ripple through the spreadsheet as we moved the cursor to an adjacent cell. We have just asked the question "How would a 25% change in inventory of ski wax affect the bottom line of specialty ski equipment sales?" We would then toddle off to cell B68, and see the number therein magically changed from 23.6% to 23.9%. Isn't that special!

Decision support and Microsoft—it's an obvious relationship. Take the biggest software giant on the globe and marry it to an exploding software requirement.

*SQL Server 7 Data Warehousing* is two—yes two, yes two—books in one. We first look at the phenomenon called data warehousing. There are so many new things to consider when planning the deployment of decision support solutions—the team players, the scope, the stakeholders, the analysis tools, the database—it would be easy to let these quandaries derail even the most ambitious projects. Once armed with this knowledge, we then show you how Microsoft's landmark database release, SQL Server 7, provides you with a complete integrated data warehouse solution at an affordable price. This winning combination—full functionality at a low price—is changing the data warehouse landscape as we now know it.

This journey into SQL Server 7 will prove to be quite enlightening. The '90s and soon-to-be '00s (odd way to look at it, but heh, we're stuck on these two digits, and we can't get rid of them) are upon us, and have been for years. So much of the theory we discuss in this book is generic, off-the-shelf advice to follow regardless of the back end (database of choice), migration and transformation tools, and the front end (analysis tools) chosen. We liken an out-of-control data warehouse project to a flash flood. One minute it's business as usual; life is good; things are moving along at a manageable pace. Then—poof—everything takes off at the same time. The work is overwhelming; deadlines are looming on the horizon; the scope of the project has crept so fast and furiously that delivery dates are missed. *SQL Server 7 Data Warehousing* will help stem the flow of those tendencies, and guide you through the design, management, and set-up of the decision support venue à la Microsoft. You will enjoy this adventure….

# CHAPTER 1

## Warehouse: What Is It, Who Needs It, and Why?

In the Beatles' film, *Yellow Submarine*, Jeremy kept complaining "So little time, so much to know." Our version of that adage is "So many acronyms, so much to know." Acronyms, acronyms—was it DSS, EIS, OLAP, or ODBC? The list could, and does, go on for pages. For many years, the computer industry has been enamored with acronyms and new terminology. In fact, the term *data warehouse* is just another iteration of a concept that has been around for years. Remember using Lotus 1-2-3? This was your first taste of "what if?" processing on the desktop. This is what a data warehouse is all about—using information your business has gathered to help it react better, smarter, quicker, and more efficiently.

Contrary to popular belief, most companies are not building data warehouses simply to test the patience of their technical staff. Data warehouses are, instead, key components of well-reasoned decision support architectures. This chapter will help you understand what users require from a decision support system and why a data warehouse is often necessary to satisfy these demands. We'll answer the following questions:

▼ What is decision support?

■ What are the business and technical goals of decision support?

■ What is data warehousing?

■ What are the business drivers of data warehousing?

▲ What are the technical drivers of data warehousing?

# A PARTICULARLY BAD DAY

Well, you've finally made it—chief information officer (CIO). Who would have thought when you started 18 years ago as an accountant-turned-COBOL-programmer that you would be sitting in such a key spot? Who would have thought that your organization would someday put you in such a strategic role? Who would have thought that all your jokes about CIOs spending their days at expensive vendor junkets or on the golf course were close to the mark? Who knew?

So, flush with the knowledge that you shot a 76 yesterday (and will likely shoot a 74 today), you check the value of your new stock options on the Internet. Suddenly, pandemonium breaks loose. You hear the angry voices outside your office. "Hey," you think, "that sounds like John Valjon, our vice president of sales and Norman Richelieu, our chief financial officer." You listen closely to the near screaming. "I don't care if he's busy, I'm seeing him NOW! Henchard just chewed us out and I want some answers!"

You think, "Now Richelieu is a bit uppity, but, I've never heard Valjon so agitated. I wonder what's up?" In storm the two gentlemen, flushed with anger, beads of sweat gathering on their foreheads.

Richelieu starts, "We spent $27 million on computers last year alone. Why is it that when John and I go into a meeting with the big man, our reports don't even match? How can it be that John thinks he sold 45,000 units in October while my reports show 42,500? How could your people possibly get such a simple thing wrong?"

John continues, "And that's just a touch of the problems I'm having with you folks. Last week I had a meeting with Ed Kramden, the purchasing chief at FutureChef Industries. I'm sure I don't have to remind you that on our list of top ten target accounts, FutureChef ranks third. I know they're having a problem with late deliveries from their current vendor. It would have been great to show up at the meeting with a report showing our delivery record to each of the cities where they have facilities. You know our logistics department is among the best and this report could be critical to winning the account.

"Anyway, the appointment was scheduled for 3:00 P.M. I called your guys at 8:00 A.M. and requested the report. Do you know what they told me? Since my request was obviously important, they would push it to the 'top of their stack.' It would only take four days to write the programs and deliver the report. Four days! What good is that? I can't imagine how long it takes a non-VP to get a critical report.

"Beyond that, we have two sales systems—one for wholesale sales and the other for retail sales. Sometimes I am interested in looking at just wholesale accounts or retail accounts. But, believe it or not, there are times when I need information about sales of particular products, regardless of where they occurred. It wastes my time and the company's money for me to have to go to two different systems, find the related figures, and plug them into a spreadsheet to figure out what the sales of product X were."

Then, it was Richelieu's turn again. "And another thing. How the heck (Richelieu has always been fond of saying, 'How the heck') can I possibly forecast our cash needs when our general ledger system keeps only six months of history online? With the seasonality in our industry, even two years wouldn't be enough.

"And hey, I'm a finance guy. I live in spreadsheets. If I can't sort it, summarize it, or chart it, I'm cranky. So, why is it that you can only give me data in paper reports? My salary costs the company over 200K per year. I'm spending half my time typing numbers from your paper reports into my spreadsheet. Does this make sense? Frankly, I'm getting a bit tired of this."

You start thinking, "200K—my deal is good but it's not that strong. Mental note: renegotiate employment contract."

"Well guys," you say, "let me chew on this for a while. I'll get back to you in a few days after I've figured it all out." The truth is, you're scared. After all, how secure is a CIO's job? You're the fourth that your company has had in the past six years. You never really asked why the others were 'shown the door.' Could it have been related to these same problems? Have there always been reporting problems here? How wise was it to take out a $450,000 mortgage last week?

# PROBLEMS WITH THE CURRENT REPORTING ARCHITECTURE

After thinking about the heated conversation, you start analyzing the issues. What were your users really saying? Their concerns seem to break into a few categories. Users are concerned about the following:

▼ **Accessibility**—Can I get to my information when I need it?

■ **Timeliness**—How long after transactions occur do I get my information?

■ **Format**—Can I get my data in spreadsheets, graphs, or maps, or using other analytic tools—or can I only get it in paper reports?

▲ **Integrity**—Can I believe the data I get?

It's not hard to see that such concerns bring into question the competence of the IS (information systems) department. Even more importantly, answering such concerns can have a huge impact on the profitability of the company. How much, for instance, would it be worth to the company to have been able to provide Valjon with the report that could have won the FutureChef account? Do you think that was the only opportunity to leverage reporting to grow the company? In all probability, similar concerns arise all the time. Support this type of request and you build a new future for your company.

# THE GOAL: DECISION SUPPORT

As we noted earlier, the data warehouse is simply one component of modern reporting architectures. The real goal of reporting systems is decision support—in other words, to help people make better decisions. While you might not realize it, virtually all computer systems have some decision support component. That component is the reports produced by these systems. People take these reports and make decisions based on the information that they contain.

Since the introduction of computer systems, decision support has evolved greatly. Originally, computer systems produced paper reports. Users generally received information on a periodic basis via daily, weekly, monthly, annual, etc. reports. To receive custom reports, users would contact the IS department and have a programmer assigned to write a program to create the report. This task would take anywhere from a few hours to, in extreme cases, months. We have heard stories about companies that had an 18-month turnaround time on report requests. Eighteen months!

Of course, paper reports provided very little formatting and analytic flexibility. For example, did you ever try to sort a paper report? It really works only if you have scissors, tape, and a lot of time. And don't try to graph the data on a paper report unless you have a box of crayons!

Around 1980, a new technology entered the scene. What was that technology? That's right, the personal computer. When we got a personal computer, we generally bought two programs to go along with it—a word processor and a spreadsheet. We used the word processor to work on our resumes. We used the spreadsheet to work with data. Did the spreadsheet give us access to any more data? Absolutely not—it gave us the ability to have our high-paid executives waste hours copying their data from our paper reports into their spreadsheets. But, at least they could now analyze and format data. Of course, the inefficiencies and possibilities for errors are obvious.

In the early 1990s, spreadsheet companies recognized these problems and started building database connectivity into their products. The only thing missing was ease of use. How many executives do you know who are masters of SQL?

This brings us to modern decision support. A decision support system is a system that gives users access to their data and allows them to analyze and format the data as needed. Figure 1-1 shows the high-level evolution of what has come to be called the *decision support* system.

Believe it or not, the fascination with end-user access to data is not quite new. Perhaps you remember a relic called COBOL—the COmmon Business-Oriented Language. When COBOL was first developed, virtually all programming was done in assembler language. COBOL was an attempt to make computers accessible to users. The first business applications were accounting systems, and therefore most users were accountants. The industry was going to give these users a tool with which to write programs and access data.

The stories of accountants who learned COBOL and thus became IS folk are legion. You've got to find it just a bit humorous that our first attempt to give end users reporting capabilities succeeded primarily in turning them into us. There have been successive attempts—each with similar, or even less auspicious, outcomes. Perhaps it's time to surrender, to realize that we really do want to turn our users into programmers, just not full-time programmers.

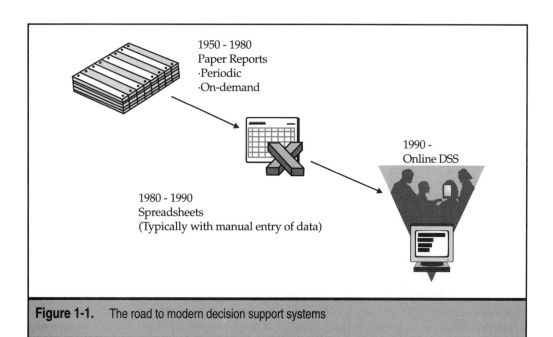

**Figure 1-1.**　The road to modern decision support systems

# AN AUTOMATIC TELLER MACHINE (ATM)—FOR DATA

Another way to view a modern reporting system is as an ATM for data. The parallels are interesting (OK, maybe not thrilling, but at least interesting) and hold a great number of lessons for the design of your reporting system.

When banks first introduced ATMs, what did they really do? In essence, they turned you into a teller, a virtual bank employee (how can anyone write a computer book nowadays without including the word "virtual"?). Now, if you consider a teller's job, you realize that it entails interacting with a complex computer system in order to execute transactions. You became a teller, but did you go through your bank's ATM training? We have yet to meet a person who answers "yes" to that question.

So, how did the bank train you to operate their complex computer system? Well, in two ways. First, they made the system so easy to use that training was a non-issue. If you could read, and press buttons, then you too could be a bank system user. Second, they limited the variety of transactions you could perform. Things that are simple and done frequently—like getting cash, making deposits, getting cash, checking balances, getting cash, and getting cash—can be done through the ATM. Things that are complex and nonroutine, like applying for mortgages, require intervention from, dare we say, a real human being. But, all things considered, that's OK. After all, how often is it that you apply for a mortgage?

But, why would you be willing to become an unpaid bank employee? Because there are benefits for you. In fact, the benefits are so great that many banks now charge $1.50 per transaction for the right to become their teller. What are these benefits? Well, you now have access to your money wherever and whenever you need it—your money is accessible evenings, weekends, holidays in New York, Chicago, Copenhagen, or Ann Arbor. Once again, can you do every conceivable banking transaction through an ATM? Well, no. There are still some complex transactions, like applying for an ill-advised $450,000 mortgage, that require help from real bank employees.

In a modern reporting environment, we are trying to do the same thing—but with data. Don't tell your users, but we are really trying to shift programming work to them (that is, make them into programmers). They'll use point-and-click tools that generate queries in languages like SQL. If we do our jobs well, these tools will be so easy to use that we won't have to expend excessive effort in training our users how to use them. Why will computer-phobic users be willing to become "virtual" programmers? Because of the benefits to them. They will suddenly be able to get the information they need when they need it. IS will no longer be a bottleneck, requiring long lead times for responding to simple requests.

If you think about it, we're really trying to shift work from IS to our users. In the past, IS was an information conduit. All requests for data flowed through the IS department. We wrote programs and the results passed back through our department to the requestors. In the future, we want to be conduit builders. We want to put the tools and structures in place that allows users to access their own data. Our jobs don't go away, they're just transformed. Instead of writing report programs, we now build data warehouses and configure query tools to give simple access to our users. Figure 1-2

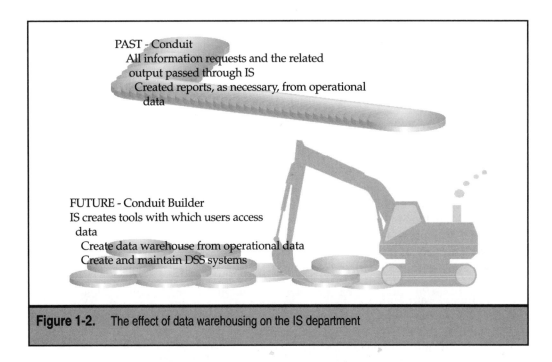

PAST - Conduit
    All information requests and the related
    output passed through IS
      Created reports, as necessary, from operational
      data

FUTURE - Conduit Builder
IS creates tools with which users access
  data
    Create data warehouse from operational data
    Create and maintain DSS systems

**Figure 1-2.**    The effect of data warehousing on the IS department

shows how IS has gone from being the conduit to being the builder of the conduit—a facilitator as opposed to a provider.

# SO, WHAT'S A DATA WAREHOUSE?

A modern reporting environment will give users access to their data, but it doesn't solve all the problems our users have. Just because users have access to data doesn't guarantee the integrity of that data. It doesn't guarantee that system response times will be adequate. It doesn't guarantee that your systems won't purge old data before its useful life is passed. In fact, giving users access to data says little about that data.

To address many of these data problems, Bill Inmon speaks of the concept of a "data warehouse." In fact, Inmon is frequently referred to as the "father of the data warehouse" (still, we recommend against calling him "dad"). In his book, *Building the Data Warehouse* (John Wiley & Sons Inc., 1996), Inmon describes the warehouse as a "subject oriented, integrated, nonvolatile, time variant collection of data in support of management decisions."

In other words, data warehouses are databases used solely for reporting. This is opposed to traditional data capture or online transaction-processing (OLTP) systems. These traditional data capture systems are frequently referred to as "operational" systems. Classic examples of operational systems include the following:

▼   General ledger

■   Accounts payable

- ■ Financial management
- ■ Order processing
- ■ Order entry
- ▲ Inventory

Data warehouses are populated with data from two sources. Most frequently, they are populated with periodic migrations of data from OLTP systems. The second source is made up of external—frequently purchased—databases such as lists of income and demographic information that can be linked to internal customer data.

While Inmon's definition refers to "management decisions," the group of users supported by data warehouses grows all the time. Now these databases support more than just managers, but the basic concepts still apply. So, let's pull apart the definition in the next section.

## Subject Oriented

OLTP databases are sometimes intended to hold information about subsets of the organization. For example, a retailer might have separate order entry systems and databases for retail, catalog, and outlet sales. Each system will support basic queries about the information it captures. But, suppose a user wants to run a query on all sales, not simply the sales captured by a particular system. In your case, Valjon wants a report that describes the sales of a particular product, regardless of the channel responsible for that sale. Your data warehouse database will be subject oriented, organized into subject areas, like sales, rather than around OLTP data sources. Figure 1-3 shows how the three sales data sources come together in the sales subject area of the warehouse.

When one of us worked for a major computer vendor early in his career, the employees could not answer a simple question like, "Who are our top ten customers?" They could tell you who the top ten mainframe customers were. They could tell you who the top ten mini customers were. They could tell you who the top ten PC customers were. But these answers in themselves were not entirely accurate; when they took the time (and were given the ability) to analyze total volume of sales of all customers across all product lines, two or three customers emerged as the best. The fact that these two or three were some of the company's best customers was lost when sales were isolated by computer size.

Imagine how much time was wasted in that company every time senior management came back with a new question. Because no central repository existed to go to, each request was a painful process. Because it was a manual process, it also had the possibility of being fraught with manual error. Yet this was the best information available, and many decisions were made based on what data the IS staff could cobble together to supply to senior management.

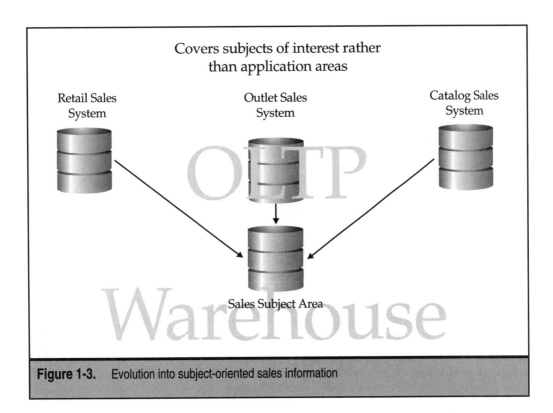

**Figure 1-3.** Evolution into subject-oriented sales information

## Integrated

Consider the situation where you're bringing together data from three order entry systems into one warehouse. It is possible, in fact likely, that each of these systems codes their data differently. Perhaps the retail system has a product code consisting of seven numeric digits (e.g., 8909321—all numbers), the outlet system consisting of nine alphanumerics (e.g., TH67AF678—letters and numbers in no special order), and the catalog system consisting of four alphanumerics and a four-character numeric (e.g., HHYU7815—letters and numbers where the last two digits are the sum of the previous two digits). To create a useful subject area, the source data must be integrated. In other words, the data must be modified to comply with common coding rules. This doesn't necessarily mean that the coding in the source systems must change but that, instead, some process must be able to modify the data coming into the warehouse to assign a common coding scheme. Figure 1-4 illustrates this difficulty—the marriage of different coding schemes into one for the warehouse data.

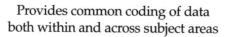

Provides common coding of data
both within and across subject areas

OLTP

| Retail Sales System | Outlet Sales System | Catalog Sales System |
|---|---|---|
| Product code: 9999999 | Product code: XXXXXXXXX | Product code: XXXX99.99 |

Product code:
Common code or a mapping of the various source codes

Sales Subject Area

Warehouse

**Figure 1-4.**   Integration of coding schemes

## Nonvolatile

*Nonvolatile* is a 50-cent word (U.S., or 75 cents CAD) meaning that the warehouse is read-only; users can't write back. As opposed to OLTP databases, warehouses primarily support reporting, not data capture. As we will see, the warehouse is a historical record. Allowing users to write back to the warehouse would be akin to George Orwell's concept of rewriting history. Figure 1-5 illustrates this fundamental difference between OLTP and the data warehouse.

## Time Variant

Much business analysis requires the identification of trends. Trend analysis requires access to historical data. Generally, more than one year of history is required, particularly when the business is seasonal. Most OLTP systems, on the other hand, do not store large amounts of history. This is because large quantities of data are the enemy of fast response times. Since OLTP systems are designed for immediate response, they often purge data within a few months of its capture. Warehouses, on the other hand, hold large amounts of history. This is one of the main reasons why warehouses are often huge databases. Figure 1-6 reiterates this time component.

Keep in mind, though, that not all history must be kept at the same level of detail. For example, one past client operated in the wholesale food business. This customer's warehouse kept track of the detail of each sales transaction for a month. When the data was a month old, it was summarized into weekly summary values. After two years, the

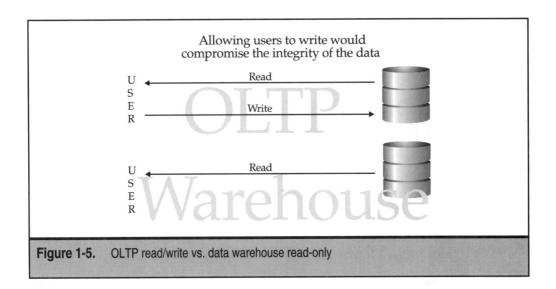

**Figure 1-5.** OLTP read/write vs. data warehouse read-only

data was kept only as monthly summaries. Not only does this help data warehouse query performance, but it also makes business sense. The details of any individual transaction generally become less important as we get farther in time away from that transaction. Three years from now, how important will it be to know that customer Y bought a sack of

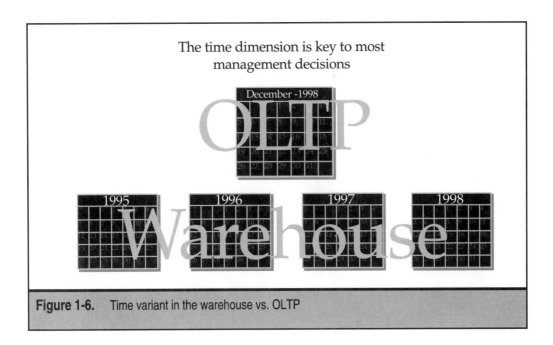

**Figure 1-6.** Time variant in the warehouse vs. OLTP

freeze-dried okra on January 26? On the other hand, if we are trying to estimate the winter demand for freeze-dried okra, it might be important to know how much freeze-dried okra was sold in total during the month of January.

# DECISION SUPPORT DIFFERS FROM TRANSACTION PROCESSING

So, we're saying that you can't do hard core reporting and OLTP work in the same database. Why not? Well, first of all, while your users will demand a reporting system that adheres to Bill Inmon's four criteria of a data warehouse, most OLTP environments do not support these. In addition, think about the differences between decision support computing and OLTP computing:

▼ OLTP systems are designed to work with small pieces of information. For example, when taking an order, an OLTP user typically works with one customer, one order, one shipment, etc. at a time. Data stored in an OLTP database is designed to support this form of use. As a result, OLTP schema are highly normalized. Decision support queries, on the other hand, frequently work with huge blocks of information. For example, imagine what happens when the president of McDonald's wants to see a report of total sales for 1997, broken down by geographic region. Running this query of the OLTP database would entail reading billions of transaction records and summarizing the results to put on the report.

■ OLTP data must frequently be updated in real time. For example, consider a bank whose systems did not provide real-time updates. A customer could go from branch to branch, withdrawing the full balance from her checking account, over and over again. In the decision support arena, on the other hand, data almost never needs to be updated in real time. This is because DSS users work with high-level, summary data. There is a real cost associated with obtaining data in real time. Before paying that cost you must ask, "Is there anything that could have happened in the past five minutes that could, or even should, have an effect on a decision that a manager will make? In fact, isn't it possible that giving managers real-time updates might cause them to overreact to 'nontrends'?"

■ OLTP schema are designed for rapid data input. Companies can't afford to make customers wait for order takers to finish transactions on slow order entry systems. In a data warehouse, on the other hand, no data is entered by users—remember, nonvolatile. Instead, the goal is to get data out as quickly as possible.

■ OLTP users need immediate response. When the "Accept order" key is hit, the screen had better be available for the next order in under a second. DSS users, while they should not have to wait months for answers, generally don't need such blazing response times. When they get a response from the system, they consider it for a while and then take the appropriate next step.

- ■ OLTP usage patterns are relatively predictable. System designers can tell how much work it will take to process a transaction and when most transactions will occur. In a decision support environment, on the other hand, usage patterns are not quite so stable. Who knows when a question might arise that requires complex analysis? Thus, the system might be heavily used for about four hours on Monday and then not touched again until Friday.

- ▲ OLTP schema are very complex. It is difficult to build an easy to use "ATM for data" on top of a complex schema.

# DATA WAREHOUSING: A DIRTY LITTLE SECRET

If you've picked up any IS-related publication over the past few years, it's apparent that warehouses are widely accepted, widely implemented tools. Database, tool, and consulting vendors love them. But amidst all the hype is buried a dirty little secret. Philosophically, in the opinion of many, data warehousing is a silly idea. Corporate data is already stored in computers that are accessible throughout the organization. Who in their right mind would get involved in moving data to new computers, cleaning it, and suffering through the headaches of making sure that this movement happens correctly, completely, and automatically? Who, in their right mind, would pick up a book the size of this one to learn how to move that data?

The original dream of relational databases was that we would store all of our organization's data in one central, integrated place. All transactions would be performed against that central database. All reporting would be out of that database. With the exception of the transaction processing, doesn't this sound a bit like a data warehouse?

Come to think of it, rather than copying data from your various OLTP systems into a data warehouse, why not get back to the original dream? Why not spend all that data warehousing money integrating your various OLTP systems? Couldn't we just place views over the new database to make it user friendly and then let users report directly from it? Wouldn't this save us from the philosophically ugly alternative of building a separate database just for reporting?

Well, an oddly related question is "How many MIPS do you have?" *MIPS* stands for millions of instructions per second, and has become one of the measurements of the processing power of a computer—more MIPS translates to faster processing. Imagine that you had infinite MIPS. Then, indeed, you could do all the processing for your company on one computer. Therefore, because you had infinite computing power, the response to any query would be instantaneous (and, incidentally, you could probably play some pretty cool computer games). Sadly, hardware vendors have let us down on this account. They have yet to deliver a computer with infinite computing power.

Instead, we live in a world where machines, including computers, can only do a fixed amount of work in a given period of time. Even large computers can only do so much work. Try, given this limitation, to run your OLTP and reporting systems on a single machine. Reporting and decision support queries frequently require a large amount of computing power as they summarize and report on millions of records. Now, imagine these queries sharing computer time with OLTP transactions and complex OLTP schema that are highly normalized. Your response time will likely be agonizingly slow. Also, these computer-intensive queries will slow down the performance of your OLTP systems. Do you want to be the one responsible for the line, "I'm sorry Mr. Kramden (of FutureChef), but we can't process your $10 million order right now because our president, Mr. Henchard, is running his monthly sales report and it's slowing down all of our systems. Could you please call back in about four hours?"

But, there is an important point here, a point that most companies don't consider. A data warehouse is not always required. For example, imagine a near-infinite MIPS situation. Suppose you run your entire company's finances on the personal finance software package called Quicken. Also, suppose this package is running on a Cray supercomputer. In this situation, you'll likely have enough MIPS to run both your OLTP and reporting systems on that one computer. While this is an extreme example, it does show that there is a range of options.

A data warehouse is frequently, but not always, the most cost-effective or even the best solution. In fact, we sometimes recommend that companies ease into data warehousing. It is often advisable to start by building summarized reporting structures in the OLTP database. These structures can eventually be ported to a warehouse as your reporting needs mature.

# RETURN ON INVESTMENT

To gain approval to pursue a systems development effort, one thing that most companies require is a financial analysis. This analysis is intended to determine whether the proposed investment will be a wise, profitable effort. Of course, no one will be sure until the effort is actually complete whether this prediction was correct or not. Even after completion, it is frequently difficult to tell whether or not a system is "paying for itself."

A number of formulae are used to determine whether or not a particular investment is wise. You've undoubtedly heard of these formulae. They have names like return on investment (ROI), internal rate of return (IRR), and payback period. Bean counters spend endless hours debating which of these is most appropriate and which is so ill-advised that the simple mention of its name will lead your project, and likely your entire organization, to certain bankruptcy.

Regardless of the formula you use, it will likely involve estimating the cost to construct your system and comparing it to the expected benefits that the system will provide. Costs include items like hardware, software, and developer and consulting fees. Benefits include items like estimated reductions in costs and increases in revenues.

In some systems efforts, the costs and benefits are relatively easy to estimate. For example, if you expect a new OLTP system to allow order entry operators to enter orders twice as fast, you can expect to need only half as many, reducing your personnel costs. In a data warehouse effort, the costs are as easy to estimate as in an OLTP environment. The benefits, on the other hand, are far less tangible.

A new sales warehouse will allow us to better market our customers, but how much better? What is the value of the following?

- ▼ More rapid access to data
- ■ More reliable reporting
- ▲ More flexible data presentation

Thus, many companies that require cost justification for every five-dollar systems purchase will forgo such analysis for the construction of a warehouse. Perhaps the exact benefits can't be quantified, but hopefully they are there.

One reason why warehouse benefits are so hard to quantify is that the exact target audience of these systems is rarely completely known when the effort is started. For example, most companies start their data warehousing efforts in the sales and marketing area. Why? Because the sales figure is usually the largest number on the company's income statement. A small percentage of improvement in this number can lead to a large dollar increase in the company's profitability. But, in our experience, while these systems are targeted at the company's sales and marketing force, an unexpected audience frequently follows close on their heels. Who? The controller's group. They're after the warehouse as an accurate place to verify exactly how the company is doing, without succumbing to the dirty data issues that are often rampant in OLTP environments.

A recent study by a company called IDC, which used information gathered from more than 60 organizations that had implemented data warehousing, found that data warehousing generated an average ROI of 401 percent over three years. Even if you're not a bean counter, 401 percent of anything is pretty good, right? With an average ROI like that, it's no wonder we see such growth in corporations developing data warehouses and data warehouse strategies.

One more point about estimating benefits. While most decision support efforts start in the sales and marketing subject area, they rarely end there. Decision support tools, such as data warehouses, are about optimizing operations—not just maximizing sales. Thus, while the sales department is generally interested in maximizing sales, other groups might be interested in helping by minimizing some factor. For example, perhaps the human resources (HR) department is trying to minimize headcount. In both the sales and HR examples, the groups are trying to optimize the company's performance.

In general, your warehousing go-no go decision should be based on questions like:

- ▼ Does it give us a competitive advantage?
- ■ Does it improve the bottom line?
- ■ Will it deliver on all its promises?
- ■ Will it be delivered on time?
- ■ What is the risk if we don't do it?

■   What is the risk if we do it?

▲   Will it be delivered on budget?

While it is important to discuss the benefits of a planned warehouse, it is usually impossible to quantify these benefits in dollar terms. Sadly, the decision to construct the warehouse must frequently be a leap of faith. This fact does, though, bring us back to our earlier infinite MIPS discussion. Sometimes it's advisable to ease into warehousing by adding reporting structures to your existing OLTP database. This can be a lower risk path that allows you to "test the waters" before diving in completely.

# THIS BOOK

The remainder of this book will discuss building your own data warehouse—the repository of information your business needs to thrive in the information age. We will help you understand what a data warehouse is and what it is not. You will learn what human resources are required, as well as the roles and responsibilities of each player. You will be given an overview of good project management techniques to help ensure the data warehouse initiative does not fail due to poor project management. You will learn how to physically implement a data warehouse with some new tools that help with the migration and transformation of legacy data into the warehouse. Once you understand how the warehouse is loaded, you will learn about query analysis and reporting software. This software is the technologist's power tool, helping you capitalize on your new information asset to mine those nuggets of value hidden in the vast expanses of data you've stored in the warehouse.

While relatively new to the field of data warehousing (given the newness of the field, who isn't), Microsoft has, for years, produced Excel—one of the strongest tools for data analysis. Throughout this book, Microsoft's traditional, and exciting new, technologies will be discussed, allowing you to leverage this powerful family of tools to your competitive advantage.

# A CAREER-SAVING HAPPY ENDING

Now it's Friday, and you have big plans for the weekend. You don't want to spend the evenings lying awake, worrying about reporting problems. You've got to go shopping for your new Mercedes. You send out an email to Valjon, Richelieu, and Henchard (as though those guys ever actually check their email). It reads as follows:

```
Folks:

It has recently come to my attention that there may be a bit of
dissatisfaction with our current reporting systems. We've been
following this situation closely over the past few months. I think I've
```

hit on a novel solution. Please expect to see a new budget request for constructing a data warehouse. I won't get into exactly what a warehouse is because you probably wouldn't understand anyway. Suffice it to say that I think this warehouse will help to solve many of our reporting problems.

With this message, you're on your way. But, there are a number of things you have to know to make the trip relatively smooth. Our next chapter discusses some of the unique things to consider in your warehousing pursuits.

# CHAPTER 2

## Things to Consider

Giving a know-it-all author a chapter title like "Things to Consider" is a bit like giving an ax murderer a chainsaw. What to do, what to do? There are a ton of things to consider. For example, consider the fact that humans have inhabited the earth for over 200,000 years but writing was invented only about 7,000 years ago (about the same time as the wheel). What does that say about the pace of technology? Well, 7,001 years ago we couldn't even write, and now we write so much that we need data warehouses to store it all!

In Chapter 1, we provided some idea of what a data warehouse is and what it isn't. In this chapter, we will address a number of "guiding principles" of data warehousing. These are insights that we've gained through years of experience and struggle. Consider them as you read the rest of this book and as you build your warehouses and marts. Let's start with a big one, one that essentially says, "Sometimes it may be a good idea to ignore what you read in this book."

# DON'T LISTEN TO WHAT WE SAY...BE PRAGMATIC

So, what are you building? Is it a data mart or a data warehouse? Can you tell the difference? Does it matter?

The data warehouse industry generates a lot of great terminology and rules. The problem with it is that people new to the field feel that they must adhere to these rules. We've been on projects where team members have told us things like, "You can't do X or Y, this is a warehouse."

At times like these, we have to ask, "Are we trying to build a warehouse to solve a set of business problems?" Our point here is that you must stay pragmatic. Build the system that solves the user's problem, not the one that looks like a pure data warehouse. Always question what you're doing. "Hey, why are we building this warehouse? Why won't a set of summary tables in our OLTP database suffice?"

# QUESTION AUTHORITY

Over the past few years there have been a lot of very intelligent individuals (and a few not-so-intelligent ones) writing and speaking on the topic of data warehousing. Magazine articles are very alluring. If it appears in print, it must be true.

Keep in mind, though, that not all words in print are gospel. *CompInfoTimes* is not the Bible. Opinions, even those of respected professionals, are just that, opinions—not facts. This, of course, puts more pressure on you. Now, the only one you can blame for mistakes is yourself. Protect yourself. Thoroughly think through your design decisions before you commit.

# START WITH BUSINESS REQUIREMENTS— NOT TECHNOLOGY

What made you interested in building systems? For many of us, it was a love of technology. We love being able to write snappy systems that put pretty pictures on some undeserving user's screen. For many of us, the answer to virtually every problem is to "build a new system."

Well, sadly, data warehousing is not about technology. Data warehousing is about solving business problems. In fact, some of the best data warehousing specialists we know have degrees in business, not in computers. One key to successful data warehousing is to start by focusing on what information the organization needs to flourish, NOT on how to deliver that information.

Query technologies are "cool," and developers want to play with them. In fact, we have seen a project where the team spent the first six months picking the query tool and then learning how to use it. Data structures were given a back seat. Managers aren't dumb people. They can tell when real progress is being made…and when it isn't. In the end, this company's managers got so frustrated that they canceled the project. It restarted, but with a new project manager who was instructed to de-emphasize tools.

It's important to remember that most properly designed warehouses will be accessed by a variety of technologies. Once the warehouse is built, it may support the following:

▼ Programs that export data to data marts

■ Report writers

■ OLAP and analysis tools

■ Data mining tools

■ Custom-coded executive information system (EIS) tools

■ Geographic information system (GIS) tools

▲ Any number of other query technologies

Thus, focusing on any one query technology can distract the team from building the necessary flexibility.

Query technologies come and go. The flavor of the day may be Cognos, but tomorrow it may be Business Objects. Regardless of what a query tool vendor may say, the real strategic piece of the warehouse is the data—not the query tool. It is vital that your data structures accurately reflect the demands of the business and that they contain correct, reliable data.

There is one caveat. Certain query tools require specific types of data structures in order to work. These can be powerful tools. We generally recommend that such tools be viewed as limited-function data mart technologies rather than enterprise-wide data warehouse tools.

# WHAT GOES INTO THE WAREHOUSE?

Many new warehouse designers view the warehouse as the final repository for all the company's data. They will make naïve statements like, "All corporate reporting will be done from the warehouse." This is generally not a viable approach. As we noted in the first chapter, the warehouse is only one component of an enterprise reporting strategy, albeit a big component.

This distinction is important for a number of reasons. For one, the vast majority of warehouses are updated by batch programs rather than in real time. Thus, transactions are not immediately loaded into the warehouse but, instead, wait until the end of the day or the end of the week. Certain reporting requests, on the other hand, require a real-time, current view of the company's data. For example, a clerk answering telephone calls from customers may need to be able to tell whether or not a particular payment has been received. Supplying that clerk only with data from a warehouse that is loaded once a week is a sure formula for customer irritation.

Another reason why it is important to "position" the warehouse in the corporate reporting architecture is to protect the project from overbuilding. In systems development, increases in size increase risk. Each new table, each new column, each new constraint increases the amount of development work that must be estimated, scheduled, and performed. They also increase the possibility that an object in the architecture will fail. Thus, positioning the warehouse effectively is a tool for managing its scope and also a tool for helping ensure success.

Given this, we recommend that in designing your warehouse you explicitly state where the warehouse will fit into the corporate reporting process. This statement should detail the rules that will be used to determine what data goes into the warehouse and what data is excluded. An example of such a statement might be, "The warehouse will focus on delivering data that has value in an aggregated format or in grouping large segments of the population. Data unique to relatively small numbers of the population, such as the second alternate address, will not be included." Statements like this (perhaps with a little more detail) give warehouse developers a basis for deciding what is included in, and what is excluded from, the warehouse. This warehouse position should be developed while you are gathering business and user requirements.

The user community should signify their understanding and agreement with the warehouse position statement. Not only does this help them understand the role of the warehouse, but it also gives them another way to plan for how to use it.

# DATA MART OR DATA WAREHOUSE?

In building a warehouse, among the first questions that always spring up are—what are data warehouses, what are data marts, and which do we build first? In this book you'll read a lot about data warehouses and data marts. One of the big topics in reporting systems nowadays is the dreaded data warehouse vs. data mart altercation (aren't automated thesauri wonderful?). Companies are trying to figure out the following:

▼ Do we need a data warehouse?

■ Do we need data marts?

■ Come to think of it, what is a data warehouse?

■ For that matter, what is a data mart?

▲ If we need both, which do we build first?

Time for some brief descriptions. As we noted in the first chapter, per Bill Inmon, a data warehouse is a "subject oriented, integrated, nonvolatile, time variant collection of data in support of management decisions." To us, a data warehouse is "broad" data store. It contains a number of subject areas. A data mart, on the other hand, typically focuses on a more narrow part of the business. It usually covers a single subject area and/or type of analysis. For example, your corporate data warehouse might include information about sales, finance, and human resources. Your company may also maintain a number of data marts. Perhaps there is a data mart targeted at analyzing product movement through the retail channel. Another, located in a regional headquarters, might be used for analyzing sales in that region. Perhaps the company has yet another targeted at employee turnover.

There are two basic ways that companies create data marts. The first is to capture data directly from OLTP systems into the marts that need it. The second is to capture data from OLTP systems into a central data warehouse and then to feed the data marts with data from the warehouse. There is a great deal of disagreement on which is the best approach. The first approach quickly gets you a data mart. But at what cost?

When you build an enterprise data warehouse, you typically start by defining an enterprise data model. This entity-relationship model shows the key entities in your warehouse and the relationships between these key entities. When you start to build your population routines, you will likely not populate all these entities at once. Still, you have defined how they relate to each other. Once the model is fully populated, users will be able to extract data that crosses functional lines (for example, the trend in sales per person employed—a measure of corporate efficiency). This query crosses the boundary between the sales and human resources subject areas. It provides a new level of information, a level not attainable in the traditional, stovepipe, transaction-oriented systems of the past.

Now, assume that you build a few data marts by extracting data directly from OLTP sources. In most cases, you get the mart up quickly, but you ignore cross-subject area relationships. Thus, the sales-per-headcount query we just mentioned remains as difficult as ever.

So, what to do? As in all our advice, the answer will vary according to a number of factors but, in general, we recommend that you adopt an enterprise-wide approach from the start. But, do this in a way that delivers results before the warehouse is complete. How do you do this? Start by quickly defining a logical, enterprise data warehouse, showing only the organization's key entities and relationships. Then attack one subject area and develop an architecture to populate that area. Determine whether queries can occur directly from the warehouse or if the relevant data must be moved into a mart. If a mart is necessary, building it will be far less complex than building it directly from OLTP systems, and it should therefore be completed fairly quickly.

One point to note: In this warehouse-feeding-mart architecture, your warehouse becomes a source system to your marts. In designing that warehouse, you can take steps to ease construction of these downstream marts. One thing, in particular, that you can do is create structures, such as last update time stamp columns, to track changes in warehouse data. While these structures will slightly increase the size and complexity of your warehouse, they will greatly ease the amount of work necessary to build downstream data marts.

Data marts can also contain data that is important for the purpose of the mart but is unimportant to the rest of the company. For example, perhaps the telecommunications department needs to analyze long-distance usage on a monthly basis. It will build its mart using two data sources:

1. It will gather data from the corporate data warehouse about every employee, their phone number, and their department.

2. It will gather data from its long-distance provider about the long-distance usage from each phone.

Notice that while the usage data is very important to this particular department, it is relatively unimportant to the rest of the company. Thus, it is unlikely that the usage data would be captured in the enterprise warehouse. Basic employee information, on the other hand, is quite important and would be captured in the enterprise warehouse.

Here's one more interesting concept about data marts: you can consider each report that your company produces to be a little data mart. This is especially true if the data is delivered in an electronic format that can later be manipulated and analyzed. Once the data is moved into Excel or Access, for example, the user can further analyze and manipulate that data. How is this different from a data mart that is explicitly called a data mart? This point is important for a few reasons:

1. It forces us to think about what it really takes to build a data mart.

2. It highlights some of the security concerns that accompany the greater access to data we are striving for when we build our warehouses and marts.

3. It also highlights the fact that a mart can be a one-time, single-use structure. Perhaps we need to do headcount reporting by race and gender to support a government audit of hiring practices. Once the audit is over, we no longer need the data. It is not necessary to build a complex architecture for every data mart needed. It is quite acceptable to use warehouse queries to build single-purpose marts to support these one-time requests.

# BIG BANG VS. SMALL ITERATIONS—DEVELOPMENT PHASES

Everyone knows that data warehouses are built iteratively, not in one large step, right? There is an endless stream of consultants and vendors screaming about rapid delivery and iterative development. Still, what do these terms really mean (we suspect that even these vendors and consultants don't always think this through)? Does this mean that a warehouse has no thought given to architecture? To user requirements? Do we just keep iterating until we get it right?

You can probably guess that the answer to those questions is "no." If you're building a system that management is going to rely upon, building one that is slapped together—missing things like basic controls and checks—is counterproductive, at least as a driver of your career success. So what, then, does this iterative development look like?

Well, the warehouse is certainly built in small pieces, or iterations. But not all of these iterations are the same size. In terms of the amount of data delivered, the first iteration is pretty small. In terms of the amount of work required, the first iteration is frequently the largest.

Why is this? Well, a good deal of the effort of your first release will focus on building a robust warehousing infrastructure. Think about it—to complete this first release, you need to do a lot of things that you'll never have to do again, at least not for a long time. These include things like:

▼ Developing the high-level enterprise warehouse model

■ Training the warehouse team on technologies and strategies

■ Selecting data movement and query technologies

▲ Creating the network and server environments and support mechanisms

Later releases will capitalize on this infrastructure, allowing you to deliver more data with far less work.

# LONG LIVE RI

Data warehouse developers have a secret weapon to help them fight their way through the administrivia that most companies force traditional applications through—administrivia like data model reviews and director sign-off. This secret weapon? The phrase, "Well this is a warehouse, and in a warehouse we do things differently." What a great cop-out! If only such excuses worked elsewhere (for example, "Well, officer, this is a Japanese car and, therefore, doesn't have to adhere to U.S. speed limits").

While we hate to give away such a powerful tool, we're afraid that the "but we're developing a warehouse" excuse (hereafter we call this the BWDAW excuse) gets used far too often. Yes, you are developing a warehouse. No, you are not developing an altogether new form of reality. Warehousing is not computing anarchy. In general, unless you can come up with a really good justification for breaking the rules we all know and live by, don't break them.

The most frequent area where the BWDAW excuse is used is referential integrity (RI). To refresh your memory, SQL Server allows a developer not only to define tables of information but also the relationships between those tables. The act of ensuring that these references are enforced is called enforcing referential integrity. You can tell SQL Server, for example, "Reject any sales transaction for which a related customer record does not exist in the CUSTOMER table." Should you try to insert data about a sale to John Smith and Mr. Smith doesn't have a record in the customer table, the database will vomit back your data (OK, perhaps vomit is a bit strong, but you get the point). Thus, though enforcing RI requires computer time when loading data into the warehouse, it does not affect query response times.

Even though tomes (yes tomes, not tones…just look it up) have been written about the need for data quality in the warehouse, developers seem dying to turn off one of their key tools for ensuring quality—RI. Why? The most frequent justification goes something like this, "We don't want to pay the performance penalty that enforcing RI entails and, besides, we're programmatically checking RI, so we don't need the database to do this for us."

Well, let's think about the "programmatically checking" argument for a moment. Who in their right mind ever wrote a serious business application that intentionally violated referential integrity? We dare say, desperately few developers who lived to tell about it. We enforce referential integrity to protect us from ourselves—to help ensure that we don't accidentally commit programming errors that violate the basic tenets of our business.

As for the performance penalty, most of the people who use this excuse have never tested the database with RI turned on. Try your system with RI turned on. In terms of performance, one of two things will happen:

1. Performance will be adequate and you'll be a referentially correct hero.

2. Performance will be inadequate and you'll have to find a way to improve it.
   In this case, you'll have a few options:
   - Analyze your load jobs to see if they can be tuned.
   - Analyze your schema to see if it can be tuned.
   - Reevaluate your hardware selection.
   - Disable referential integrity (if you're willing to take the risk).

The point here is that you shouldn't start your project by turning off one of your best data quality tools. Turn it off only if there is no other way to get the load performance you need.

One last note about RI. Frequently, you will validate the data from your source against a list of valid values before you put it into the warehouse (i.e., programmatically check referential integrity). What do you do with "bad values?" Do you reject them? Well, one technique we've used is to insert the bad records into the lookup tables when you need them. The technique involves inserting a record to fix the problem into the related lookup table. In the key of that lookup table, put the value you are looking for. Fill the rest of the fields of the lookup record with some recognizable bad value—such as question marks.

This approach has a lot of value. For one, it allows you to completely populate your warehouse—thus, users running summary queries will get the correct totals. Second, it adheres to referential integrity rules while still keeping a record of data that must be investigated. Third, and most important, it allows you, or a user, to run queries showing the impact of "bad data." Suppose you run a sales query and get a result indicating that 20 percent of all sales were to customers that the system could not identify. You can now start to look at your OLTP systems with an eye toward forcing those systems to capture this essential data.

# QUERY TOOLS—YOU WILL HAVE MORE THAN ONE

As we noted earlier, you may very well build a data mart specifically to support a particular query tool—especially if that tool requires its own proprietary data structures. On the other hand, other marts and most data warehouses should be tool independent. To get the warehouse's full value, it will likely be queried by a variety of tools. These might include things like:

▼ Report writers

■ Online analytical processing (OLAP) databases and tools

■ Statistical analysis and data mining packages

■ Client/server programming languages

■ Geographic information system (GIS) mapping tools

▲ Executive information systems (EIS)

Thus, developing the warehouse should not be viewed as an exercise in query tool selection. Instead, it should be geared toward developing and populating powerful, tool-independent data structures. Data structures and data are a strategic investment. Well done, these will last for years. Query tools, on the other hand, are nonstrategic. The "flavor of the day" will change from year to year. Design specifically for today's flavor and you'll have a bad taste in your mouth tomorrow.

# DATA WAREHOUSE DIFFERENCES—A DEVELOPER'S PERSPECTIVE

Skills and habits formed while building an assortment of operational system work have prepared many DSS analysts and developers for data warehouse project work. All that operational system "big bang" work is not out the door. In many ways, data warehouses are not that different from those systems that you've always built. Think of a data warehouse as consisting of two separate yet intertwined architectures—the data loading architecture and the end-user data access architecture. To a great extent, the loading architecture is really just a well-designed batch system in a client/server environment. The data access architecture may be a bit different, but it really just builds on tools that you've already acquired—tools like SQL and client/server and/or Internet concepts. Chapter 18 speaks at length about the Internet, and the data warehouse Web solutions.

In other ways, data warehouses—systems for delivering rather than capturing data—are vastly different than anything you've ever built before. In Chapter 1, you learned that data warehouse projects are different by nature. Now you will see how participants in data warehouse projects must learn how to deliver a system that is radically different from any other they have delivered before.

This reorientation is good for IT professionals who are fortunate enough to participate in warehousing projects. Not only does it allow them to hone their client/server skills, it also gives them an opportunity to work on projects that are typically very visible to management and the company at large. This visibility, though, does have its downside. Because they gather data from other systems using other technologies (that were possibly built at times when the business looked very different than it currently does), data warehouse projects can be quite demanding and, at times, tense. Participants on data warehouse projects should be prepared to accept the visibility that comes along with such a project, and at the same time be prepared to deliver under some very demanding conditions.

Developers new to the data warehouse world must be ready for a significant mind shift, a shift away from a data-capture mindset to one of data distribution. Warehouse developers must develop a mindset that focuses on rapidly delivering large quantities of data. The question is no longer, "How quickly can I insert this row in the database?" The question now becomes "How can I deliver results to a query that summarizes 10 million rows in a reasonable amount of time? Beyond that, how can I ensure adequate performance to a variety of similar queries that I can't even foresee today?"

The thinking is very different. For example, in a data-capture world, you index your data very lightly. In a reporting world, you put a lot of indexes on your data, paying a price when loading in batch that pays off in faster response time when users run a variety of unforeseen queries.

Another example, one that data modelers in particular have difficulty grasping, is the concept of denormalization. In the OLTP world, schema are highly normalized. A transaction may need to join a few tables together, generally accessing only a few records in each of these tables. If you were to join the same tables in a reporting environment and try to bring back millions of records, your query would die—and you'd get an angry phone call from some disgruntled user (and his boss). Thus, you denormalize tables together in the data warehouse.

Think a minute about denormalization. What are you really doing when you denormalize? In a way, aren't you doing the following?

1. Predicting the work that a user will request.

2. "Predoing" it in a batch job so that the system doesn't have to do it when the user submits his or her query.

A good way to approach many of the performance issues you'll encounter in the data warehousing world is to ask yourself, "Is there anything else I can predo when I load the data to save the user from having to do it at run time?" Hey, what about creating summary tables to support certain summary queries that I know the user will run? Etc., etc., etc.

The point? Developers moving from an OLTP environment to a data warehousing environment must get used to the fact that they are going to break some of the traditional rules in order to satisfy their users' lust for data (did you ever think you'd see the words "lust" and "data" in the same sentence?).

# DATA WAREHOUSE DIFFERENCES— THE USER'S PERSPECTIVE

Here's a sobering thought: In many cases, use of the data warehouse is optional. If a user doesn't want to use the warehouse, she won't. If using the warehouse is more trouble than it's worth, the user will circumvent it. "Circumvent it how," you ask? Well, remember that the warehouse contains data gathered from other systems. Perhaps our user will get reports directly from those systems. Perhaps she'll set up her own mini IS department to write programs and circumvent the overbearing, central IS department that tried to force her to use that damned warehouse. Perhaps she'll do her best to go without reports altogether.

Clearly, a warehouse holds a ton of promise. What would make a user avoid it? Well, how about the following:

▼ **Unreliable data**—how many times does our user have to make bad decisions or look bad in front of her boss, because your warehouse delivered bad data, before she loses interest?

■ **Poor response time**—perhaps immediate response time isn't necessary, but how user-friendly is it to lock up the user's PC for four hours waiting for a report to run?

▲ **Complex user interfaces**—have you ever tried to teach an executive how an outer join differs from an inner join? Do it once and you'll never try again (assuming, of course, that you remain employed). How willing will your user be to use your warehouse if you give her a tool that requires her to define her own joins?

Of course, this is different than the OLTP world. In OLTP, for the most part, users have to use the system that they're given. If your job is to enter sales transactions into a database, the only way you'll be able to do this is to use the system that the IS department gave you.

The point here is that the data warehouse is one of the few places where the user really can vote on whether or not she likes the system. If she likes it, she'll use it to no end. If she dislikes it, she'll avoid it like the plague. How would the face of business change if users had such voting power over all the systems we gave them?

## EMPOWERING USERS

How many times in the past few years have you heard that company X or Y is restructuring? Everyone's doing it. If you read deep enough into the details of restructuring announcements you usually find somewhere that management in the new organization will empower its (remaining) employees. What do they mean by "empower?" Well, they mean that now employees will be allowed to make many of the decisions that used to be directed up the management chain. Think about it, though. How effective will employees be at making decisions if they don't have data with which to make those decisions?

Implementing a data warehouse is one way to deliver this data. Not only is it tied to freeing users from running to management, but, surprisingly, it also frees users from having to run to IS.

*Empowerment* gives users control of their own destiny—no more running to programmers asking for reports programmed to satisfy burning needs. How many times in operational environments are new reports identified, scoped, and programmed, after which the developer discovers that, by the time they are ready, the user has found other sources for the desired output? An inevitable time delay exists between the identification of new requirements and their delivery. This is no one's fault; it is simply reality.

Using reporting tools against a data warehouse empowers users to get and analyze data and make informed decisions by themselves. For example, OLAP tools allow users to do forecasting, drill-down, and digging for trends in all aspects of their business. The data warehouse user can slice and dice data in ways never dreamed of before. New information is uncovered and new ways of thinking are born. When users are armed with the freedom to report on what they want, when they want, the operational application development personnel are free to build new applications. These applications may be tailored to implement business decisions made by executives and management, based on information gleaned from the data warehouse. They may even be applications to correct some of the dirty data issues that the warehouse uncovers. If this sounds like the best of both worlds, it is.

## WHY CHOOSE MICROSOFT FOR DATA WAREHOUSING?

Let's face it—Microsoft is a relative newcomer to the enterprise-scale database market. The current version of SQL Server has an upper limit of 100–200Gb for database size, well within the range of some of the larger decision support repositories being deployed worldwide. Even more to the point, Microsoft is also relatively new to the data warehousing market. So, why choose Microsoft as your data warehousing platform? Among the reasons are

▼   The price/performance ratio inherent in Microsoft's offerings

■   Ease of use

■   Comprehensive solution out of the box

■   Integration across a wide variety of tools

▲   Choosing a long-term partner

Let's have a look in more detail at these reasons.

## Price/Performance

Traditionally, technologies start out as expensive tools and then, over time, become more cost-effective. Microsoft has been a leader in reducing the cost of technology. Until recently, enterprise-wide data warehousing has been a tool only of very large companies—the companies that could afford it. Microsoft's push into the data warehousing market will, undoubtedly, lead to the ubiquity of warehouses and affordable reporting and analysis tools.

## Ease of Use

Microsoft's database has always been easier to use and manage than other relational database products in the market. SQL Server 7 builds upon this heritage while also scaling up to support larger, more sophisticated databases.

## Comprehensive Solution Out of the Box

SQL Server 7 offers a robust data warehouse solution out of the box. Out-of-the-box features in addition to the core database and tools include an integrated OLAP engine, data extraction and transformation tools, a built-in metadata repository, a natural language interface, a workload analyzer, and a database tuning tool; the list goes on.

## Integration Across a Wide Variety of Tools

Microsoft already supplies a number of tools for accessing databases. For example, while Excel is a great data analysis tool, did you know that it can directly access databases? What about Word? Did you know that Word can directly access databases? What a great tool for a "proactive" warehouse. Even today, if you have a database that contains information about customers and their purchase levels, you can hook that database to Word and use it to generate sales letters to key customers. Close integration with Microsoft Front Office tools, as well as Back Office integration with Web servers, messaging systems, mainframe connectivity, provide an organization with a comprehensive integrated solution.

## Choosing a Long-Term Partner

Choosing an enterprise database and data warehouse vendor is the beginning of a long-term partnership. The last few years in the database industry show how important it is to choose a database vendor with staying power. Microsoft has a proven track record for building and improving its software products. The team Microsoft has assembled for SQL Server is all-star quality. With its existing tools, its new SQL Server 7 database, and 7x24x365 support, clients can be confident when making a decision to go with Microsoft as a long-term partner.

Time to move on. An all too easily forgotten aspect of the data warehouse development exercise is the people involved in the process. Building that team is the subject material of the next chapter. So many people with a wide range of skillsets belly up to the bar when delivering a decision support solution. Leave your prejudices behind; sometimes there are more politics involved as the many neophytes are molded into a cohesive team. Leading that team can be a course fraught with pitfalls and potholes. There is such a demand for data warehouse specialists that we all cannot forget that we got started, too, sometime in the past; be patient and work together!

# CHAPTER 3

## Building the Team

When we began writing this chapter, the intent was to supply you with a successful organizational chart, which could be used as the basis to build a data warehouse team. But, the more we thought about it, the more we realized that would be the equivalent of implying only one correct way exists for you to organize a data warehouse team. In truth, correct ways to solve any problem or meet any challenge depend upon many factors, all of which are specific to available resources and your particular time constraints.

With this in mind, it became clear this chapter would be of more value if it discussed various roles that should be part of a successful data warehouse initiative. After looking at the individuals—their unique abilities and time constraints—you have available, you can use this chapter as a sounding board when you build your team. In addition, it will act as a reference tool to see if you have covered all necessary bases.

# THE DATA WAREHOUSE TEAM CHECKLIST

No matter which task you choose to analyze, as you break it into its various components, you quickly realize that no matter how simple the task seems, it is not as easy as it looks. To illustrate this point, look at how complicated it is simply to take a container of milk from a refrigerator and pour that milk into a glass. As you look at this problem in more detail, you might derive the following task list:

1. Locate the refrigerator.
2. Open the refrigerator door.
3. Scan the current contents of the refrigerator to locate a container of milk.
4. Determine how to move any items in the refrigerator that stand in your way so you can obtain the milk.
5. Remove the milk container from the refrigerator and place it on the kitchen counter.
6. Remove the milk cap.
7. Place the milk cap on the kitchen counter.
8. Determine where the clean glasses are located.
9. Open the kitchen cabinet door that contains the clean glasses.
10. Determine which hand to use and how to hold and retrieve the clean glass.
11. Inspect the glass for chips because it is breakable.
12. Bring the glass to the bottle of milk.
13. Pour the milk into the glass.

This list represents the task list of pouring a glass of milk in its simplest form, but what if a problem occurred? What if the bottle of milk was almost empty? What if the bottle of milk was a paper carton? What if the milk was in a plastic container? What if the glass you were about to use was chipped? What if the glass you picked up was not properly cleaned? What if you wanted the milk warmed?

As you can see from this simple example, many tasks must be performed and many different scenarios must be considered. Each one of these situations will affect how long it takes to get a glass of milk. The old native saying, "Don't judge people until you have walked in their moccasins," applies here. The significant attribute of a professional athlete is the ability to make a sport look so easy you want to try it yourself. When we watched Larry Bird of the Boston Celtics play basketball or Bobby Orr of the Boston Bruins play hockey, they made it look so easy. (It's not hard to see a few of us are very big Boston sports fans. On a side note, we do not want to hear how good the Chicago Bulls are until they win 16 world championships. They are still a very far cry from the legacy of the Boston Celtics—sorry, Boston pride overwhelmed us there for a minute.) Yet when we pick up a hockey stick or a basketball, we are very quickly brought to the realization that it's not so easy.

When you look at the listing of data warehouse roles, do not underestimate the complexity of the undertaking on which you are about to embark. Be it a data mart or a full-blown, enterprise-wide data warehouse, it is a lot of work to take your organization's data, scrub it, clean it, and repackage it so that you have easy access to slice and dice it any way you want. No matter how easy your team makes it look, under the surface, a lot of effort was expended to get you there. In much the same way the professional athlete makes a particular sport look so easy, a successful data warehouse implementation team will make what they do look easy at first glance. Yet, when you take the time to look behind the scenes, a lot of tasks were completed and a lot of time-consuming effort made it all possible.

Let's take a high-level look at a data warehouse roles checklist; these are some of the areas of responsibility you need to cover in your effort to build a warehouse. Since there is a great deal of overlap, we will only go into detail on the major items. The next listing shows a data warehouse roles checklist—use this as your guideline when building the team.

```
Data warehouse project manager
Data warehouse architect
Database administrator
System administrator
Data migration specialist
Legacy system specialist
Data transformation/grooming specialist
Data provision specialist
Data mart development leader
Operations/data center
Configuration management
Organization consultant
Change management consultant
Quality assurance/testing specialist
Infrastructure specialist
Production control analyst
```

```
Power user
Trainer
Technical writer
Public relations person
Metadata steward
Corporate sponsors
Help desk functionality
End-user business executive
Tools specialist
Vendor relations person
Web master
Metadata repository manager
New technologies analyst
New technologies manager
End users
Consultants
```

**TIP:** Your particular situation will determine how these roles are allocated. On a very large data warehouse effort, these roles would be spread among 7 to 30 individuals; on a smaller warehouse effort, a single person might accomplish two, three, or even all these roles.

As you can see from reviewing the data warehouse roles checklist, you must think through and account for many different roles. Your level of success will depend on how you manage the resources you have available to accomplish the tasks associated with these roles. On a very large data warehouse effort, each of these roles might represent a particular individual; on a smaller effort, a single person might accomplish two or more of these roles.

## ROLES NEEDED FOR YOUR DATA WAREHOUSE TEAM

As you read the detail of these roles, remember your particular situation and the personalities involved. Review your situation from two different perspectives:

▼ **The job function**—the nature of the job that has to be performed

▲ **The person or individual**—the nature of the person performing a task

For example, you must decide which person or what team will be responsible for the functions of a system administrator, who should be responsible for determining whether or not the backups are working, and if the correct system patches are installed. As we stated before, you must determine if the person you choose has the right technical breadth of experience coupled with an appropriate personality. If not, perhaps a team should fulfill this function. Let's proceed by having a look at the major players on the data warehouse team, particularly their abilities, and their responsibilities.

# Data Warehouse Project Director

The person you consider for project director should have a quick wit and a solid understanding of the business and its technology vision. More importantly, this person must understand why the business needs a data warehouse and how to sell this concept to senior management to obtain the needed funding. The project director must have the ability to talk about the data warehouse initiative from the 10,000-foot view. Project directors should spend much of their time working with senior management to keep them up to date on the status of the project and to ensure that the direction of the warehouse project will meet the business directives. A project director typically holds the purse strings for the project; he or she is the type of person who can take the vision of the corporation and make certain everyone in the team understands it. The project director must have strong leadership qualities. The project director must "sell" the warehouse to both senior management and potential users; yes, many users are part of the design team. This selling job is to users that may end up coming on board after seeing the results of the warehousing initiative (i.e., screens full of analytical query data) on corporate desktops around the organization.

## Abilities/Responsibilities

▼ This is the person responsible for the strategic initiatives for the overall data warehouse. They must be able to aid the organization by envisioning how the warehouse will be utilized and deployed to meet the organization's information objectives.

■ The perspective of this person is that of a bird flying over a maze. This image represents the project director's need to take a global view of the project to see where it is headed. Like the bird, a project director sees the paths of the maze and where they all head, yet he or she may not see every pitfall hidden within the maze.

■ Must have strong leadership skills. The project director should constantly communicate the vision of the project. This ability to motivate and inspire will, in effect, energize all team members and enable them to overcome any barriers to change. These barriers will come in many forms, from political obstacles to resource problems.

■ Must know how to establish a vision for the future and how to relate this vision to the needs of the business. They must develop strategies to produce all necessary changes to accomplish the vision.

■ Must have strong political skills. The project director must know how to package and sell the efforts of the team to senior management. He or she must understand the importance of each business unit within the company and ensure that the priorities of the warehouse project are in synch with the priorities of the business.

- Must have strong communication skills, including written ability, oral ability, and the ability to listen effectively.

- Must have strong financial skills. The project director will have ownership of the warehouse budget as well as ownership of the preparation of the budget. He or she will also have to ensure this budget adheres to the standard corporate practices.

- Must have power over the technology. The project director must be able to talk the talk but not necessarily walk the walk.

- Must be responsible to senior management for the status of the project. The buck stops with the project director. If anything goes wrong, the problem rests on his or her shoulders.

- Must be responsible for monitoring the major milestones of the project and for making certain the milestones are in tune with corporate needs.

- Must be able to educate top management on the various applications and the impact data warehousing will have on those applications.

- Must be adept at obtaining the necessary economic support within the business units.

- Must be able to educate users on the data warehouse and its capabilities.

- Should be participating in user group meetings and industry associations.

- Must be able to define budgets and schedules.

▲ Must be able to identify applications and prioritize between applications.

## Data Warehouse Project Manager

Unlike the data warehouse director, the data warehouse project manager does not need a quick wit. He or she needs sound organizational skills and sound management capabilities. The data warehouse project manager should spend time managing the initiative and directives of the project. He or she must understand the data warehouse initiative from a rat's view of the maze; however, having the ability to see over the maze is also very important.

The project manager must understand and oversee all the details of the project. He or she owns the project plan and oversees it daily. This person must understand how to be a great negotiator because he or she will constantly be dealing with conflict resolution and task prioritization. The project manager must understand what a critical path is and how to manage a project against it. He or she should constantly be working with the team leaders to appraise the technical soundness of each task.

When you visualize a project manager, you may have a mental image of a burly sort of person who has an ability to hold people's feet to the fire physically. The project manager's role is not that of a visionary, but he or she must know how to follow the vision. This is not the job of a corporate politician, but he or she must understand the politics of the team members. The project manager needs to be a great negotiator; success on the job hinges on the ability to navigate through the stakeholders' convergent needs. He or she understands that a successful project plan contains tangible results. The project manager must understand that a task is either 100 percent complete or it is not done at all. He or she understands that no task should take more than three weeks. The best analogy to this position is that of the majority whip in the U.S. Senate. The whip makes certain the right players are present; he or she pushes what must be pushed through and delegates what must be delegated. The whip is skilled at sidestepping the non-issues and overcoming the hurdles. He or she is the person who drives the car.

*TIP:* The most important attribute of a great project manager is the ability to keep an eye on milestones constantly and never lose sight of the project commitments.

## Abilities/Responsibilities

▼ This person is not a corporate politician but, instead, a person with strong team-building skills. The project manager understands how to make a group of people work together as one toward a common goal.

■ Must be able to align the project deliverables with the business needs. They must have the vision to understand the business objectives of the warehouse while still providing the leadership to help the team deliver in a timely manner.

■ Must have strong organizational skills and pay very close attention to detail.

■ Must have strong planning skills.

■ Must have strong management skills, but also must understand technology. On the job, the project manager will constantly be dealing with team members who have varied skill sets. He or she must understand technical mumbo-jumbo. Put another way, they should have a good idea how long a particular task should take. When a task falls behind schedule, they should be able to look under the covers to ensure the process and procedure the technical staff member is using is appropriate.

■ Must be able to plan effectively and allocate available resources. A staff member with too little to do is as dangerous for a project as a team member with too much work to do. Both these situations will lead to team member fatigue.

■ Must be able to deal with resource shortages effectively. People leave projects and move on. This is a fact of life. A project manager who does not deal with this easily is sure to fail. A project manager who panics every time a resource leaves is not in control and is not doing his or her job.

- The project manager must be a diplomat. The project manager will constantly deal with stakeholders who feel their needs are the most critical. Stakeholders typically only see their needs. A good project manager must assess each stakeholder's need and see where those needs fit into the overall vision of the project.

- Must know how to deliver bad news and how to circulate good news. They realize one of the keys to success is a well-informed team member.

- Must be able to set up and *control* a meeting. They must be able to provide team members with the needed nudge when they don't appear for meetings.

- Must be in control of the project scope. The project manager must be able to control scope creep. *Scope creep* happens when requests come in that will affect the delivery date of a project. The project manager must know how to take this problem to the appropriate ears, and then he or she must obtain the necessary documentation to support the approval of the scope creep.

- Must be able to do appropriate risk management. For example, when the project manager is working with new technology, he or she must understand how this new technology may affect the project plans. In a data warehouse environment, this is critical because you are constantly dealing with bleeding-edge technology. *Bleeding-edge technology* is state of the art and introduces new ways to do something with new functionality. If you don't want your project to die from this, the project manager must understand risk assessment.

- Must listen well. The project manager must pay attention; he or she must know when to interrupt and when to listen.

- Must have the ability to harmonize the team. The project manager must be able to reconcile disagreements.

- Must be able to play the role of gatekeeper. The project manager helps facilitate participation by the team members. He or she must constantly monitor to see if everyone is satisfied with the approaches. The project manager should make certain the team understands the priorities.

*TIP:* Project managers must take the time to understand the contribution of everyone on the team. Team members that are treated like mushrooms do not thrive. Only mushrooms thrive in the dark.

- Must be an excellent negotiator—able to admit an error and to look for the compromise that will get the project back on track.

- Must be able to determine the performance of the project. They realize tasks are not 50 percent complete—it's all or nothing. A task is not done till it's 100 percent. Trying to manage a project by partial completion does not work.

- Must realize that sick projects will not get better on their own. The project manager knows sick projects require corrective action immediately.

- Must realize he or she cannot be a developer at the same time. The position of a data warehouse project manager is a full-time, dedicated position.

- Must be able to select team members and then motivate them.

- Must be able to evaluate team members and perform performance appraisals.

- Must be able to run a project to a budget.

- Must be able to educate users on the data warehouse and how it will impact the particular business unit.

- Must be able to monitor industry trends and identify emerging technologies that should be considered for adoption.

▲ Like the director of data warehousing, he or she should be able to identify and solidify economic support for the project.

# Data Provision Specialist/Business Analysts

Data provision specialists are the people who go out and meet with various department heads and key end users to define the business needs of the organization; then, they communicate those needs to the rest of the team. To be successful, data provision specialists must have strong people skills. They must be able to extract information from nontechnical people and convey pertinent information to the technical teams. This information takes many forms—from current business practices to the current invoice forms used. They must have enough political savvy to identify the key decision makers and power users. In a nutshell, data provision specialists must be able to determine what information must be available if the warehouse is to meet various business unit needs.

## Abilities/Responsibilities

▼ Must serve as the conceptual business advisor for the project.

- Must know how to phrase questions to determine the end users' needs.

- Must have excellent writing skills and the ability to convey the end users' needs to the technical teams.

- Must be able to develop the database schema and be familiar with data concepts like the star schema.

- Must take responsibility for defining the scope statements. Must work with the technical teams and the user community to obtain the necessary consensus so the project moves forward.

- Must have excellent people skills. Data provision specialists not only must be diplomats, they must also be eloquent communicators. Much of the success of the data warehouse project hinges upon the ability of the data provision specialist to work well with the user community.

■ Must have enough political savvy to identify key decision makers. They must then know how to make the best use of the key decision-makers' time when they have it.

■ Must be able to assist the end users in how to find the information they need from the warehouse.

■ Must be able to help train the end users.

■ Must be able to develop EIS and decision support systems.

■ Must be able to develop and implement test plans for new applications. This includes monitoring data quality. Dirty data will destroy a data warehouse project very quickly.

■ Must be able to gain consensus among different users' departments for the good of the warehouse. This means helping to develop and implement common data definitions and key performance indicators.

■ Must be able to identify and document the inflows and outflows of data to the warehouse. This includes identifying possible incompatibility of data in the warehouse to other systems. For example, he or she must ensure that the financial data in the warehouse reconciles to the source financial systems.

▲ Must be able to evaluate new software—from middleware, reporting tools, and front-end software to data mining "OLAP" software.

## Data Warehouse Architect

The data warehouse architect is a technical Jack or Jill of all trades. To achieve success in this career, the architect must understand both the technical side (i.e., familiarity with the software and hardware involved) and the business needs. He or she will take the findings of the data provision team and interpret those findings into a road map of the data warehouse. This road map is typically the *entity relationship diagram* that maps out the tables and the relationships between the assortment of tables in the data warehouse. If you think of the data warehouse project team as a basketball team, the data architect is the point man; this is the person who guides the team to the opposing team's net.

The data warehouse consists of information from the various operational areas of the company and some external systems. The data warehouse architect team understands all these data feeds and weaves them into a single integrated data reservoir. In a successful data warehouse implementation, the various business units will gain access to all the necessary information they need to stay competitive.

An architect who understands the business needs and implements them into a functional database design has the key to success. No substitute for real-world experience exists, because this is what teaches a good data architect when to break the rules and when to follow them. What is important is that the architect has the ability to remove him or herself from daily details and to take a more global view.

## Abilities/Responsibilities

▼ Must take ownership of the entity relationship diagram and all the corresponding documentation. An example of other documentation the person should be responsible for is a corporate data dictionary, which contains all the attributes, table names, and constraints.

■ Must be able to articulate the overall architecture and establish and maintain standards.

■ Must possess a thorough knowledge of database design and associated tools.

■ Must have good peer-to-peer communication skills. Does not require corporate political skill—but it doesn't hurt either.

■ Must be fluent in evaluating and selecting appropriate hardware.

■ Must be fluent in evaluating and selecting appropriate networking facilities.

■ Must be fluent in evaluating RDBMS software.

■ Must be fluent in evaluating and selecting the appropriate extraction, transformation, and loading products.

■ Must have good business analysis skills.

■ Must be able to evaluate new software—from middleware, reporting tools, and front-end software to data mining "OLAP" software.

■ Must be able to educate users and technical staff on data warehouse capabilities.

■ Should be monitoring industry trends and identifying technologies that should be adopted.

■ Must be responsible for managing the data warehouse metadata, which is data about data. The data warehouse architect is king or queen of the data.

■ Must be the watchdog of data warehouse standards. It is his or her responsibility to maintain all the documentation about the warehouse database design. The data warehouse architect is responsible for adopting database design and naming standards; he or she must also make certain these are followed. These standards should be used in all future application development.

■ Is the primary person responsible for the development and delivery of the subject models and logical warehouse models.

▲ Provide expertise in the area of data volumes, network capacities, storage volumes, and growth projections.

# Database Administrator

A description for the perfect database administrator (DBA) would be a benevolent king or queen. To achieve success at this job, the database administrator must have a tight reign over his or her database kingdom. He or she must surround the database castle with a moat, lowering the drawbridge only to those who have earned the right to use the database. Only friends—not foes—can enter the database. Like a benevolent king or queen, the ideal database administrator is concerned with the safety and security of the castle. This means appropriate measures are taken and procedures are established to make certain the database is backed up and secure. He or she measures the response of the database and takes corrective action to ensure response time is adequate.

This is a critical role, which should be present early in the process. Many organizations make the mistake of not keeping a full-time DBA in the process. The database administrator should be a normal extension of the team from the beginning for complete effectiveness.

## Abilities/Responsibilities

▼ Must have some political skills. For example, the database administrator might not want to upgrade the system on the busiest business day of the year. Common sense is a requirement.

■ Must ensure appropriate backup and recovery procedures are in place to meet the business requirements. If a project is not backed up and a database is lost, a month of the project team's work could be lost.

■ Must be fluent in how to design the logical database, then take that logical database and implement the physical model.

■ Must be responsible for putting security in place to make certain only the right people can look at the right data. In other words, the DBA uses SQL Server mechanisms to control all access to the database, as discussed in Chapter 12. The database administrator works closely with the data architects to implement the database design. In addition, he or she must be able to set up a procedure that logs usage of the warehouse.

■ Must be able to implement processes that monitor query and database performance.

■ Must work closely with the technical team to ensure they adhere to corporate policies and procedures pertaining to the database. This includes development of policies to control the movement of applications onto a production database.

■ Must monitor the growth of the database to ensure the smooth running of daily activities.

■ Must monitor performance. This is a critical function of the DBA. He or she must establish baselines and compare the database performance against the baselines to ensure it is performing adequately.

■ Must tend to daily administration of the database.

■ Must be able to tackle issues as soon as they spring up. The database administrator position is one of the most technically challenging roles that exist within all the teams.

■ Must have minimum writing skills, although email etiquette is a plus.

■ Must be available to work 24×7. This is not a 9 to 5 job.

■ Must work closely with the system administrator to install all database software and patches.

■ Must be able to establish procedures that monitor the loading of the database. These procedures should ensure that adequate database space is available. The procedures should make sure that data is loaded in the most efficient manner. Data loading is discussed in Chapter 8.

■ Must be able to monitor data quality. The DBA is concerned with data quality.

■ Must be able to select and size hardware platforms.

▲ Must be able to select and implement middleware.

# System Administrator

The system administrator (SA) must understand the ins and outs of the chosen data warehouse environment. The SA is responsible for administering the computer systems, whereas the DBA is responsible for administering the databases. The SA is responsible for system backups, installation of new hardware, upgrading the hardware, system software, firewall creation, and any other daily activities concerning the computer system. A *firewall* is a set of computer programs restricting network access to the data warehouse. Think how much project time would be lost if your development environment were destroyed!

In today's world, the system administrator is the cowboy or cowgirl of computers. Many times they work alone and during off-hours. They are constantly on call and dealing with show-stopping problems. This gives them an attitude and tends to make them stand alone. You can spot many a male SA, by the ponytail—that's why we call them the cowboys of computers.

## Abilities/Responsibilities

▼ Must have some political skills. For example, the system administrator may not want to upgrade the system on the busiest business day of the year. Common sense is a critical requirement.

■ Must be available 24×7. When things happen, the system administrator must respond immediately.

■ Must ensure appropriate backup and recovery procedures are in place to meet the business requirements.

■ Must take responsibility for putting security in place to make certain only the right people can look at the system. In today's environment, the SA typically gets involved in firewall creation.

■ Must work closely with the technical team to make certain they adhere closely to corporate policies and procedures pertaining to the system. This includes development of policies to control the movement of applications onto a production system.

■ Must be able to do performance monitoring; this is another critical function of the system administrator. He or she must establish baselines and compare the performance of the system against the base to ensure it is performing adequately.

■ Must have minimum writing skills, although email etiquette is a plus.

■ Must be able to access the system remotely. When something happens after hours, the SA must be able to respond.

■ Must be fluent at administering user access and security.

■ Like the DBA, they must be able to account for users' activities.

▲ Must be capable of evaluating and selecting hardware and software—that includes the network hardware and software.

## Data Migration Specialist

This is a cornerstone position. If you can't get the data out of the legacy system, your warehouse project will fail. The data migration specialist is responsible for the development and acquisition of software that enables your organization to move data from legacy systems and external data sources into a staging area for the transformation effort. The *staging area* is a holding area for some data before it is moved into the SQL Server data warehouse repository.

The data migration specialist must understand the relationship and the differences between the legacy system and the warehouse. The role of the data migration specialist is to transfer the knowledge and data from the legacy system into a format with which the data transformation team can work. The goal of *data migration* is to move this data into a new format without compromising data integrity and to maintain all the business rules. This is such a critical task, with so many intricacies, that it is useful to break it into a separate effort from transforming the data. Many times, a major role data migration plays is getting the data into an SQL Server table or an ASCII file. An *ASCII* file contains text data. These formats make it easy for the new technology tools to manipulate the data.

If you were looking for a data migration specialist, you should look within your organization for a long-time player who possesses an intimate working knowledge of the legacy systems and a strong desire to learn the new technology. This is typically a person within your organization who has chosen the technical route vs. the management route. In this position, technical prowess is king.

You need to write or develop internal tools to facilitate migration because this is an evolving area within building a warehouse. The data migration specialist must be open to third-party solutions. There are many new solutions coming to market every day. This individual should be able to evaluate these tools and be able to make reasonable business decisions—to determine, for example, if buying a solution is better than building it in-house.

## Abilities/Responsibilities

▼    Must have intimate knowledge of the current legacy system and understand the data stored within the system. This knowledge must include the internal structure of the existing legacy systems or the ability to analyze the legacy system to learn the data structures. This is a highly technical area where strong programming skills are a must.

■    Need not be political. Like the rat mentioned earlier, the data migration specialist must know how to navigate through the maze to find the cheese. His or her nose and wits are all they need—political savvy is just plain not needed.

■    Must be competent with legacy tools. Communication or writing skills are not important. This is a highly technical slot.

■    Must work closely with the legacy technology specialist to learn necessary information.

■    Must be proficient at developing data cleaning and data migration programs, or in using the appropriate automated toolset available today for this task.

■    Must be proficient at identifying data sources. Like a bird dog, he or she needs to be able to follow the scent and bring home the bird.

■    Must be able to automate the entire migration process. Many times, these programs will be running for quite some time. This includes procedures to ensure the process works correctly.

▲    Must be able to develop test plans.

# Data Transformation/Grooming Specialist

People in this position are concerned with migrating the data into the appropriate SQL Server tables with their associated attributes. Many times, this includes cleaning the data, making certain all the codes are standardized. One record in the legacy system can become split into multiple table rows, which can quickly become very complicated. What sounds like a simple task is not. This effort will consume a major portion of the project. In essence, the data transformation specialist makes an apple into an orange or tries to fit a round peg into a square hole.

Unlike many of the existing legacy systems, SQL Server is not as forgiving of inconsistencies. For example, if an attribute is defined as "not null," you must supply a value. There is an old saying, "garbage in, garbage out," (GIGO) that applies here. If you don't take the time to convert and load the database correctly, then don't start the project.

The bottom line? The data transformation/grooming specialist is concerned with the actual transformation of the data into the new database design. This is where the old system becomes the new one.

## Abilities/Responsibilities

▼ Must be highly technical. The data transformation/grooming specialist position requires a strong working knowledge of SQL Server 7 loading techniques and Transact*SQL.

■ Must be a perfectionist. The data transformation specialist position contains the "bean counters" of the technical world. If they are not perfectionists, you will be in trouble. Dirty data is worthless data. The value of the warehouse correlates directly to the quality of the data.

■ Need not be political.

■ Must develop the code needed to groom the data into the new data structure, meeting all the new standards.

■ Must work closely with the data architect and data provision specialist to make certain all business needs are met.

■ Should be proficient at being able to search for causes of incompatibility of data. If you want a warehouse to be successful when you first turn it on, don't expect your users to find data problems. If you do, they will quickly not trust or use the warehouse.

■ Responsible for developing and implementing the software that will clean and scrub the data.

▲ Must be able to develop and implement test plans.

# Data Mart Development Leader

A *data mart*, by definition, is a subset of the data warehouse. The required skills for the data mart development leader closely mirror those of the data provision specialist. The only difference is the effort of a data mart development leader concentrates on a particular business area. For example, the data mart development leader might be working on the marketing data mart. His or her effort is focused on how to present the key components of the warehouse in which the marketing group is interested—no more and no less.

## Abilities/Responsibilities

▼ Must know how to phrase questions to determine the end users' needs.

■ Must have excellent writing skills and the ability to convey the end users' needs to the technical teams.

- Should be proficient in the business area the data mart is being built for.

- Must be able to develop the data mart schema and be familiar with data concepts like the star schema.

- Must take responsibility for defining the scope statements. Must work with the technical teams and the user community to obtain the necessary consensus so the project moves forward.

- Must have excellent people skills. Data mart leaders not only must be diplomats, they must also be eloquent communicators. Much of the success of a particular data mart hinges upon the ability of the data mart leader to work well with the user community.

- Must have enough political savvy to identify key decision makers. He or she must then know how to make the best use of the key decision-makers' time.

- Must be able to assist the end users in how to find the information they need from the data mart. He or she must also structure the data mart so that it makes sense for end users to navigate.

- Must be able to help train the end users.

- Must be able to develop EIS and decision support systems.

- Must be able to develop and implement test plans for new applications. This includes monitoring data quality. Dirty data will destroy a data mart very quickly.

- Must be able to gain consensus among different users' departments for the good of the warehouse. This means helping to develop and implement common data definitions and key performance indicators.

- Must be able to identify and document the inflows and outflows of data to the mart. This includes identifying possible incompatibility of data in the warehouse to other systems. For example, he or she must ensure that the financial data in the warehouse reconciles to the source financial systems.

- Must be able to evaluate new software—from middleware, reporting tools, and front-end software to data mining "OLAP" software.

- Must be able to deploy the data mart quickly. In today's world, users must see results every 60 to 90 days.

## Quality Assurance/Testing Specialist

"A job worth doing is a job worth doing well!" Quality is something you achieve the old-fashioned way—you work at it. Someone within the team must be focused on quality. If the culture of your warehouse team has strong roots in quality, then the product built will be one of quality. One way to obtain a high-quality product is to have a thorough testing process. The quality assurance team is established to play the role of "gatekeeper" who is responsible for quality.

The quality assurance/testing specialist works with stakeholders to make certain everyone works together to deliver a finished product. Typically, this function is responsible for creating and approving testing plans. This specialist is responsible for reviewing test results, which may mean making certain the code compiles cleanly before it moves into production or comparing the legacy system results to the warehouse results. He or she must be adept at tracing problems back to their source and have enough political savvy to get source systems to correct the problem at the start and not make the warehouse have the horrendous job of fixing all data problems within the warehouse.

Someone once told us that we do not release data for consumption of the users, we publish data. It's funny that when we read our daily newspaper or read this book, we do not expect to see any errors. However, when we happen upon a typo or a grammatical error, we are surprised. Maybe this surprise is a result of our expectation that newspapers and books are reviewed and checked by many people before they ever see the light of day, so mistakes should be caught. We do not live in a perfect world, so errors happen; they also occur since our world is ever changing. We must stop and constantly review how we are doing. The quality assurance individual or team must be the one place in the business that constantly asks, "How are we doing?" The answer may be, "OK!", but they must be ready and able to say, "Houston, we have a problem." They are the last line of defense, and as such will be ultimately responsible for publishing the data that will be used to help the organization make decisions, so do not underestimate the need for data warehouse and data quality assurance.

## Abilities/Responsibilities

▼ Must be responsible for creating and reviewing all test plans. This includes identifying the appropriate warehouse team members and members of the user community who should participate in the quality/testing process.

■ Must be aware that this is a cooperative effort of all the stakeholders. To obtain a quality product, the quality assurance/testing specialist and all the stakeholders must make a concentrated effort throughout the project. A quality product will not be obtained if the effort occurs only at the technical end.

■ Need not be political, except team members will always have good reasons why they do not have to comply with the rules. We suggest you have the quality team report to the project manager. Otherwise, they will not be effective.

■ Need not be a highly technical role. The position of quality assurance/testing specialist is primarily one of user testing.

▲ For this process to work, a plan must exist. Without proper preparation, you will not achieve the results you want.

# Infrastructure Specialist

The infrastructure specialist is the person responsible for crossing all the *T*s and dotting all the *I*s. This person or team makes certain all the pieces are in place. Do all new users have appropriate hardware? Do they have proper system accounts? Are all the database access roles defined? Do they have the appropriate training to do the job? As you can see, a successful data warehouse has thousands of intricate details, each of which must be attended to for a successful project. The infrastructure specialist is the person responsible for all the nitty-gritty details.

The infrastructure specialist must be a good technical coordinator to be successful. He or she must be able to develop an implementation plan and track its progress throughout the organization. The infrastructure specialist must know when to raise that alarm bell and when to do careful prodding. You can build the greatest system in the world, but if your users can't access it, your work was for naught.

## Abilities/Responsibilities

▼ Must be able to see the bigger picture. For example, you don't want to order a personal computer (PC) for the field a year ahead of time. And you don't want to give end users PCs without making certain they know how to use it.

■ Must be moderately technical. It helps if the infrastructure specialist can talk the terminology.

▲ Must have excellent organizational skills. He or she must be able to hold people's feet to the fire. If the network specialist promises to have network software installed on Thursday, the infrastructure person needs to make certain it happens.

# Power User (Legacy System Specialist)

No one understands the application better than end users. They are the ultimate customers. If you want to be successful, keep the end users happy and involved. They have a much better understanding of the business than the technical team. Look for those power users who typically love technology and will work with you, quickly embracing the new system. A system must be used if it is to be accepted. The sooner you can get users using and embracing the system, the sooner the warehouse will be accepted.

These power users typically help your team bridge the gap of knowledge between the old system and the new system. You need them to help you understand the current operational systems (from which data is extracted for the data warehouse).

### Abilities/Responsibilities

▼   Must have an intimate working knowledge of the current legacy system.

■   Must have a strong working knowledge of application, but technical ability is not a requirement.

■   Must have strong communication skills, because you want them to help teach the new system to other end users.

■   Must have political savvy and connections. You want them to spread the good news. A classic trait of a power user is someone the rest of the organization uses for information. He or she becomes the answer person within the department.

■   May or may not be technical, yet power users are adept at making the system work for them.

▲   Must love technology.

## Trainer

A big mistake many organizations make is to put technology on the desks of users without formal training. If you want to be successful, you must teach the community how to use the warehouse. The best trainers are typically in-house power users that know and understand the business. We recommend you have a trainer who develops strong training material to provide to the power users for teaching their departments. In other words, train the trainer. This way, power users reinforce their own knowledge and enhance their standing in the department. You want to help strengthen their power base because they are on your side. Power users know their peers better than anyone. The more they spread the good news, the better.

### Abilities/Responsibilities

▼   Must have excellent communication skills and infinite patience.

■   Must have excellent user knowledge of the warehouse and its tools.

■   Must have excellent writing skills. A difference exists between good technical documentation and good training materials.

▲   Must have the ability to laugh. A good smile is a plus.

## Technical Writer

What if a developer gets hit by a truck on the way to work? Would the necessary documentation exist to protect the interests of your company? Many times, the answer to this question is "No!" Most developers do not want to write technical documentation.

This is a fact we must face. You need good documentation to help get the word out about the work you are doing. Does it make more sense to have a programmer writing documentation or to have a technical writer doing the documentation? Which choice leads to better job satisfaction and a better product? The answer is the technical writer; let the writer write.

The position of technical writer is frequently overlooked. A data warehouse is a complex application. Having good standardized technical documentation is helpful. This is one of the ways your user community will judge the effort.

## Abilities/Responsibilities

▼ Must have excellent communication skills and infinite patience, because the technical writer is dealing with developers with little to no program documentation.

■ Must have a good working knowledge of the warehouse.

■ Must write clearly and concisely; must employ good standards within the documentation.

■ Need not be political.

■ Must have a working vocabulary of data warehousing.

▲ Must have the needed credentials. This is a professional skillset and you want it done right.

# Public Relations Person

The public relations (PR) person should have a quick wit and a great smile. Typically, he or she must know how to play golf. You want the PR person to get the word out to senior management wherever possible. He or she must understand the business and how the warehouse will impact it. The idea with this role is for the PR person to provide management with the status of the project in a controlled manner. He or she needs to know how to distribute bad news softly and good news with a bullhorn. The PR person is responsible for corporate-wide communication, which includes overseeing such activities as newsletters, power user meetings, senior management meetings, and participating in key presentations.

## Abilities/Responsibilities

▼ Must know how to let senior management win the golf game.

■ Must have excellent communication and presentation skills.

■ Should have attended a "dress for success" seminar.

■ Should know how to turn a challenge into an opportunity.

■ Must know how to turn a project delay into a respite.

- Must be a great politician, with an ear constantly against the wall.
- Must be loyal to the cause.
- Must like to travel, to get the good word spread.
- ▲ Must never talk technical. This frightens the nontechnical community.

## Corporate Sponsors

If the project is to be successful, you must know who backed the project in senior management. Then, you can use the backers to break down the large barriers in your way. Look for ways to enhance their standing in the company. Know who your strongest ally is and what his or her agenda is. Make certain the PR person works closely with your strongest ally. This will help you understand how to keep the project healthy and happy. Beggars can't be choosers. Corporate sponsors come in all sizes and shapes, and you get what you get.

## Help Desk Functionality

An undertaking of this magnitude will have problems. Your ability to get users working painlessly with the warehouse is critical. A help desk is a great way to diffuse anxiety. If users know someone is listening and cares, they will give you the needed break. Don't go live until you have a functioning help desk—a one-stop place for answers. Monitoring the volume and types of calls is critical so that the quality team is aware of trouble points and can address them early in the process.

**TIP:** Do not turn on your warehouse until you have figured out how your help desk function will be handled.

### Abilities/Responsibilities

- ▼ Must have a trained person who understands how to use the warehouse properly.
- Must have infinite patience and understanding.
- Should have good technical knowledge so he or she can communicate the problem to the team.
- A help desk must be organized.
- ▲ Must have excellent communication skills and know the terminology of the community of users. Don't have propeller heads answering the phones.

# Tools Specialist

A successful data warehouse implementation consists of many sophisticated tools. You need good application developers who understand the tools you are using to build and deploy the warehouse. The tool specialist's ability to use these tools will help minimize the risk of the project.

## Abilities/Responsibilities

▼ Must be highly technical.

■ Should be aware of and have a good working knowledge of the core third-party tools in the marketplace.

■ Should have the ability to choose the right tool for the right job. For example, this person would know when it makes sense to use one tool rather than another, driven by knowledge acquired of the SQL Server 7 data warehouse solution.

▲ Must be a worker rat. The tool specialist builds the maze and, thus, needs no political skills.

# Vendor Relations Person

Building a data warehouse in today's world requires the use of many key vendors. No one vendor yet—not even Microsoft—can supply you with one-stop shopping. Your ability to manage your vendor relationships is critical. You need vendors who bring real solutions to the table and who do not waste your time with immature products that someday may be ready. This position requires a dedicated eye to the problem. If this position is filled correctly, you will be successful much quicker.

## Abilities/Responsibilities

▼ Must have good technical skills and understand the warehouse requirements.

■ Must be able to develop criteria that can be used to determine if a vendor product makes sense. From day one, the vendor relations person should be aware of the core data warehouse products.

■ Must have good communication skills.

■ Must have good writing skills.

■ Must have good negotiation skills, which includes the ability to review the contracts.

▲ Must understand the political relation between the vendors and your company.

# Web Master

Face it, we live in an Internet-enabled world already. Many people consider the pace at which PC usage has grown around the world frightening. Well, Internet technology is growing at a rate three times faster than the PC. An Internet year is like going from the 80386 chip to the Pentium Pro in just one year. Recently at an industry show, the president of the United States' adviser on Internet technologies stated that by the year 2002, the industry expects $400 billion USD to be spent online. It's no wonder the Internet age is heating up so fast—the private sector of the world smells opportunity and is gravitating to it very quickly.

The Internet is also revolutionizing how we deploy software. With software based on a universal browser, you have a very easy way to deploy and maintain applications. With all this in mind, the Internet landscape is changing every day and requires someone who is responsible for paying attention to it and how it should impact the data warehouse.

## Abilities/Responsibilities

▼ Responsible for being quickly abreast of emerging Internet technologies as they apply to the warehouse.

■ Should be familiar with key vendors' Internet strategies.

■ Must be able to evaluate and install Internet technologies.

▲ Must be able to install and implement the network. This includes firewall technologies and developing processes to identify performance bottlenecks.

# Consultant

Face it, you can't be all things to all people. Sometimes you need to reach outside your organization and bring in the experts. Just be smart about it. Check resumes and check references.

As you can see, many roles and individuals are necessary for a successful data warehouse project. In this chapter, we took time to highlight some of the key roles. Since many of the roles overlap each other, we did not describe in detail all the roles—only the key ones. Don't get hung up on titles, since they are constantly changing and many titles mean the same thing. For example, to many people a system administrator is the same as a system manager, which is the same as a network administrator. Focus in on what jobs you need done and make sure you cover as many bases as possible. This chapter should have given you the information you need to put a successful team in place. Chapter 4 discusses managing the data warehouse team. Suggestions will be offered on some sound and proven project management techniques. The techniques presented helped us deliver projects on time and on budget.

# CHAPTER 4

## Managing the Data Warehouse Project

What are the correct expectations for managing a data warehouse project? Simply stated, no data warehouse project will ever stay on target as originally planned. Anyone who tells you it will stay on target has never actually managed such a large undertaking. It has been the author's experience that no large project is ever accomplished on plan or on target. The goal to good project management is to pick goals and targets you can manage. We all know problems will arise, so you must set up policies and procedures to deal with the rough spots. You must make sure you set proper user expectations. If you do all this correctly, you will have a successful implementation of your data warehouse or data marts. You will see the yellow warning flags coming up the pole long before a red flag appears and stops the entire project.

The key to successful project management is to develop standards by which you can judge the success or failure of the project and all its undertakings or individual tasks. By establishing these standards down to the task level, you will very quickly be able to determine problems at a micro level as they arise and make the needed adjustments quickly. This is a very important point. By setting up performance standards down at the task level, you will be able to quickly catch problems as they arise. Our experience has taught us that catching the problems at the task level is key if you want a successful data mart or data warehouse implementation.

The best analogy to this is how a doctor or nurse works with a patient in the hospital. No two patients are the same. Likewise, no two projects are the same. Because each project is unique, you know the techniques you choose to apply may not always work as expected.

When a doctor or nurse works with a patient, he or she is constantly reviewing the patient's progress against predetermined milestones and benchmarks. Based on the measured results, appropriate changes are made to the care given. Many times this includes changing the dose of medicine, or even the type of treatment given. This chapter will discuss some project management techniques you can apply to ensure the success of your data warehouse project.

## WHAT IS PROJECT MANAGEMENT?

As a senior manager of a consulting company doing larger and larger projects, one thing has become clear to the firm: good project management is essential. Our proficiency at being able to manage a project will make or break us. Even though we have a successful track record, it was clear that as a company we could improve upon the process. So, we went in search of project management experts who would take our combined project management skills in the company to the next level. In the quest for experts, we engaged the services of a company called Duncan Nevison in Lexington, Massachusetts. They taught a course for us entitled "Mastering Modern Program Management." Much of the following material is based on years of practical experience and the guidance of the project management experts from Duncan Nevison.

During this project management course, a slide was held up with a quote from the *Harvard Business Review*: "High performing companies boast . . . we've got the best project managers in the world." This quote certainly reflected how we felt as a company. Our track record of meeting or exceeding customers' expectations has been excellent but as the data warehouse initiatives we were undertaking became more and more complex, we knew we must improve our project management capabilities.

Having the best talent is not enough. If having the best technology meant you would always be successful, wouldn't we all be using the NeXT operating system? Having the best technologist was also not enough. We had to become the best project managers. At my firm, we agree completely with the quote from the *Harvard Business Review*: high-performing companies have the best project managers in the world.

Failure on the project management front could put the firm at risk on two fronts: with our customers and with our employees. As a company, we have an obligation to communicate in an open and honest manner with our customers concerning the status of their projects and the likelihood of coming in on time and on budget. To be successful, we needed to apply good project management techniques. At the same time, we have an obligation to our internal staff to work hard at fine-tuning necessary resources so we will be neither overstaffed nor understaffed. In today's world there is a critical shortage of good technical talent. We could not afford this risk on either front.

Companies around us who did not manage projects correctly either burned out good staff members or overcharged customers for resources they did not need. In addition, an overstaffed project meant a waste of good talent, which, if not challenged, would leave the company. As we are all well aware, with the extreme shortage of good Microsoft developers in the marketplace, we cannot afford to overstaff a project. If we wanted to continue as a high-performing company, we had to improve our project management skills. Our desire to be the best was used as an opportunity to reevaluate how we managed our projects. This chapter represents an overview of some basic "best practice" project management techniques. We encourage you to use this as a test to see if you are on the right track. If the answer is "NO," then take the time to learn more.

**VIP:**   Failure on the project management front could put you at risk on two fronts: with your customers and with your employees. With the shortage of good Microsoft talent, we cannot afford either risk.

Exactly what is project management? *Project management* is the application of knowledge, skills, tools, and techniques to project activities in order to meet or exceed stakeholders' needs and expectations.

What we especially like about this definition is the use of the term "stakeholders." Yes, stakeholders. Like all corporations, we have a fiduciary responsibility to our stockholders, just as a project manager has a fiduciary responsibility to those individuals and organizations affected by the project plans and their execution. So, a *stakeholder* is any group or individual affected by the project and all its activities. These stakeholders include the customers as well as all the people involved in the project internally. Yes, everyone involved has a stake on the successful implementation of the plan. The sooner you recognize this, the more likely you are to be successful.

**VIP:**   A stakeholder is any group or individual affected by the project and all its activities.

If you want to have a successful project, you must take the time to identify all your stakeholders and to understand what impact they will have on the project. You must take the time to understand what their needs and expectations are. Without understanding a stakeholder's needs and expectations, you can never manage or influence them. If you do not take the time to understand your stakeholders needs and expectations, your project will fail. The better you understand your customers, the greater chance you have of being successful. Like all choices you make in life, there are trade-offs; successful project management is about making trade-offs.

**VIP:** You must take the time to understand what a stakeholder's needs and expectations are. Without understanding their needs and expectations, you can never manage or influence your stakeholders.

In many ways, the project manager needs to be a great diplomat, because some of the customers' needs and expectations may be in conflict. This is not uncommon. The project manager must be someone who can look at the problem from each person's perspective and then work toward decisions that ultimately meet the needs of the organization in the most cost-effective and resource-efficient manner.

Another painful lesson we have learned over the years is that no good tools exist to provide project management. Project managers provide project management. Many organizations let "the project management tool" tail wag the dog—they start to manage the project according to the strengths and weaknesses of the particular tool. This does not work. We have been at companies that think sending someone to a Microsoft Project class is sending them to a project management class. What these companies are doing is sending someone to a class that will concentrate on how to use the tool, not on good project management techniques. These are two distinctly different things. Microsoft Project is a great project management tool, but it is not a great project manager; this is commonly called "the tail wagging the dog."

**VIP:** Project managers provide good project management. Stated in another way, project management tools do not provide project management. Many people think that if they use Microsoft Project, this will give them good project management. This is simply not true. This way of thinking will get you in big trouble. The best analogy to this is a carpenter—the carpenter builds the house, not the hammer. Like the hammer, Microsoft Project is a great tool when used appropriately.

What we recommend, and also implement, in our company is that you concentrate on giving everyone within your firm an understanding of good project management techniques. Create special project management courses for each employee within the company. Some people receive a course that introduces them to the terminology, while others receive a course that teaches them critical skills like understanding the critical path. We do this to make sure we have a team of cathedral builders. You might be asking, "What's a cathedral builder?" Well, read on.

There is a very old story about a gentleman who walks up to two masons hard at work. He asks the first mason, "What are you working on?" The first mason replies, "I am building this walkway." He then asks the second mason, "What are you working on?" The mason replies, "I am part of a team building this cathedral." Which mason would you want on your team? Well, at our firm, we want a team of cathedral builders. The more they understand project management, the smoother the process will work and the happier everyone will be.

What we are not doing is getting people hung up on how to use the tool. Many times, good project managers fail because they are too busy trying to make a project management tool do the job. Instead, they should be spending their time managing the staff, customer expectations, and communication. Trying to make a project management tool do the job is like trying to make a round peg fit into a square hole. As a company, we also have decided to hire a management tool expert and leave the project managers free to manage the projects. This brings us back to the key point: don't let the project management tool tail wag the total project dog. Develop internal staff members who are "tool du jour" experts. This leaves your project managers free to be doing what they should do best:

▼ Appraising each stakeholder and determining his or her needs.

■ Influencing stakeholders to move the project forward.

■ Setting the right customer expectations.

■ Looking for the yellow warning flags and dealing with them.

■ Taking the time to manage the project and not letting the project manage the players on the team.

■ Managing the team members tasks to make sure they are not overutilized or underutilized.

▲ Setting up a realistic window to manage the project by. Our experience has taught us that is 30, 60, and 90 day increments.

Let's back up a bit now and talk about a project—the atomic commodity of the management initiative.

# WHAT IS A PROJECT?

Here we are talking about project management when we haven't yet defined the term "project." For this definition, we go to the source—the Project Management Institute. The Project Management Institute is a nonprofit professional organization dedicated to advancing the state of the art in the management of projects. Membership is open to anyone actively engaged or interested in the application, practice, teaching, and researching of project management principles and techniques. (One of the best ways to contact the institute is on the World Wide Web at www.pmi.org.)

According to the book, *A Guide to the Project Management Body of Knowledge,* published by the Project Management Institute Standards committee, a *project* is a temporary endeavor undertaken to create a unique product or service. One key point here is *temporary endeavor.* This means the project must have a defined start and end. If you are unclear about what must be done to complete the project, don't start it. This is a sure path to disaster. In addition, if at any point in the project it becomes clear that the end product of the project cannot be delivered, the project should be canceled. This also applies to a data warehouse or data mart project.

**VIP:** A project is a temporary endeavor undertaken to create a unique product or service. A project must have a defined start and end.

Another key point of the definition is to create a *unique* product or service. You must have a clear idea of what you are building and why it is unique. It is not necessary for you to understand why your product or service is unique from day one, but through the process of developing the project plan you will uncover the unique attributes of this project. Once you understand the uniqueness of the project, you will then be able to determine what constitutes a completed project. Only with a defined end do you have a project that can succeed. It's easy to be successful when you have a clear goal of what you want to accomplish.

## THE SCOPE STATEMENT

One of the proven techniques we can use to help us with this discovery process is called a scope statement. A *scope statement* is a written document by which you begin to define the job at hand and all its key deliverables. In fact, we feel it is good business practice not to begin work on any project until you have developed a scope statement. These are the major elements in the breakdown of a scope statement:

1. **Project title and description**—Every project should have a clear name and a description of what you are trying to accomplish.

2. **Project justification**—A clear description of why this project is being done. What is the goal of the project?

3. **Project key deliverables**—A list of key items that must be accomplished so this project can be completed. What must be done for us to consider the project done?

4. **Project objective**—An additional list of success criteria. These items must be measurable—a good place to put any time, money, or resource constraints.

**VIP:** Every project must have a scope statement. A scope statement is a written document that defines all the deliverables.

Think of a scope statement as your first stake in the ground. What's important is that a scope statement provides a documented basis for building a common understanding among all the stakeholders of the project at hand. It is crucial that you begin to write down and document the project and all its assumptions. If you do not do this, you will get burned. Our experience has taught us that without a scope statement listing assumption and constraints, you will get into trouble.

All a stakeholder remembers about a hallway conversation is the deliverable, not the constraints. Many project managers have gotten into trouble by making a hallway statement such as, "If the new network is put into place by July 1, I feel comfortable saying we can provide you with the legacy data by July 10." All the stakeholder will remember is the date of July 10, not the constraint associated with it. Make sure you document all assumptions and constraints.

Don't be alarmed as you continue down the scope statement path if it is reworked. That's a good thing, because through the process of discovery, the project plan and associated scope statement will change. This is a discovery process. Just make sure you always maintain a clear vision of what constitutes a completed project. It's very easy to succeed when you have a very clear target of success.

To illustrate this point better, let's say a major publisher approached you to write a book on data warehousing for the newest version of Microsoft SQL Server, about to be released. Let's see what a starting scope statement might look like, as shown in Figure 4-1.

As you can see from Figure 4-1, we have created a document that attempts to articulate the job at hand. This is our first stake in the ground.

In the project justification statement, we try to say why we are doing it. If we can't state this in clear terms, we should question even doing the project. In the project deliverables section, we try to identify major components that must be completed for us to say the job is done. In the project objectives, we try to discuss additional success criteria, which includes any time constraints. For example, we now know it would not be acceptable to deliver a document of 100 pages in length.

**VIP:**  If you can't state in clear terms a project justification statement, you should question even starting the project.

This becomes a powerful tool when working with the stakeholders. It becomes a common point of reference for all stakeholders. The scope statement should be written so anyone can understand it. You should have one scope statement for all users. You do not create different scope statements depending on the audience.

# WORK BREAKDOWN STRUCTURE

Once you have completed your project scope statement, another technique we find useful is called a work breakdown structure. We use this technique to help fill in any gaps or missing items. In *A Guide to the Project Management Body of Knowledge*, "a work breakdown structure" is defined as "a deliverable-oriented grouping of project elements, which

### SQL Server 7 Data Warehousing Project Scope Statement Overview

A 300-400 page book that will explain to the reader what a data warehouse is, provide an overview of how you manage the effort, and discuss in detail how you use Microsoft SQL Server 7 and its associated software to implement a warehouse.

#### Project Justification

- It is clear that to implement a data warehouse is a very complex process and there is not an existing book today that teaches Microsoft users how to do this taking full advantage of the SQL Server 7 software.

- It is clear that this book will enable the Microsoft community to better understand how to correctly use Microsoft tools when building a data warehouse. This will generate additional software sales and improved customer satisfaction.

- There is a hot market for data warehousing material. It is critical that the Database Professional's Library series develop a warehouse offering or run the risk of losing the business to competitors.

- Without a data warehouse offering, the credibility of the Database Professional's Library series is at risk.

#### Project Deliverables

- A technical editor must be chosen.
- A work breakdown structure must be completed.
- A signed contract must be delivered.
- A finished manuscript must be delivered.
- A draft of all artwork must be finished.

#### Project Objectives

- The finished manuscript must be at least 300 pages.
- The finished manuscript must be delivered by November 12, 1999.
- Each chapter should be at least 20 pages in length.
- The book should teach people how to effectively implement a data warehouse using Microsoft SQL Server 7's technology.

**Figure 4-1.** Sample scope statement

organizes and defines the total scope of the project. Each descending level represents an increasingly detailed definition of a project component. Project components may be products and services."

A work breakdown structure is exactly as it sounds—a breakdown of all the work that must be done. This includes all deliverables. For example, if you are expected to provide the customer with weekly status reports, this should be in the structure. If you expect to hold a kickoff meeting, this should also be in the structure. Both these items would fall under the category of project management.

When we create a work breakdown structure, we show it to our customers and say, "If you don't see it in here, don't assume it's being done." To illustrate this point better, Figure 4-2 shows a high-level view of a work breakdown structure.

## How to Create a Work Breakdown Structure

One of the easiest ways we have seen to create a work breakdown structure is to find a blank wall and a pack of sticky yellow notes. Put the project name on a note on the wall. Next, from the scope statement, write majors deliverable on a note and add them to the wall. Write, "project management" on a note and add it. Then, under each of these areas, start to decompose all the deliverables (i.e., split them up into smaller pieces). Figures 4-2 and 4-3 show the start of a work breakdown structure based on the sample scope statement shown in Figure 4-1.

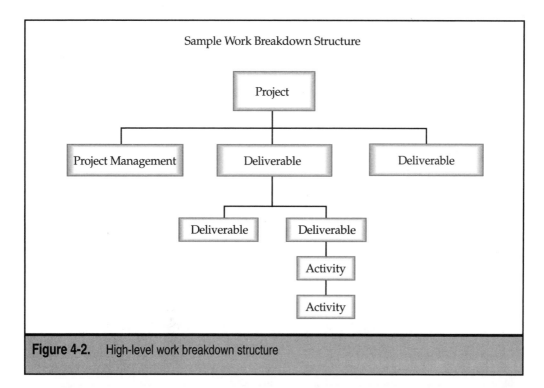

**Figure 4-2.**   High-level work breakdown structure

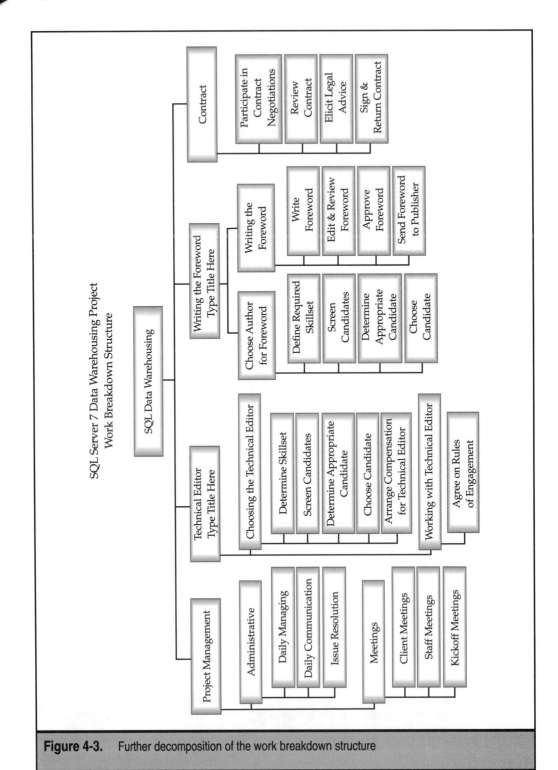

**Figure 4-3.**   Further decomposition of the work breakdown structure

As you can see, this exercise quickly makes you think about all the required steps. When you review this document with the stakeholders, you are well on your way to having enough detail to estimate the project. In addition, you can now start to apply some resources to each of the items in the work breakdown structure. This work breakdown structure should be at a level where any stakeholder can understand all the steps it will take to accomplish each task and produce each deliverable.

After you have completed the work breakdown structure on the wall, we find it helpful to write it down in outline form. Look at this work breakdown structure in outline form:

```
SQL Server 7: Data Warehousing Project Work Breakdown Structure
                     Outline Form


1.  Project Management
    1.1    Administrative
           1.1.1  Daily Management
           1.1.2  Daily Communication
           1.1.3  Issue Resolution
    1.2    Meetings
           1.2.1  Client Meetings
           1.2.2  Staff Meetings
           1.2.3  Kickoff Meetings
2.  Technical Editor
    2.1    Choosing the Technical Editor
           2.1.1  Determine Skillset
           2.1.2  Screen Candidates
           2.1.3  Determine Appropriate Candidate
           2.1.4  Choose Candidate
    2.2    Technical Editor Compensation
           2.2.1  Sign Contract
           2.2.2  Send Check
    2.3    Working with Technical Editor
           2.3.1  Establish Procedure
           2.3.2  Agree On Rules Of Engagement
3.  Writing The Foreword
    3.1    Choosing Writer For Foreword
```

Once you have this work breakdown structure in outline form, you should then start to describe each item and create a description of what must be done. These descriptions should be at a level any stakeholder can understand, as illustrated in the next listing:

```
SQL Server 7: Data Warehousing Project Work Breakdown Structure
                     Detail Form


1.  Project Management

This activity is not normally thought of as a deliverable but,
```

because it consumes up to 25 percent of the total project budget, we recommend you include it.

```
1.1 Administrative
    This includes the overhead items associated with a project.
    1.1.1 Daily Management
        This includes gathering time cards, status reports,
        dealing with vacations, project costs, attrition, and
        training.
    1.1.2 Daily Communication
        This includes a combination of ongoing formal and informal
        discussions. The communication with the client is vital to
        the project delivery and will be the primary vehicle for
        potential problem resolution.
```

After you have completed the work breakdown structure, you should review it to make certain any stakeholder can understand it. With the proper level of description, this should not pose a problem. Make sure the work breakdown structure contains enough detail so you can begin to make educated guesses on the resource requirements. Ensure the work breakdown list is as complete as possible. For example, many times people forget to include meetings, documentation, training, demonstrations, equipment setup, time for review, time to learn new tools, weekly status reports, and many other tasks that are implied yet take significant time and resources to accomplish.

## PROJECT ESTIMATING

Now that you have a breakdown of what needs to be done, you can begin to estimate how long it will take and how much effort it will require. Clearly, your customer will want you to determine the cost—this means you need to know how long each activity will take so you can accurately price it. Recent studies show that approximately 47 percent of all consulting jobs performed were fixed-price bids. With the trend for consulting services moving rapidly toward fixed-price bids, we may soon be building software systems the way we build a house. There will be a detailed project plan and severe penalties when we are late. In the field of project management, the construction industry is way ahead of the software industry. When you decide to build a house, they can give you great detail on how much and how long it will take.

By using good project management techniques today, your organization can gather the necessary information to price and predict jobs correctly in the future. Here are two types of activities you can estimate:

1. **Activity estimates** are low-level educated guesses as to how long a particular task will take within a given project. They are your primary tools when gauging the progress of a project.

2. **Project estimates** are high-level guesses to help you make funding decisions. Many times, your initial project estimates have no bearing on how long it will take to accomplish the project or how much it will cost.

This leads to an important point: *activity estimating is not a negotiation.* If it takes two hours to create a database, it takes two hours. Never lower your estimates. If your manager or another team member thinks your estimate is too high, find out why they think it is too high. They may have a good reason and you may agree.

> **VIP:**   Activity estimation is not a negotiation. If it takes two hours to build a database, it takes two hours. Don't be persuaded into agreeing to time frames that are not realistic.

If your time line is too long, look at other ways to get around this obstacle. Perhaps having two people working on the task will bring it in by the needed date. As the old saying goes, it is what it is.

## Probability and Risk

In life, most things result in a bell curve. Figure 4-4 shows a sample bell curve that measures the likelihood of on-time project delivery. The graph measures the number of projects delivered late, on time, and early.

As you can see in Figure 4-4, the most likely outcome falls to the center of the curve. This type of graph is skewed in the center; hence, the terminology *bell curve* is taken from the shape. Table 4-1 summarizes the data presented in Figure 4-4.

What this teaches us is that we currently do time estimates incorrectly. That is, trying to predict a single point will never work. The law of averages works against us.

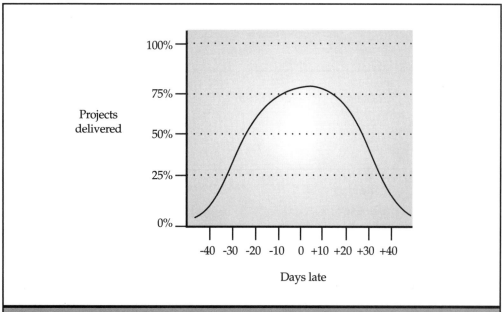

**Figure 4-4.**   Project delivery bell curve

| Percentage of Projects Completed | Days from Expected Delivery |
|---|---|
| 25 | 33 days early or 35 days late |
| 50 | 25 days early or 25 days late |
| 75 | 8 days early or 13 days late |

**Table 4-1.** Bell Curve Data Summary

We should predict project time estimates like we predict rolling dice. Experience has taught us that when a pair of dice is rolled, the most likely number to come up is 7. When you look at alternatives, the odds of a number other than 7 coming up are less.

A craps table is an excellent way to observe this. When you play at a craps table, you can place a bet on what the next number rolled on the dice will be. Based on the number you pick, you will get a corresponding payoff based on the casino's risk. For example, if you predict the next number rolled is 7, that prediction will pay far less than if you bet the next number rolled is 12. The casino has looked at the probability of any outcome and determined its associated risk. Why not do this with project managing? For example, why not get a 3-point estimate—the optimistic view, the pessimistic view, and the most likely answer? Based on those answers, you can determine a time estimate. Table 4-2 shows an example of a three-point estimate worksheet.

| Task | Subtask | Best Case | Most Likely | Worst Case |
|---|---|---|---|---|
| Choosing the technical editor | Determine skillset | 1.0 | 3.0 | 5.0 |
| | Screen candidates | 1.0 | 2.0 | 3.0 |
| | Choose candidate | 0.5 | 1.0 | 2.0 |
| Total | | 2.5 | 6.0 | 10.0 |

**Table 4-2.** Three-point Time Estimate Worksheet

As you can see from Table 4-2, just the task of choosing the technical editor has considerable latitude in possible outcomes, yet each one of these outcomes has a chance of becoming reality. Within a given project, many of the tasks would come in on the best-case guess, and many of the tasks will also come in on the worst-case guess. In addition, each one of these outcomes has an associated measurable risk.

We recommend you get away from single-point estimates and move toward 3-point estimates. By doing this, you will start to get a handle on your true risk. By doing this exercise with your team members, you will start everyone thinking about the task and all the associated risks. What if a team member gets sick? What if the computer breaks down? What if someone gets pulled away on another task? These things do happen, and they do affect the project.

**VIP:**   Get away from single-point estimating. It is better to establish a pessimistic and optimistic range for a task to be done.

You are now also defining the acceptable level of performance. For example, if a project team member came in with 25 days to choose a technical editor, we would consider this irresponsible. We would require a great deal of justification. Another positive aspect to the 3-point estimate is that it improves the stakeholders' morale. The customer will start to feel more comfortable because he or she will have an excellent handle on the project. At the same time, when some tasks do fall behind, everyone realizes this should be expected. Because the project takes all outcomes into consideration, you could still come in within the acceptable time lines. An entire science exists within project management that allows you to take 3-point estimates and improve the level of accuracy.

# Types of Risk

Let's take a closer look at risk. When you do get caught (i.e., the project gets out of control and unmanageable), this is typically due to one of three situations:

1. **Assumptions** —You get caught by unvoiced assumptions, which were never spelled out.

2. **Constraints** —You get caught by restricting factors, which were not fully understood.

3. **Unknowns** —Items you could never predict, be they acts of God or human error.

The key to risk management is to do your best to identify the source of all risks and the likelihood of their happening. For example, when we project plan, we typically do not take work stoppages into account. But if we were working for an airline that was under threat of a major strike, we might reevaluate the likelihood of losing valuable project time.

Calculate the cost to the project if the particular risk happens and make a decision. You can decide either to accept it, find a way to avoid it, or try to prevent it. Always look for ways around the obstacles. For example, on one particular client site, we have a complicated transformation process running every weekend on Tandem hardware. Because we are running on a Tandem, we have decided the likelihood the system will not be available is nil. At the same time, we have a staff member who covers this job all weekend to make certain it is successful. Duncan Nevison lists the following types of *internal* risks:

1. Company politics
   - Corporate strategy change
   - Departmental politics
2. Project stakeholders
   - Sponsor
   - Customer
   - Subcontractors
   - Project team
3. Project characteristics
   - Schedule bumps
   - Cost hiccups
   - Technical surprises

They also list the following *external* risks:

1. Environment
   - Fire, famine, flood
   - Pollution
   - Raw materials
2. Government
   - Change in law
   - Change in regulation
3. Economy
   - Currency rate change
   - Market shift
   - Competitor's entry or exit
   - Immediate competitive actions
   - Supplier change

By looking at these risks, you get a sense of all the influences that may impact your particular project. You should take the time to assess and reassess these. For example, if your project is running severely behind schedule, is there another vendor waiting to try to take the business? If your project is running way over budget, is there a chance the funding may get cut? We must always be aware of the technology with which we are working. Familiarity with technology is important; we need to know, for example, if what we are working with is a new release of the software or a release that has been out for a long time.

## Critical Path

After you determine what must be done and how long it will take, you are ready to start looking for your critical paths and dependencies. These critical paths are yet another form of risk within a project. For example, there are inherent dependencies among many project activities. A chapter must be written before it can be reviewed. A technical editor must be selected before the editing cycle of a chapter can be completed. These are examples of dependency analysis.

Let's say we are working on a project with three unique lists of activities associated with it. Each unique path (A, B, C) of activities is represented based on its dependencies. Each cell represents the number of days that activity should take. By adding all the rows together, you can tell the duration of each path. This is shown in Table 4-3.

Start A represents a part of the project with three steps, which will take a total of eight days. Start B represents a part of the project with three steps, which will take a total of six days. Start C represents a path with two steps, which will take a total of 20 days.

The critical path is *Start C*. You must begin this as soon as possible. In fact, this tells us the soonest this project can be done is 20 days. If you do not start the activity that takes 15 days first, it will delay the entire project ending one day for each day you wait.

**NOTE:** Be aware that as any project continues, the critical path can change over time.

| Unique task | Part #1 | Part #2 | Part #3 | Total |
|---|---|---|---|---|
| Start A | 1 | 3 | 4 | 8 days |
| Start B | 1 | 2 | 3 | 6 days |
| Start C | 15 | 5 | | 20 days |

**Table 4-3.** Critical Path Analysis

# A JOB IS NOT DONE UNTIL THE WORK HAS STOPPED

There is a very old saying—"Fool me once shame on you, fool me twice shame on you, fool me three times shame on me." How many times have you asked an application developer for the status of a project and been told the task is 80 percent complete. Yet that last 20 percent takes longer to accomplish than the first 80 percent. Well, shame on you. Our experience has taught us a task is either 100 percent complete or it's not completed. There are no partially accomplished tasks.

Best practices have taught us—when managing a project, a particular task has only two states. Just like a computer chip that has *on* or *off*, a task is either *completed* or *not completed*. To determine the percentage complete of the entire project add up the total number of tasks, and divide into it the number of tasks deemed 100 percent complete. For example, in writing this book, we decided there were 100 individual tasks. Of those 100 tasks only 14 tasks are 100 percent complete. Ignore any task that is not 100 percent completed. This means the overall project to create the book is 14 percent complete. Even if 50 tasks were reported back as 90 percent finished, we ignore them. Our experience has taught us this is the only way to gauge the true progress of any project. Anything less than this is fooling yourself.

# 90 DAYS—PLANNING FOR SUCCESS

We started this chapter saying no project schedule is ever on target as originally planned. That's because as project managers, we are expected to look too far into the future. To try and plan the success of an undertaking a year out is just too far. Our experience has taught us to manage your data warehouse and data mart implementations in approximately 90-day increments. This actually works. It's enough time to get a substantial number of efforts accomplished and too short a window for the project goals to change.

You succeed because you can get your hands around the effort. The team understands the problem at hand and is able to work on it in a targeted manner. The bottom line—90-day increments or plans work.

# PROJECT MANAGEMENT SUMMARY

A data warehouse initiative could be one of the toughest projects you will ever work on—without good project management, you will fail. We have given you an overview of the major concepts of project management and some good project management techniques to follow, but this chapter was not intended to replace the need for good project management training or experience. Its purpose was to provide a good framework by which to begin the complexities of managing a data warehouse initiative.

All projects have stakeholders. Stakeholders are the individuals or organizations affected by the project and all of its activities. You must take the time to understand their needs or you will never be able to manage or influence them. Without understanding your stakeholders, your project will fail.

Project managers—not project management software—manage projects. Do not expect Microsoft Project to manage your project, because it is just one of many tools you might use to help you succeed. A project is a temporary endeavor; it must have a defined start and end.

A scope statement is an excellent starting point for any project and a common technique to help you identify and scope the tasks to be done. In the process of discovery for the scope statement, you will identify what must happen for a project to end. Following the initial scope statement, we recommend you develop a work breakdown structure to help you find any missing components in your project. During the process of developing a work breakdown structure, you will discover any existing holes. When you develop the work breakdown structure, list all activities that must happen for the project to be a success. The example we used to illustrate this was the project management activity. This activity alone can account for as much as 20 percent of a team member's time, yet it is commonly overlooked.

Once you have identified all the activities, it's time to start placing resources and estimates against them. Our experience has shown that three-point estimates work, but single-point estimates do not work. Single-point estimates do not reflect the real world because they do not take risk into account. By applying all the techniques covered in this chapter, your data warehouse project will run smoother.

A project time line of about 90 days works. It's enough time to accomplish a significant effort but not enough time for the world to change its mode.

Time to move on. Let's get into some of the meat of data warehouse theory—data marts. We are unsure whether a small data warehouse can/should be called a collection of data marts or a small data warehouse can/should be called a data mart. Regardless of what it's called, the setup, design, deployment, and completion of a data mart happens in a much shorter/less expensive time frame than its larger sibling—the data warehouse. Whatever it's called, make sure the data mart is in the users' hands in the three-to-five-month time frame.

# CHAPTER 5

# Data Warehouse Design

T he design of a data warehouse is a paradigm shift from the way that operational systems are designed. Data warehouse designers must now contend not only with designing a database and a user interface; they must also contend with data loading strategies, data access tools, user training, and ongoing maintenance issues. The data warehouse requires a strong database design with many facets. When embarking upon a data warehouse design, you must now consider numerous issues that did not have to be considered in operational design. This chapter is intended to help you gain a better understanding of how the warehouse is built and the issues that you must consider in achieving a complete data warehouse design.

One may even say that data warehouse designers are not as "normal" as operational system designers. In this chapter, we will provide you with the guidance necessary to design a data warehouse. We will focus on design theory and dimensional modeling, and provide a proven approach to designing a robust data warehouse.

# DESIGN—THE NEXT LOGICAL STEP

Most definitions of data warehouses start with a few baseline concepts of what they are supposed to do and who uses them for decision making. Ask the question, "What is a warehouse?" Depending on who you ask, you will probably get an equal number of different answers. The data warehouse is not just a database; it is an entire system. From the extraction of data from operational systems, to the loading and management of data within the warehouse, to end-user data access, the warehouse is a system to help people better understand and analyze their organizations. In Chapter 1, we looked at how we see the data warehouse within your organization. Now that we are designing the warehouse, we must be sure to design a system that meets the needs of both users and developers.

At its most granular, atomic level (we will get to this later), the *warehouse* is a repository for detailed, nonvolatile, time-based information. The warehouse must also serve as a tool to perform summary-level, strategic analysis of this information. The warehouse may also act as the source for high-performance query structures such as specialized data marts or multidimensional databases such MicroStarategy's DSS Agent. Achieving both purposes in an effective manner is the focus of this chapter.

Building an enterprise data warehouse or a focused data mart is a process that merges the business users directly to the corporate data they need in order to make informed strategic, effective, and detailed business decisions. The design of the warehouse must therefore be easily understood and manipulated. Because end users will be directly querying the warehouse, this design must be simple to understand and navigate. When you create a complex data warehouse that contains structures that are difficult to navigate, you expose your warehouse to being misunderstood. This can result in invalid assumptions and misinterpretation by decision support system (DSS) users and, ultimately, incorrect and even dangerous business decisions.

The warehouse, when designed in an intuitive manner, allows business users to easily understand the data that they are viewing and interrogating. These users intuitively understand the data that helps them run their business—items such as product numbers, corporate regions, product lines, customer types, and so on. This information is the window into the data that the users can quickly incorporate into their information analysis. Data warehouses that are created in isolation of end-user requirements are doomed to failure. By creating your data warehouse with end users in mind, you help them to quickly embrace the new technology and ensure the success of your data warehouse design and implementation.

# ONGOING INTERACTION WITH THE USERS

Building an enterprise data warehouse is a full-fledged development project—one that requires a focused group of users and developers to come together in the development process. In many ways, it is more difficult than developing an operational system. The requirements are more ambiguous, given the necessity of ad hoc analysis. Designers must contend with uncertainties in the major components of data to be stored and the methods of accessing that data.

Understanding the requirements is imperative. We must understand a number of areas, including the following:

▼ User reporting requirements

■ Historical data retention

■ Nature of the data to include

■ Nature of the data to exclude

■ Where to get the data

■ How to get the data from point A (its source) to point B (the warehouse), and possibly onto point C (a high-performance query structure)

■ How to ensure that the data is properly replicated (*replication* is one of the approaches used to ensure a change to operational system data is reflected in data warehouse data)

▲ How to provide enough flexibility so we do not limit the long-term viability of the warehouse

In analyzing requirements, we need to ask users to provide examples of the reports they currently use. Analyzing these outputs gets you well on your way to identifying the data that must be in the warehouse. In addition, if you can replace these, you may be able to eliminate the subsystem that produces them, thus enhancing the return on investment (ROI) of your warehouse. Questions we frequently ask users when designing a data warehouse include the following:

▼ What is your department's role within the enterprise?

■ What is your role within the department?

- What reports do you use to fulfill that role?
- Where do you currently get this information?
- What do you do with this information after you've obtained it?
- Is this information typically produced at your request or is it found on some periodic report?
- Do you ever type this information into a spreadsheet to analyze it further?
- ▲ How timely must this information be?

The design of a data warehouse is not simply the design of a data repository; it's the design integration of many components. There is the consideration of the operational data sources, the staging area, and the data repository and aggregation structures when designing the data warehouse. The other item that must always be considered when designing and implementing the warehouse is the types of reporting that the system will be required to perform. In our experience, we have seen many data warehouses that have failed to provide the necessary performance and flexibility because they were built in isolation from the reporting requirements. In addition, it is rare that a single reporting tool can satisfy all reporting uses of the warehouse. In general, most warehouses are accessed by a variety of different users and tools, each optimized for a particular reporting purpose: report writing, batch file creation, online analytical processing, data mining, and others. To be successful in designing your data warehouse, you must ensure that all factors affecting your design are considered. Better to overdesign than to find that you have missed some critical information once the system has been implemented.

Designing the data warehouse is an iterative experience. The design team is not your typical operational system design team. When building the data warehouse team, the most important members of the design team are the target users and business analysts. In Chapters 3 and 4, we looked at the data warehouse project team and managing the project. The target users provide us with the details on the purpose of the warehouse. These users have an important perspective on the way that the warehouse will be used.

**NOTE:**    The user community must be an active participant in the warehouse design process. Without user involvement, the warehouse will cough, sputter, and die!

A successful warehouse effort teams users and designers from the start. These user teams perform a number of roles, including the following:

- ▼ Providing user requirements
- Signing off on the development team's interpretation of user requirements
- Acceptance testing the completed system
- ▲ Suggesting enhancements after the warehouse is released into production

The designers must act as the facilitators in the design effort. An experienced data warehouse designer who has a variety of experiences building data warehouses can be a major asset to the overall success of the project. The designer acts as a facilitator, ensuring that all aspects of the warehouse are analyzed and that the design is accurate and complete. The business analysts should be people from your organization who understand how your business is run and the processes that are in place to collect information. They may have been part of your operational system's design team or may be business users of your warehouse. These people will contribute an interesting perspective for the design team. They understand the business processes and business rules that will be stored by the warehouse and how and where operational data required for the warehouse resides.

The design team can be quite large; make sure that your team does not grow too large, where useful discussions are difficult to carry out. We have been working in design teams as small as three individuals (facilitator, business analyst, and end user) and as large as 20 people. When forming the team, focus on a complete team since everyone must come together to create a dynamic and robust data warehouse.

# DATA WAREHOUSE DATABASES VS. OPERATIONAL DATABASES

Since the introduction of relational databases, data modelers have been trained to build normalized databases for operational information systems. Normalized structures store the greatest amount of data in the least amount of space; hence, we define *normalization* as a method of designing a database. At its simplest level, normalization is a process of decomposing data structures into their smallest components. The emphasis in normalization is on flexibility and efficiency of storage. Normalization also supports data-driven systems that can frequently be enhanced with changes only to data, not to data structures and programs. These systems need to be shared and nonredundant within the corporation. For years, we have been building our operational systems with the idea of normalization as our only goal. The warehouse is a paradigm shift in database design. While flexibility and efficiency are lofty goals in a warehouse, they are not the ultimate goal.

**NOTE:**   The ultimate goal in the data warehouse arena is rapid access to large amounts of data.

In fact, warehouse designers will frequently trade off flexibility and efficiency for query performance. Warehouse table structures can take on a number of forms. Pilots frequently state, "If a plane looks good, it flies good." The sad truth of warehousing is that, frequently, the uglier the structure (in terms of maintenance and space required), the better the performance. Table 5-1 shows you that the different characteristics between data warehouses and operational systems are great enough that they must be designed uniquely. So if it smells like an operational system and barks like an operational system, it must be an operational system—not a data warehouse.

Operational transactions become historical events in the warehouse. In many operational systems, simply retaining the expired operational data permits strategic reporting from the operational database. This arrangement sounds good in theory, but has proven to be impractical—the real-world performance, capacity, and technology limitations cannot be ignored. Therefore, building the warehouse becomes an integral part of your organization's data strategy.

Realistically, few operational systems can provide truly ad hoc data access or at least queries that perform well (i.e., run to completion in a short amount of time). The warehouse asks you to provide the access. Data warehouse designers must generally understand the access needs and specifically understand the data to be used as a basis of that access. Users may have some chance of making up a query on the fly, but they have no chance of making up the data from which the query is derived. In many ways, the data model is more important than the data analysis.

## Types of Data in the Warehouse

We think of the data warehouse as a collection of historical transactions and summarizations. It may be thought of as the giant spreadsheet that sits on that big computer. The warehouse is much more than just a simple collection of information. It can hold many different flavors of data. The following is a common sampling of the types of data that are contained in the warehouse:

▼   Transactions downloaded from operational systems—this data is time stamped to form a historical record.

| Data Warehouse Data | Operational System Data |
|---|---|
| Long time frame | Short time frame |
| Static | Rapid changes |
| Data is usually summarized | Record-level access |
| Ad hoc query access | Standard transactions |
| Updated periodically | Updated in real time |
| Data driven | Event driven |

**Table 5-1.**   Differences Between Data Warehouse Data and Operational Data

- Dimensional support data (customers, products, time).
- Table to support the joining of dimensional data and numeric facts relating to this data.
- Summarization of transactions (e.g., daily sales by department). These are really preemptive queries; the data is aggregated when it is added to the warehouse rather than when a user requests it.
- Miscellaneous coding data.
- Metadata, the data about the data. This category might include sources of warehouse data, replication rules, rollup categories and rules, availability of summarizations, security and controls, purge criteria, and logical and physical data mapping.
- ▲ Event data sourced from outside services, such as demographic information correlated into the geographic areas in which your company operates.

These types of data that we have just described are all contained in the warehouse. It shows us that the information that we hold in the data warehouse is vastly different from the information that is contained in an operational system. When looking at designing a data warehouse, you must keep in mind that "I am not designing an operational system! I am not designing an operational system!" This mantra will be your guide: do not design a "normal" database for your warehouse without understanding the end use of your information. By the end of this chapter we will have shown you the concepts behind database design, data warehouse design, and a proven approach to warehousing; you will see that "You're not in Kansas anymore!" and that designing the warehouse is a paradigm shift from operational system design. Let's then move forward so we can change your way of looking at data. This process could be irreversible—look both ways before crossing.

# "NORMAL" OPERATIONAL DESIGN

Operational system design and creating databases to serve operational purposes differ significantly from the goals of data warehouse design. When creating a database for an online operational system in a relational model, the concern is with quick response time and efficient data storage. Therefore, when designing with these goals in mind, we create a data model that is in third normal form. There are other higher forms of normalization, but the description to the third level suffices for describing the differences between operational and data warehouses. Nowadays, many operational systems are designed to levels higher than third normal form. Normalization of a database is a concept developed by Dr. Codd and a number of other database theorists to design databases that achieve the goals necessary to deploy efficient operational systems. Each step in the normalization process addresses a single issue. The following sections will help you better understand what has come to be called normalized relational design.

# First Normal Form

The first step of the normalization process is the removal of repeating groups. The resultant tables are said to be in the first normal form. First normal form has the following attributes:

▼ All attributes are atomic.

■ They cannot have a set of values.

▲ They cannot have any nested relations.

The structure pictured in Table 5-2 is in first normal form. As you can see, all the items are at their lowest form—this is placing items at the atomic level. As well, there are not repeating groups. For example, you could think of listing all of this person's projects in

Employee ID

First name

Last name

Street address

City

Province

Country

Home telephone

Office telephone

Cellular telephone

Job description

Salary

Project number

Project name

Budget

Duration

Start date

Projected end date

Manager

**Table 5-2.** Structured Data in First Normal Form

one record. This would then limit the flexibility of your information, so we ensure that we do not have any repeating groups. First normal form is a place to start, but it is only one stop on our normalization adventure.

## Second Normal Form

The first normal relations are then decomposed stage-wise by addressing each of the normalization criteria. When dependencies on part of the key are removed, the relations are said to be in the second normal form. Second normal form ensures that the relations of all nonprimary attributes are fully dependent on the primary key. Table 5-3 illustrates a few relations in second normal form, with the primary key attributes underlined.

Let's dissect the relations pictured in Table 5-3 and show how the nonkey attributes are fully dependent on each relation's primary key. In the Employee Data entity, all of the nonkey attributes are dependent on the Employee ID. For example, picking an employee with ID 100720, that person's name is directly hooked to the ID, as is that person's street address of 60 Cocksfield.

The EMPLOYEE and PROJECT tables have now been separated such that all nonkey attributes are now fully dependent upon their respective primary keys. We have therefore created three datasets: one for the employee; another for the project; and, finally, a table that relates the two, the assignment data. As you can see, all nonprimary attributes are fully dependent on the primary keys.

| Employee Data | Project Data | Assignment Data |
|---|---|---|
| <u>Employee ID</u> | <u>Project number</u> | <u>Employee ID</u> |
| First name | Project name | <u>Project number</u> |
| Last name | Budget | Duration |
| Street address | Manager | Start date |
| City | | Projected end date |
| Province | | |
| Country | | |
| Job description | | |
| Salary | | |
| Home telephone | | |
| Office telephone | | |

**Table 5-3.**   Relations in Second Normal Form

## Third Normal Form

The transitive dependencies (dependencies on nonkey attributes) are removed by further decomposition. The result is the third normal form, or the so-called Boyce-Codd normal form. Third normal form is characterized by the following:

▼ All nonprime attributes are fully dependent on every key.

■ All prime attributes are fully dependent on the keys that they belong to.

▲ No attribute is fully dependent on any set of nonprime attributes.

The entities shown in Table 5-4 are in third normal form, again with the primary key attribute(s) underlined and the foreign keys underlined and bolded.

Let's dissect the relations pictured in Table 5-4 and show how the nonprime attributes are now fully dependent on every key:

▼ In the Employee Data entity, the nonprime attribute Job type is now dependent upon the Job type data entity. For example, people who all are consultants will have their job type being defined in the Job type data entity.

| Employee Data | Pay Data | Project Data | Manager Data | Assignment Data |
|---|---|---|---|---|
| Employee ID | Job type | **Project number** | Manager ID | **Employee ID** |
| First name | Description | Project name | Name | Project number |
| Last name | Salary | Budget | Location | Duration |
| Street address | | **Manager ID** | | Start date |
| City | | | | Projected end date |
| Province | | | | |
| Country | | | | |
| **Job type** | | | | |
| Home telephone | | | | |
| Office telephone | | | | |

**Table 5-4.** Entities in Third Normal Form

▲   In the Project Data entity, we have defined a link to the Manager Data entity. So, if a manager manages multiple projects, this information can be linked via this common key.

The data objects have now been brought into third normal form. The exercise to go from first to second, and then on to third normal form, shows how we must focus on the following steps:

▼   First normal form: remove all repeating groups

■   Second normal form: link all entities by primary keys

▲   Third normal form: link nonkey attributes by keys to supporting foreign keys

Further decomposition to remove multivalued dependencies may then be used to produce a set of relations in the fourth normal form. Some designers recognize a domain key normal form (or DKNF: Fagin 1981) in which every constraint on the relations is the result of only two variables—the key and the domains of the nonkey attributes. No generalized method for achieving this state has been proposed.

Operational database design, by convention, will be based in a normal form. The data warehouse, by comparison, will usually be denormalized for efficient retrieval of information. By denormalizing the structures contained in the data warehouse, we improve performance and usability of the information. The design of the warehouse is a paradigm shift in the way that we design and implement a database.

# DIMENSIONAL DATA WAREHOUSE DESIGN

Since we have looked at operational system design at a high level, we can now look more closely at the components that constitute the data warehouse. The data warehouse database is a combination of many different components, including the following:

▼   The staging area

■   The data warehouse

▲   The focused data marts

The staging area is a set of database tables that will be used to receive the information from the operational data sources. The information will be populated with data from the operational systems. Often, we get flat files containing the data. The staging area mirrors these structures. By creating a staging area, we can then accelerate the data loads and more easily manipulate the data within the SQL Server 7 database. The staging area provides a simple environment from which we can create the data transforms and load the data into the warehouse. The data warehouse is a set of data tables that will contain all of your data. The structures in the warehouse simplify the enterprise's data while still retaining a nonprocess-oriented database structure. The data here is time stamped to allow for time-based analysis. The level of normalization or denormalization within an integrated warehouse database structure is determined based upon the requirements for this database. Now these structures will be used to drive the structure to the warehouse. The final data storage format is a high-performance query structure such as a data mart or a multidimensional database. Data marts are normally created using a star schema to enhance data retrieval by end users. This concept will be detailed in Chapter 6.

Each component is built in the warehouse based on user requirements. If the user is looking at creating a complete enterprise-wide data warehouse, you should plan to build all three parts. However, in the case of the creation of an individual data mart, you may be able to satisfy the user's requirement with a stand-alone data mart. The truth is usually somewhere in the middle of all this. Figure 5-1 illustrates at a high level how all of the components within the data warehouse are integrated and shows you how the data will flow through an enterprise data warehouse.

The topology of the warehouse is a varied affair. The data is extracted from sources such as operational systems and flat files. This data is then loaded into the data warehouse using a number of methods, some proprietary to SQL Server 7 and some third party data warehouse loading tools. The warehouse will be created at the highest detail level of information required by the users. The data warehouse is then used to populate the various process-oriented data marts. These data marts will be structured in a star schema topology to achieve maximum retrieval performance. The entire data warehouse then forms an integrated system that can serve the end-user reporting and analysis requirements of the user community.

We now move on to discussing the famous star schema. You can't spend more than a few minutes looking at data warehouse design or conversing with your colleagues

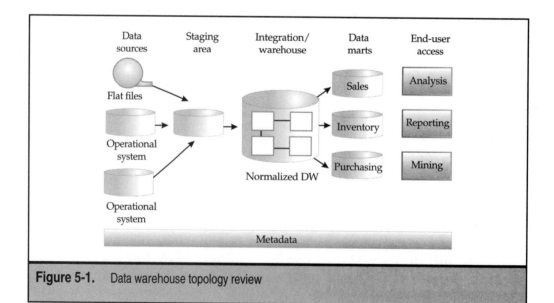

**Figure 5-1.**    Data warehouse topology review

without running across these two words. The star schema can help you to optimize data warehouse performance, so leverage this knowledge when designing your overall data warehouse implementation.

# THE STAR SCHEMA

The *star schema* is a concept that provides superior data retrieval power to the data warehouse and can help accelerate the deployment of decision support systems. Companies like A. C. Nielson and IRI have shown over time that the concept of the star schema is necessary to top-performing data warehouses. The design idea of the star join schema has allowed us to better empower the data warehouse to more directly meet the needs of the end users. The name "star schema" is derived from the appearance of the data model, with a large central table surrounded in a star formation by subordinate tables. Many dimension tables surround the central table, known as the fact table. This type of modeling is known as *dimensional data warehousing*.

Fact tables contain measures that are used to perform analysis, and also contain the keys that link the dimensions. *Measures* are the numerical information used to perform analysis; they are often used in functions like sum, average, median, and standard deviation. Measures include items such as total sales, monthly bank balance, quantity shipped, and so on. The dimension tables contain the attributes that describe the data components and provide the information to do comparative analysis. The star schema is another way to model transactions. For example, *performance measures* are some of the ways to judge how the organization is performing. The schema describes those measures. For example, dollar sales are a measure of how well the organization is performing. Sales can also be described or measured according to the following:

▼ Where they took place (location)

■ Who they were made to (customer)

■ When they occurred (time of year)

■ What was sold (product)

▲ Who sold it (sales personnel)

The star schema is designed with a great deal of redundant dimension data, which is provided in this manner only to improve performance of information retrieval. By creating a data model in the star schema design, we prejoin the dimension information for the users and simplify the relationships that will need to be analyzed by the users. The following describes facts and dimensions and helps you to relate these in your own data warehouse.

## The Fact Table

The fact table is a table that may be viewed in two parts. The first part defines the primary key; the other holds the numerical measurements on the warehouse. These measures are defined and calculated for each derived key and are known as facts or measures. Measures should have the following characteristics:

▼ Numeric

▲ Additive (usually)

However, at times you may find that a measure is required in the warehouse, but it may not appear to be additive. This is known as *semiadditive facts*. An example of a semiadditive fact would be room temperature in different parts of an office tower. If we would add together the temperatures in all the locations in the building, a completely meaningless number will be derived. By averaging this number, a more meaningful conclusion will be reached. Another example is inventory balances, which are not additive over the dimension of time. This value again lends itself to aggregation using an SQL function other than **sum**, such as **average**.

## Dimension Tables

The dimension tables can be viewed as the windows through which users will analyze their data. They contain the text descriptions of the items that support business operations. The design of the dimensions provides for the definition of the dimensions' attributes. These attributes should be plentiful. A product dimension could easily contain 50 or more attributes. These attributes should have the following characteristics:

▼ Be textual

■ Be discrete

■ Define constraints

▲ Provide row headers during analysis

When looking at the dimensions, the attributes of a dimension can be seen as information to describe the item. So, for a product information dimension, we may say that it can be described as having a certain color. This attribute would be textual, such as "blue." Each product with a different color would have its own record within the dimension, making it discrete. This attribute for color could then be used to define your comparative analysis—such as give all the sales for blue products—thereby defining your constraints. Finally, the attribute can be used as a heading during analysis, so we could use the attribute name of color, or we may use the name of each distinct color. Attributes are very powerful for analysis of your data within the data warehouse. Some may say that the attribute is your window into your data.

As we have discussed previously, the following example shows the power and depth of attributes. If we want to determine the number of sales of blue-colored ice creams, we would enter the data structures via the product dimension, which contains the color attribute for our products. This dimension provides users with a number of analysis windows, which are opened by accessing the attributes in a conditional manner.

Let's look at what types of data components will more than likely become a dimension vs. a fact or a dimensional attribute:

▼ When a component is a number, and is additive or semiadditive, it will likely be a measure.

▲ When a component is a description, it will likely be a dimensional attribute.

Table 5-5 shows some examples of dimensions and the types of attributes that would form the dimension definition, again with primary key columns underlined.

As you can see in Table 5-5, every dimension has a surrogate key. A *surrogate key* is a system-generated primary key used to designate individual records in each dimension of the data warehouse. The surrogate key removes any requirement to use an implied key from your operational systems. This is required so that when we determine how we will manage changes within a dimension, we are not confined by a key implied from an operational code. Also, by removing the dependence on operational keys, heterogeneous codes from multiple operational systems can be collected in common warehouse coding structures. Surrogate keys also have better performance: they are limited to one column rather than concatenations of columns and they are generally integer data types, which are processed more quickly than character data types. The power of the star schema comes in its simplicity.

Table 5-6 describes how these keys (underlined as usual) are linked in a fact table, along with some measures that can be used during data analysis.

So, as you can see, the fact table is composed of two distinct sections: the primary key, comprised of the keys from the dimensions, and the numeric measures. This simple structure allows for very interesting and detailed data analysis.

| Time Dimension | Product Dimension | Customer Dimension |
|---|---|---|
| <u>Time key</u> | <u>Product key</u> | <u>Customer key</u> |
| Date | Operational ID | Name |
| Month | Product name | Street address |
| Day | UPC code | City |
| Year | Product class | State/province |
| Quarter | Color | City |
| Fiscal year | Flavor | Country |
|  | Product size | Type |

**Table 5-5.** Dimensions and Their Attributes

| |
|---|
| <u>Time key</u> |
| <u>Product key</u> |
| <u>Customer key</u> |
| Sale amount |
| Quantity |
| Discount |

**Table 5-6.**    Dimension Keys Linked in Fact Table

Figure 5-2 illustrates how users can easily navigate and understand the model to create interesting queries. The schema that we provide you with is a simple one to understand, and with simple training can be used by all users in your organization. The database schema described shows a PRODUCT_SALES fact table and TIME, PRODUCT, and CUSTOMER dimensions. The dimensions are joined together in the fact table by

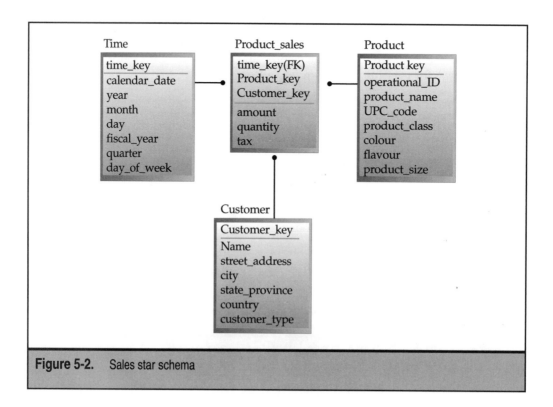

**Figure 5-2.**    Sales star schema

foreign keys defined for each dimension. The foreign keys ensure that we create a consistent view of the data, with all records related by our generated surrogate keys. We will discuss how to guarantee that when you load data into the warehouse, the data consistency is retained.

**NOTE:** The primary key of the fact table is comprised of foreign keys to the dimension tables and numeric measures.

**NOTE:** The fact tables are actually highly normalized (except in unusual situations where the fact tables might be denormalized by a dimension like time). Dimension tables are highly denormalized.

Let's continue the design discussion by looking at granularity.

# GRANULARITY

*Granularity* is defined as the level of summarization that will be maintained by your warehouse; however, a warehouse will usually contain many levels of granularity. When creating your data warehouse or data mart, you must define the granularity of the data as part of your warehouse definition. Table 5-7 provides a quick reference on the relationship between granularity and data detail.

*Grain* can be defined as the highest level of detail that is retained in the warehouse, such as the transaction level. This data is highly detailed and can then be summarized to any level required by your users. It is imperative when designing your data warehouse that you define the granularity of the data at the outset of your analysis effort, since it will affect your database design. If you define the grain improperly, you can handicap your warehouse and defeat the purpose of creating it. When defining granularity within the warehouse, consider the following factors:

▼ Type of analysis you will be performing

■ Acceptable lowest levels of aggregation

▲ Volume of data that can be stored

| Grain | Data Detail |
| --- | --- |
| Low (e.g., transactional) | Very high |
| High (e.g., summarized) | Medium to low |

**Table 5-7.**    Relationship Between Granularity and Data Detail

The types of analysis you plan to perform with the warehouse will directly affect your warehouse's granularity. If you plan to use the warehouse to perform analysis based on information summarized at the daily level, then you would not want to define the grain at the weekly level.

**NOTE:** If you define your level of granularity too high, you may not be able to perform some more detailed operations within your warehouse.

The data warehouse will usually have multiple levels of granularity within the same schema. You may have one level for data that was created within the current year and another for data in the previous two- to five-year window. This is based upon the lowest level of aggregation required in the warehouse. You may find that your users will need transactional data in the warehouse, but this data is only applicable during the current year; after that period, the data can be summarized at a weekly or monthly level. These decisions are critical to your overall data warehouse design and must not be taken lightly.

Finally, the last contributing factor to defining your warehouse's granularity is the amount of disk space that you can make available to the warehouse. If you have limited resources, you may find that you can only handle data volumes if your data is summarized at a weekly level. This analysis must be performed based upon your knowledge of your data requirements and the amount of space that this information will take up within the database. We find that if you design your warehouse based on hardware limitations, you will impose artificial limits on the warehouse, which could defeat the long-term viability of the system. Today, the price of disk space is cheap, so make every attempt to define your level of granularity based on information requirements.

Now that we have defined the components of a data warehouse, we must put it all together. To that end, we provide you with an approach that has proven successful in designing data warehouses.

# DATA WAREHOUSE DESIGN APPROACH AND GUIDE

We have discussed the components of the data warehouse and some of the concepts that we will use during the analysis and design of a warehouse. The most important step towards the design of the warehouse is to create a design team that represents all parties concerned with delivering and using the data warehouse. For years we have been developing systems with little or no user representation. The data warehouse embraces the users and their requirements.

The design of the data warehouse is iterative and requires careful planning and analysis. The following is a methodology that has proven successful in designing and deploying data warehouses. Through this process, you will design and develop your data warehouse topology. This will include the database structure, the extraction methods and procedures, the data loading and transformation techniques, and the end-user reporting and retrieval strategy.

# Project Analysis and Planning

This phase of the project is crucial to successfully delivering data warehousing solutions. Analysis and planning are often the least appreciated phase of any project.

We prefer the use of joint application development (JAD) sessions as the vehicle to bring the team together to qualify and quantify the details for the project. In commencing the process, we (along with the design team) will identify the goals and direction for the data warehouse. We will confirm the warehouse's focus, its target audience, and its purpose within the corporation. This will then lead into defining the project, scope, and tasks. The definition of the scope allows the team developing the plan to review and analyze the details of the project in order to identify the tasks, deliverables, dependencies, and assumptions of the project. We first looked at scope in Chapter 2, when looking at the data warehouse project team. When defining your project scope, you need to capture the following information:

▼   Subject areas

■   Number of tables

■   Amount of history

■   Number of target users

■   The summarization level of the warehouse

■   Management of individual data changes within the warehouse

▲   The window available for data warehouse extraction and cleansing

Two streams of thought that are pursued during the JAD sessions will satisfy distinct components of the complete data warehouse solution. The first stream will focus on the data storage side of the solution, and the second will focus on the reporting requirements. It is imperative to the success in architecting a sound data warehousing solution that a high-level understanding of the reporting requirements be achieved.

During the analysis phase, we determine the processes within the business that we are trying to model with the data warehouse or data mart. Initially, one must define the processes that will be satisfied by the warehouse. The process could be any of the following or another as defined by your own business:

▼   Point of sale transactions

■   Healthcare claims

■   Manufacturing analysis

■   Insurance claims

■   Bill of materials

■   Purchase orders

▲   Plant logistics

As you can see, there is no limit to the types of analysis you will need to support with the information contained in your data warehouse. Now that you have started to define the business foci of your warehouse, you are ready to start defining your supporting details. The dimensions of your data model will form this supporting information for your warehouse. Now that we have defined the processes, we can take an initial run at defining the required dimensions.

A very useful tool in performing this analysis is the process/dimension matrix. This matrix defines the processes that will support the business processes and specific information that will be required to satisfy the reporting needs. Table 5-8 is a sample matrix developed for a banking system, with dimensions across the top and processes down the leftmost column.

A review of the operational information systems will be performed. This review will allow the design team to better understand the current data sources and data flows. These systems form the operational foundation of the business, and this review will identify the data that is being used within the company. The understanding of these processes allows us to define a clear vision of the current business processes related to the collection and dissemination of information required for the data warehouse. Based on the scope and requirements that you have defined, time and resource estimates for delivering the required solution are established. The entire data warehouse team reviews the scope and systems requirements, and any missed items are then included for completeness. This review also serves as a way of further enhancing user involvement in the project by allowing users to understand the direction that the project is taking and ensuring that all their requirements are being addressed.

| | | | | Dimension | | | |
|---|---|---|---|---|---|---|---|
| **Process** | **Time** | **Account** | **Product** | **Customer Rep.** | **Branch** | **Securities** | **Customer** |
| Track customer account | X | X | X | X | X | | X |
| Security transaction | X | X | X | | X | X | X |
| Monthly account balance | X | X | X | | X | | |

**Table 5-8.** Dimensions and Processes Matrix

## High-Level Design

The high-level design phase of the methodology builds towards the goal of delivering the data warehouse. This phase focuses on integrating the business processes and business needs that will drive the construction of the data warehouse and the related decision support system.

Merging the information related to your current business process and the goals intended for the data warehouse, the data warehouse architect will create a high-level entity relationship diagram (ERD). The *ERD* is a diagram that shows us all the objects in the database. It describes all the tables (entities) and how each one relates to the other. By creating your ERD in a CASE tool, you can provide a graphical description of your database. This ERD will start to form the database road map of the data warehouse. It will show the major objects and their relationships to each other. It will document the data transformations from operational systems to the data warehouse. The ERD will form the starting point for creating the staging area and/or *operational data store* (ODS) and the data warehouse dimensional models. These will be refined in future phases of the life cycle.

Once your entities are defined, you must also define the level of granularity of your warehouse. This definition will then help in defining your objects. Figure 5-3 shows the high-level version of such an entity relationship diagram.

As you can see from Figure 5-3, we have defined the major objects and the relations between them. This will form the initial database structure. This step allows us to see that

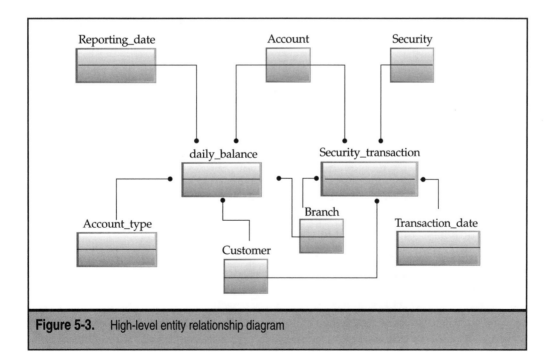

**Figure 5-3.** High-level entity relationship diagram

we have identified the major objects in our data warehouse. We would also define the major objects required by any staging objects in the database. The initial design allows us to validate the design direction that we have chosen with our data warehouse. Together with the target user group, we will review and ensure that we have created a design that collects and collates the information in a simple and efficient manner.

Defining a staging area within your data warehouse topology depends upon the detail requirements of the end users. The staging area can be a time-based data structure that holds the information from your operational systems in common structure and coding standards. The time component of the staging area allows you to track the changes in the data over time, allowing for very detailed analysis and trending of your operational data. It will be structured in a manner similar to the operational system; this structure can be used for quick loading of information into the database and allows you to work within a simple environment from which to populate the warehouse and standardize the data. The staging area allows for a simpler method of loading the data, since loading a normalized schema that contains a minimum of information requires a minimum amount of reformatting. This will reduce the amount of user programming to guide the load before the data is moved into the data warehouse. If you do not want to refer back to your operational database platform, then storing detailed data in your staging area would be the valid direction to resolve this issue. If you do not require this level of detail or do not have the resources to support it, then a simple staging area will suffice and data would be purged after that warehouse's high-performance query structures are populated. If you create a time-based staging area, you will then have a platform from which your data warehouse will be populated. Regardless of how you stage and store your raw data from your operational systems, you must first consider how this information should be integrated into your overall data warehouse strategy. Although this method offers a more robust data warehouse architecture and a more flexible data mart strategy, how users plan to access and manipulate the data must be considered. When you retain the data within the staging area, you then have available to you an area of the warehouse that can be used to populate historical information into the warehouse as the mandate of the warehouse changes.

At the conclusion of your high-level design, you will be able to show a low-detail version of your data warehouse. This will then serve as a vehicle to confirm that you have collected the requirements correctly and that your model can satisfy the information requirements of the warehouse's users. At this point, we should also confirm that we have satisfied our reporting requirements at a high level. In cooperation with the end users, the model should be reviewed against the reporting requirements that were defined during the early stages of the design process.

**NOTE:** The high-level design is concerned with understanding the business. This level ensures that all the business processes of the data warehouse are documented and that we get a basic understanding of the information that will need to be collected.

# Mid-Level Design

The mid-level design refines the information collected during the previous phases of the project. The mid-level design will create a more detailed definition of the data warehouse. The focus at the mid-level is detailing the data.

The review of your operational systems will continue. It will now focus on the detailed data attributes that these systems provide. The ERD will be further refined to include the individual attributes in the data model. As well, the review will include the definition of standards that will be adhered to for the data attributes. Since information sources have diverse information standards that need to be coalesced into a common information repository, the definition of standards is imperative.

During refinement of the ERD, the data warehouse architect will map the data sources to their respective data warehouse destinations. He or she will also identify information that may be required in the data warehouse that is not currently available in the operational sources and must be derived from other information sources.

At this point, we can start to integrate some aggregation and focused dimensional modeling into the ERD. This design consideration will be based on the high-level business intelligence requirements that were captured and compiled within the project analysis and planning phase.

At the conclusion of the mid-level design, we will once again present the results to the user community. This will ensure that the business requirements are being met by the design. At this point, we will also encourage feedback on the direction the data warehouse is taking. It is imperative that we continue to inform and discuss the data warehouse design with the parties involved to ensure that we are building a warehouse that meets the users' needs. Figure 5-4 shows a mid-level design diagram.

Figure 5-4 documents the results of the mid-level design. As you can see, the dimensions and facts now have a number of attributes. These attributes are developed based upon user input, reporting requirements, and operational data sources. This model is moving us closer to the physical model that we will need to then implement the data warehouse.

**NOTE:** The mid-level design is concerned with structure and completeness. This level ensures that all the data elements required by your business warehousing needs are now included in the model. We are less concerned with how and where the data will come from, and more interested in satisfying information requirements.

# Low-Level Design

This phase of the project focuses on creating the physical database design and the processes required for creating and populating the data warehouse. Based on the results of previous project phases and feedback acquired during each phase review, the physical data model will now be completed. The model will include all entities, relationships, attributes, and attribute definitions. The model will identify all data sources for each

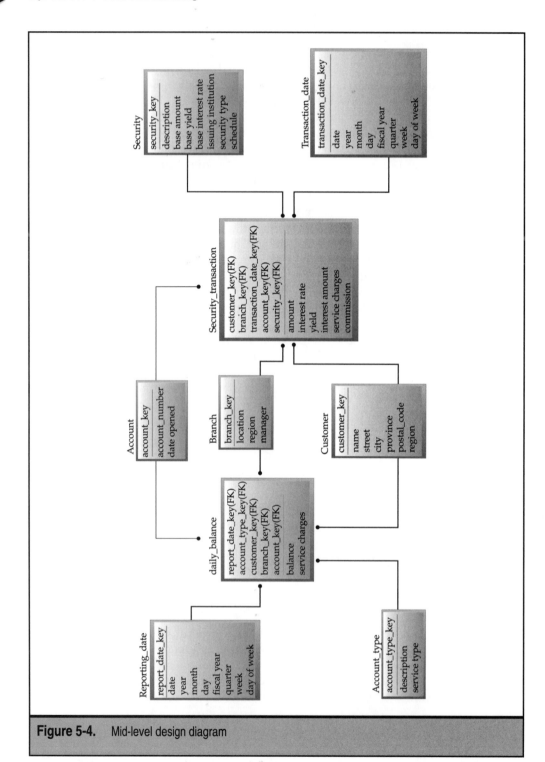

**Figure 5-4.** Mid-level design diagram

attribute and the extraction and construction methods for information that is being transformed from its original format or derived from other sources.

The processes required to load and transform the data from the operational data sources will be defined. The process definitions will identify the source and target hardware platforms, the methods for transmitting data across the network, the data loading methods, the data cleansing methods, and data transformation methods and techniques.

We will then create an implementation plan that will address and schedule the implementation and development of the system. This will be the final checkpoint before full development commences. The database design will be completed, the storage requirements defined, the data growth predicted, the hardware configured, and user approvals obtained. The implementation plan will describe the system in its entirety, documenting all data, interfaces, and methods that will be used to create the physical data warehouse solution. This plan will serve as the baseline for the development phase of the project.

A complete review of the database, the data interfaces, and the planning will be carried out at the end of this phase to ensure that the users understand the system that they have helped to design. Any changes that are required will be incorporated before development is initiated, thus maximizing the development team's productivity. With our data warehouse design, we are now ready to move forward into the development and deployment of the data warehouse.

Speaking of deployment, let's move on to discussing data marts. In the first version of this work, we struggled over calling them "datamarts" or "data marts." Now that we have come to a unanimous decision that they are "data marts," we feel we have been able to gain a consensus among the four of us. Hopefully this will inspire the players in the potential warehouse vs. data mart struggle to reach a quick agreement as well. After all, life is a series of concessions—being willing to listen to others when they make sense, and being willing to listen to others when they don't.

# CHAPTER 6

## Data Marts

This chapter is dedicated to data marts—the dimensional solution that holds the information key to the decision-making process. Unlike the enterprise data warehouse, the data mart supports specific processes in segments of a corporate suite of decision support systems; however, by linking data marts we can achieve a detailed view of our business and find trends that may have been previously unknown.

We first defined a *data mart* as a subject-oriented business view of the warehouse. It usually contains significantly smaller amounts of data than the warehouse and it is the object of analytical processing by the end user. In a corporate data warehouse solutions environment, there may be marts set up for pockets of the company, such as sales, manufacturing, and billing. Data marts enable pockets of a company's organization to make better-informed and more accurate strategic business decisions. Data marts commonly are less expensive and much smaller than a full-blown corporate-wide data warehouse. Organizations that intelligently implement a number of data marts find it provides their users with a quick introduction to warehousing. By allowing users to use and understand the power provided to them by the data mart, they can then embark on a more complete corporate warehouse. As the corporate enterprise data warehouse is built, the user community always has access to their own data marts, which evolve over time. The old saying of "If you build it, they will come," is very true during data warehouse development—by having users better understand the analyses that they can perform on their data, the more complete the warehouse will evolve into. So, get your users involved in a data mart initiative, building toward the enterprise data warehouse.

The current industry trend is to build the enterprise data warehouse with an "architected solution approach," which means to build each data mart taking into account corporate information issues. As a result, we create the true customer list at the true atomic level; thus, as more marts come online, their dimensions are consistent and reusable, and the mart is more easily modified over time. The atomic level of data—the data staging area—makes it possible to join across marts, and your collection of marts becomes the enterprise data warehouse—ever evolving and no single mass project is ever embarked on.

Classic operational systems concentrate on high-level requirements that cater to the needs of all the users. When the global system is ready, the lower-level detailed needs of segments of the user community are met. This type of implementation is called *top-down*. A common example of top-down development is a financial management application. Specific modules are planned to deal with transactions as they move through the life cycle from budgets to expenditures. All the needs of all the users are attended to and the final product is delivered according to the big bang theory of system development. Data marts are usually developed in the opposite way, which is called *bottom-up*. The specific needs of small, focused locations within a business are addressed using the bottom-up approach.

*Trade-offs* is an interesting word when you think of designing data marts. Visions of a multiterabyte (a terabyte is 1,024 gigabytes) warehouse conjure up scenarios where end-user queries take forever to complete and cause endless frustration in the community. Because the data mart can check in at a fraction of the size of the enterprise data warehouse, analysts, development staff, and users may feel this is definitely the way to go based on size and size alone. This approach may be an easy sell to management in the short term, but, as all our experience has shown, it is not the way to proceed. Granted, current and future hardware acquisitions may be driven by the plans for data mart/warehouse rollout, but the business needs of your organization's decision makers outweigh all other factors. The data mart is developed using the dimensional modeling methodology, as discussed in Chapter 5, but focuses on only a single business process.

# DATA MARTS

*Data mart*—these words evoke visions of a 24-hour convenience store with specific goods that are tailored to meet consumer needs. In the data mart, you could not be closer to the truth. The specialty item is data—data designed to solve the business requirements of a pocket of corporate data warehouse users. Data marts are subject-oriented dimensional databases with a normal life expectancy of three years. Unlike the enterprise data warehouse, they can check in with a figure under $250,000. Most data marts ring in at 25 gigabytes and support a user community of between 10 and 25 users.

Vendors of tools that build, and then manage, data marts must provide a cost-effective, rapid solution that can be used on any-sized project. The results of the build effort must be made available to the user community in a timely fashion. *Timely fashion* means a time to market of two to four months. Prospective users of corporate data marts can easily lose interest when turnaround times are longer. Data mart software must leverage existing operational and other DSS repositories during their build phases. Providers of technology must be able to read data directly from a suite of legacy systems implemented on IBM mainframe servers using products such as IMS and DB2, as well as newer systems such as SAP and PeopleSoft running on UNIX servers. Data can be extracted directly from these systems using COBOL modules, and the results moved into the data mart from flat files.

The model of the data mart is driven by the ways the user needs to view and use the information. Rather than paying so much attention to the physical layout of the data, the data mart model reflects what the users want to be able to do and how they wish to have it presented. Data mart implementers interview the users and, with their input and the knowledge the implementers have about the technology, design a model that is ideally suited to the users' requirements. This is an iterative process, which sometimes goes on for the life of the data mart. An *iterative process* is one that is repeated, but this does not mean the iteration is repeated because its previous execution was flawed. An iterative process is simply executed over and over again, usually in response to changing corporate uses of the data. Grocery shopping or paying the phone bill are parts of everyday life that are iterative processes.

## Stand-Alone Data Marts

Pockets of some organizations have beaten a trail on their own to the data mart solution. Sometimes, in a largely decentralized company, segments of the business community have funded, developed, and deployed the data mart solution virtually without the involvement of the personnel tasked with the management of computer system solutions. These are known as *stand-alone data marts*. As the 1990s come to a close, and with the parallel-capable hardware and software products in the marketplace, these stand-alone data marts are difficult if not impossible to integrate into a larger corporate data mart or data warehouse initiative. Too many discrepancies exist between different stand-alone data marts in the way the data is structured and how the data is encoded. It is virtually impossible to merge these data marts' contents when looking for ways to share data between the corporate segments of an organization. As with data that comes from many data sources, the coalescing of the information can be difficult. The lessons that we learn from the building of data warehouses should be used when designing data marts—the data marts must form consistent views of our business. Data marts should not be built in isolation, and organizations must develop an overall data mart strategy that incorporates all lines with the business.

Many data marts are a *subset* of a large data warehouse's information, centrally designed, built, maintained, and distributed to groups of DSS users throughout a company. Today, the thrust is towards centralized management. This reduces the administrative redundancies inherent in a decentralized model. Companies are building data marts that feed on a combination of larger operational and decision support data sources. These data marts incorporate a company-wide approach to delivery of decision support systems; this is only possible in businesses that are committed to deploying systems from a central point under the auspices and supervision of a company-wide systems development and deployment group. The types of processes that lend themselves very well to data mart development include sales, purchasing, customer service processes, logistics, and manufacturing. The model shown in Figure 6-1 demonstrates how a process, such as Pay-TV Orders can form a data mart using a star schema. The data mart is a simple one, yet you can already realize the types of queries you could write, even with what at first glance appears to be a simple model.

Data marts often share information portions within the organization and an overall data mart strategy. In the banking industry, many business processes share the account dimension. These processes will include bank balances, loans, credit cards, and marketing. The account is a common concept in almost all areas of the bank's business. By creating an account dimension and then sharing this dimension among the data marts, we allow the bank to form a common view of their account holders within many business focus areas. The idea of shared dimensions has been called "conformed dimensions" by Ralph Kimball. Dr. Kimball says that through the sharing of information contained in these conformed dimensions, we can join information together in what would have been independent data marts. This idea is critical to allow data marts to exceed the information limitations that a stand-alone data mart provides. With conformed data marts, you can now analyze your data across data marts. Remember that the granularity of your data marts must be the same for this analysis to be useful. The diagram in Figure 6-2 shows how our original data mart of Pay-TV Orders can be related to a customer product transaction data mart. Through the subscriber dimension we perform analysis, such as how many customers with a particular cable service have ordered Pay-TV family-rated movies.

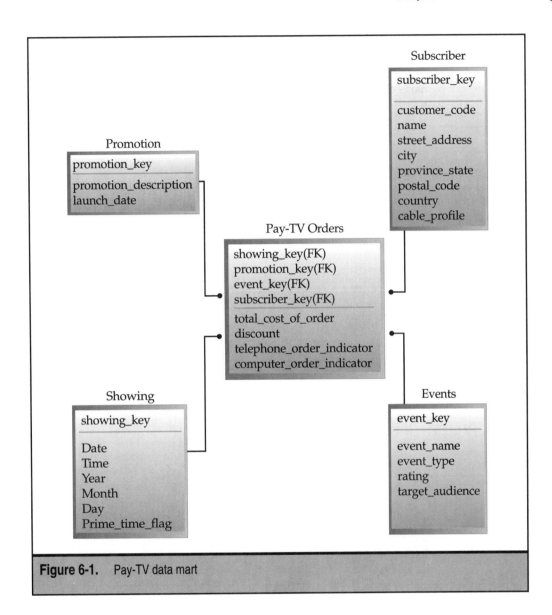

**Figure 6-1.**   Pay-TV data mart

## Dimensional Database

Data marts are dimensional. A *dimensional* database allows for decision support queries using a wide range of criteria combinations, so many queries using the data in a data mart are ad hoc. An *ad hoc query* is one whose selection criteria are chosen by the user as the query is formulated. Many queries against operational systems are canned or preprogrammed. A *canned query* is one set up to run at the user's request and to bring

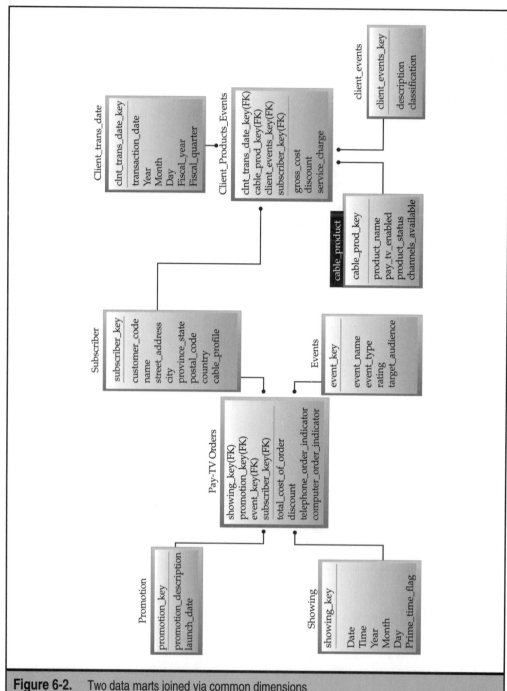

**Figure 6-2.** Two data marts joined via common dimensions

back data in a predetermined format; they always access the same tables. That is why it is so important to design your data mart with query efficiency in mind. The star schema provides a high degree of performance and the simplicity that power users and occasional DSS users require. As we have already discussed, the star schema is a simplistic approach to database and data warehouse design. The schema developed for a data mart appears simple for users to navigate; its power is based in this simplicity. By creating the data mart with query in mind, we provide ad hoc users with a schema that is both simple to navigate and that is tuned specifically for query performance.

**NOTE:** It has been shown that 90 percent of all queries are driven by canned queries in a data warehouse environment, with only 10 percent being ad hoc queries.

The data mart must support *n*-way queries with a network of indexes constructed in such a way that the operator can use an OLAP tool and:

▼ Report on the information in one table in the data mart using any column as a selection criterion.

▲ Assemble data from two or more tables in the data mart, joining the objects using foreign key relationships; one query may join tables X, Y, and Z, and the next minute, the same user could join A, B, and C in a way that may never happen again.

The data mart serves as a foundation for online analytical processing (OLAP) in a decision support system. As a result, the DSS architect listens to the users and collects information on factors, such as:

▼ What information do they wish to glean from the data mart?

■ How do they want that information presented?

■ What level of summarization (granularity) do they want?

▲ What tables will be commonly joined together in OLAP query processing?

Armed with the answers to these questions, the analyst begins the data mart design process and arrives at a physical model that will suit the needs of the most important commodity in the entire process—the *user*. We apologize to all users now for using the term—it seems as if the term "user" has negative connotations. In the data warehouse the user is king or queen, and to that end we will also call you knowledge workers. Without users, your data mart and data warehouse are destined to problems, so involve your knowledge workers (users) in every aspect of the construction and implementation to allow yourself the best opportunity for success.

## Dimensions Affect Design

Dimensions together with facts form the basis of the star schema. The star schema is the basic unit of design in the data mart. Please refer to Chapter 5 for a more complete discussion of star schemas. Designing the data mart utilizing dimensional modeling will enable you to maximize the effectiveness of the data mart. Often, after a mart has been used for a period of time, users identify new information requirements. When the original design of the data mart was developed, it was created by defining the business process and the dimensions and facts to support this requirement. Each dimension in a data mart requires storage of another column in the central fact table. So, when designing the data mart, we try to predict all the types of uses for that data mart. The initial design will address the dimensions and the facts that will satisfy the analytical processing requirements of the data mart (i.e., its raison d'être). However, there are times when you discover that a new dimension is required in the mart. A careful review of this addition must be done, because we will be changing the fact table in our star schema. Your review must include the following details:

▼ Define the new dimension requirement (e.g., product, promotion, salesperson).

■ Is this a new data requirement or can we add additional attributes to an existing dimension?

■ If this can be satisfied by new attributes, the impact is that we need to add the new attributes to an existing dimension.

■ If this requires a new dimension, we must design the new dimension by defining the new table. This will include the primary key and all attributes for the new dimension.

■ How will the dimension be incorporated into the fact table? We must define how we will rebuild the data contained in the fact table, because the dimension will form a new part of the primary key.

■ Define how historical data will be reconciled with the dimension.

■ Define the impact to the loading, extraction, and population routines currently involved in the data mart.

■ Develop a plan for implementing the new dimension.

▲ Implement the new dimension.

As you can see from this list, the impact of what may be considered a simple dimension change in an existing data mart or data warehouse is no small exercise. Your analysis may show you that the current operational system does not allow us to rebuild the existing data, so you may be required to deploy a new data mart to satisfy this new requirement. Remember that your data warehouse is only as good as your operational data sources and the historical data that they contain. Figure 6-3 shows the star schema with a new dimension and attribute.

## Drill-Down Requirements Impact Design

As data is moved into the data mart, it usually undergoes some form of summarization. The statement, "The company grossed $26 million last year" does not mean much to the

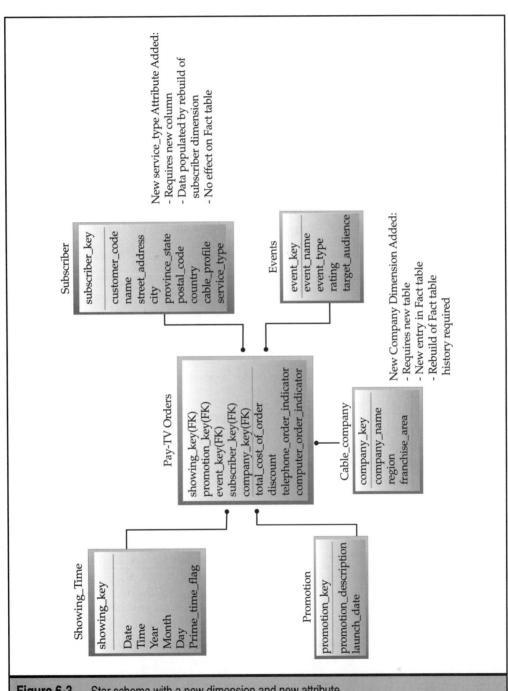

**Figure 6-3.** Star schema with a new dimension and new attribute

DSS user. When users are presented with this information, they inevitably want to get at the underlying information that rolls up to the multimillion-dollar figure. This process of digging deeper into data is referred to as *drill-down*. The data mart implementation team has the responsibility to decide the following:

1. What level of drill-down does the data mart user wish to have available?
2. Based on the answer to the first question, what information will be stored in the data mart and what information will be derived at run time?

Table 6-1 illustrates how complex drill-down can get for a sales data mart.

| Country | Continent | Region | State/Province | City |
|---------|-----------|--------|----------------|------|
| USA | North America | East | Florida | Miami |
| | | | | Orlando |
| | | | | Tampa |
| | | | New York | New York |
| | | | | Albany |
| | | | | Lake Placid |
| | | West | California | San Francisco |
| | | | | Los Angeles |
| | | | | San Diego |
| | | Central | Michigan | Detroit |
| | | | | Ann Arbor |
| | | | | Taylor |
| Canada | | East | Nova Scotia | Halifax |
| | | | | Yarmouth |
| | | | Newfoundland | Cornerbrook |
| | | | Quebec | Montreal |
| | | | | Sherbrooke |
| | | | | Sainte Agathe |
| | | Central | Ontario | Ottawa |

**Table 6-1.**    Sales Data Mart Drill-Down Example

| Country | Continent | Region | State/Province | City |
|---------|-----------|--------|----------------|------|
| | | | | Nepean |
| | | | | Toronto |
| | | | | Hamilton |
| UK | Europe | Central | London | London |
| | | | | Ealing |
| | | | | Brentford |
| | | Northern | Yorkshire | Birmingham |

**Table 6-1.**   Sales Data Mart Drill-Down Example (*continued*)

Design decisions impact the performance of queries against the data mart. As we can see, a simple dimension such as a location dimension can break down into many combinations that allows for a strong ability to analyze your data from many different directions. From the data shown in Table 6-1, Table 6-2 illustrates the types of analysis that can be performed.

As you can see, the types of analysis and the number of ways that you can slice and dice the data provide for a great deal of flexibility. The data mart may store summary data at the city level and roll up to the continental level as a query is processed. A point exists where the drill-down capability stops. When first contemplating where to stop the process, the DSS analyst needs to converse with the user of the data mart and ascertain when the loss of detail does not affect the ability to make informed decisions. In the design illustrated in Table 6-1, once the user has drilled down to the city level, there is nowhere else to go.

| Type of Analysis | Columns to Satisfy Requirement |
|------------------|-------------------------------|
| Sales for the entire organization | Summary of all data in data mart |
| Sales by country | Summarize by country |
| Sales in North America by region | Summarize by continent and region |

**Table 6-2.**   Types of Analysis on Sales Data Mart

# QUERIES AGAINST THE DATA MART

Query criteria can be lumped together into four main categories:

1. Inclusion operations, where data is selected based on its passing one or more comparisons. This includes the three mechanisms shown in bold in the following listing:

```
-- Equality
select promotion_description
from promotion
where promotion_key = '123'
go
-- Equality within a set
select name
from subscriber
where city in ('TORONTO','OTTAWA','MONTREAL')
go
-- Bounded range
select sum(total_cost_of_order)
from    pay_tv_orders
where   showing_key between 10 and 27
go
```

2. Exclusion operations, where data is eliminated based on its not conforming to one or more comparisons. This operation usually uses some form of negation construct. These are shown in bold in the next listing:

```
-- Not equal
select promotion_description
from promotion
where promotion_key != '123'
go
-- Not in a set
select name
from subscriber
where city not in ('TORONTO','OTTAWA','MONTREAL')
go
-- Not within a bounded range
select sum(total_cost_of_order)
 from    pay_tv_orders
 where   showing_key not between 10 and 27
 go
```

3. A combination of inclusion and exclusion operations, where some data is eliminated and qualifying data become part of the result set. The following listing illustrates this type of query:

```
select isnull(sum(total_cost_of_order),0)
  from    pay_tv_orders
  where   telephone_order_indicator != 'N'
  and     showing_key not between 10 and 27
  go
```

4. Arithmetic functions, such as **sum, min, max, or avg**, where a function is applied to numeric fields in the query, coupled with any combination of inclusion and exclusion operations. Usually, character fields are either left as is or become the sources of grouping operations. Examine the following SQL statement for an example of this type of query selection criteria:

```
select sum(total_cost_of_order)
from        pay_tv_orders
inner join showing
on          pay_tv_orders.showing_key = showing.showing_key
inner join subscriber
on pay_tv_orders.subscriber_key = subscriber.subscriber_key
where   showing.year  = 1998
and     showing.month = 4
and     subscriber.city = 'PHOENIX'
go
```

The data mart is heavily indexed, with the anticipation that the users will base query results on large amounts of data using a wide range of selection criteria.

## Sum of This, Sum of That

Aggregates play a vital role in the decision support data mart. *Aggregation* is a process whereby multiple detail records are combined into a single data mart record. The numeric data stored in each aggregate record represents the sum of the corresponding fields from all the operational records it summarizes. The rows in a data mart can be thought of as a slice of operational data, with an added dimension involving time and a level of summarization. Data is no longer atomic, where each row contains information related to one and only one transaction. In Chapter 5, we discussed granularity and how highly granular data equate to highly summarized—that is, low-detail data—and vice versa. As data is brought into the data mart, the analyst decides with what level of granularity to begin. The SQL **sum** function accomplishes the aggregation operation, coupled with the **group by** statement as the data is moved into the data mart. Additional types of aggregation are identified once the end users start to work with the data marts.

# DATA WAREHOUSE VS. DATA MART

One of many intriguing factors about data warehousing in general, and data marts in particular, reminds us of the saying, "You can't see the forest for the trees." In this context, this familiar metaphor illustrates how data mart data can reveal remarkable similarities among previously unrelated data. The trees are represented by the seemingly isolated occurrences of data, and the forest is the total set of data, which has previously unforeseen similarities. Just remember that although you can find a correlation between two previously unrelated facts, does not mean that the facts are related. You may find that the sales in your organization are affected by the season, but the relationship between the ambient room temperature and the sale of gum may not be a true relationship. So, when relating two or more factors in a DSS system, remember that you may be able to relate apparently unrelated attributes and come to a conclusion. However, this conclusion may be coincidental, so care must be taken in defining the types of analysis you plan to perform.

The data mart is the target of a number of data warehouse steps; it is where the DSS end user will spend most of the day. The sheer size of an enterprise data warehouse can make some decision support tools balk. Also, the navigation of the enterprise data warehouse may be difficult, which may intimidate a certain portion of your users. The smaller data mart, containing less data, is set up to optimize the analyst's access to information. Many vendors exist who market data mart software that is designed to help complete the journey that data make out of operational systems into the warehouse environment. Figure 6-4 shows the major components in this journey.

Some data mart providers read operational system data dictionaries, make sense out of the relationships, wade through the inherent complexities, and provide the analyst with choices on how the data can be loaded into the data mart. Assistance with this time-consuming activity is fundamental to a mature data mart solution provider.

An interesting benefit of sinking time and money into developing data marts is they can cost a fraction of the money needed to implement a full-blown enterprise data warehouse. Analysis dollars are eaten up quickly when companies embark on a project, insisting that the be-all, end-all warehouse is the only acceptable output. Experience has shown that warehouse development checks in with a three- to five-million dollar price tag and up to three years for delivery. Figures like these are within the grasp of large corporations, but data marts help provide solutions for smaller businesses as well as focused segments of a company's decision makers. The enterprise data warehouse may be a longer-term goal for some smaller companies but, as previously mentioned in this chapter, data marts are rapid development outputs that implement a bottom-up approach. They get the information required for smart business decisions out to the consumer in shorter time periods.

Data marts are the new breed of data warehouse solutions. Being bottom-up, they are driven by consumers in cooperation with a team of information technology (IT) experts. Many enterprise data warehouse projects have floundered, just as many of their

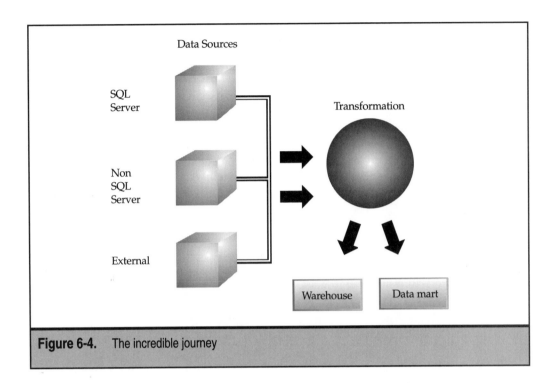

**Figure 6-4.**    The incredible journey

operational system predecessors have. Companies end up biting off more than they can chew; the initiative comes in way over budget, coughs, and dies. This is a reality of data warehousing; they are often developed, and when they are finally launched to the user community, they do not meet the user's information needs. This could be a result of changes in requirements during the long time needed for development. Data marts address this concern directly by ensuring that users are involved from the inception of a data mart project. The users drive the process, since they are the business users and the owners of the data. However, remember, as we stated previously, data marts need to be built with the enterprise in mind as well. Stand-alone data marts that do not play nice with the other data marts can lead to difficult and costly integration efforts.

Recently a number of sophisticated tools have been developed to access the data mart. Previously, data warehouse projects made use of a hodgepodge of 3GL and 4GL tools. *3GL* refers to the family of computer languages (or generation of languages) such as C, COBOL, Pascal, and PL/1. *4GL* refers to a later breed of languages such as Transact-SQL used in tools such as PowerBuilder and Visual Basic. Data warehouse teams were tasked with building their own management mechanisms, and could be said to be "reinventing the wheel" with every step (just as was said of their operational system counterparts). How many times have organizations decided to develop their own custom solution, only to realize in several years that they should have purchased commercial off-the-shelf

(COTS) software? In the late 1980s, we were looking at some COTS for a client to solve their financial management requirements. Now, in 1998, they are still kicking themselves for doing their own solution, which is riddled with unnecessary complexities. As we will discuss, these tools for managing and populating your warehouse are reaching a level that allows data warehouse and data mart designers to leverage them during their implementation process.

The data warehouse industry is exploding, especially in the area of managing data marts. A next-generation set of tools is so data warehouse sensitive that it automates collection of metadata as the project progresses. *Metadata* is data about data; it describes what type of data is stored where in the warehouse, and it leads you through the network of relationships that exist within the data.

# REFERENTIAL INTEGRITY

*Referential integrity* (RI) plays a big role in the data mart and the data warehouse. RI is a mechanism used in relational databases to enforce relationships between data in different tables. RI also enforces business rules, such as:

▼ No building address may be entered into the client address table until the street on which that building resides has been recorded.

■ No part number may be recorded in inventory until the manufacturer of the part has been recorded.

▲ No small business may use the quick method for filing the goods and services tax until it has received notification from Revenue Canada Taxation.

Star schema was first discussed in Chapter 5. This special schema will take advantage of SQL Server 7's referential integrity mechanisms for the optimizer to correctly plan its execution path. The data mart builders pay special attention to this schema because it provides the optimal access to data in many data marts or full-blown data warehouse repositories. For the schema to be set up, you must define primary and foreign keys in the SQL Server 7 source data before the schema can be designed and implemented. Let's discuss setting up primary and foreign keys in your data mart.

## Primary Keys

You have probably heard of primary keys, but many developers and administrators have little or no experience with how they are defined in SQL Server 7. A *primary key* is one field or a combination of fields in a table that can uniquely identify each row in that table. The SQL to set the table is as follows:

```
create table subscriber (
        subscriber_key          numeric(10) not null,
        customer_type           varchar(1) null,
        name                    varchar(30) null,
        street_address          varchar(30) null,
        city                    varchar(30) null,
        province_state          varchar(2) null,
        postal_zip_code         varchar(10) null,
        map_area                numeric(5) null,
        demographic_rating      numeric(3) null
)
go
```

Then, after a table is created, the **alter table** construct is used:

```
alter table subscriber
        add primary key (subscriber_key)
go
```

SQL Server 7 creates a unique index on the combination of one or more columns defined as the primary key. Some additional specifications can be used when creating primary key constraints. These additional parameters and options can be found in the Transact-SQL help files.

# Foreign Keys

When a column has been defined as a primary key in one table and is included in a different table, that column is called a *foreign key*. Note that foreign key columns can only reference columns in other tables that have already been defined as part of that table's primary key. The syntax for defining a foreign key is

```
alter table pay_tv_orders
        add foreign key (subscriber_key)
        references subscriber
go
```

To put it another way, a foreign key is the primary key from one table stored in another table. In the relational database model, foreign keys define relationships between common columns in different tables. Figure 6-5 shows two relationships based on foreign keys.

**TIP:** The SQL statements shown for setting up primary and foreign keys are the tip of the iceberg on a large topic, which you should study before setting up a system of RI in a data mart or data warehouse.

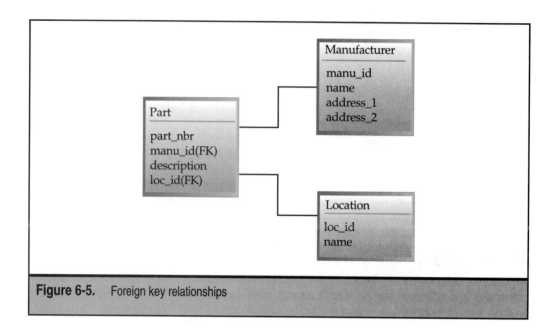

**Figure 6-5.**     Foreign key relationships

Once primary and foreign keys are defined, the DSS architect can begin to map the tables in the data mart, leveraging the existence of primary and foreign keys as the way data are related to one another.

# BEST-OF-BREED DATA MART TOOLS

With the onslaught of data mart solutions providers, consumers are looking for the following before deciding which set of tools is for them:

1. Consumers want a cost-effective toolset that can deliver solutions in less than six months, with a price tag of less than $250,000.

2. Consumers want a toolset that is an example of "one-stop shopping." Consumers insist that whatever vendor they do business with must bundle the core data mart functions into a single engine. These functions are discussed in the following section.

3. Consumers want a tool that can facilitate rapid inclusion of existing metadata, which already resides in operational systems.

4. Consumers want a toolset that can take advantage of the gains in parallel processing facilitated by multi-CPU computers, which serve as the host for many large data warehouse and data mart implementations.

5. Consumers want a tool that can grow to be used in an enterprise DWH.

# Core Data Mart Tool Functions

Consumers are looking for a set of core modules when evaluating vendors whose products provide a data mart solution to the marketplace. The next few sections cover some of these core modules.

## Extraction and Loading

Data mart software providers must play a role in facilitating this extraction process. *Extraction* is closely related to transformation because data representation can be so radically different in unrelated systems that serve as source data for the data mart. A data mart tool that can provide a standard interface for extracting data from source systems can aid you to significantly save time during this time-consuming phase of the project. The tool must also be able to read from heterogeneous data sources. Just like people, data sources come in all different shapes and sizes. So, even if you are populating a SQL Server 7 data mart, the sources can be a mixed affair. Sources could include a SQL Server 7, Oracle, or DB2 Relational database, flat files, or a mainframe's DB2 or IMS database. So, ensure that the tool you select can address all the types of databases and data sources that you may encounter in your data mart and in your overall data warehouse strategy, and you may make the right purchase the first time.

The other aspect of the tool must be its loading facility. The simplest way to move data into the data mart is to use the standard SQL **insert** statement. For some small data marts, you may be able to get away with SQL because of very low volumes, but a loading tool that can also do bulk loads is far more valuable and flexible. Disabling the generation of transaction log information while moving data into the warehouse will be discussed in Chapter 8. So, the tool must provide you with a flexible enough architecture to select the most efficient method of loading possible.

## Transformation

*Transformation* ensures that as data is moved into the data mart, it conforms to a standard system of codes and abbreviations. Decisions are made on which way to indicate code fields and which descriptions to use if the code data is extracted from tables in different systems that use the same code but a different method of representation. Many transformations can be handled by straight SQL functions and operations, but some data mart vendors have decided to complement the SQL functionality with their own proprietary mechanisms. We find that we are often required to program a very complex transformation with a variety of tools to meet the requirements of the data mart. Tools from suppliers such as Sagent, Ardent, and Prism are used to complement transformation requirements. These tools usually have proprietary languages that are used to program complex transformation rules. Remember that you will spend most of your development time creating your data transforms. It is not a small or a simple task, so plan this step wisely and evaluate the various programmatic alternatives available to you.

## Load

Moving the data into the SQL Server 7 repository can be a challenge. As the size of your data mart increases, the problem's complexity is magnified. Chapter 8 will speak about moving data between other SQL Server 7 systems using export and import and other systems using Data Transformation Services as well as a handful of third-party products. Adopters of data mart tools are looking for assistance with this load process. They want the ability to schedule loads, and to specify what data should be replaced, and where the data resides in the data mart.

When loading data into the SQL Server 7 data mart, the data can be put directly into the target tables or moved into intermediary tables; then, the data can be further processed as they are moved into the actual target tables. Using a set of intermediary tables can be the most efficient way to load information into the data mart. The structure of the intermediary tables is often radically different from the target tables. Many of the current generation of loading and transformation tools create these tables as part of their implementation strategy; these tools then manage these tables.

**TIP:** If you do use this technique, remember to delete the data from the intermediary tables when you are done with them. To avoid generating transaction logs when these tables are wiped, use the SQL Server 7 **truncate table** construct rather than a **delete** method.

**TIP:** Another possibility is that these intermediary tables stay in existence and become your atomic level, so that it keeps a historically correct data layer that can be used to rebuild or change your data marts.

A data mart tool must be able to leverage the parallel processing power of many high-end processors because so many loads involve vast amounts of data. A *high-end machine* is one that has the strong processing power coupled with fast parallel I/O operations. Machines with more than one processor (referred to as MPP or SMP, depending on how they are configured) are ideal candidates for housing the data mart and warehouse.

# DATA MART OR DATA WAREHOUSE?

Should we build a data warehouse or a data mart? This question has been asked many times, and it has many different answers. Often, those two words that serve as a catch answer to many difficult questions creep up in response to this query: *good question*. Our experience has shown you should not begin a turf war—the "must be a data warehouse" on one side and the "must build a data mart" on the other side. We like to use the term "datahouse" or "waremart." In other words, it does not matter what you build, but decide now and do it, or create an enterprise warehouse over time from an architected set of marts with a common atomic layer. We have developed a set of questions to ask customers when they are seeking guidance on making this hard decision. This is actually a score sheet. As indicated in the right column of Table 6-3, mark "1" for each YES and "0" for each NO (except in questions 7 and 10, as noted). Tally up your score; then we will discuss the outcome.

So, how did you do? Tally your score. If you got 10, you are definitely data warehouse bound. If you scored 0, you are definitely data mart bound. A tally between 2 and 6 indicates that the data mart way is the best way to proceed. A tally between 7 and 10

| | Question | YES = 1<br>NO = 0 |
|---|---|---|
| 1. | Is your business able to commit to a multimillion-dollar project that will span many fiscal years? | |
| 2. | Are your business units selling or servicing customers who fall into similar profiles? | |
| 3. | Do management personnel in the business units normally agree on data definitions of your business commodities? | |
| 4. | Are your corporate decision makers capable of sitting and waiting for their turn, or do they have a "me first" attitude? | |
| 5. | Is your organization centralized? | |
| 6. | Is there a consensus on the amount of historical data that your organization needs to maintain? | |
| 7. | Are there certain business areas that are much more interested in starting a focused DSS initiative? (YES = 0 and NO = 1) | |
| 8. | Does your organization have the hardware in place to support a very large data warehouse? | |
| 9. | Do the decision makers agree on the level of summarization that they need to make decisions? | |
| 10. | Are there any data marts currently in use in the organization? (YES = 0 and NO = 1) | |

**Table 6-3.**   Data Mart Vs. Data Warehouse Checklist

suggests data warehouse. If you threw your hands into the air, waffling about some yes and no answers, if you have more yeas than nays—data warehouse; if you have more nays than yeas—data mart. Also, review how you answered certain questions. For example, if your business users are not dedicated to developing a data warehouse or a data mart, you must first get them involved for any initiative. If you find that there is an individual or group of individuals within your organization that have read the magazines and believe the gospel of the data warehousing singers, then a focused data mart for this group may provide the best payoff. This group will be motivated to work with you to develop their data mart solution. This group can then be used as a strategic vehicle to educate the rest of your organization on the power of a data mart and data warehouse. Sometimes, until the users can look at it and touch it, they cannot see the benefit. Providing a concrete solution and a review of how the data mart has been leveraged by the group can help to launch an enterprise warehouse project. Data marts are often used to provide companies with a proof of concept when they are first embarking into the data warehouse world.

Key to the successful building and deployment of data marts is the users' ability to understand what data it contains and how the objects are related to one another. Integrating data marts within the data warehouse allows users to more quickly grasp the benefits of data warehousing. These data marts can be used to leverage and market your overall data warehousing strategy.

The data mart is focused on providing a solution to a business process while providing high-powered analysis support. It primarily deals with satisfying a single business process. It is a more inexpensive alternative to an enterprise data warehouse. Finally, it can serve as a vehicle for an organization to launch a full data warehousing strategy. Although they may appear to be small, the data mart is anything but small when it comes to delivering strategic power within your organization. We think it would be good to point out that the warehouse project does not have to be a data mart or a warehouse with no middle ground. A process for going from an initial data mart strategy to an eventual warehouse is a key competitive strategy for many large and small organizations during the construction of a data warehouse and data marts.

You are now leaving the data mart…ensure the checkout person looks under the cart for some of the bulkier items. You also may want to keep a close eye on the prices being rung up on the cash register. There have been known to be glitches in the bar code to price programming in some large data marts. Pay attention to the sign at checkout #6—"Data warehouse solutions ONLY!" The next chapter looks at the SQL Server 7 specifics with setting up the data warehouse. Much of the material covered throughout this book is theoretical and, regardless of the database of choice, offers suggestions of what to accomplish when. Chapter 7 starts to marry a great deal of the theory to the SQL Server 7 database, introducing some jargon specific to Microsoft's solution.

# CHAPTER 7

# The Physical Data Warehouse

A typical data warehouse will check in at a size substantially larger than the databases we support underneath our operational systems. This chapter looks at setting up the data warehouse using the SQL Server 7 Server as its repository—that is the physical layout of the warehouse. We'll take some of the material we discussed in Chapter 5 and translate it into a living/breathing SQL Server 7 set of tables. Some of the material is aimed at technical administrators, but the ideas presented will assist all readers when asked to participate at some level in setting up the physical data warehouse. Many readers have managed large databases over varying periods of time. This chapter will look at some additional issues that come up in a decision support system (DSS) repository related to issues such as warehouse population, managing historical data, and optimal placement of database files to support the warehouse. Let's start out by looking at the very large database (VLDB), then start discussing setup issues for these large information repositories.

# THE VLDB

VLDB—four letters one hears everywhere in one's travels around the data warehousing technical community. The classification of a very large database usually starts based on size. People speak of managing a 30Gb (3,072Mb or 32,212,254,720 bytes), calling it a VLDB; then, other people turn around and say they manage a 10Tb database (10,995,116,277,760 bytes) and the 30Gb is not a true VLDB. Our definition for a VLDB is a lot simpler, and is applied regardless of the size of your database.

## Window of Opportunity

This *window of opportunity* is the amount of time in a 24-hour period that the data warehouse is quiet and maintenance operations can occur. Within a data warehouse, these maintenance operations typically include getting operational information into the data warehouse, database maintenance tasks, and backing up your database.

With high-speed tape drives, many installations need a window of only a few hours (if that) to copy their database to tape nightly. As the size of the database increases, many sites require more time to write these backups. Now that most tape hardware and software technology copies files at speeds well in excess of dozens of gigabytes per hour, many multigigabyte databases can be backed up in a window of opportunity of less than two hours. Simply put, one way we define a *very large database* is one that cannot be backed up to tape in its entirety during the nightly window of opportunity.

Based on that definition, if one needs 2½ hours to copy a SQL Server 7 database to tape and the window is only 1½ hours, that person is managing a VLDB regardless of the total database size. The layout and management techniques that come into play with the VLDB have to be followed for the 100Gb database that cannot be backed up during its window as well as the 900Mb database that does not fit into its window.

Based on this discussion, let's look at our definition of a VLDB. A *VLDB* is

▼   A database for which a consistent backup cannot be written in a DBA-defined window of opportunity. A *consistent backup* is one that can be used to restore all or part of a SQL Server 7 database.

▲   A database whose size requires it to be broken into smaller, more manageable chunks that permit DBAs to work with portions of the repository at a time.

## Care and Feeding of a VLDB

A VLDB must be handled with care. The same management approach you use with smaller information repositories may not work with a VLDB. Both sheer size and disk input/output (I/O) activity determine how you should organize the physical structure of your VLDB. When we discuss the physical structure, we're talking about how the information is encoded on disk and how the information is organized on disk. The remainder of this chapter focuses on this and the supporting functions in SQL Server 7 to provide for VLDB data warehouse support.

SQL Server 7 is the most significant release in the SQL Server product cycle. SQL Server 7 focuses on ease of use, scalability, and data warehousing. This focus has resulted in significant changes in the core components: the storage engine and query processor. To review, the storage engine is responsible for managing the on-disk structure and transactional integrity of the data. The query processor is responsible for taking the incoming SQL and determining the most efficient means of dealing with the storage engine. It's important for you to understand these since they will form the bedrock of your VLDB.

Before getting into this, let's first look at how SQL Server 7 encodes information and how it handles internationalization and worldwide database installation details.

# NATIONAL CHARACTER SUPPORT

In the midst of implementing a multinational data warehouse, you need to pay attention to some issues related to the storage and display of extended characters in the SQL Server 7 database. Some of this must be done on the client, some on the server. Without taking the time to set this up properly right from the start, characters such as "éâæôöòûùÿÖÜ£¥áíóúñÑ¿" will be displayed as "ibftvr{y#%amszqQ?." Better believe it—if Rolf Gröenveld's name is displayed as "Rolf Grvenveld", you will certainly hear about it (not to mention that if it is displayed properly, you won't hear from anyone).

## Setting Options

This falls onto the shoulders of the database administrator responsible for the setup and minding of SQL Server 7. SQL Server 7 offers a robust multilingual solution through the use of character sets and sort orders as well as Unicode support—new to SQL Server 7. Back in the old days, each character that the computer stored or displayed consisted of eight bits, which allows for 256 distinct values. At the time, this seemed like a lot as it let you use all the uppercase and lowercase letters, numbers, symbols and some graphics characters. It did not, however, leave room for international characters, especially when you consider languages such as Japanese or Chinese that have many more characters than English. The answer to this was Unicode, a system that allowed for 16-bit characters—a total of 65,536 different characters. SQL Server 7 supports both Unicode and individual code pages. Selection of the character set, sort options, and Unicode options are specified using the SQL Server 7 installation screen shown in Figure 7-1. This screen shows the default settings for the character set, sort order, and Unicode support. This screen is not displayed as part of the typical, or default, installation. To activate this screen, within the Setup Type screen, choose Custom when presented with the options Typical, Minimum, and Custom.

The settings that you choose on this screen affect how characters are displayed, as well as the order in which the data will be sorted. For example, does "é" get sorted before or after "e" or does the accent get ignored for sorting purposes? In the default setup, we are using the International Standards Association (ISO) character set sorted in dictionary case-insensitive order. In addition, we are sorting accent characters in order rather than grouping them with the unaccented version of the same character.

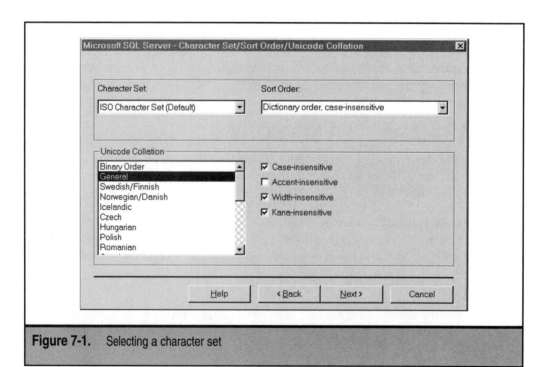

**Figure 7-1.** Selecting a character set

**NOTE:** The value you set at installation time cannot be changed without reinstalling SQL Server 7, re-creating the database, and loading all the data! Do yourself a favor and make sure that this setting is correct the first time.

SQL Server 7 now supports Unicode data types. Unicode stores character data using two bytes for each character rather than one byte. Unicode can use one standard set of bit patterns to encode each character in all languages, including languages such as Chinese that have large numbers of characters. Unicode data does need twice as much storage space—for example, the new Unicode data types *ntext*, *nchar*, and *nvarchar*. These extra space requirements are offset in many international organizations by the need to convert code pages between databases supporting different languages.

# National Character Sets on the Client

When a query or online analytical processing (OLAP) tool on the client is used to access the warehouse, the Windows setup file must properly reflect the desired character set to display information correctly. On a Windows 3.x or DOS (16-bit) client, the following text will be displayed in the config.sys file to indicate the desired setup:

```
country=001,850,c:\dos\country.sys
device=c:\dos\display.sys con=(ega,850,2)
```

This prepares the system to use code page 850. Windows code pages define how values in a byte map to characters in a specific language. Most warehouses are set up to display multilingual character sets that cover most European languages. In order to tell the system to actually use this code page, you need to also add three lines to autoexec.bat, the Windows batch file that is invoked at startup time:

```
nlsfunc
mode con cp prep=((850,437)c:\dos\ega.cpi)
chcp 850
```

The **mode** command instructs the computer to allow either code page 850 or code page 437, a U.S. English setup that supports graphical characters for lines and borders. The **chcp** command then sets code page 850 as the default.

On a Windows 95, Windows 98, Windows NT 3.5, or Windows NT 4.0 client, the code page is set in the registry. The Windows registry is a repository that contains information used by the system and programs to define the operating environment and to save the state of the environment when the server has to be rebooted. Use the Regional Settings control panel applet to change this setting to the code page that you need.

 **TIP:** Regardless of the client software, the code page setting is the first place to look when trying to figure out why extended characters are not being displayed properly.

We recommend visiting language and character display issues along the way with the users of the warehouse. It can be a real nuisance—not to mention a political nightmare—to deploy the warehouse to the user community only to have them discover character set problems that you missed. It's now time to cover the architecture of SQL Server 7. In one of our previous works, we discussed how important a basic understanding of software architecture becomes the more time we spend with a vendor's software solutions.

# SQL SERVER 7.0 ARCHITECTURE

Before getting started on this important section, let's spend a bit of extra time on some terminology. Jargon, we have jargon, we have lots and lots of jargon (with due respect to Perry Como).

▼ **API**—Applications programming interface. This is used to define the interface that a programmer uses to access functionality by the providers of the assortment of software programs with which other software interacts.

■ **ODBC**—Open database connectivity. This is the industry standard API for accessing relational databases. Typically, products and programs requiring access to one or more relational databases will write once to ODBC, as opposed to once for every separate database's proprietary API.

■ **OLE DB**—Microsoft's strategic API moving forward. Microsoft will continue to support ODBC since it is a mature standard. New API features and innovations (e.g., an interface to provide fast bulk insert capabilities) will be added to OLE.

■ **DB2**—IBM's relational database offering, initially available only on mainframes—now deployed on some other platforms.

▲ **Flat files**—Text or binary file containing tabular information. Flat files typically are references to relational database transfer formats, e.g. comma-separated values (aka CSV).

The SQL Server 7 architecture provides clean layering between components. The query processor communicates with the relational engine via OLE DB, Microsoft's strategic database API. This well-defined OLE DB interface, along with SQL Server 7's support of four-part naming provides SQL Server 7 users with the ability to issue distributed heterogeneous joins—that is, one query can access multiple SQL Server databases on different servers, a flat file, an Oracle database, and a DB2 database. Four-part naming means that a SQL object can be uniquely identified by server machine or external link definition, database, schema, and object. This capability, new to SQL Server 7, allows the Query Processor to include remote SQL Server databases and other OLE DB and ODBC-compliant databases into a distributed heterogeneous join. SQL Server 7 ships with OLE DB drivers for Oracle and Microsoft Access, as well as functionality to map ODBC drivers to this OLE DB interface. Figure 7-2 illustrates the SQL Server 7 architecture in a nutshell.

The query processor has added some very sophisticated algorithms for optimizing large, complex queries, including star schemas. We will cover the query processor in detail in Chapter 9. It's important to mention it here because the query processor is responsible for creating parallel query plans that take advantage of NT's multithreaded SMP architecture.

## SMP

*Symmetric multiprocessor* operating system architectures provide scheduling services that allow tasks to execute on all CPUs in a symmetrical fashion. NT Server supports SMP at the operating system level. NT threads are the units of execution for SMP machines. Previous versions of SQL Server maintained a thread pool and would schedule tasks on this thread pool. SQL Server 7 improves SMP utilization by providing user-mode scheduling services and by implementing NT fibers. We won't drill down into the minutia here; the key point is that SQL Server 7 scales better on large SMP systems than previous versions by minimizing context switching and reducing contention on the NT spin-lock coordinating thread dispatching to processors.

SQL Server 7 scales down as well as up. It will run on Windows 95, Windows 98, and NT Workstation 4.0. For VLDB, you will only want to use NT Server, which is optimized for multiprocessors. Windows NT Server 4.0 standard edition currently supports up to a four-processor configuration. For VLDB, the best solution is NT Server 4.0 Enterprise Edition, which supports up to eight processors and 3Gb of memory. There are specialized hardware vendors that support versions of NT that will run on computers with more than 16 processors. Unless you require these systems, we recommend that you stay with four-processor configuation for data marts and eight-processor configuration for your large data warehouses.

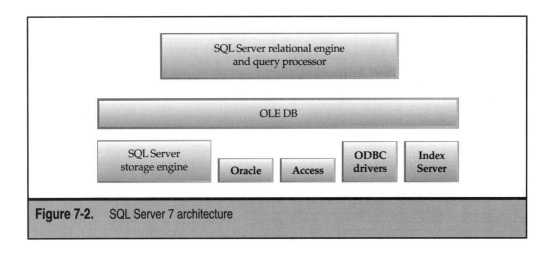

**Figure 7-2.**   SQL Server 7 architecture

# PARALLELISM

*Parallelism* involves the ability of software to take advantage of multi-CPU machines to reduce response time when queries are passed to the database engine for processing. Parallelism is especially important for complex data warehouse queries against VLDB databases. The difficult feature to implement is intraquery parallelism, the ability to break a single query into multiple subtasks and distribute them across multiple processors in an SMP machine for execution. The SQL Server 7 query processor builds upon SQL Server's existing parallel I/O and interquery capabilities by introducing a parallel operator that allows for intraquery parallel processing. The advantage to this architecture is that the operations (e.g., sorting) do not have to know about the parallelism. Figure 7-3 illustrates this parallel-processing feature.

Unlike other relational databases, parallel-query processing is determined dynamically by the SQL Server query processor and requires no special tuning or add-ons to the base configuration. SQL Server does provide some configuration of

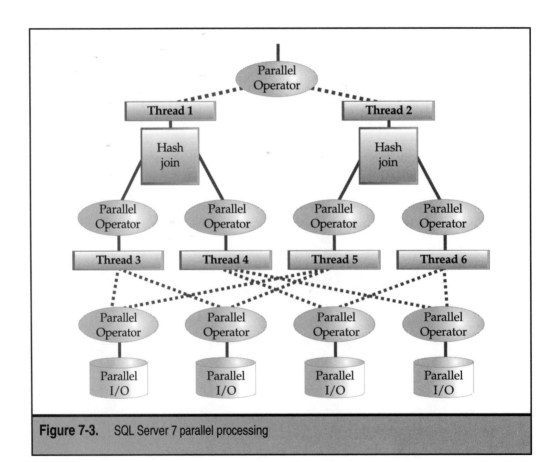

**Figure 7-3.** SQL Server 7 parallel processing

parallel queries through the Enterprise Manager. Figure 7-4 is invoked by modifying the properties of a server within the Enterprise Manager. You are able to allocate the number of processors available for SQL Server multiprocessing, the number of processes to allow parallel operations to run on, and a minimum query plan threshold for considering parallel query. Figure 7-4 shows the SQL Server 7 dialog box where the multiprocessors are specified. Take the time to perform this activity; it will pay off big time down the road.

# QUERY PROCESSOR OPTIMIZER AND STATISTICS

The query plan (aka access path) is what SQL Server 7 query processor builds when selecting the most efficient method for returning results for a query. A query plan is based on the indexes on the objects and relevant statistics. The module responsible for building the query plan is the query processor's *cost-based optimizer* (CBO). There are other optimizer techniques used by relational database query processors; however, CBOs

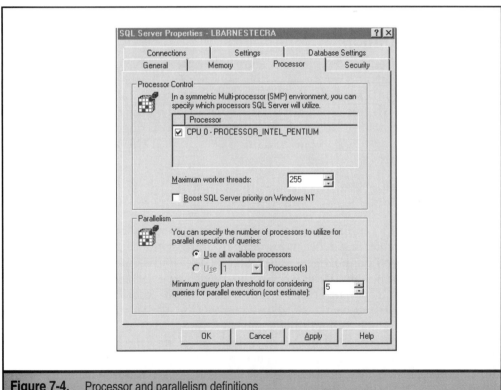

**Figure 7-4.**   Processor and parallelism definitions

are the prevailing technology in the industry and represent the best mechanism for optimizing queries, especially those seen in large data warehouses.

The statistics accessed by the QP contain information about distribution and selectivity of data. The distribution describes how the key values are spread across the data. The selectivity represents how selective the key value will be in retrieving data. For example, gender has a low degree of selectivity, while a social security number has a high degree of selectivity.

The CBO is heavily dependent upon the accuracy of the statistics that it accesses. No relational database keeps a real-time version of statistics because of the prohibitive cost of recalculating these statistics upon every database modification. The fact that statistics can get out of date is one of the largest issues for VLDB sites.

## Automatic Statistic Calculation

The SQL Server 7 team recognized that keeping up-to-date statistics is often a maintenance issue—or worse, an ignored issue. SQL Server 7 proactively addresses this issue by periodically updating index statistics automatically. This is a huge feature, especially for the low- to medium-sized data warehouses and data marts that may not have a DBA assigned to manage the environment.

## Statistic Administration

DBAs have the flexibility to disable this feature if they prefer to have explicit control over when the **update statistics** operation occurs. SQL Server 7's **create index** syntax has a **statistics_norecompute** attribute. The **update statistics** statement also provides the DBA with flexibility on what index statistics get recomputed and the sampling used when recalculating. For example, the statement shown in the next listing updates the statistics for the Last Name and First Name columns of the AUTHORS table by sampling 50 percent of the table rows:

```
update statistics authors(au_lname, au_fname)
with columns, sample 50 percent
```

Note the flexibility in this command. When you invoke **update statistics**, you can choose an entire table, a specific index, and columns within a table. This is a very powerful feature; you can now generate statistics pages for columns that don't have an index associated with them. This provides the query processor with more information about the data that it's operating on. The more data, the more accurate the resulting query plans. The **drop statistics** command allows you to drop all statistics associated with a table, its indexes, and the columns that you have defined.

SQL Server 7 has changed the on-disk structure of statistics within the database. Previous versions stored this information in one database page. SQL Server 7 now stores this information as a Text column. Text columns now use a B-tree-like structure to efficiently store the information across one or many database pages.

*TIP:*   Choosing to sample a percentage of the total rows is a viable strategy, especially for large data warehouse tables. Statisticians have shown that sampling a small percentage of the total population produces a very accurate result. We highly recommend that you use this feature with your large data warehouse tables.

The sp_autostats stored procedure allows you to modify the behavior of the automated statistics operation. The next listing shows how you turn off the automated update statistics for the au_id index on the AUTHORS table in SQL Server 7's sample PUBS database.

```
exec sp_autostats authors, 'off', au_id
```

## Viewing Statistics

Last, but certainly not least, the **dbcc show_statistics** command provides you with current statistics on the target index or column. The following example shows you how to retrieve statistics for an index and the results for a star schema fact table with a five-column primary key:

```
dbcc show_statistics (sales_facts, pk_sales_facts)
go
statistics for index 'PK_SALES_FACTS'.
UPDATED              ROWS    ROWS    SAMPLED STEPS   DENSITY        AVERAGE KEY LENGTH
AUG 20 1999 6:36AM  234716  234716       100       1.001001E-3     17.954601
ALL DENSITY    COLUMNS
1.001001E-3    TRANSACTION_DATE
1.001001E-3    TRANSACTION_DATE, STORE_NUMBER
1.0344792E-5   TRANSACTION_DATE, STORE_NUMBER, CUSTOMER_NUMBER
4.2604679E-6   TRANSACTION_DATE, STORE_NUMBER, CUSTOMER_NUMBER, SKU
4.2604679E-6   TRANSACTION_DATE, STORE_NUMBER, CUSTOMER_NUMBER, SKU, PROMOTION_CODE
STEPS
NOV  1 1994 12:00AM
NOV 11 1994 12:00AM
NOV 22 1994 12:00AM
DEC  2 1994 12:00AM
.    .    .    .
```

Time to move on to looking at SQL Server 7 database configuration and setup.

# DATABASE SETUP AND CONFIGURATION

Before we look at how to manage database objects in the warehouse, it's important to understand how SQL Server 7 stores the data internally. Let's discuss some of the underlying fundamentals of the SQL Server 7 storage engine that have changed with the latest version.

## SQL Server 7 On-Disk Structure (ODS)

The base allocation unit for SQL Server is a *page*; for SQL Server 7, this size increased from 2,000 bytes to 8,000 bytes. The allocation unit for SQL Server consists of eight page blocks called *extents*. SQL Server 7 keeps track of extents on-disk using two bitmap structures—a global allocation map (GAM), which provides information about free extents, and an index allocation map (IAM), which provides information for extents used by tables and indexes.

These bitmap structures represent a major improvement over the previous versions of SQL Server, which used doubly linked lists to navigate extents. Bitmap structures make the ODS less susceptible to hard disk hiccups. In addition, combining bitmap structures along with NT scatter/gather I/O allow the query processor to request pages from the storage engine efficiently with one disk head pass over the data.

Rows are identified within SQL Server 7 by an eight-byte row identifier (RID) consisting of a file number, a page number, and a slot number within the page. Note that rows cannot span pages. However, with the new ODS, the maximum size of a SQL Server varchar has increased from 255 to 8,000 bytes—a major improvement. SQL Server 7 now fully supports row-level locking. In data warehouses, this is typically not a key issue since data warehouses are mostly read only with bulk updates occurring at scheduled times, typically daily. Row identifiers are used by clustered indexes and heap table indexes as pointers to the rows. But we are getting ahead of ourselves here. Let's get back to the user-visible mechanisms for maintaining databases.

## Organizing Information in Your Data Warehouse

SQL Server 7 users create and maintain their databases using a hierarchy of *databases*, *filegroups*, and *files*. Let's look at this hierarchy.

### Databases, Filegroups, and Files

Previous versions of SQL Server had the concept of first creating devices and then allocating databases on these devices. This structure sometimes resulted in a design where one database spanned multiple devices and one device contained multiple database fragments. SQL Server 7 eliminates this by creating a hierarchical structure for defining databases: databases contain one or many filegroups, which contain one or many files. Filegroups and files cannot be shared across databases. Figure 7-5 illustrates the relationship between these three entities.

## Creating the Database

The SQL Server 7 Enterprise Manager allows you to create a sophisticated database structure directly from its user interface. In Figure 7-6, we create a Sales98 database with one filegroup for each month and one or more files for each of the month filegroups.

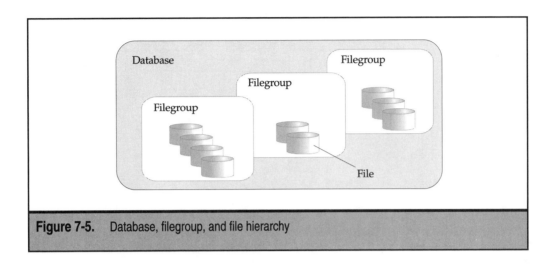

**Figure 7-5.** Database, filegroup, and file hierarchy

Figure 7-6 shows the Sales98 database creation in the Enterprise Manager where the properties are defined, the transaction logs specified, and other options set up. Figure 7-7

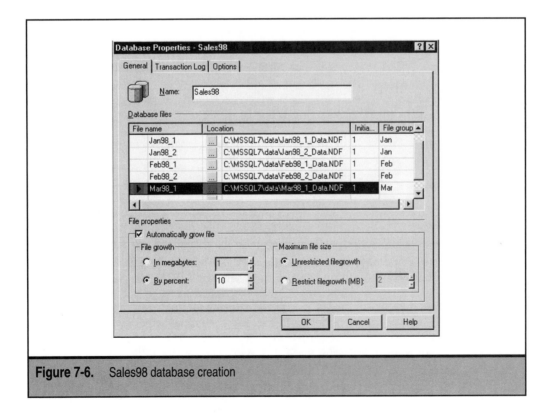

**Figure 7-6.** Sales98 database creation

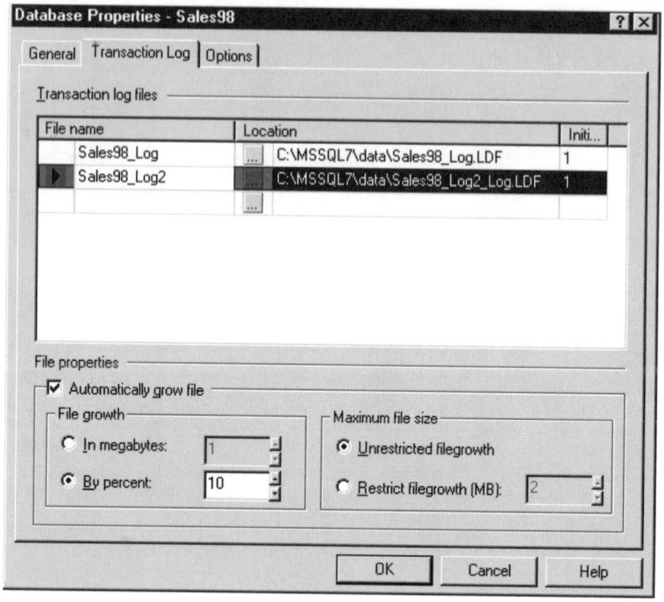

**Figure 7-7.** Sales98 transaction logs definition

shows the transaction log setup and definition; notice we have defined two transaction logs.

Let's pick apart the makeup of the Sales98 database. It consists of eight files consisting of three separate file types:

▼ One primary datafile called Sales98_Data.MDF. This file is always stored in the primary filegroup.

■ Two transaction log files called "Sales98_Log.LDF" and "Sales98_Log2.LDF". These files are used to manage and store database transaction log information.

▲ Five secondary datafiles: There are three filegroups—Jan, Feb, and Mar. Jan and Feb both consist of two files whereas Mar consists of one file.

The SQL Server 7 user interface greatly simplifies database management and maintenance. It's also useful to understand the SQL language used to create the above database. The SQL Server Profiler ships with SQL Server 7 and provides you with a mechanism for capturing all traffic for the SQL Server 7 server. We will be covering the SQL Server Profiler in more detail later in this book. Using SQL Server Profiler, here's what the SQL Server 7 Enterprise Manager sent to the server to create the Sales98 database:

```
create database [Sales98]
on primary
( name = n'Sales98_data',
  filename = n'c:\mssql7\data\sales98_data.mdf' ,
  size = 1, filegrowth = 10%)
log on
( name = n'Sales98_log',
  filename = n'c:\mssql7\data\sales98_log.ldf' ,
  size = 1, filegrowth = 10%),
( name = n'Sales98_log2',
  filename = n'c:\mssql7\data\sales98_log2_log.ldf' ,
  size = 1, filegrowth = 10%)
```

Note the default use of bracketed identifiers (i.e., for the **create database** syntax) and the Unicode literal used for specifying filenames. After the primary datafile and the transaction log files are created, the Enterprise Manager uses the following syntax to add a filegroup to the Sales98 database:

```
alter database [Sales98] add filegroup [jan]
```

After the filegroup is created, files are created and added to the filegroup with the following code.

```
alter database [Sales98] add file
( name = n'jan98_1',
  filename = n'c:\mssql7\data\jan98_1_data.ndf' ,
  size = 1, filegrowth = 10%)
to filegroup [jan]
```

This filegroup and file syntax is repeated for each file and for each filegroup. Filegroups are important for data warehouses. The reason why you will create filegroups other than the default primary filegroup can be summed up in one word—performance. Performance for a data warehouse is not only about query speed, it's also about database load time, backup and recovery time, and database maintenance operations. Backup and recovery can operate directly on filegroups. This provides you with the capability of implementing a robust backup strategy within your window of opportunity. A backup strategy that includes filegroups allows you to restore one filegroup instead of the entire database when one disk on your system is corrupted.

Once filegroups are created, and filegroups are assigned, you can start to create your database objects. All SQL Server 7 database objects are created within a filegroup; when you create a table and an index, you specify the filegroup in which the table or index will reside.

Files are important for very large databases. SQL Server 7 files allow you to determine the physical placement of your filegroups on your disk farms. SQL Server 7 also allows you to add files to your database after the initial database creation; this is important because this gives you the ability to grow your VLDB without having to restructure your entire database. In addition, you can choose whether you want to use a RAID 5 configuration to evenly distribute your data over your disk farm, or you can choose to design this yourself.

Adding a file to a filegroup gives us the flexibility of adding to a disk configuration for a VLDB. Data objects belonging to the filegroup will have their data proportionally striped across the child files. The decision to place an extent (i.e., an eight-page cluster) on a particular file is a function of the amount of free space that currently exists for each file in the filegroup. In our earlier example, we can add an additional file to the Mar filegroup when we notice that our nightly data loads are higher than expected and we want to distribute this load to another disk.

```
alter database [Sales98] add file
( name = n'mar98_2',
  filename = n'd:\mssql7\data\mar98_2_data.ndf' ,
  size = 1, filegrowth = 10%)
to filegroup [mar]
```

Another reason that file design is an important consideration for your VLDB is related to SQL Server 7's new on-disk structure. Designing your files correctly allows you to take advantage of SQL Server 7's parallelism. SQL Server 7 parallelism, described earlier in this chapter, can optimize its database operations by initiating multiple operations on multiple disks in parallel. Before moving on, let's look at a few features with SQL Server 7 that prove especially helpful in the data warehouse arena.

## Auto-Grow and Auto-Shrink Feature

One major feature for SQL Server 7 is that both datafiles and log files can autogrow and autoshrink. *Autogrow* means that the file is automatically extended when it reaches capacity. *Autoshrink* means that a background process wakes up and checks to see if it can automatically shrink files to reclaim space. These features are less important for VLDB systems than they are for smaller SQL Server installations. Large VLDB systems will have DBAs who understand the total space requirements for the database and allocate space accordingly. However, the auto-grow feature is useful for the cases where disk space estimates have been underestimated. With auto-grow, you no longer have to worry about database operations failing as a result of a database (or database log) filling up—no more 1105 errors (for you seasoned SQL Server readers!), and life doesn't get any better than this!

Database auto-shrink can be enabled by SQL Server, but should never be enabled for a VLDB. This feature, when enabled, results in the SQL Server Agent scheduling a background process that wakes up occasionally and shrinks the database when possible. Shrinking a database is still possible—for example, a CURRENT_YEAR_SALES_FACT table that auto-grows as sales are added throughout the year can be shrunk after it's emptied at fiscal year end. The following SQL Server command will shrink this file to its original 10Mb size:

```
dbcc shrinkfile  cur_year_fact_file, 10
```

This **dbcc shrinkfile** is also a very useful command for restructuring your database objects on your datafiles. The **emptyfile** option migrates all the data in the file to other files in a filegroup. This is useful in cases where you have significantly truncated the size of a table and want to remove the file from the filegroup.

## SQL Server Clustered and Nonclustered Indexes

SQL Server 7 supports two index structures: clustered indexes and nonclustered or heap indexes. The heap index root node contains a pointer to the data row id, while the clustered index root node points directly to the data, which is stored on-disk by the clustered key. With SQL Server 7, the on-disk structure for indexes changes as well. Clustered indexes retain the same behavior—their root node points to the data instead of a row locator. Figure 7-8 illustrates how secondary indexes are structured in SQL 7.

Previous versions of SQL Server stored a logical/physical pointer in the index, both clustered and heap, to the actual data. SQL Server 7 secondary indexes now store the clustered indexes' key value instead of the row id. This results in more efficient **insert**, **update**, and **delete** operations on the database. Previous versions had to update all secondary indexes when the clustered index database **update** operation resulted in a page split. Page splits occur in B-trees, the base format for relational database on-disk

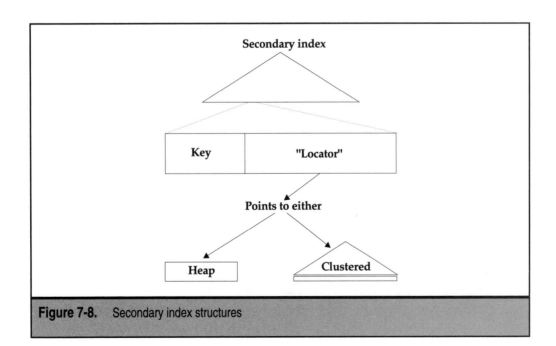

**Figure 7-8.**   Secondary index structures

structures, when the new or modified data no longer fits on the underlying physical page when the underlying data is sorted. Figure 7-9 illustrates how data is retrieved from a clustered index.

In this example, when we use a secondary index to retrieve the row with the clustered index value of "Adams," we identify the clustered index key value, 6, and use this to retrieve the row. Note that there's an additional level of database lookup here. However, research has shown that clustered indexes rarely have more than two levels and will typically exist in the database's data cache. Tandem has been using this approach successfully since the 1980s. However, migrating from prior versions of SQL Server to SQL Server 7 requires that the DBA review each clustered index. Clustered indexes should be compact in SQL Server 7.

One reason for clustered indexes in prior SQL Server versions was that database fragmentation was avoided by using clustered indexes. SQL Server 7 now recognizes gaps in heap file structures and will insert a new record in these gaps. The advantage to clustered indexes is now solely whether the organization, by primary key, will eliminate an additional sort operation for database queries.

*TIP:* Only use clustered indexes in SQL Server 7 when your queries will benefit from the implicit sort order by primary key on-disk.

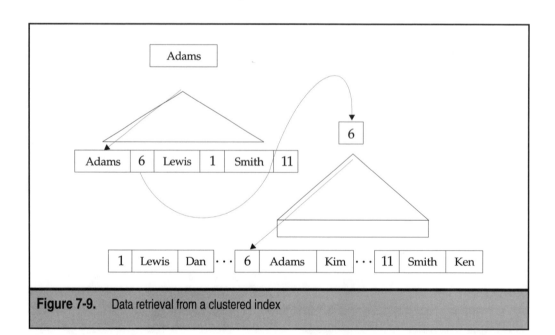

**Figure 7-9.** Data retrieval from a clustered index

For example, consider a clustered key for the Date field for tables where queries commonly select by date as shown in the next listing:

```
DateField > '12-may-2000' AND DateField < '17-June-2000'.
```

SQL Server 7 has enhanced space management for heap tables, so the earlier benefits of using clustered indexes to eliminate holes in your database pages are no longer an issue.

## Database Log Files

SQL Server 7 database log information, used for database rollback and roll forward, is now maintained as a separate set of files. Previous versions of SQL Server maintained transaction log information in relational tables. Separating transaction log information into its own file and format, as well as using *fuzzy backup techniques*, has simplified the access code and has significantly improved database backup and recovery performance.

Fuzzy backup is a common technique used by many relational vendors today. Simply stated, it means that the current state of the database is backed up with the transaction log. Compare this with the previous versions of SQL Server, which had to perform weird contortions (so to speak) to ensure that a transactionally accurate version of the database was being backed up while online.

**NOTE:**   Database backup and recovery, along with database maintenance, was the limiting factor in SQL Server databases prior to SQL Server 7.

This limit has now been removed. Microsoft has run some internal tests where SQL Server 7.0 backup now scales to the speed of the tape backup system. You will want to place your transaction logs on a mirrored device (RAID 1) as opposed to RAID 5 striped devices. You will want to do this because transaction I/O is sequential, and current disks process sequentially at a factor of three to four times faster than random I/O. Placing transaction log files on a disk array with other activity will slow down sequential I/O to random I/O speed.

SQL Server 7 also provides for efficient backup while the database is online. Tests run by the SQL Server 7 testing team show only a 10 percent degradation in TPC-C benchmark numbers when the test was being run during a full backup! This is significant because now your window of opportunity for backup can extend to production hours.

## Don't Forget the Temporary Work Area

*Tempdb* is SQL Server's temporary database work area. As with open datafiles, Tempdb can auto-grow when more storage is required than currently exists on the file. The new query processor has many new sophisticated join algorithms that require significant Tempdb resources. For VLDB, we recommend that you initially allocate a significant amount of disk to tempdb. This initial allocation avoids the potential fragmentation of your tempdb as it grows to accommodate large, complex queries. Note that since tempdb is a database, it can be spread across multiple files on your disk array.

> *TIP:* For VLDB databases, consider placing tempdb within its own filegroup and its file on a separate disk.

## Other SQL Server 7 System Databases

The other system databases resident on a SQL Server 7 system include *MASTER*, *MODEL*, and *MSDB*. MASTER is the primary database for a Server 7 system and contains the system-level database information. MODEL defines the default database metadata loaded into newly created databases. Modify the MODEL database to reflect your desired default database configuration. The MSDB database contains metadata and data for the SQL Agent scheduler and the SQL Server replication mechanism. It can be viewed as the repository for information for SQL Server 7 system tasks.

Note that you will not be able to view system databases and system objects by default. To enable the viewing of this system information, right-click the mouse on the server within Enterprise Manager, select Edit SQL Server Registration, and select the Show System Databases and System Objects checkbox.

# TRANSLATING THEORY INTO PRACTICE

There are two sides to the data warehouse implementation approach: design and physical implementation. The data model for many OLTP systems has been normalized as discussed in Chapter 5. In the next section, we are going to look at the process of denormalization, an activity where normalized operational data is mapped differently to satisfy the processing and query requirements dictated by decision support systems.

## Systematic Denormalization

As data is moved from operational systems into the warehouse, you go through a process called *systematic denormalization* that violates all the rules relational database architects apply when modeling most systems. Systematic denormalization is done to enhance the performance of the warehouse by reducing join operations that are resource intensive. Compared to single table **select** statements, join operations:

▼ Consume significantly more CPU

■ Require gobs more temporary workspace (on disk and in memory) for sorting

■ Require temporary tables for holding of intermediary results

▲ Perform more I/O since at least one I/O is required per table in the query

In the midst of studying relational database theory, you ran (or will run) across problems with data that was not properly normalized. Storing the data in one and only one place is a fundamental requirement as normalization is performed. For example, problems can creep up when a vendor record is stored in the VENDOR table for the accounts payable application and the same vendor information is stored in the SUPPLIER table for purchasing. Suppose the company moves and the data is updated in accounts payable but not in purchasing. Picture the difficulty (not to mention embarrassment!) if one application believes the Newport Technology Group's offices are in Crystal Beach and the other thinks they're in Ottawa! (ha, ha...)

Picture a few small tables from an OLTP environment as shown in the next listing.

**NOTE:**   This sample is oversimplified to allow us to lead you through the denormalization exercise. Naturally, in a real-life example, PURCHASE would trap much more information, such as customer name, and ITEM would hold the UNIT_COST and then some.

```
PURCHASE:
     PURCHASE_ID            INT
     PURCHASE_DATE          DATETIME
     TERMS                  CHAR(2)
LINE ITEM:
     PURCHASE_ID            INT
     LINE_NO                INT
     ITEM_ID                INT
     QUANTITY               INT
ITEM:
     ITEM_ID                INT
     ITEM_DESCRIPTION       VARCHAR(40)
     MANU_ID                INT
MANUFACTURER:
     MANU_ID                INT
     MANU_NAME              VARCHAR(40)
     ADDRESS_ID             INT
ADDRESS:
     ADDRESS_ID             INT
     SEQ                    INT
     ADDR_TEXT              VARCHAR(40)
```

Figure 7-10 shows the relationship between the objects in this schema.

**NOTE:**   SQL Server 7 has an entity-relationship design tool shipping with the product out of the box!

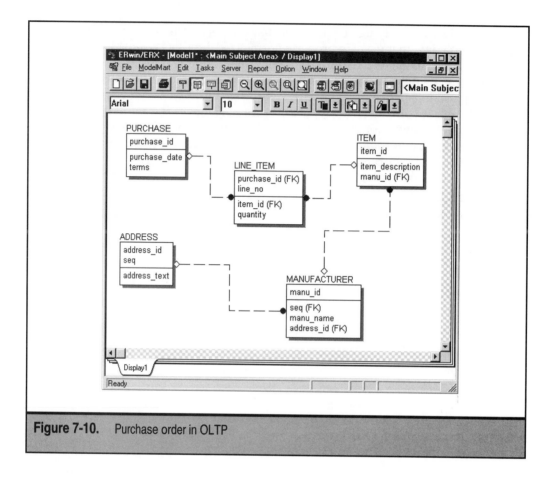

**Figure 7-10.** Purchase order in OLTP

After loading a few seed rows for purchase order number 9002 into these five tables, let's look at their contents, then show the SQL used to construct the order on a data entry screen in the OLTP system:

```
select  * from purchase
PURCHASE_ID PURCHASE_DATE    TERMS
----------- ---------------  -----
9000         1997-12-12      CA
9001         1997-12-22      SX
9002         1997-12-25      NY
(3 row(s) affected)
select  * from line_item
PURCHASE_ID LINE_NO     ITEM_ID     QUANTITY
----------- ----------  ----------  ----------
9002         1          881991      9
```

```
9002          2              992811      10
9002          3              221221      90
(3 row(s) affected)
select  * from item
ITEM_ID       ITEM_DESCRIPTION                                MANU_ID
----------    -----------------------------------------    -----------
881991        Diagonal flange B67                             90
992811        Circular blade                                  90
221221        Ford Fiesta                                     89
(3 row(s) affected)
select  * from manufacturer
MANU_ID       MANU_NAME                                      ADDRESS_ID
----------    -----------------------------------------    -----------
90            Daves Part Mart                                 9095
89            Tamara Car                                      2355

(2 row(s) affected)
select  * from address
ADDRESS_ID  ADDR_TEXT                                ADDR_TEXT2
----------  ----------------------                   --------------------
9095        Bay 16, 789 Flora                        2 Toronto ON M8U 7Y6
2355        1 General Delivery                       2 Chapman AB T5Y 6Y7

(2 row(s) affected)
select a.purchase_id,a.purchase_date,a.terms,
       c.item_description,b.quantity,d.manu_name
from   purchase a,line_item b,item c,manufacturer d
where  a.purchase_id = b.purchase_id
       AND b.item_id = c.item_id
       AND c.manu_id = d.manu_id
       AND a.purchase_id = 9002
order by b.line_no
PURCHASE_ID PURCHASE_DATE TERMS ITEM_DESCRIPTION    QUANTITY MANU_NAME
----------- ------------- ----- ------------------  -------- --------
9002         1997-12-25    NY   Diagonal flange B67     9    Daves Part Mart
9002         1997-12-25    NY   Circular blade          10   Daves Part Mart
9002         1997-12-25    NY   Ford Fiesta             90   Tamara Car
(3 row(s) affected)
```

To wrap up this section, let's look at how the normalized purchase order information could be denormalized and brought together in the decision support arena. We create the denormalized table using the same type of SQL query used in the previous listing to build the purchase order image, but this time store the results in a table:

```
create table dwpurchase AS
select purchase.purchase_id, purchase.purchase_date, purchase.terms,
       item.item_description, line_item.quantity,
manufacturer.manu_name
from item
inner join line_item on item.item_id = line_item.item_id
inner join manufacturer on item.manu_id = manufacturer.manu_id
inner join purchase on line_item.purchase_id = purchase.purchase_id
(3 row(s) affected)
select * from dwpurchase
```

| PURCHASE_ID | PURCHASE_DATE | TERMS | ITEM_DESCRIPTION | QUANTITY | MANU_NAME |
|---|---|---|---|---|---|
| 9002 | 1997-12-25 | NY | Diagonal flange B67 | 9 | Daves Part Mart |
| 9002 | 1997-12-25 | NY | Circular blade | 10 | Daves Part Mart |
| 9002 | 1997-12-25 | NY | Ford Fiesta | 90 | Tamara Car |

```
(3 row(s) affected)
```

After so many relational years, pursuing the $n$th degree of normalization, some people find it difficult getting their heads around the way tables are constructed in the decision support environment. Interestingly enough, some people find the normalization process drudgery and find the systematic denormalization exercise refreshing.

**NOTE:** Denormalization is not a consideration in OLTP systems; data normalization is a matter of fact for operational systems, and there is no way around it. Strict adherence to data normalization protects the integrity of the data in the operational database.

In the next section on star schemas, we will show you how to build a star schema for the SQL Server 7-based data warehouse using the data mart first introduced in Chapter 5. When you see the entity-relationship diagram from which the schema is built, compare it against the report shown in Figure 7-11 listing some of the entities in the operational systems whose data comes together in the mart. Notice how the SUBSCRIBER entity in the data mart pulls data from SUBSCRIBER, SUBSCRIBER_ADDRESS, and SUBSCRIBER_PRODUCT in the operational and PAYTVORDER contains information pulled from PPV_RATE, PPV_ORDER, and PPV_PROMOTION_COUPON.

## Star Schema Implementation

The famous star schema—it's all fine and dandy to discuss the theory and give recommendations as to where it makes sense, but let's look at implementation to complete the discussion. Especially for organizations in the prototype phase or the early

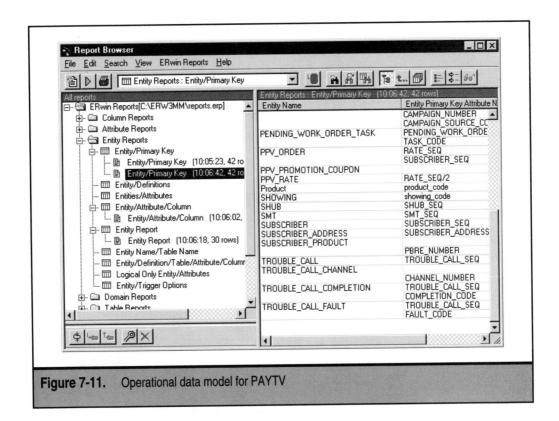

**Figure 7-11.**   Operational data model for PAYTV

adoption of the data mart approach, the acquisition of tools may still be somewhere down the road. What we are going to do in this section is look at the building of a star schema from the ground up. The schema, first introduced in Chapter 5, is shown again in Figure 7-12. The schema is comprised of PAYTVORDER as the fact table, and SHOWING_TIME, PROMOTION, CABLE_COMPANY, EVENTS, and SUBSCRIBER as the dimensions.

The next listing shows the creation of the fact and dimension tables, then the setup of the infrastructure to allow for star query processing. Regardless of whether you point and click using a GUI interface (SQL Server 7 Enterprise Manager or the like) or do it manually in SQL Server 7 Query Analyzer, the SQL passed to SQL Server 7 is similar to what you see next. When doing the physical implementation, we have made the following changes to the schema to satisfy SQL Server 7 and one logical preference we have with table naming:

▼ We have changed the DATE,TIME,YEAR,MONTH and DAY attributes in the SHOWING_TIME entity, to eliminate SQL Server 7 reserved word conflicts.

▲ We have made the physical table name for the EVENTS entity singular (i.e., EVENT).

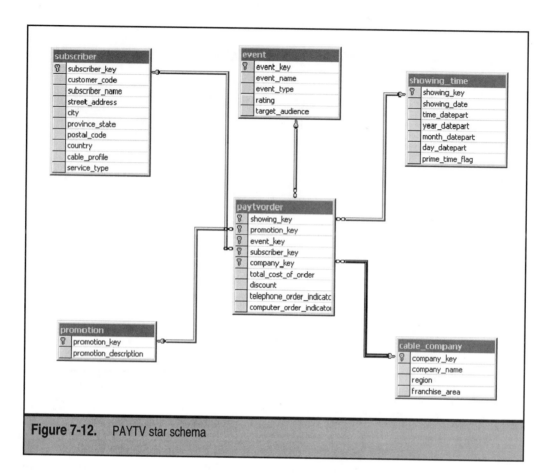

**Figure 7-12.** PAYTV star schema

**NOTE:** We are placing the PAYTVORDER table and indexes into one filegroup and all of the dimension tables and indexes into a second filegroup. As we mentioned before, filegroups and files allow you to determine the physical structure of your VLDB on your disk farm.

```
/* ------------------------------------------------------ */
/* SQL Server 7 Data Warehousing OMH 1998                 */
/* *                                                       */
/* Corey, Abbey, Abramson, Taub, Barnes, Venkitachalam */
/* ------------------------------------------------------ */
--
-- Create the fact table
--
create table paytvorder(
    showing_key int not null,
```

```
    promotion_key int not null,
    event_key int not null,
    subscriber_key int not null,
    company_key int not null,
    total_cost_of_order money,
    discount int,
    telephone_order_indicator char(1),
    computer_order_indicator  char(1) )
on fact_fg
go
--
-- Build the primary key for PAYTVORDER.
--
alter table paytvorder
add constraint paytvorder_pk
primary key ( showing_key,promotion_key,
    event_key,subscriber_key,company_key )
on   fact_fg
go
--
-- Build SHOWING_TIME, PROMOTION, CABLE_COMPANY, EVENT,
-- and SUBSCRIBER. Remember, these are the dimension tables and are
-- nothing like their OLTP counterparts. Only the columns needed for
-- analysis are included.
--
create table showing_time (
    showing_key      int not null,
    showing_date     datetime,
    time_datepart    varchar(10),
    year_datepart    smallint,
    month_datepart   tinyint,
    day_datepart     tinyint,
    prime_time_flag char(1) )
on   dimension_fg
go
create table promotion (
    promotion_key    int not null,
    promotion_description varchar(100))
on   dimension_fg
go
create table cable_company (
    company_key      int not null,
    company_name     varchar(60),
    region           char(2),
```

```
        franchise_area char(2) )
on   dimension_fg
go
create table event(
     event_key        int not null,
     event_name       varchar(40),
     event_type       char(2),
     rating           int,
     target_audience char(3) )
on   dimension_fg
go
create table subscriber (
     subscriber_key        int not null,
     customer_code         varchar(10),
     subscriber_name       varchar(30),
     street_address        varchar(40),
     city                  varchar(20),
     province_state        varchar(2),
     postal_code           varchar(10),
     country               varchar(20),
     cable_profile         varchar(8),
     service_type          char(3) )
on   dimension_fg
go
--
-- Create the primary keys for the dimension tables.
--
alter table showing_time add constraint showing_time_pk
     primary key (showing_key)
on   dimension_fg
go
alter table promotion add constraint promotion_pk
     primary key (promotion_key)
on   dimension_fg
go
alter table cable_company add constraint cable_company_pk
     primary key (company_key)
on   dimension_fg
go
```

```
alter table event add constraint event_pk
     primary key (event_key)
on  dimension_fg
go
alter table subscriber add constraint subscriber_pk
     primary key (subscriber_key)
on  dimension_fg
go
--
-- Add foreign keys to fact table pointing at all the dimensions.
--
alter table paytvorder add constraint showing_key_fk foreign key
     (showing_key) references showing_time
go
alter table paytvorder add constraint promotion_key_fk foreign key
     (promotion_key) references promotion
go
alter table paytvorder add constraint cable_company_fk foreign key
     (company_key) references cable_company
go
alter table paytvorder add constraint event_fk foreign key
     (event_key) references event
go
alter table paytvorder add constraint subscriber_fk foreign key
     (subscriber_key) references subscriber
go
```

# PHYSICAL IMPLEMENTATION CHECKLIST

We are going to close this chapter with a list of SQL Server 7-specific items that need to be part of the physical data warehouse. Some relate to client issues, some to server, some to the communication between the two. Table 7-1 lists these items, in no particular order, and offers some notes on the particulars of each step.

**NOTE:** This checklist is gleaned from our experience with warehouses, data marts, and other large information repositories. We have probably thought of some points you may not have, and there is more than likely some stuff here you had not considered.

| Software | Server | Client | Notes |
|---|---|---|---|
| NT 4.0 Server | X | | For VLDB, you will want NT Server 4.0 Enterprise Edition. |
| SQL Server 7.0 Server | X | | SQL Server 7 ships with a rich set of features and utilities out of the box. For large databases, you will want to use SQL Server 7.0 Enterprise Edition. |
| Client network and ODBC drivers | | X | Windows NT, 95, and 98 install the network drivers that you will need to access SQL Server 7.0. TCP/IP is the recommended network transport. Windows 3.1 will require you to install the network drivers separately. SQL Server 7.0 ships with a client installation utility that allows you to configure client machines accessing SQL Server over a variety of networks. |
| OLAP engine | X | | The SQL Server 7.0 installation includes Microsoft OLAP Services. |
| Extraction, transfer, and transform (ETT) tools | X | | SQL Server 7.0 ships with Data Transformation Services (DTS), base facilities to allow you to move and transform legacy information into your data warehouse. For advanced ETT services, you may want to look at other vendors' products. Some popular ones include Sagent, Informatica, DataStage, Data Junction, and Platinum. |
| Data staging area | X | | Most, if not all, data warehouses will have an intermediate staging area where information is initially loaded and massaged. |
| Operational data store (ODS) | X | | Many VLDB data warehouses now include an intermediate database that leverages the data warehouse cleansed data. This information is not necessarily part of the official data warehouse, but it is many times very useful. For example, many groups within an organization may need to do a lookup from a common pricing product list that spans operational databases and groups within the controlling organization. |

**Table 7-1.** Physical Implementation Checklist

| Software | Server | Client | Notes |
|---|---|---|---|
| Hardware configuration | X | | CPU: SMP configuration.<br>Memory: As much as possible. For VLDB, consider gigabytes.<br>Disks: A combination of RAID 5 and RAID 0 is the most common. RAID 5 for data and indexes, RAID 0 for the transaction log files.<br>Look to fiber channel moving forward for speed. |
| Backup and recovery and database maintenance plans | X | | A key part of any production database. These plans must fit into your data warehouse's window of opportunity. |
| Disaster recovery plan | X | | Again, a key part of any production database. What's the strategy for the data warehouse when an earthquake hits the data center? |

**Table 7-1.** Physical Implementation Checklist (*continued*)

We now move on to the data transport piece. In the next chapter, we will have a look at extraction, transformation, and loading of information into the warehouse. There is quite the hodge-podge of solutions out there to assist the process. The key, once the source data is identified and mapped to target locations, is ensuring the feed of data from operational systems and other sources is robust and easy to set up, maintain, and change. Easier said than done? We'll see.

# CHAPTER 8

# Moving the Data into the Warehouse

One of the biggest challenges an organization will face in building a data warehouse or data mart is getting diverse sources of information into or accessible to the warehouse. Think about it. A typical system we use every day of our lives was built to process a distinct transaction, not to analyze the effect of a series of transactions. For example, a payroll system was built to cut a paycheck and a point of sales system (like you see at your local grocery store) was built to process an order.

These types of systems are called *online transaction - processing* (OLTP) systems. Just as the name implies, they process a transaction, whether that is a paycheck, a grocery receipt, or getting money from your local automated teller machine (ATM). What a great trivia question—how many of your friends know what ATM really stands for? How many of your friends will actually admit they don't know and will just make an acronym up. Imagine if the typical OLTP system that is used every day were built to provide the functionality of a data warehouse. This means that any time of day a user of the system could request to slice and dice the data. Think of the analogy of an automobile. A car can be built for performance or the car can be built for fuel economy. But rarely would you ever see a race car that got great gas (or as our friends overseas say, petrol) mileage. The point is very clear—there would be long lines at the grocery store, the ATM machine would take a couple of hours to give you your money, and everyone's paycheck would be delayed three weeks.

For good reason, OLTP systems are streamlined for a transaction, where a single transaction consists of a very small quick burst of information. The good news is we all don't wait in line at the ATM machine, whereas the bad news is getting this OLTP data into the warehouse is one of the biggest challenges you will face. As you will learn in this chapter, SQL Server 7 has many new features to help you extract and transform the data so that it can be made accessible to the warehouse. Let's get started.

# DATA TRANSFORMATION SERVICES OVERVIEW

In SQL Server 7, the tools to help you extract, transform, and load data are known as the Data Transformation Services (DTS). DTS has many aspects to it:

1. *Extraction*  This involves the identification of data elements in source systems and use of a tool to pull out the needed information from those repositories. We use the term *repository* since we are typically talking about a collection of data or information that is stored in a particular location.

2. *Transformation*  This involves the process of mapping source system data elements to their final destination. Many times, transformation process includes converting the data into more usable format. Rather than bring every given OLTP transaction into the warehouse, it is very common to see data stored in summary fashion only.

3. *Loading*  This involves exactly what the name means. This is the physical process of taking the transformed data and adding it into the warehouse.

4. *OLE-DB architecture*   This is an architecture that supports the reading of data in its native format. By utilizing a framework of OLE-DB providers that support reading data in its native format, the process of extraction is greatly simplified. By being able to read the data natively, it can make the extraction process a very efficient operation in certain situations. OLE stands for object linking and embedding.

5. *OLE-DB providers*   These are part of the OLE-DB architecture that actually allow you native access to the data stores. Table 8-1 shows the major OLE-DB providers.

6. *SQL Server Agent*   This is an intelligent software agent that allows you to automatically schedule many of the DTS services. Services are discussed in depth much later in this chapter.

By utilizing DTS services and OLE-DB, you have a flexible architecture to deal with what most would consider the biggest challenge to building a warehouse. The biggest challenge is, of course, making data available to the warehouse. Let's now take a closer look at how you can use DTS to help you validate the data you will add to your warehouse.

# VALIDATING DATA

There is a very old saying—*GI/GO*. For those of you who have never seen the acronym it is referred to as garbage in means garbage out. Your warehouse is only as good as the quality of information you place into it. Pay attention (we can tell you're starting to doze off). Your warehouse is only as good as the quality of information you place into it. If you

| Providers | Notes |
|-----------|-------|
| SQL Server | You use this to go from one SQL Server database to another. |
| Microsoft Excel | Yes, even your spreadsheets are easily available natively. |
| DB2 | Watch out IBM. A migration from DB2 to SQL Server can be made easy. |
| Microsoft Access | Access to Access (this is a joke—think about it). |
| ASCII | Both fixed field and variable length. |
| Oracle8 | Please don't tell our Oracle Press readers. |

**Table 8-1.**   Quick Summary of Major OLE-DB Providers

do not pay attention to this fact, you will build what we commonly refer to as the data outhouse, which is illustrated in Figure 8-1—look familiar?

To avoid the data outhouse syndrome, it is very important to recognize the fact you will have to do some data validation before data can be loaded into the warehouse. If data validation is not performed, you risk the integrity of the business analysis relying on the warehouse. The best resource for helping you validate the data is the source system experts. Source system experts include personnel with both technical and nontechnical expertise.

**Figure 8-1.** The data outhouse

Validating data in the warehouse is a very time-consuming but necessary process. We recommend that the process of validation be highly automated. SQL Server 7 has many native features to help you with automating the validation process, so take advantage of them.

# Simple Validation

A good example of simple validation can be found in even the most common of data definition language (DDL) statements, the **create table** command. When you create your tables, make sure you make full use of the **not null** property where appropriate. When columns in a table are defined as **not null**, rows must contain values for these columns or they cannot be inserted into the table. The next listing is an example of creating a table using SQL Server 7:

```
create table [customer]
([customer_id] [integer] not null,
 [customer_last_name] [varchar](40) not null,
 [customer_mi] [char](1),
 [customer_first_name] [varchar](40));
```

We think it's important to spend a few minutes on the **not null** definition shown in the previous listing. It plays a huge part in operation systems as they are developed, and likewise in the data warehouse arena. When you assign the property of **not null** to a particular column in the database, you are forcing a value to be stored in that column. In our example, you must always supply a value for the column Customer_Last_Name and the column Customer_ID. If you do not have values for these two columns, the SQL Server 7 database engine will not allow the data to be stored in the database. On the other hand, the values for the columns Customer_MI and Customer_First_Name are optional.

There are a few ways to enforce uniqueness in column values found in rows in the same table. For example, as shown in the next listing, you can create unique indexes:

```
create unique index indx_cust_id on [customer] (customer_id)on primary;
```

By creating the index indx_cust_id, we are not allowing any two values of the Customer_ID column to be identical. Where appropriate, create compound indexes to help with validation. A compound index is shown in the next listing:

```
create index [state_city] on [customer] (state_cd, city_cd) on [primary]
```

In the example of creating the state_city index, you now prevent two cities from having the same name within a given state. Regardless of the source of the data, through the proper use of table properties and indexes you can ensure the source system data will meet certain minimum requirements. Lets take a closer look at how we can use other features of SQL Server 7 to automate complicated validation.

## Complex Validation

For more complex validation, you can always create a stored procedure. Think of a stored procedure as a miniprogram that you can write to perform a specific task within a SQL Server 7 database. It is precompiled and preparsed. This means it is a very efficient way of executing SQL statements. Like any other programming language, a stored procedure accepts parameters or arguments that control its behavior and can optionally produce outputs. Unlike a traditional programming language like COBOL or C, a stored procedure is optimized to run against the SQL Server 7 database. The next listing illustrates the creation of a simple procedure:

```
create procedure fix_missing_prices as
update titles
set price = compute avg(price)
from titles
where price is null
```

As you can see in this example, we are establishing a price for those titles that currently have no price stored in the database. This is a very simple example of what a stored procedure is capable of. Our point is to let you know that you have a very powerful tool for performing complex data validation in an automated manner. To learn more about stored procedures, we recommend you consult your SQL Server reference manual or Books Online.

## More Complex Validation Using DTS Scripts

With DTS, you also have the added capability of creating a DTS script that is tightly integrated with a language such as Visual Basic Script or JavaScript. This offers you a great advantage when creating validation scripts. You can use a widely accepted scripting language such as Perl with native support for SQL Server 7. The next listing shows a script that simply copies column values elsewhere:

```
'***************************************************************
'  Visual Basic Transformation Script
'  Copy each source column to the destination column
'
'  Corey, Abbey, Abramson, Taub, Barnes, Venkitachalam
'  SQL Server 7 Data Warehousing          1998
'***************************************************************
Function Transform()
    DTSDestination("au_id") = DTSSource("au_id")
    DTSDestination("au_lname") = DTSSource("au_lname")
    DTSDestination("au_fname") = DTSSource("au_fname")
    Transform = 1
End Function
```

Sorting through the myriad ways you can validate your data is an education onto itself. It is no surprise that the actual task of validating the data itself can consume such a large amount of the effort in building the data warehouse. In fact, we could have written a book on just the material covered in this chapter alone. Our goal for this section is to explain your many options on validation so you can make intelligent choices. Don't overlook such actions as creating the tables with the proper properties and indexes. After that has been accomplished, choose the techniques you are most comfortable with, be that JavaScript or just a plain SQL Server stored procedure. Let's now take a closer look at grooming or scrubbing the data to make it meet acceptable standards for placement in the warehouse.

# SCRUBBING DATA

Validation is the process of determining if the data is within acceptable standards. Standards are installation dependent, and those developed and implemented for one site may not make any sense elsewhere. When that data falls outside the accepted limits, it is now a candidate for the process we call *scrubbing*. Scrubbing data involves taking corrective action to data that falls outside of acceptable standards.

A good example of this is to take a closer look at one of the challenges one of our telecommunications customers faced. They provided homes across the United States and Canada with cable service. Each of their operational systems across North America represented the cable channel Home Box Office differently, as shown next:

▼   H.B.O

■   HB

■   HOME

■   HOME BOX

▲   Home Box Office

For the purposes of this warehouse, it was best to make this data consistent. If these many values for Home Box Office were migrated to the warehouse as is, any queries using the data would have evaluated these many values for Home Box Office as different channels. Suppose you ask, "Show me all the revenue dollars we received in the month of May by channel." The output may resemble the following without any data scrubbing:

May Revenue by Channel

```
History             100,000
HBO                 500,000
H.B.O               250,000
HB                  100,000
HOME                100,000
HOME BOX            200,000
Home Box Office     100,000
Weather Channel     200,000
```

The resulting query would be useless, making it very difficult to produce consistent information. What the user expected to see is this:

```
May Revenue by Channel

History              100,000
Home Box Office    1,250,000
Weather Channel      200,000
```

Trying to get the numerous source systems to correct this problem in this situation was not very practical. We were dealing with many heterogeneous systems and operating systems. It was determined that it was easier to correct this problem as the data was being migrated into the warehouse—in the process we refer to as scrubbing the data. With SQL Server 7, data scrubbing can be achieved in a number of ways.

**NOTE:**   Don't assume it always makes sense to scrub the data. Many a data warehouse effort has failed trying to correct the problems of the past. This is a very delicate balancing act. You need to go over the business justification of grooming the data vs. making the source system correct the data at the source.

Our experience has taught us, many times, that trying to correct the problem in the warehouse is cost prohibitive. Don't expect to solve these problems after the fact. Push back on the operational system to correct them at the source. Many times this can be best. This way, both the warehouse and the operational system maintain integrity. As you could see from our telecommunications example, sometimes correcting the problems in the warehouse makes sense.

# TRANSFORMING DATA

During the data migration step, it is often necessary to transform operational data into a different format more appropriate to the data warehouse design. Our experience has taught us that the majority of the time transformation involves aggregation to the data to make it more meaningful. Simple examples of data transformation are as follows:

▼ Changing all alphabetic characters to uppercase.

■ Calculating new values based on existing data. For example, the total amount of clam chowda (for those of you not from New England, it is known as clam chowder) sold in the company might be stored by state vs. each individual city.

■ Breaking up a single data value into multiple values, such as a product code. For example, the product code "1998XLBLST" might be broken up to mean

   ■ Year manufactured—1998

   ■ Size—extra large

- Color—blue
- Clothing item—suit

▲ Merging separate data values into a single value, such as concatenating separate Year, Date and Month fields into a single value of year and month. For the purpose of the warehouse, we might not need to go down to the day a particular item was sold.

As we have talked about before, how data is stored in a warehouse is different than how it is stored in an OLTP system. Let's now take a closer look at a star schema, a very common database approach that is used in a data warehouse.

## Star Schema and Fact Table

These two terms are mentioned in many places around this book. A very common technique when building a data warehouse is to use a star schema. A *star schema* is a database design optimized to support queries that are typically requested of a data warehouse.  It accomplishes this optimization by reducing the number of I/Os a typical request would generate. As most information system professionals know, even though we have made great advances in computer processing power, a physical request to a disk is still one of the slowest tasks a computer can accomplish. Any time an I/O can be eliminated, you will greatly increase performance.

Figure 8-2 shows a typical schema from an operational system. It represents a typical database design to support an OLTP system where the design is optimized to process transactions one at a time, day in and day out.

Figure 8-3 shows an OLTP system design transformed into a star schema for the data warehouse.

The table at the center of the star is known as the *fact table*. In the data warehouse, the fact table is usually very large (row-numberwise and also in comparison to some other tables) and serves as the holder of the main portion of the warehouse that supports analysis. Refer to the "Star Schema Implementation" section in Chapter 7 for more star schema/fact table details. This is almost opposite to the traditional relational design, which breaks things down using database normalization theory and techniques. *Normalization* involves implementing a regimen where data is stored once and only once and objects are linked together by relationships based on common column values. As well, fact tables contain data that describes a specific event. In this example, the star schema represents a specific event as an order. The tables surrounding the fact table or hub of the star schema are called dimension tables. Dimension tables are categories of information that organize the data in the fact table. For example, in an order entry system, you are dealing with orders. This is the very foundation upon which the whole business is based. An order by itself is not very useful to helping the business stay competitive. When you add to it the dimension of who, where, and when, you have now added tremendous value to the order information. For example, you can now ask questions like the following.

▼ How many green Ford pickups where sold during the month of May that had air-conditioning?

■ Who are my top ten customers for 1998?

■ Who are my top ten customers in New England?

▲ What is my best-selling product by state?

Because fact tables contain the vast majority of the data stored in a data warehouse, it is important that the table structure be correct before data is loaded. It is much cheaper to alter a design on paper than after it has been implemented. Expensive table restructuring

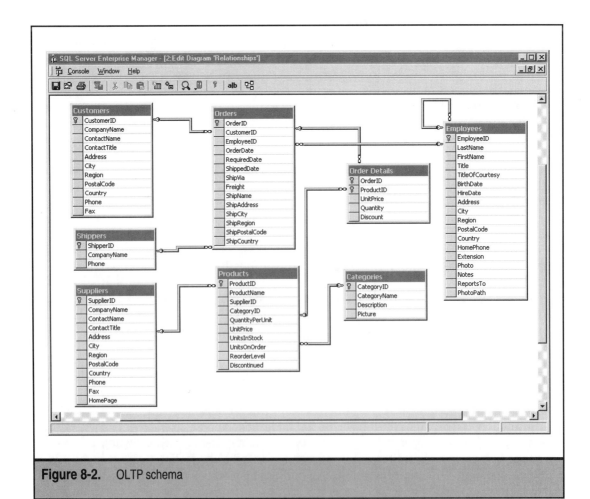

**Figure 8-2.**  OLTP schema

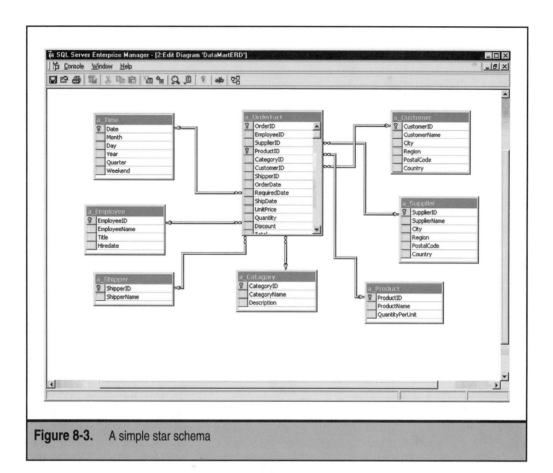

**Figure 8-3.** A simple star schema

can be necessary if data required by decision support queries is missing or incorrect. Some of the characteristics of fact tables are as follows:

▼ Many rows—possibly billions. With SQL Server 7, the size of the database is virtually unlimited.

■ Primarily numeric data; rarely character data.

■ Multiple foreign keys (into dimension tables).

▲ Static data.

Let's move on to data migration.

# MIGRATING DATA

Our experience has taught us that the migration of data from operational systems typically involves copying the data to an intermediate location before it is finally copied to the data warehouse. Copying data to an intermediate location is necessary if data should be scrubbed, as discussed in the "Scrubbing Data" section earlier in this chapter.

## Move Data During Off Hours

The process of copying data should ideally occur during a period of low activity on the operational system. Be smart; don't be a Rambo. Operational systems support day-to-day business—don't mess with them. Pick a slow time to migrate your data from the OLTP system into the warehouse.

Make sure you understand your business and its supporting systems. Don't migrate data if the nightly batch updates have not completed. If the data warehouse is composed of data from multiple interrelated operational systems, it is important to ensure that data migration occurs when the systems are synchronized. Your source system experts are your friends. Listen to them, they will help you avoid these common pitfalls. These source system experts will help you understand these operational systems better than you will ever be able to learn on your own. To help you simplify the process of migration, we will now take a closer look at the DTS Import and Export Wizards.

# DTS IMPORT AND EXPORT WIZARDS

The DTS Import and Export Wizards allow the user to interactively create DTS packages that can be used to import, export, validate, and transform heterogeneous data using OLE-DB and *open database connectivity* (ODBC). ODBC is common standard for providing access to data. Data transformation services can also be used to copy schema and data sources. However, DTS does not copy indexes, stored procedures, or referential integrity constraints. To state this more plainly, DTS will copy the data, the table, and its columns and properties. None of the additional information about how a table interacts with other tables and programs will be copied. With DTS Wizards you can do the following:

▼ Specify any custom settings that are supported by a particular OLE-DB provider.

■ Copy the entire contents of a table from one source to another.

■ Copy the results of any given SQL query from one source to another. The results of any query, no matter how complicated, can be moved. Yes, even distributed queries can be copied. A distributed query is one that involves data from multiple sources and locations. Yes, even data from Boston to Mumbai, India (aka Bombay—nice trivia question, eh?).

■ Use the query builder functionality within the DTS Wizards; even an inexperienced user can build a query and move its results to a data warehouse.

■ Change the name, data type, size, precision, scale, and even nullability of a column when copying from a source to a destination. Of course, you can't perform illegal-type conversions—for example, trying to store a letter of the alphabet in a column designed to hold only numbers.

▲ Execute a Microsoft ActiveX script that can modify (transform) the data when copied from the source to the destination, or perform any operation supported by the JScript, PerlScript, or VBScript languages. Wake up, this is *real* important!

After a wizard has created a DTS package, you have the option of storing the package to the SQL Server MSDB database, the Microsoft Repository, or a COM-structured storage file. For those of you new to SQL Server, MSDB is a special system database you get with every installation of SQL Server. MSDB is a database that stores data that allows SQL Server to manage itself. Using wizards, you can easily schedule the DTS packages for later execution.

**NOTE:** DTS is just a tool that will help you move the information around. It cannot, however, overcome the limitations of any given source or destination system.

If the given destination system does not support special data types (e.g., blobs or *binary large objects*), don't expect a DTS Wizard to move that data representation into the destination.

In the DTS Wizard's efforts to make the movement of data as painless as possible, if you do not tell it exactly what you want, it will make decisions for you. For example, if the destination system does not support blobs, DTS might convert blobs into a varchar field. As powerful as this feature might be, it is not immune to lack of operator instruction. Our experience has taught us that when you choose to make data type conversions, tell DTS what you want. Let's take a closer look at DTS Wizards and how you use them.

## Using Import and Export Wizards

To use the Import/Export Wizards, you must first invoke the Enterprise Manager (referred to as EM sometimes). There are a number of ways to get to EM (especially if you have created a folder on your desktop for SQL Server 7); Figure 8-4 shows getting there from the Start menu.

Once in EM, you will be presented with a series of choices. One of the choices will be to invoke the Import and Export Wizards. A wizard is a graphical user interface that guides you in a process. For example, when using Microsoft Word, a wizard might help you navigate a feature you are not familiar with. Perhaps that is creating an addressed envelope or a mail merge document. For the purposes of this discussion, we will take a closer look at the Import Wizard.

Figure 8-5 shows the sign-on information screen presented when using the SQL Server 7 DTS Import Wizard.

The major purpose of a wizard is to prompt you for the needed information to accomplish the particular task at hand. In our example, you must inform DTS what type of OLE-DB provider is needed for the destination. To make this task easier, you are provided with a pull-down menu of just the appropriate choices.

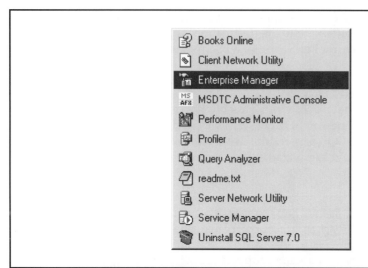

**Figure 8-4.** Enterprise Manager from the Start menu

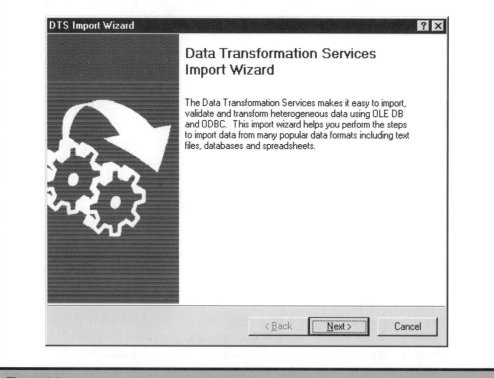

**Figure 8-5.** Import Wizard startup

The Server field prompts you for identification of the machine you will be migrating information from. The wizard will provide you with a pull-down menu of all valid choices. As you can see, the wizard provides you a framework to make this task very simple. Figure 8-6 shows a data source context-sensitive dialog initiated by the wizard once the source has been specified; in this case, we selected the OBDC Data Source Driver.

There is an old saying that a picture is worth a thousand words. For your sake, be thankful that is true. We get compensated based on page count. The larger the book, the more they can charge. Imagine what this book might cost if we could not show you those pictures. Imagine what it would cost your organization if you had to pay a programmer to write code for each extraction you might need. Well, this is just the tip of the iceberg. Let's take a look at more advanced features of wizards.

## Advanced Features of Export/Import Wizards

As mentioned earlier, the transformation process can be fairly complicated. With the advanced features of these wizards, you can easily do data type conversions, column mappings from source to destinations, and much more. Figure 8-7 illustrates how the Import Wizard simplifies tasks such as column mapping and transformation.

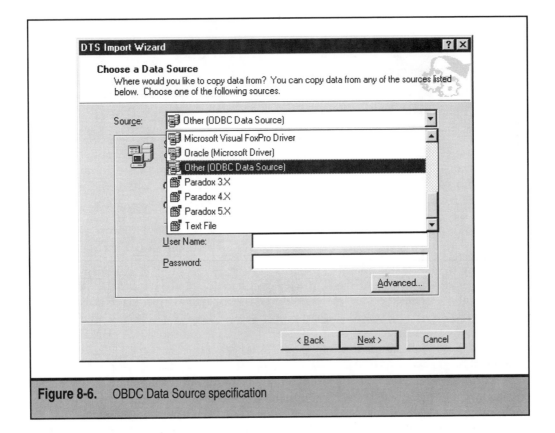

**Figure 8-6.**    OBDC Data Source specification

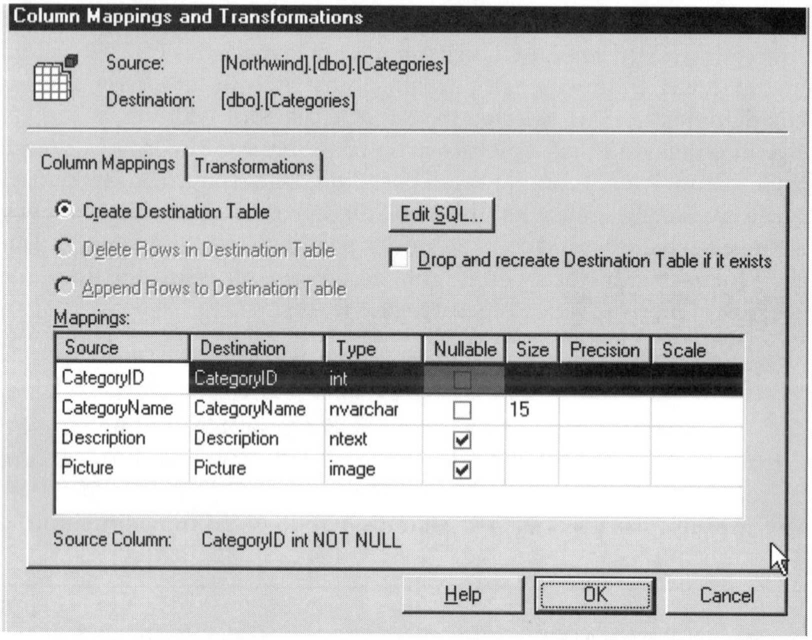

**Figure 8-7.** Column mapping and transformations

Many times, the transformation process can't be handled in such a simplified manner. Have no fear—DTS scripting is here. Figure 8-8 shows how you can easily manipulate DTS transformation scripts while using the Import Wizard. Notice you have a pull-down menu of all the scripting languages available—JScript, PerlScript, and VBScript. One of the things we found particularly useful about wizards was that even the advanced users found them quite useful.

## Scheduling and Wizards

Once you create these DTS packages, you may want to use them over and over. Of course, you remember our earlier warning—don't do it during prime time. Have no fear—DTS wizards are here. You guessed it; they even have a wizard for scheduling. Figure 8-9 shows the Wizard dialog box where you save, schedule, and replicate a package via the SQL Server 7 DTS scheduling module. Figure 8-9 shows how a recurring job is set up and scheduled to run every second day starting August 26 and ending December 12.

You can choose to execute now or at some future date and frequency. What we did not begin to show you is just how thorough the wizards are. For example, when you copy

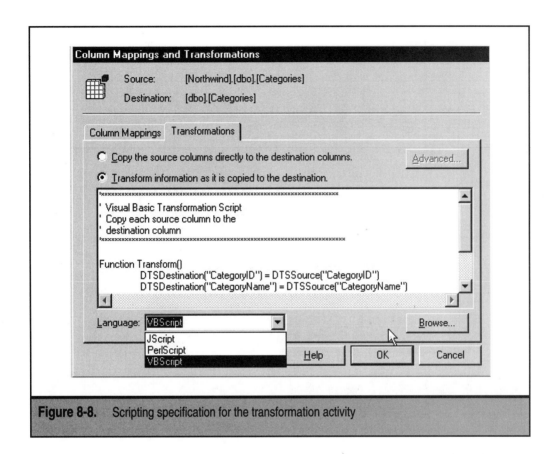

**Figure 8-8.**    Scripting specification for the transformation activity

a table from one SQL Server database to another, if the table already exists on the destination, the wizard prompts you with an option to drop and re-create the destination table. On the other hand, if the destination table did not exist, the table would be created.

Literally, the series of prompts any given user might see could be different. If a table already exists, the Import Wizard gives you the choice of dropping and re-creating it during the exercise. That is different than what you would see if the table did not exist. The wizards adapt to the particular situation at hand, which is why they are so powerful.

## Importing Data from a Text File into a SQL Server 7 Database

Many times you will be faced with migrating data from a flat file of ASCII data into a SQL Server 7 database. Table 8-2 shows a number of ways fields in text files are delimited and how DTS deals with that particular delimiter.

Once again, have no fear—a DTS Wizard is here. Had we chosen Text File in Figure 8-6, the wizard would have presented us with a series of boxes where we could specify these delimiters. Using the information in Table 8-2, you are now armed with the

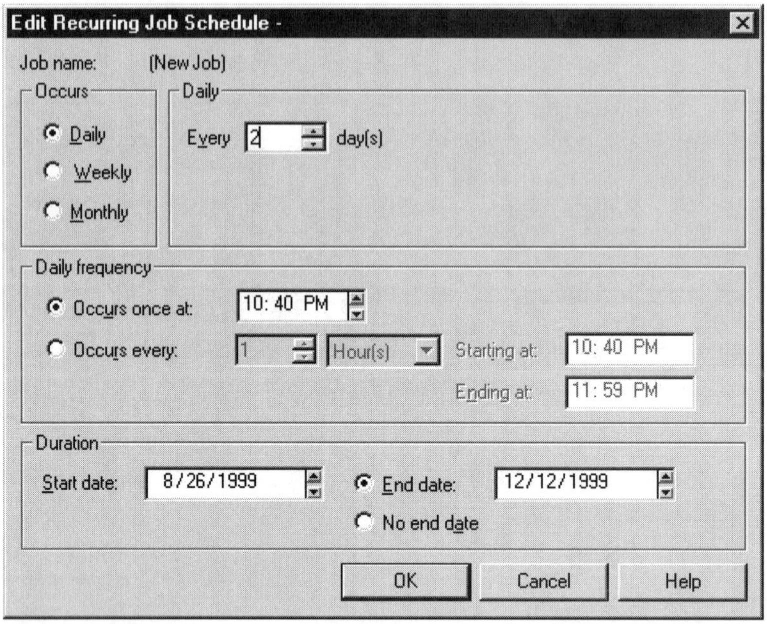

**Figure 8-9.** Scheduling via the Import Wizard

introduction that allows you to try it on your own. With the wizard, even the novice user can migrate information into SQL Server 7 database.

## CREATING A DESTINATION TABLE FOR REPLICATION

When creating a DTS package using the DTS Import or Export Wizards, you can specify that the destination will be a replication publication. That's a mouthful; let's discuss this for a while.

*Replication* is the ability to store multiple copies of a database in different locations. Be it Boston and Mumbai or even just two computers in the same building. SQL Server allows you to keep these "replicated" copies of the database always synchronized and up to date. It does that with the publisher/subscriber model—that is, some database publishes an event and the subscribers receive and update their copies upon notification. There are three basic types of replication:

▼ *Snapshot* Just as it sounds. At any given point in time, it is a snapshot of the PUBLISHER database. Think of it as purge and rebuild.

- *Transactional*   As events occur in the PUBLISHER database, the events or transactions are propagated to the subscribers.

▲ *Merge*   Send off the transaction. Only the differences are applied.

| Format | Explanation of What DTS Will Do |
|---|---|
| Delimited | Align data within the file into fields, each delimited with a terminating character. All fields must be delimited with the same terminating character. |
| Fixed field | Align data within the file into fields of equal width. A field within the file has the same width for all rows of data. Each field can have a different width to other fields within the same row, however. |
| File type | Choose ANSI or Unicode, depending on the type of data in the file. |
| Row delimiter | Separate one row in the file from the next with a character sequence. Choose from the following:<br><br>{CR} {LF} carriage return line feed<br>{CR} carriage return<br>{LF} line feed<br>Semicolon<br>Comma<br>Tab<br>Vertical bar<br>\<No delimiter><br>Any other character to use as the row delimiter |
| Text qualifier | Enclose text fields character used. Choose from: Double quotation mark {"}<br>Single quotation mark {'}<br>\<None><br>You can also type in a character to use as the text qualifier. |
| Skip rows | Enter the number of rows from the start of the file to skip being copied. |
| First row has column names | Specify that the first row in the text file has column headings rather than data. |

**Table 8-2.**   Common Delimiters in Text Files

In fact, replication can be done from many heterogeneous data sources. You do this by using SQL Server 7 as the information pump. Food for thought.

# DTS COMMAND LINE—NOT FOR THE FAINT OF HEART

Do not try this at home. It is recommend that the command line be used by advanced users only. Through the use of the command-line option, it is possible to pass parameters that will allow you to bypass the dialog boxes normally required by the wizard.

For example, the following command line can be used to launch a wizard that will create a DTS package. This package can export data from the ORDERS database on the server named PRODUCTION, using the OLE-DB provider for ODBC (MSDASQL), and connecting to the SQL Server 7 database as the user sa with a password turday.

```
dtswiz /x /Sproduction /Usa /Pturday /dORDERS /rMSDASQL
```

After a DTS package has been created and saved, it is completely self-contained and can be retrieved and run using the SQL Server 7 EM.

# DTS BULK COPY PROGRAM (BCP)

One of the features the authors really like about SQL Server 7 is the fact that DTS takes advantage of the *bulk copy program* (BCP) as the default way to migrate data into the warehouse. BCP avoids the expense associated with many normal **insert** operations.

Every time you do an **insert** into a SQL Server 7 database, the event is logged. The good news is the event is logged. This gives you the ability to roll forward in the event of a database failure. For example, if the system were rebooted due to a power failure, this logged event would allow you to recover from the failure.

When you are initially loading a large amount of data, this feature creates a lot of overhead that slows you down by a factor of at least ten times. In the case of a data migration, in the event of a failure, you can always go back to the source system. So, if you could eliminate this logging, you could speed up the migration process. By using DTS and BCP, you can now load many gigabytes of data in a reasonable amount of time.

**VIP:** Using BCP is a very fast way to migrate data into the warehouse.

BCP and DTS accomplish this boost in performance by writing the data directly into the database, circumventing all logging.

## More Neat Stuff You Can Do

During our research for this book, we found two features worth mentioning; we call this more neat stuff you can do:

▼ The ability to export data and create pivot tables in Microsoft Excel. We thought this was great stuff. A pivot table is an interactive table that quickly summarizes, or cross-tabulates large amounts of data. You can rotate its rows to see different summaries of source data by displaying different pages or displaying the details for areas of interest.

▲ Support for creating customized data sources and destinations. For data sources and destination not typically supported by OLE-DB providers, DTS supports creation of on the fly custom format and access mechanisms. For example, we can establish a business rule that states, "If plane utilization exceeds 85 percent, place a row into my high-performing plan route spreadsheet."

# DTS PACKAGE DESIGNER

Packages are a series of actions, which you can use to automate data into and out of your warehouse. So once you have created a package, it is important you have a way to manage it. Let's quickly go over management of DTS packages.

Using the SQL Server 7 Enterprise Manager, you will be able to organize and manage DTS packages. Actions include the following:

▼ Creating new DTS packages.

■ Viewing existing packages.

■ Modifying DTS packages. This includes all property attributes.

■ Saving DTS packages. This includes local and repository formats. The former involves the ability to store the package in an efficient file format. This is the most common way we see packages stored. The latter entails the ability to store the package in a database.

▲ Deleting packages from storage—both local and the repository.

## Modifying DTS Package Properties

As you are well aware, properties contain valuable information that determines a package's behavior. These are two basic types of collections of properties:

▼ **Package properties**—Accessed through the Package tab. This deals with properties that are specific to a particular package.

▲ **Global variables**—Accessed through the Global Variables tab. This deals with information passed between steps in a package.

Let's now take a closer look at these tabs.

### Package Tab

The Package tab is used to specify general DTS package properties. Table 8-3 offers suggestions and information about the types of information entered in this tab.

| Property | Notes |
|---|---|
| Name | Specify the package name. |
| Description | Specify the package description. |
| Creator Name | View the Package.CreatorName property. |
| Computer Name | View the Microsoft Win32 computer name (Package.CreatorComputerName property). |
| Date | View the Package.CreationDate property. |
| Error File | Specify the Package.LogFileName property. This can be in UNC format. |
| ... (browse) | Specify the log filename location. |
| Fail Package on First Error | Specify whether package execution aborts if the first step fails. |
| Write Completion Status to Event Log | Specify whether to write the package execution status to the Microsoft Windows NT application event log. This is only available on computers running Windows NT. |
| Priority Class | Specify the Microsoft Windows process priority (Package.PackagePriorityClass property). Possible values are Lowest, Low, Normal, High, Highest. |
| Limit the Maximum number of tasks executed in parallel to | Specify the maximum number of tasks that can execute concurrently. This can be any positive 32-bit integer (default = 10). |

**Table 8-3.**   Information Entered in Package Tab

## Global Variables Tab

The Global Variables tab is used to display information about variables that pass between steps in a package. Table 8-4 provides you with a quick definition of the different properties you will find.

# DEVELOPING WITH DTS

As you have already read about for these many pages, DTS provides you with a very powerful and extensible framework for migrating data from your operational stores into

| Item | Notes |
|------|-------|
| Name | Specify the global variable name. |
| Type | Specify the global variable data type. |
| Value | Specify the initial value assigned to the variable. |
| New | Add a global variable to the package. |
| Delete | Delete a global variable from the package. |

**Table 8-4.** Items in the Global Variables Tab

your data warehouse. We have shown you how using the DTS and wizards can get you 80 to 90 percent of the way there. The problem is that the race is not won until you cross the finish line. Well, have no fear—DTS can get you there. Do what any blue-blooded programmer would do when faced with this situation—write custom code.

Does this mean you throw out the DTS architecture? No. You just incorporate those packages' objects into your code. They are fully reusable; they are the building blocks. DTS was designed with this type of extensibility in mind. What is very clear to me after working with SQL Server 7 is that many of the toughest challenges you face, you no longer face alone. SQL Server 7 will help you overcome them.

Now that's quite a mouthful! Wizard this, wizard that, export this, import that. What with so much automation, we'll all be better SQL Server 7 experts by dawn! The next chapter in the never-ending SQL Server 7 journey deals with indexing and query processing. This may indeed be the technical heart of this work. Fill up the coffeepot, put on the kettle, warm the milk, or whatever fancies your suit! Meet us at the third post on the left....

# CHAPTER 9

# Query Processor—Indexing the Warehouse

This chapter of *SQL Server 7 Data Warehousing* discusses indexing the warehouse. *Data warehouse administrators* (we call them DWAs) are responsible for ensuring the warehouse is set up in a way that supports optimal access to the information using the least amount of CPU, disk access, and other precious computer resources. This chapter is aimed at these administrators, and is one of the few chapters in this book that contains some material specifically for the technical readership. We will look at different approaches to indexing data in the SQL Server 7 database, then discuss the ways indexes are created and maintained, the benefits of each approach, and some caveats we have experienced with their implementation and usage.

An *index* is, in most cases, a structure separate from the table data it refers to, storing the location of rows in the database based on the column values specified when the index is created. Indexes are like minicopies of the table data they refer to. Examine the query in Figure 9-1 and its results, showing the contents of the TITLES table (no big deal, but it's a start!).

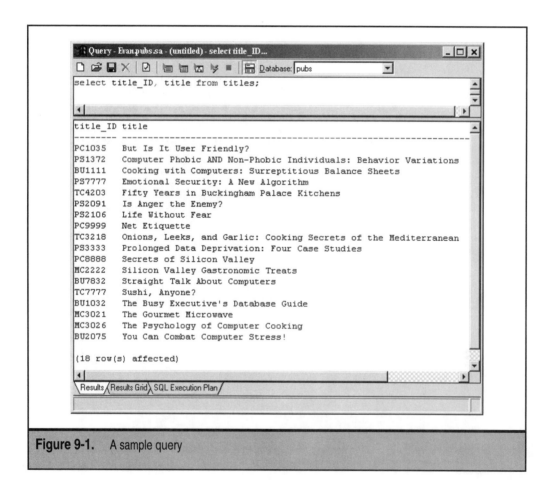

**Figure 9-1.**   A sample query

Suppose a query were to restrict the Title, looking for names that started with the text "SM" (called the *lookup string*). Without an index on Title, SQL Server 7 would read from the first row to the last row, looking for the rows with the desired lookup string. With an index, SQL Server 7 would proceed to the index, obtain an address of the qualifying row, then present the data in the qualifying row to the process that issued the query. In a nutshell, that is what indexes are all about.

**TIP:**   Index lookups are the secret to optimizing the response time to most queries, and are used systematically in a data warehouse to improve warehouse throughput.

Enhanced throughput contributes three words crucial for the success of a data warehousing project—*enhanced customer satisfaction*. Let's get started by having a look at the types of indexing available with SQL Server 7.

# WHAT COLUMNS TO INDEX

Two main rules or guidelines exist concerning what columns to index in the SQL Server 7 database. First, some terminology. *Selectivity* is a measurement of the number of distinct values in a table column compared to the number of rows in the whole table. The *predicate* of a SQL statement is that part where the selection criteria are specified. The *selection criteria* specifies which rows of information are to be included in the query result set. The first criterion starts with the **where** keyword; all subsequent criteria start with the keyword **and**. The *result set* is a set of one or more rows that qualify for inclusion in a specific query.

## Selectivity Consideration

Using the Rows column value from the **sp_spaceused** stored procedure, coupled with the Cardinality column value from the **sp_statistics** stored procedure, you can assess the selectivity of a column. Suppose there were 79,000 rows in a table in a finance data mart and the Acc_Type column had eight distinct values. The selectivity of any row in a table is calculated according to the following formula:

```
                rows in table         1
selectivity =   --------------    *   ------------
                distinct values       rows in table
```

This is the same as saying the selectivity is the inverse of the value found in Cardinality for that column. In this example, the selectivity equals the inverse of 8, which is .125, or 12.5 expressed as a percent. This leads to the following guideline:

**TIP:**   When a column value is found in less than 5 percent of all the rows in a table, that column is a good candidate for an index.

## Mentioned in Predicate Consideration

Say a purchases data mart continually processed queries using the Purchase_Date and Cust_Num columns as part of the predicate. These two columns should be considered for indexes.

Columns displayed as part of the query results but not used as part of a predicate are not good index candidates. In other words, the italicized column in the following listing may not be considered for an index, whereas the one in boldface may be a candidate:

```
select sum(aggr_day),region,
  from day_summary,region
 where trans_date between '01-JAN-1999' and '31-JAN-1999' ;
```

*TIP:* Columns that are commonly parts of query selection criteria are candidates for indexes.

Naturally, because this is a rule (actually a guideline), exceptions exist. Columns continually mentioned in a predicate, but upon which a function or operation is performed, are not candidates for indexes. If a function is to be performed on a column, the column's index is not used. We call this *index suppression*. The following listing shows two examples of how the Trans_Date column from the previous listing may be used that do not warrant an index:

```
select sum(aggr_day),region,
  from day_summary,region
 where datepart(dy, trans_date) in (1,2) ;
select sum(aggr_day),region,
  from day_summary,region
 where datediff(mm,trans_date,sysdate) >> 6 ;
```

There is one more guideline about columns mentioned in predicates with and without a function. Suppose the Trans_Date column from DAY_SUMMARY is used in the SQL statement:

```
select ..
  from day_summary ..
 where cast(trans_date as char(19)) ..
```

as well as in the SQL statement:

```
select ..
  from day_summary ..
 where trans_date between (..
```

*TIP:*  A column that is used in a predicate with and without a function performed on it may still be a candidate for an index. Analyze the number of SQL statements using a function and implement an index if it optimizes the statements without a function.

## Data Warehouse Uniqueness

In a way, we have found that indexing a data warehouse or data mart is a dream come true. A common occurrence when designing operational systems is that the database the programmers use during development contains only a small subset of production data. The tables used during program development are a fraction of the size they are in production. Some of our clients have very large tables with 30,000,000 or 40,000,000 rows in production and a 30,000- or 40,000-row subset in development. In the data warehouse or data mart, enough data exists throughout development that tough indexing decisions can be made against realistic volumes of data. With this volume of data, it is easier to assess the efficiency of indexes and run tests to zero in on additional indexes that could aid performance. Tables can be analyzed and calculations about selectivity can be made to decide appropriate columns for indexing.

*TIP:*  Columns that are indexed in operational systems are not necessarily good candidates for indexing in the DSS.

A well thought out and meticulously implemented indexing scheme for an operational system needs careful review and ongoing scrutiny as the data is moved into the decision support arena.

# SINGLE-COLUMN AND COMPOSITE INDEXES

SQL Server 7 uses a B-tree index, which you can think of as containing a hierarchy of highest-level and succeeding lower-level index blocks. There are two types of blocks in the B-tree index:

- ▼ Branch blocks, or upper-level blocks, simply point to the corresponding lower-level blocks.
- ▲ Leaf blocks, where the actual meat of the indexing method lies, contain a reference that points at the location of the actual row the leaf refers to.

SQL Server 7 has stuck to the B-tree organization for so long mainly due to its simplicity, ease of maintenance, and retrieval speed of highly selective column values (high cardinality). This organization is especially suited to queries looking for index column values in equality (i.e., **where colA = 'ABC123'**) and range searches (i.e., **where colA between 'A12' and 'R45'**). The size of a table, be it a few hundred or a few million rows, has little or no impact on the speed with which B-tree-indexed data can be fetched from its corresponding tables. When working with one or more large objects, the B-tree index is not the culprit when queries take long times to return the result sets. The culprit is the massive amounts of information that make up that set.

There are two types of indexes that can be built using the traditional SQL Server 7 B-tree index mechanism—single-column and composite. *Single-column* indexes are built on one column of a database table using code similar to that shown in the next listing:

```
create index purchase_1
   on purchase (purchase_id)
 on index_filegroup;
```

A *composite index*, or concatenated index, is built on two or more columns in the same table, as shown in the following listing:

```
create index purchase_2
   on purchase (cust_id,purchase_date,total_amt);
```

The same activity is accomplished using Enterprise Manager, using the Create Index Wizard—of which the final screen is shown in Figure 9-2.

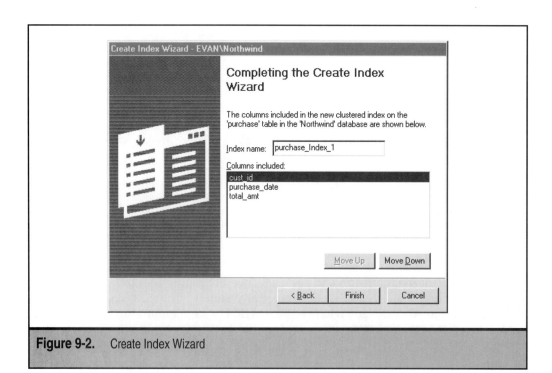

**Figure 9-2.**   Create Index Wizard

# CLUSTERED INDEXES

SQL Server 7 delivered a new type of structure that can prove beneficial for some requirements in a data warehouse. Traditional database tables have a data segment (the area set aside for storage of the column values for all columns defined for a table) and an index segment (where quick reference information is stored by column value). Clustered tables with SQL Server 7, on the other hand, merge the two traditional segments into one. Thus, the data is the index and the index is the data.

## Defining Clustered Tables

Let's look at creating a clustered table in the following listing:

```
create table country (
        country_code    char(3),
        name            char(30),
        capital         char(30),
        free_form1      char(1200),
        free_form2      char(1200),
        constraint country_pk
        primary key clustered (country_code))
```

Notice the use of the **clustered** keyword immediately after the **primary key** keywords. In SQL Server 7, new tables automatically default to clustered if the constraint is a primary key, and nonclustered if the constraint is unique. You can only define one index to organize by, so if you specify **clustered** on both a primary key and a unique index in the **create table** statement, then the table will be created with a clustered index on the unique key only.

## Benefits of Clustered Tables

The major benefit when using clustered tables is the retrieval time to get at the data. In the traditional table with one of the normal index approaches, retrieval can involve two reads. The first is to scan the index segment looking for column values matching the desired selection criteria. The second gets the rows from the data segment to which the qualifying index entries refer by using a rowid fetch. The first operation is referred to as an *index range scan* and, in most (but not all) cases, is the way SQL Server 7 processes a query. There is only one segment with the clustered tables; in other words, the index is the data.

Queries involving exact match or range searches will run faster using clustered tables. With a separate data and index segment and traditional tables, the index duplicates column values from the data segment, thereby consuming double the space for those indexed columns.

*TIP:* The data warehouse is an ideal location for clustered tables, but don't rush out and implement them everywhere without testing their performance in your SQL Server 7 databases.

## Where to Use Clustered Tables

Code tables are ideal candidates for clustered tables. Retrieval is done using the primary key columns; most of the time, the Description field populates a drop-down picklist. Applications that support text searches on document collections may also benefit from using clustered tables. OLAP applications, being multidimensional in nature, benefit from a clustered methodology because it speeds up access to portions of the multi-dimensional blocks.

*NOTE:* Not all tables seeming to meet the requirements for the clustered approach should be set up using this SQL Server 7 feature. Experience and familiarity with your data warehouse data will assist with deciding whether or not to use this method.

# PRIMARY KEY INDEXES

The data warehouse is chock full of *referential integrity*, designed through a network of primary and foreign keys, to ensure parent-child relationships are maintained and enforced. We call referential integrity by its initials—*RI*. There are a few ways to define primary keys in the SQL Server 7 data warehouse, but there is really only one way to do it properly. Inspect the following listing, commented to illustrate the points we are making:

```
-- The table already exists, so must be altered to set a primary key.
alter table sale add constraint
sale_pk primary key clustered (sale_id)
```

*TIP:* Use the **alter table add constraint** ... convention to build all primary key constraints with the **clustered** keyword, naming the constraint as it is built. Make the name meaningful.

We recommend using primary key constraints to enforce uniqueness for tables in your data warehouse repository rather than unique indexes. This is a double win since many query tools are sensitive to the primary key/foreign key relationships defined in the data dictionary, as well as SQL Server 7's star schema optimization technique. This optimization technique in particular is discussed in Chapter 20. Inspect the following SQL statements that these tools pick up automatically:

```
alter table customer add constraint customer_pk
    primary key clustered (cust_id)
go
alter table sale add constraint sale_customer_fk
```

```
    foreign key (cust_id) references
    customer (cust_id)
go
```

We have defined the primary key for the CUSTOMER table using the appropriate **alter table** command. We then reference that primary key using the next **alter table** command against the SALE table whose Cust_id column values are related to the primary key in CUSTOMER.

> **NOTE:** When designing the layout and location of tables in the data warehouse, pay attention to the relationships between columns in different tables as the network of objects is mapped.

## Fast Index Rebuild

SQL Server 7 allows you to perform a quick index rebuild. SQL Server 7 reads the information in an existing clustered index, rewriting the index from start to finish in a new area in the database where the index currently resides. By using the existing index as input (rather than reading the table data as it does with the **create index** statement), the operation runs to completion in far less time than the traditional approach of dropping and then creating the index. You must add the **with drop_existing** clause to your SQL statement, and the index must be identical to the index that is being replaced; otherwise, the existing order is ignored and you will not see any speed improvement over a standard **create index** statement. The following listing illustrates fast index rebuild:

```
create unique clustered
  index customer_pk on customer (cust_id)
  with drop_existing
```

> **NOTE:** The table upon which the index is built must be quiet when the index is rebuilt since the rebuild writes the new index based on the makeup of the old.

# THE SQL SERVER QUERY PROCESSOR

The query processor is one of the fundamental components for every relational database. The query processor receives compiled SQL requests and determines the most efficient access plan to satisfy the SQL statement request. Like the storage engine, the query processor has been rearchitected for SQL Server 7. This new architecture contains well-defined interfaces, which allows the query processor to easily add new innovations into future versions of SQL Server.

A perfect example of this modular, well-defined interface is the parallel operator described in Chapter 7. Query parallelism is achieved by inserting a parallel operator into a query plan tree. Contrast this with the other approach where parallelism intelligence has to exist in all components of the query processor.

SQL Server 7 has added to SQL Server 6.5's capabilities by considering multiple indexes when determining a query plan. SQL Server 6.5 would only consider one index—more specifically, the first column in an index. The query processor also supports index intersection, another important feature for large databases.

The SQL Server 6.5 query processor had limited query optimization techniques. In fact, there was only one algorithm for optimizing joins—the nested loops/inner join. This algorithm will iterate through all tables in the join operation in a nested fashion. This algorithm works very well if the top-level tables in the hierarchy have low levels of cardinality. If this isn't true, then this is not an optimal strategy.

SQL Server 7 has also added additional algorithms for addressing complex joins, including sophisticated hashing algorithms. These new query-processing techniques are quite sophisticated, but rather than describing them in detail, let's use the SQL Server Query Analyzer to demonstrate these features.

## SQL Server Query Analyzer

The SQL Server Query Analyzer is the next generation of what was previously known as ISQL, the interactive SQL Server Query utility. Rather than explain the utility in words, let's see what it looks like. The following query, seen in Figure 9-3, is issued against the

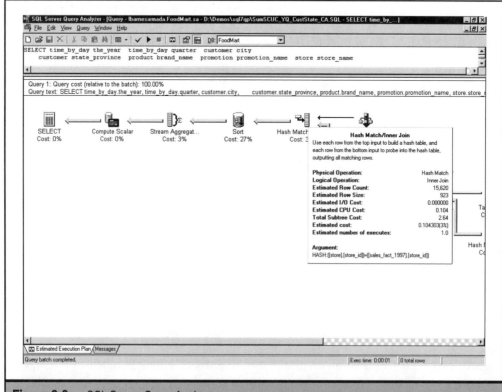

**Figure 9-3.** SQL Server Query Analyzer

FOODMART database that ships with SQL Server 7. FOODMART is a data mart for a chain of food stores throughout North America.

SQL Server 7 has added a Results Grid feature, which makes displaying result sets a lot friendlier than in previous versions. What's really exciting about this tool is the graphical SQL Execution Plan or show plan capabilities that have been added. Let's take the identical query and instead of choosing Execute query into grid toolbar, let's choose the Display SQL execution plan toolbar, shown in Figure 9-4.

SQL Server 7 now produces a graphical query plan, which provides you with detailed information about how the query processor has decided to satisfy your SQL request. This is state-of-the-art technology and will be your intimate friend as you build and optimize your data warehouse queries. Looking at the first part of the display, you notice two new query optimizer operators—hash match/aggregation and hash match/inner join.

The store clustered index icon is in red. This means that the query processor has identified an index or table where the statistics are either missing or out of date. This is another great feature since one of the primary culprits for a poorly performing data

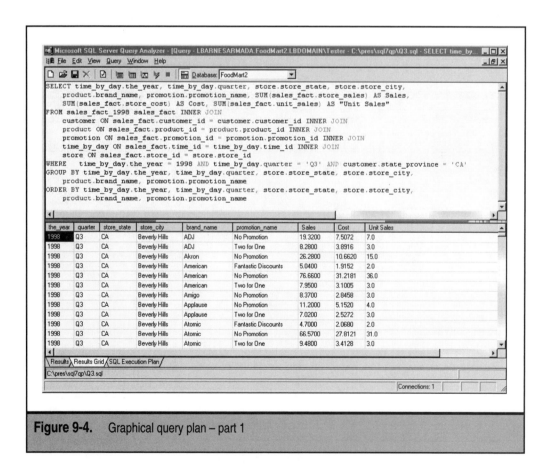

**Figure 9-4.**   Graphical query plan – part 1

warehouse is up-to-date statistics. Let's find out precisely what the issue is. Moving the cursor and holding it over the entry in red produces the screen in Figure 9-5.

Notice that there's a description at the top that explains why this portion of the query plan was flagged as a potential performance problem. In this case, the statistics for this clustered index are missing. In addition, notice that the estimated query statistics the query processor calculates are displayed. These estimates are totaled as we move from right to left, with the total estimated query cost displayed as the last statistic.

SQL Server 7 supports automatic statistics generation. The query processor will initiate an update of a table or index statistics as part of its normal execution. You, as the query designer, also have the option of updating statistics. If you right-click the mouse on the item, the Query Analyzer allows you to explicitly create or update statistics, or enter the Index Maintenance dialog box. Notice how SQL Server 7 suggests this maintenance dialog box should be visited as shown in Figure 9-6. The query processor helps you zero in on potential problems during SQL statement analysis operations.

We will talk more about updating statistics in Chapter 19. The goal here is to make you aware of the powerful tools available to you, as the data warehouse query designer and administrator. Let's look at one more item before we move on. Remember when we

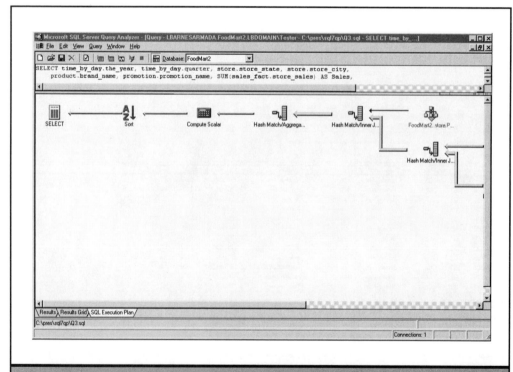

**Figure 9-5.**    Query plan – detailed analysis

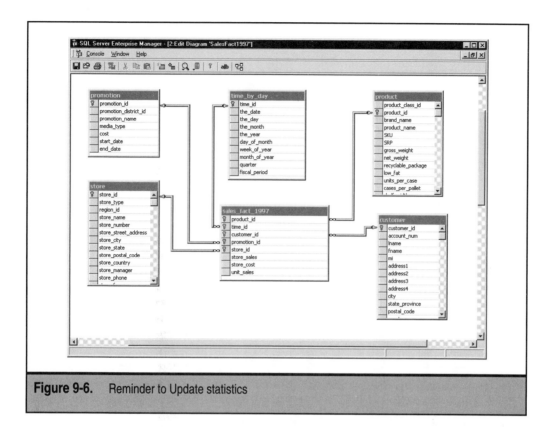

**Figure 9-6.**   Reminder to Update statistics

mentioned the new sophisticated join algorithms? You can learn more about these yourself by hovering the mouse over the particular icon. In the following example, Figure 9-7, we're looking at the Hash Match/Inner Join icon.

The goal of this section is to provide you with a brief review of the query processor and a glimpse at the Query Analyzer tool and its capabilities. The query processor adds state-of-the-art optimizer capabilities. This utility provides an order of magnitude increase in usability and power for the data warehouse query designer and database administrator. These features ship with SQL Server 7 out of the box and are alone worth the price of admission.

# INDEX CREATION AND MAINTENANCE GUIDELINES

Before moving on to the next episode in the SQL Server 7 data warehousing opera, let's close this chapter with some guidelines that will ensure your successful implementation of an indexing approach and help you deliver a decision support solution that leads to a satisfied user community.

## Use the Index Analyzer

SQL Server 7 Query Analyzer contains a great tool to help you index your warehouse. By entering actual queries that are sent to the warehouse, SQL Server 7 will advise you of

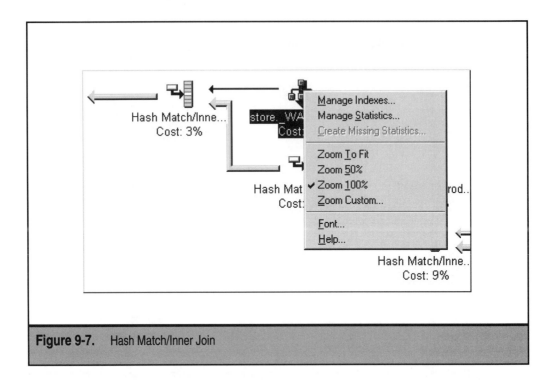

**Figure 9-7.**    Hash Match/Inner Join

indexes that would speed up that particular query. If users are complaining about slow response time on a specific query, use the Index Analyzer to determine an optimum indexing strategy, then decide if the cost of the additional index is worth it. An example of this is shown in Figure 9-8, where we include OrderDate in the query and there is no index on this column.

## Load Data, Then Create Indexes

It is best to load the data into your warehouse objects, then create the indexes manually. If indexes exist on tables as they are populated, the indexes must be updated as the data is inserted. In an OLTP environment, as you will see shortly, the number of indexes that may exist can greatly slow down this process since each index needs to be updated with every row that is inserted into the database.

## Number of Indexes per Table

Since tables in the data warehouse are primarily read-only by the user community, you should not worry about the number of indexes, unlike the approach taken with operational system indexing. In the operational system, we caution creating indexes for

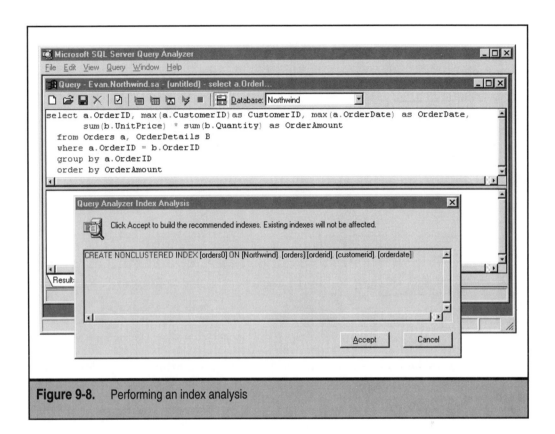

**Figure 9-8.**   Performing an index analysis

applications light on reporting and heavy on transaction processing. With a large number of indexes in place, each time rows are added or deleted and the indexed column values change, index maintenance can be costly. It's a balancing act as well as a trade-off—there is work involved in keeping the index up to date; however, the index may be required for reporting requirements.

**TIP:**  In the data warehouse, you may find yourself "overindexing" tables if you come from a transaction processing background. Minimizing retrieval time for query processing is the primary concern in the data warehouse at almost all cost.

The gist of the previous tip is not to worry about placing more indexes on your DSS tables than you may be accustomed to doing in the operational systems environment. It is the nature of the beast, and something you will have to get used to in the data warehouse. In OLTP environments, most of the time, a check against the TXN_DETAIL table will display the following results as displayed in Figure 9-9.

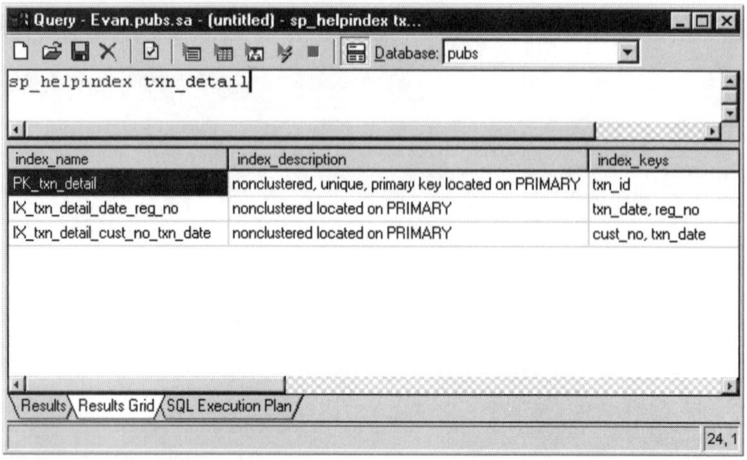

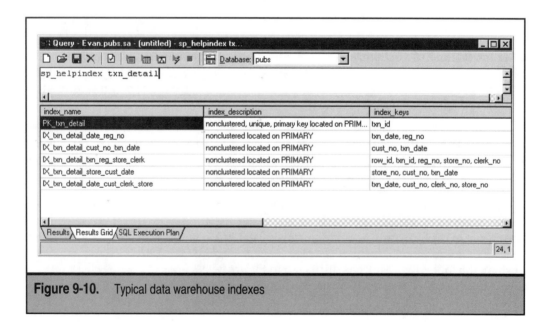

**Figure 9-9.**　Typical OLTP indexes

This indicates there are three indexes (one of which is the primary key index) and five columns indexed in total on TXN_DETAIL. In the data warehouse, it is not uncommon to return results as seen in Figure 9-10 on some heavily accessed tables.

**Figure 9-10.**　Typical data warehouse indexes

If we looked at the total space consumed by a table of 400Mb and an index allocation of 800Mb, we identify a characteristic of the data warehouse repository built on SQL Server 7—often, the index space requests will be significantly larger than the allocation requested for the data segment.

As you no doubt have seen from the preceding pages, indexing the warehouse is a job that requires decision making. Those decisions will contribute down the road to the success or failure of your warehouse built on the SQL Server 7 technology. Follow the suggestions and tips presented in this chapter and devour any recommendations you run across elsewhere. The choice of indexing approach need not be all-consuming. The next chapter discusses advanced data warehousing techniques. You've already cut your teeth on eight previous chapters, and now you should no longer regard yourselves as neophytes. You will, should you decide to accept this mission, become a more enlightened technologist in the decision support arena after reading and memorizing the material in the next and subsequent chapters.

# CHAPTER 10

## Advanced Data Warehousing Techniques

There are two ways you arrived at this chapter. The first (which many of us are typically guilty of) could be you came directly to this chapter thinking you know all the other material. The other reason is that you have survived the preceding chapters (if we did not write that particular chapter, we might be so bold as to say dull, tedious, monotonous, uninteresting, tiresome, wearisome, irksome and ho-hum). Either way, when the authors got together and decided to write this book, we all agreed that every good book has to have an "advanced" section. So here it goes....

By utilizing the information obtained in this chapter, we feel that you will learn information that will be the difference between just building an average data mart and building a great data mart. SQL Server 7 introduces a number of radically new concepts. Among those concepts are files, filegroups, and a whole list of new data types. We will instruct you in the proper use of this new capability, which will have significant impact on the performance of your data mart. Let's start off by taking a closer look at files and filegroups.

# DATABASE FILES

By default, when you create a SQL Server 7 database, it will map the database over a set of operating system files. An *operating system file* is just like a folder of information in a filing cabinet. It holds a collection of information. By default a SQL Server 7 database will create two sets of files. One set, which includes primary and secondary components, is to hold the data. This set includes database objects such as tables, stored procedures, triggers, and views. The other set of files is used to hold the transactions. These transaction files are also known as log files, or as Old Gus to its friends. Let's take a closer look at each of these files:

▼ **Primary datafile**—This file is the starting point of the SQL Server 7 database. Every database can only have one primary datafile. The recommended file extension for a primary datafile is .mdf.

■ **Secondary datafiles**—These files are optional and can hold all data and objects that are not contained within the primary datafile. You can have one or more secondary datafiles. Think of secondary datafiles as extensions of the primary datafile. The recommended file extension for a secondary datafile is .ndf.

▲ **Log files**—Every database must have at least one log file. The log files hold all of the transaction information needed to recover the database in case of a failure. The recommended file extension for log files is .ldf.

SQL Server 7 does not require the use of .mdf, .ndf, and .ldf file extensions, but our experience has taught us it is a good idea; remember, this could affect your job status one day. When you create these files, you have two names associated with each file: The physical name and the logical name.

▼  The *logical_file_name* is the name used to refer to the database file in all Transact-SQL statements. The logical filename must conform to the rules for SQL Server identifiers and must be unique within the database.

▲  The *os_file_name* is the name and location of the physical file, used to store the information. It must follow the rules for Microsoft Windows NT or Microsoft Windows 95 filenames.

For example, in Figure 10-1, we can see that we have one primary file with a logical name of mydb_primary and a physical name of mydata1.mdf. We also have two secondary files and two log files. We could have easily given the primary file a logical name of ACCOUNTING while leaving the physical name untouched. It is advised that you make the name meaningful, as it will simplify tracking many files that tend to accumulate as the system grows.

In the old days (with computers, this could be as old as yesterday, but we are referring to SQL Server Version 4), each file could only be associated with a single device. It severely limited your ability to stripe the data. *Striping data* is the ability to spread data across multiple physical storage devices. Today, CPUs keep getting faster and faster, and

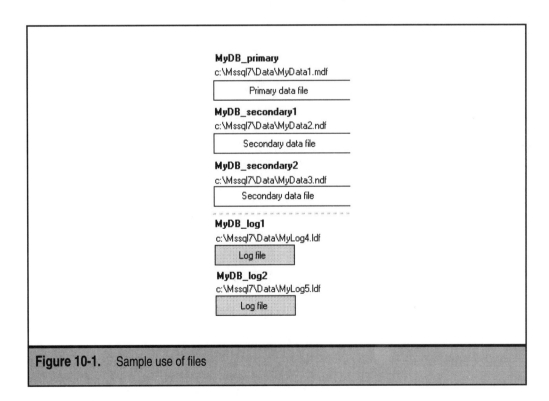

**Figure 10-1.**  Sample use of files

disk speeds have not kept pace (speed...pace, get it—neither do we). Your ability to maximize I/O throughput will greatly affect the performance of your database. Let's now take a closer look at how SQL Server 7 stores data within these files.

# Database Pages

All data within a SQL Server 7 database is stored and accessed via a database page. A *database page* is the fundamental unit of data storage in SQL Server 7 database. The best analogy to a database page is the pages of a book. Think of a book as the database. If you want to access some information within the book, you must first find the page you need and then turn to the page in order to retrieve this information. Even if you just want one word from the book, you must first turn to an actual page and view the page in its entirety. A database works in much the same way. If you want information from the database, you must first retrieve the physical database page where the data is stored in order to view the information within it.

A database page in SQL Server 7 is an 8Kb block of information. In SQL Server 7, each database page has a unique number associated with it. These numbers are assigned sequentially, starting at 0. To differentiate one page 0 from another, each page also has a file ID associated with it. In Figure 10-1 , the mydb_primary file might have a file ID of 7. So, to access page 0, you would need the file ID and the page ID. This way, each page within a file is unique. Figure 10-2 illustrates how page numbers are used.

One of the nicest new features of SQL Server 7 is that files can automatically grow from their originally specified size. As you have already learned, a file is made up of many database pages. When you run out of database pages, the file can be configured to grow automatically. When you define a database file, you can specify a growth increment. Each time all the pages within a file are filled, it then increases the size of the datafile by the growth increment. Each database file can also have a maximum size specified at creation. This is a part of the properties associated with a datafile. It's interesting to note that if a maximum size is not specified in the properties, the datafile can continue to grow until it has used all available space on the disk. This feature is especially useful when SQL Server 7 is used as a database embedded in an application where the user does not have ready access to a system administrator. The user can let the files auto-grow as needed to lessen the administrative burden of monitoring the amount of free space in the database and allocating additional space manually. Another new concept in SQL Server 7 is the use of filegroups. Let's take a closer look at this exciting feature.

# Database Filegroups

Up to now, we have learned about datafiles and pages. One of the nicest features of SQL Server 7 is the ability to organize datafiles into groups. By working with a collection of datafiles as a group, it eases the administrative burden greatly. The other major reason

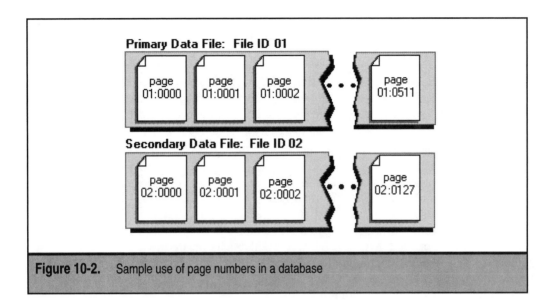

**Figure 10-2.**   Sample use of page numbers in a database

you group files is to help facilitate disk striping. Let's move on to a sample use of file groups.

In this example, we have three files (data1.ndf, data2.ndf, and data3.ndf), that are created on three disk drives, respectively, and then assigned to a single filegroup myfilegroup1. Suppose you then create a table called VISA_CARD_TRANSACTIONS in the filegroup myfilegroup1. This means the contents of tables placed in this file group will automatically be spread across three physical disks. The key to getting the best performance out of a database is typically minimizing I/O. If you get anything out of this book, get this. I/O is the slowest operation a computer can do. Anything you do to facilitate I/O will make your application run faster. In this example, queries against VISA_CARD_TRANSACTIONS table would be spread across the three disks, thereby improving performance. Three disk heads are faster than one. The impact of this feature puts SQL Server 7 in a new league.

## The Importance of Secondary Files

Now let's talk about why secondary files are so important. Let's say you work for Visa International, a wholly owned subsidiary of Database Technologies Inc. You have been given the task of storing all the VISA transactions within a SQL Server 7 database. You start to load the transaction in your primary file. You quickly find out that your primary file has exceeded the maximum file size supported by an NT file system. Do you go off in a corner and cry? No, you call super secondary file to the rescue. This ability to create multiple secondary files associated with a primary file gives you virtually limitless storage capacity. You got it—with the ability to support secondary files, SQL Server 7 allows you to build multiterabyte databases. This is just the tip of the iceberg. You can use this concept to separate tables from indexes, and so on and so on.

> **VIP:** Our experience has taught us that you must pay attention to the size of the primary filegroups. It contains all the system tables. System tables are the tables a database uses to manage itself. If the primary filegroup runs out of space, no new catalog information can be added to the system tables. This will stop your database, and in turn your data mart or data warehouse, from working.

## Creating a Filegroup

Now that we have discussed the concept of filegroups, let's put it to use. In the following example, we will show you how to create a database named MYDB. The datafile named mydb_primary will be associated with the primary filegroup. It will have a default size of 4Mb and grow up to 10Mb using 1Mb increments.

The datafile named MyDB_FG1_Dat1 will be associated with the user-defined filegroup MyDB_FG1_Dat1. This filegroup does not have system catalog information stored with it. This filegroup will have a default size of 1Mb. It will grow up to 10Mb in size. It will do this using 1Mb increments.

Associated with every database must be a log. In this case, the log is on a separate filegroup called MyDB_log. It has an initial size of 1Mb. It can grow to a max of 109Mb using 1Mb increments. At the very end of this stream of code, we show you how to make MyDB_FG1 the default filegroup. This is very advantageous. Many times, you want the system catalog information separated from the data. The next listing brings the preceding theory to life:

```
use master
go
create database mydb
on primary
( name='mydb_primary',
filename='c:\mssql7\data\mydb_prm.mdf',
size=4mb,
maxsize=10mb,
filegrowth=1),
filegroup mydb_fg1
( name = 'mydb_fg1_dat1',
filename = 'c:\mssql7\data\mydb_fg1_1.ndf',
size = 1mb,
maxsize=10,
filegrowth=1),
log on
( name='mydb_log',
filename='c:\mssql7\data\mydb.ldf',
size=1,
```

```
maxsize=10,
filegrowth=1)
go
alter database mydb
modify filegroup mydb_fg1 default
go
use mydb
create table mytable
( cola int primary key,
colb char(8) )
on mydb_fg1
go
on mydb_fg1
go
```

As you can see, you can very easily separate the I/O stream across numerous devices. This includes data, indexes, and logs. Figure 10-3 is a graphical representation of what we have just accomplished with the previous listing.

Using Transact-SQL is great for the code warriors among us, but we know that there are some among us that are not code warriors. For these mouse babies, you

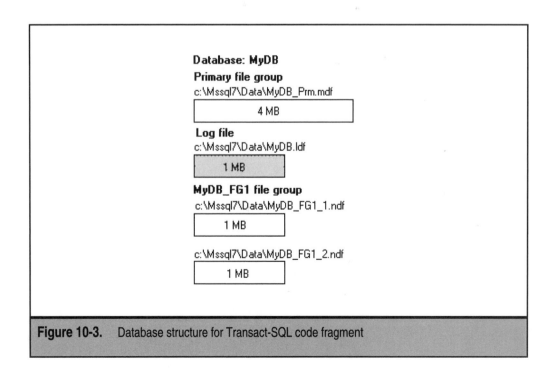

**Figure 10-3.**    Database structure for Transact-SQL code fragment

can accomplish this same task using SQL Server Enterprise Manager. It takes just a few easy steps:

1.  Open SQL Server 7 Enterprise Manager.

2.  Expand a server group, then expand a server to display a screen similar to that shown in Figure 10-4.

3.  Expand databases.

4.  Right-click the database to increase. Figures 10-5 and 10-6 show you what your options are after selecting this step.

5.  Click Properties.

6.  To increase the dataspace, click the General tab. To increase the transaction log space, click the Transaction Log tab.

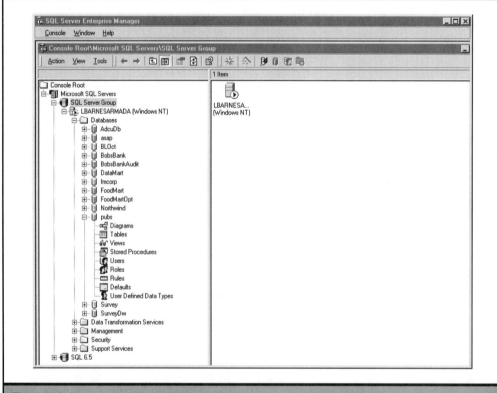

**Figure 10-4.**  SQL Server Enterprise Manager

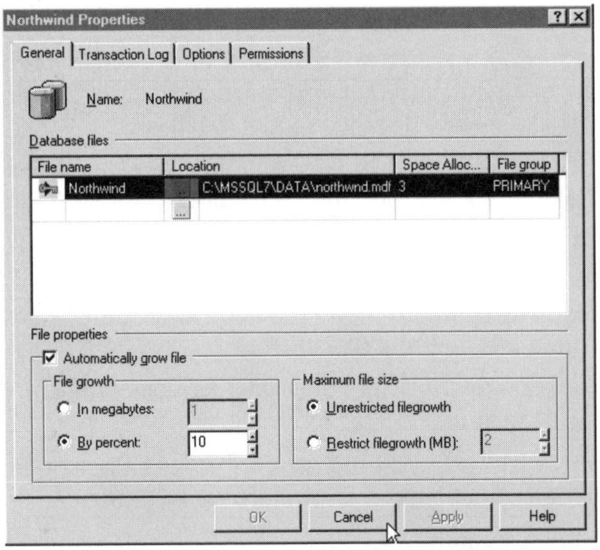

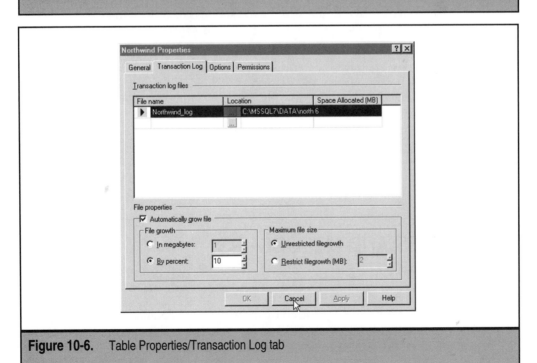

**Figure 10-5.** Table Properties/General tab

**Figure 10-6.** Table Properties/Transaction Log tab

7. In the File name column, click the next empty row and enter the filename that will contain the additional space.

8. The file location is generated automatically and given the .ndf suffix for a database file, or an .ldf suffix for a transaction log file. The initial size of the file is the default size specified for the model database.

9. To change the default values provided in the File name, Location, Space Allocated (MB), and File group (not applicable for the transaction log) columns, click the cell you want to change and enter the new value.

10. Specify how the file should grow:

   ■ To allow the currently selected file to grow as more data space is needed, click Automatically grow file.

   ■ To specify that the file should grow by fixed increments, click In megabytes and specify a value.

   ■ To specify that the file should grow by a percentage of the current file size, click By percent and specify a value.

11. Specify the file size limit:

   ■ To allow the file to grow as much as necessary, click Unrestricted filegrowth.

   ■ To specify the maximum size the file should be allowed to grow to, click Restrict filegrowth (MB) and specify a value.

The maximum database size is determined by the amount of disk space available and the licensing limits determined by the version of SQL Server you are using. An option you have is to make user filegroups read-only. The data cannot be altered, but the catalog can still be modified to allow work like permissions management.

Another interesting feature is that SQL Server 7 databases can be detached from a server and reattached to either another server or the same server. This is especially useful in making databases that are distributed for use on a customer's local SQL Server.

Now that we have you excited about using files and filegroups, we should also warn you about the rules that you must play by; these are discussed in the next section.

# RULES OF FILES AND FILEGROUPS

You thought you were going to get off easy...we think not! Rules, rules, and did we mention rules? Considerations for files and filegroups include the following:

   ▼ A file or filegroup cannot be used by more than one database. For example, the files sales.mdf and sales.ndf, which contain data and objects from the SALES database, cannot be used by any other database.

■ A file can only be a member of one filegroup.

■ Tables, indexes, and text, ntext, and image data can be associated with a filegroup—in which case, all their pages will be allocated in that filegroup.

■ Data and log information cannot be part of the same file or filegroup. Datafiles and log files are always separate.

■ Log files are never part of any filegroups. Log space is managed separately from data space.

▲ Files in a filegroup will not auto-grow as long as there is no space available on any of the files in the filegroup.

Now you could easily say, "I know what they are, I know what my rules are, how do I use them?" Funny you should ask; this is exactly what we will discuss next. Let's take a closer look at how you can put this awesome feature to good use.

## Using Files and Filegroups

Filegroups use a proportional fill strategy across all the files within each filegroup. As data is written to the filegroup, an amount proportional to the free space in the file is written to each file within the filegroup, rather than writing all the data to the first file until full, and then to the next file. For example, if file myfile1 has 100Mb free, and file myfile2 has 200Mb free, one extent is allocated from file myfile1, and two extents from file myfile2, and so on. This way, both files become full at about the same time and simple striping is achieved.

As we learned earlier, using files and filegroups improves database performance by allowing a database to be created across multiple disks and multiple disk controllers. For example, if your computer has four disks, you can create a database that comprises three datafiles and one log file, with one file on each disk. As data is accessed, four read/write heads can simultaneously access the data in parallel, which speeds up database operations.

Another fact is that files and filegroups allow better data placement because a table can be created in a specific filegroup. This improves performance because all I/O for a specific table can be directed at a specific disk. For example, a heavily used table can be placed on one file in one filegroup, located on one disk, and the other less heavily accessed tables in the database can be placed on the other files in another filegroup, located on a second disk. The authors have found the following to be good rules to live by when using files and filegroups:

▼ Most data marts will work well with a single log file. However, in a high-OLTP environment, this may not be appropriate.

■ Only use the primary file for system tables and objects, and create at least one secondary file to store user data and objects.

■ To maximize performance, create files or filegroups on as many different local physical disks as are available, and place objects that compete heavily for space in different filegroups.

■ Use filegroups to allow the placement of objects on specific physical disks.

■ Place heavily accessed tables and the nonclustered indexes belonging to those tables on different filegroups. This will improve performance due to parallel I/O if the files are located on different physical disks.

▲ Do not place the log file(s) on the same physical disk with the other files and filegroups.

Another big value added to the entire data mart strategy is the data type you can choose to use. SQL Server 7 gives you access to many efficient data types. The data type you choose to use can affect the overall performance and storage requirements for the data mart. Let's take a closer look at the data types available in SQL Server 7.

# DATA TYPES

Each column, local variable, expression, and parameter has a data type. The set of system-supplied SQL Server 7 data types is shown next. User-defined data types, which are aliases for system-supplied data types, can also be defined.

## Using Data Types

Objects that contain data have an associated data type that defines the kind of data (character, integer, binary, and so on) the object can contain. The following objects have data types:

▼ Columns in tables and views

■ Parameters in stored procedures

■ Variables

■ Transact-SQL functions that return one or more data values of a specific data type

▲ Stored procedures that have a return code, which always has an integer data type

Assigning a data type to an object defines four attributes of the object:

1. The kind of data contained by the object—for example, character, integer, or binary

2. The length of the stored value, or its size

3. The precision of the number (numeric data types only)

4. The scale of the number (numeric data types only)

If an object is defined as money, it can contain up to 19 digits, four of which can be to the right of the decimal. The object uses 8 bytes to store the data. The money data type therefore has a precision of 19, a scale of 4, and a length of 8. Transact-SQL has base data types as described in the next few sections.

## Integers

▼ **Bit**—Integer data with either a 1 or 0 value.

■ **Int**—Integer (whole number) data from -2^31 (-2,147,483,648) through 2^31 - 1 (2,147,483,647).

■ **Smallint**—Integer data from 2^15 (-32,768) through 2^15 - 1 (32,767).

▲ **Tinyint**—Integer data from 0 through 255.

## Decimal and Numeric

▼ **Decimal**—Fixed precision and scale numeric data from -10^38 -1 through 10^38 -1.

▲ **Numeric**—A synonym for decimal.

## Money and Smallmoney

▼ **Money**—Monetary data values from -2^63 (-922,337,203,685,477.5808) through 2^63 - 1 (+922,337,203,685,477.5807), with accuracy to a ten-thousandth of a monetary unit.

▲ **Smallmoney**—Monetary data values from -214,748.3648 through +214,748.3647, with accuracy to a ten-thousandth of a monetary unit.

## Approximate Numerics

▼ **Float**—Floating precision number data from -1.79E + 308 through 1.79E + 308.

▲ **Real**—Floating precision number data from -3.40E + 38 through 3.40E + 38.

## Datetime and Smalldatetime

▼ **Datetime**—Date and time data from January 1, 1753 to December 31, 9999, with an accuracy of three-hundredths of a second, or 3.33 milliseconds.

▲ **Smalldatetime**—Date and time data from January 1, 1900 through June 6, 2079, with an accuracy of one minute.

## Numerics

▼ **Cursor**—A reference to a cursor.

■ **Timestamp**—Database-wide unique number.

▲ **Uniqueidentifier**—A globally unique identifier (GUID).

## Character Strings

▼ **Char**—Fixed-length non-Unicode character data with a maximum length of 8,000 characters.

■ **Varchar**—Variable-length non-Unicode data with a maximum of 8,000 characters.

▲ **Text**—Variable-length non-Unicode data with a maximum length of 2^31 - 1 (2,147,483,647) characters.

## Unicode Character Strings

▼ **Nchar**—Fixed-length Unicode data with a maximum length of 4,000 characters.

■ **Nvarchar**—Variable-length Unicode data with a maximum length of 4,000 characters.**sysname** is a system-supplied user-defined data type that is a synonym for **nvarchar(128)** and is used to reference database object names.

▲ **Ntext**—Variable-length Unicode data with a maximum length of 2^30 - 1 (1,073,741,823) characters.

## Binary Strings

▼ **Binary**—Fixed-length binary data with a maximum length of 8,000 bytes.

■ **Varbinary**—Variable-length binary data with a maximum length of 8,000 bytes.

▲ **Image**—Variable-length binary data with a maximum length of 2^31 - 1 (2,147,483,647) bytes.

## Synonyms

As we can see in Table 10-1 data type synonyms are included for SQL-92 compatibility within SQL Server.

All data stored in SQL Server 7 must be compatible with one of these base data types. You also have the option of creating your own data types as extensions or supersets of the base types. Let us take a closer look at how that can be accomplished, and more importantly, once you have created your data type, how to use it in a table.

## User-Defined Data Types

Another powerful capability in SQL Server 7 is that you can also create your own user-defined data types. For example, you may want to create a data type called "birthday," a datetime that allows NULL values. From SQL Server Query Analyzer, you would enter the following Transact-SQL statement. The *SQL Server Query Analyzer*

| Synonym | Mapped to System Data Type |
|---------|---------------------------|
| Binary varying | varbinary |
| Char varying | varchar |
| Character | char |
| Character | char(1) |
| Character(n) | char(n) |
| Character varying(n) | varchar(n) |
| Dec | decimal |
| Double precision | float |
| Float[(n)] for n = 1-7 | real |
| Float[(n)] for n = 8-15 | float |
| Integer | int |
| National character(n) | nchar(n) |
| National char(n) | nchar(n) |
| National character varying(n) | nvarchar(n) |
| National char varying(n) | nvarchar(n) |
| National text | ntext |
| Numeric | decimal |

**Table 10-1.**   Synonyms Mapped to System Data Types

allows you to create and run Transact-SQL; it can be accessed from the SQL Server 7 Program Group.

Next is an example of the Transact-SQL used to create the new data type of birthday.

```
exec sp_addtype birthday, datetime, 'NULL'
go
```

Once you have created your new data type, you could use it in a table in your data mart. Again, in SQL Server Query Analyzer, you would type in Transact-SQL statements similar to the following, then execute them:

```
create table mytable
(emp_id char(5),
emp_first_name char(30),
```

```
emp_last_name char(40),
emp_middle_initial char(1),
emp_address char(40),
emp_birthday birthday)
```

User-defined data types are always defined in terms of a base data type. They provide a mechanism for applying a name to a data type that is more descriptive of the types of values to be held within the object, or to save you time by defining a type that will have common properties and be used often. This can make it easier for a programmer or database administrator to understand the intended use of any object defined with the data type.

Now that you know everything about data types, how would you use that knowledge? The next section takes a closer look at setting data types to columns of a table.

# ASSIGNING DATA TYPES TO A COLUMN

A column's data type determines what kind of data can be stored in the column. When creating a table, after entering the column name, the next choice presented to you is a list of system-defined data types that appears in the Datatype property column. Figure 10-7 shows an example of creating a new table.

You can choose the appropriate data type for the information you want to store in the column. If user-defined data types exist for your database, they appear at the end of the data type list. The system-defined data type that corresponds to the user-defined data type appears in parentheses at the end of the user-defined data type name. For example: "ssno (varchar)."

## Assigning a User-Defined Data Type to a Column

The following points are worth noting when doing this assignment:

▼ Selecting a data type automatically sets the length, precision, and scale for the column, based on the data type's definition.

■ You cannot change these settings for user-defined data types.

■ You can change the Allow Nulls setting only if the user-defined data type allows null values.

▲ When you select a user-defined data type, the default setting is blank, even if a bound default is defined for the data type.

Changing the data type re-creates the table in the database when you save the table or diagram. If this column is related to columns in other tables, then the data type of the related columns must also be changed to preserve referential integrity. If your organization has a multinational presence, you will be very interested in the next section.

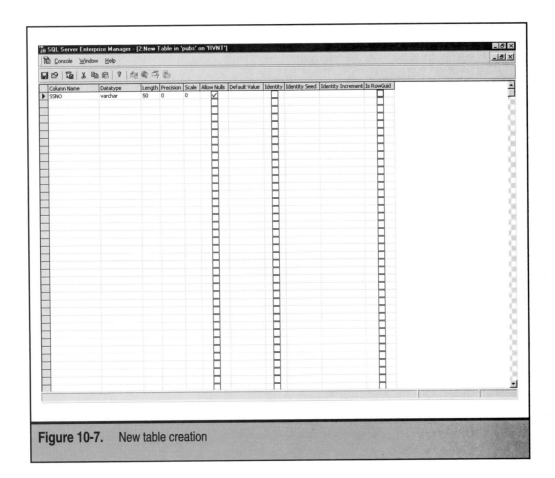

**Figure 10-7.**    New table creation

In that section, we discuss the use of Unicode data. Let's take a closer look at what Unicode is, and how you may put it to use.

# USING UNICODE DATA

The Unicode specification defines a single encoding scheme for practically all characters widely used in businesses around the world. All computers consistently translate the bit patterns in Unicode data into characters using the single Unicode specification. This ensures that the same bit pattern is always converted to the same characters on all computers. Data can be freely transferred from one database or computer to another without concern that the receiving system will correctly translate the bit patterns into characters.

One problem with data types that use one byte to encode each character is that the data type can only represent 256 different characters. This forces multiple encoding specifications (or code pages) for different alphabets such as European alphabets, which are relatively small. It is also impossible to handle systems such as the Japanese Kanji or Korean Hangul alphabets that have thousands of characters.

SQL Server 7 translates the bit patterns in char, varchar, and text columns to characters using the definitions in the code page installed with SQL Server. Client computers use the code page installed with the operating system to interpret character bit patterns. There are many different code pages. Some characters appear on some code pages, but not on others. Some characters are defined with one bit pattern on some code pages, and with a different bit pattern on other code pages. When building international systems that must handle different languages, it becomes difficult to pick code pages for all the computers that meet the language requirements of multiple countries. It is also difficult to ensure that every computer performs the correct translations when interfacing with a system using a different code page.

The Unicode specification addresses this problem by using two bytes to encode each character. There are enough different patterns (65,536) in two bytes for a single specification covering the most common business languages. Because all Unicode systems consistently use the same bit patterns to represent all characters, there is no problem with characters being converted incorrectly when moving from one system to another. In SQL Server 7, these data types support Unicode data:

▼ nchar

■ nvarchar

▲ ntext

The "n" prefix for the above data types comes from the SQL-92 standard for national (Unicode) data types. Use of nchar, nvarchar, and ntext is the same as char, varchar, and text, respectively, except:

▼ Unicode supports a wider range of characters.

■ More space is needed to store Unicode characters.

■ The maximum size of nchar and nvarchar columns is 4,000 characters, not 8,000 characters like char and varchar.

▲ Unicode constants are specified with a leading N (e.g., N'A Unicode string').

## Unicode Data

Traditional, non-Unicode data types in SQL Server 7 allow the use of characters, which are defined, by a particular character set. A character set is chosen during SQL Server setup and is immutable throughout the lifetime of the installation. Using Unicode data types, a column can store any character that is defined by the Unicode standard, which includes all of the characters that are defined in the various character sets. Using Unicode data types takes twice as much storage space as non-Unicode data types.

Unicode data is stored using the nchar, nvarchar, and ntext data types in SQL Server. Use these data types for columns that store characters from more than one character set. Use nvarchar when a column varies in the number of Unicode characters (up to 4,000) between rows. Use nchar when every row has the same fixed length (up to 4,000 Unicode characters) for the same column. Columns of the ntext data type can be used to store more than 4,000 Unicode characters in each row for the same column.

As mentioned at the beginning of this chapter, the purpose was to give you the knowledge to take your data mart from a good one to a great one. Use data types to your advantage. Use file groups to help stripe your data. With this bag of tricks, you are well on your way. After this exposé of things you can do for your data mart using SQL Server 7, we are confident that you can see why we are absolutely excited about these advanced features. Which ones you choose and how you deploy your data mart are your choices. Now you know what options you have to tweak your data mart. In the next chapter, we will take an in-depth look at backing up you data mart or warehouse.

# CHAPTER 11

## Backing Up the Warehouse

P rior to addressing backup, it is helpful to review how SQL Server 7 stores your data—the manner in which it stores data is crucial to a successful backup. Let's get started by first looking at how data is stored in SQL Server 7. Our experience has shown that coming to grips with issues such as storage enhances one's overall understanding of the product.

# SQL SERVER 7—HOW DATA IS STORED

SQL Server 7 is structured into databases and files. Out of the box, SQL Server 7 has four system databases, each of which consists of two files—a data file with an .mdf extension and a log file with an .ldf extension. If you are using SQL Server 7 replication, another system database called DISTRIBUTION will be created to handle the replication settings. *Replication* allows you to share the load among two or more servers, and SQL Server 7 will automatically transfer the data between servers, allowing the user to specify when and which data is transferred. You might have users from accounting on one server while marketing users connect to the other server, or you might have one server in Tokyo and a second in Tel Aviv. All data and log files are created by default in the C:\MSSQL7\DATA directory. The next listing shows a directory listing after SQL Server 7 is installed and replication is enabled, assuming you accepted the suggested defaults.

```
Volume in drive C is C DBTECH
Volume Serial Number is 243E-16FB
Directory of C:\MSSQL7\Data

.                    <DIR>          17/12/99   10:41 .
..                   <DIR>          17/12/99   10:41 ..
DISTMDL    LDF      1,048,576   19/12/99    0:48 distmdl.ldf
DISTMDL    MDF      2,621,440   19/12/99    0:48 distmdl.mdf
DISTRI~1   LDF      1,048,576   19/12/99    0:48 distribution.LDF
DISTRI~1   MDF      3,145,728   25/12/99    9:58 distribution.MDF
MASTER     MDF      7,602,176   23/12/99   22:29 master.mdf
MASTLOG    LDF      1,048,576   23/12/99   22:29 mastlog.ldf
MODEL      MDF        786,432   23/12/99   22:29 model.mdf
MODELLOG   LDF        786,432   23/12/99   22:29 modellog.ldf
MSDBDATA   MDF      7,340,032   25/12/99    9:57 msdbdata.mdf
MSDBLOG    LDF      1,048,576   25/12/99    9:59 msdblog.ldf
NORTHWND   LDF      5,832,704   23/12/99   22:29 northwnd.ldf
NORTHWND   MDF      3,080,192   23/12/99   22:18 northwnd.mdf
PUBS       MDF      1,835,008   25/12/99    9:58 pubs.mdf
PUBS_LOG   LDF        516,096   23/12/99   22:29 pubs_log.ldf
TEMPDB     MDF      2,097,152   25/12/99    9:55 TEMPDB.MDF
TEMPLOG    LDF        786,432   25/12/99    9:59 TEMPLOG.LDF
16 file(s)     40,621,408 bytes
        2 dir(s)    1,528,549,376 bytes free
```

Together, these files make up the MASTER, MODEL, MSDB, TEMPDB, DISTRIBUTION, PUBS, and NORTHWIND databases. The first three are system databases that must exist just for SQL Server 7 to start. TEMPDB is used for temporary storage and is automatically re-created at startup, if it does not already exist. *PUBS* and *NORTHWIND* are sample databases that can be used for training, testing, or tutorials. Table 11-1 describes the physical configuration of the databases highlighted in the previous listing.

| Database | Description | Data File | Log File |
|----------|-------------|-----------|----------|
| MASTER | Contains a record of all other databases in the system. Without a MASTER database, SQL Server 7 will not start. | MASTER | MASTLOG |
| MODEL | This database contains a template for new databases, except DISTRIBUTION. Like the MASTER database, MODEL must exist when SQL Server 7 starts. | MODEL | MODELLOG |
| MSDB | Contains all scheduled jobs and alerts. Must exist at startup. | MSDBDATA | MSDBLOG |
| TEMPDB | This file is automatically deleted on shutdown, re-created on startup, and autogrows as needed. You should not back up this table. | TEMPDB | TEMPLOG |

**Table 11-1.**    SQL Server 7 System and Sample Databases

| Database | Description | Data File | Log File |
|----------|-------------|-----------|----------|
| DISTRIBUTION | This database maintains all the settings for replications to successfully work. | DISTRIBUTION | DISTMODEL_LOG |
| PUBS | A sample database. | PUBS | PUBS_LOG |
| NORTHWIND | Another sample database. | NORTHWND | NORTHWND |

**Table 11-1.**    SQL Server 7 System and Sample Databases (*continued*)

Enterprise Manager is Microsoft's graphical interface that allows you to administer SQL Server 7, displaying all the databases, tables, backup devices, and other attributes of SQL Server 7. If you go into Enterprise Manager, most of these databases will be hidden by default, and only PUBS and NORTHWIND (two sample databases) will be visible. In order to view the system databases, you need to right-click on the server icon in the left pane of the Enterprise Manager main console, select Edit SQL Server Registration, and mark the Show System Databases and System Objects check box.

Do yourself a favor—don't try to modify the system databases directly. For example, the MASTER database contains a table with all the backup devices. Rather than modifying this table, use stored procedures, which are precompiled miniprograms that perform specific functions. Microsoft has thoughtfully provided a number of stored procedures to maintain the server, such as **sp_addumpdevice**, which creates a dump device for backup. Let's now move on to the meat of backing up the warehouse.

# BACKING UP THE WAREHOUSE

Many moons ago, Thak the caveperson drew pictures of each hunt on the walls of the cave. After a while, soot from the fire started to build up on the walls and obscure the drawings, so Thak decided to copy the drawings onto the walls of a spare cave in order to preserve the memories. The result: the first backup. In this particular case, it didn't help because Thak was eaten by a saber-toothed tiger as he left the cave.

A backup may not have helped Thak, but in the age of data warehousing it's critical. The warehouse may contain huge amounts of data that has taken years to accumulate. SQL Server 7 now accommodates single files of up to 32Tb (where a terabyte is 1,099,511,627,776 bytes), and a database can now be as large as 1,048,516Tb! Users have become accustomed to, and expect access to, this data without impediments, and a database crash can take a system offline for days. The key to recovering quickly is a carefully thought out and implemented backup strategy. We will take a look at the why, what, when, and how of backing up your server. If it initially seems overwhelming, welcome to the club! The first question that always comes up will be addressed next.

# Why Bother with Backup Anyway?

The "why" of backing up is obvious–you probably like your job, and as a database administrator (DBA) you have a responsibility to keep the users working. People who maintain database servers the likes of SQL Server 7 back up because "stuff happens," or something like that. In an online transaction-processing system (OLTP), every minute that the database is down could mean dollars, jobs, or—in the case of critical systems— even lives. Backups are used in cases of both system and user errors. In a warehouse environment, you may be able to re-create your data by reloading from your OLTP systems, but the time needed to transform terabytes of data from multiple systems could leave your warehouse down for days. Your backup is insurance for your data and just like deciding on the appropriate amount of insurance for your car, you need to decide how long you can afford to be without the warehouse. The answer to this question will shape your decisions regarding backup. There are people out there that wouldn't think of driving an uninsured car, but go along either unaware or ignorant of the fact that the only thing that is keeping the warehouse running is the thin cushion of air between a read/write head and a metal disk that's spinning at 5,400 rpm. The next few sections will help shape your backup strategy.

# What to Back Up

The obvious answer to the previous question is "the database," but that will only get you partial credit. SQL Server 7 requires three items to properly operate the warehouse:

▼   The system databases

■   The user databases

▲   The user database logs

All these items need to be backed up on a regular basis. The problem arises when you take into account the size of the warehouse. Current tape backup formats such as *digital linear tape* (DLT) can back up 70Gb in about 2 hours, but a large warehouse on the order of 1Tb would take 24 hours to complete—you would have to continuously run the backup just to keep up!

There are two ways to reduce the volume of data that needs regular backup:

▼   **Separating files into live and static data**—Live data is data that grows and changes with feeds from your OLTP systems, whereas static data is data that will not change, such as sales transactions from the previous year.

▲ **Taking advantage of differential and log file backups**—Rather than backing up the entire database with every backup, you can just store the changes to the database since the last backup (a differential backup), or a list of transactions needed to bring a restored database back to the current state (a log file backup). As you create or update information in the database, you not only update the data itself, but you add to a list of changes made to the data. If the server crashes, you just need to restore the database's last full backup and apply the changes that were recorded.

Let's go down one more level in the great backup discussion and look at some SQL Server 7 specifics.

## Filegroups

With SQL Server 7, *filegroups* are logical groupings of data onto one or more physical files. Filegroups allow you to optimize how the server accesses data on the disk by specifying that tables exist on specific physical drives. They also make backups easier in some cases by grouping data into smaller chunks that can be backed up more quickly. Another use of filegroups is to allow static data to be backed up only when it is manually modified. Some data, such as your sales for 1997, is inherently static, and this makes backups much easier. SQL Server 7 makes this easy by providing file and filegroup backups. Normally, you wouldn't use a filegroup backup on live data unless your warehouse was much too large to back up any other way. In order to make use of this feature, you need to create at least one additional file segment for the database, giving it a different filegroup name. Depending on the size of your static data, you may want more than one filegroup so the data can be divided up logically. In order to do this, through Enterprise Manager, select the database and edit the properties as shown in Figure 11-1.

The act of creating multiple datafiles can also be done using a Transact-SQL script, as shown in the following listing:

```
alter database warehouse
add filegroup static
go
alter database warehouse
add file
( name = 'Warehouse_Static',
filename = 'c:\mssql7\data\warehouse_static_data.ndf',
size = 5mb,
maxsize = 100mb,
filegrowth = 5mb)
to filegroup static
go
```

SQL Server 7 will respond with the following:

```
Extending database by 5.00 MB on disk 'Warehouse_Static'.
```

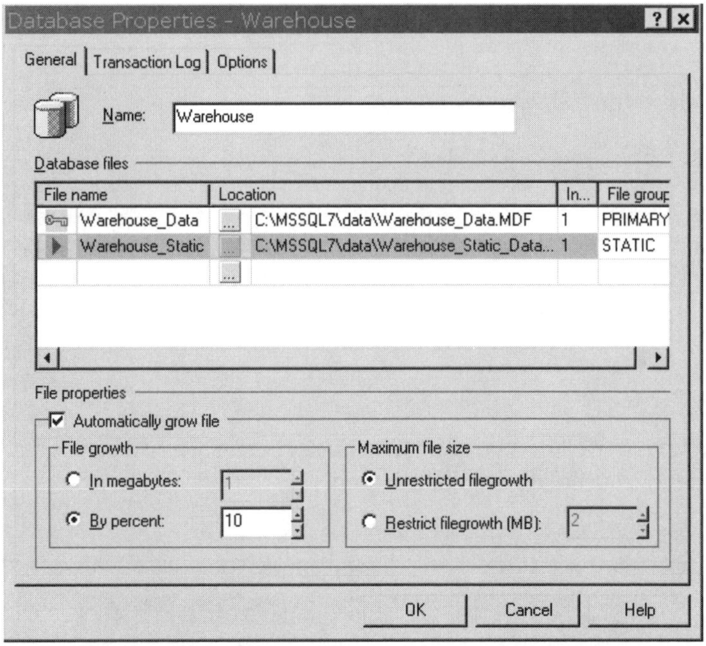

**Figure 11-1.** Creating multiple database files with Enterprise Manager

Once you have defined the filegroup, you can then place the file into the filegroup by using the Action | Design Table menu and selecting Table and Index Properties as shown in Figure 11-2.

The task is accomplished by selecting the Table File Group and the Text File Group and setting both to STATIC, the filegroup we created in the previous step. Close the window and save the changes to the table. Enterprise Manager will create a new table, copy all data, constraints, and indexes over to the new table, drop the old table, then rename the new table to the old name. If you have a large table, this process may take a while. There isn't an easy procedure for this in Transact-SQL, so it is advisable to use Enterprise Manager to make this change.

Dividing even dynamic tables into filegroups is another great way to limit the amount of data or the frequency of backups. If you have a limited window in which to perform your backups, filegroups will let you back up some tables in one window and other tables during the next window.

In order to make sure that static data is not changed without your knowledge, it is critical that you mark the filegroup as read-only with a SQL statement similar to that shown in the following listing:

```
alter database warehouse
modify file
group static readonly
```

This should return the following message:

```
The filegroup property 'READONLY' has been set.
```

If this message doesn't appear, you may not have exclusive access to the table. Make sure that there aren't any users accessing the table, and ensure that the database is not selected in Enterprise Manager. If, at some point in the future, it does become necessary to load additional data into a read-only table, mark the table as read/write as shown here:

```
alter database warehouse
modify filegroup static readwrite
```

After you have performed your maintenance, perform a full backup of the filegroup, then mark the filegroup read-only once again.

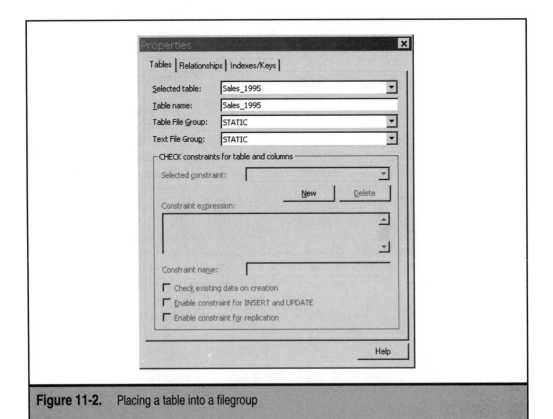

**Figure 11-2.** Placing a table into a filegroup

## Differential and Log File Backups

In addition to backing up the complete database, there are two additional types of backups that can be performed—log file and differential backups. A *log file* backup contains all the transactions that have been performed on a database since the last full backup or the last log file backup. Log files contain all transactions that have changed data on the database. During a full backup, all transactions are committed to the database and the logs are then truncated. As transactions occur, the log file grows. When these files are backed up, they are automatically truncated to keep them from growing too large. If you need to restore the database using log files, you must restore the last full backup of the database, then restore each and every log file in order to make sure that data integrity is maintained. The problem is that this procedure could be very slow if you have many log file backups. One important thing to note is that when you define a database, you must make sure that the database option for Truncate Log on Checkpoint is disabled. If it is enabled, SQL Server 7 will automatically purge the log every time a transaction hits a checkpoint such as a **commit** statement. If you do not intend to use log file backups, then enable the option to prevent the log files from growing until they consume all disk space.

A differential backup contains all the changes to a database since the last *full* backup. In order for a database to be successfully restored to the point it was before the restore became necessary, you need to have a full backup and any changes made since that backup was written. Differential backups are usually only a fraction of the size of the full database and can consequently be performed much more quickly. If a restore becomes necessary, all you need to do is restore the full backup followed by the differential backup. The drawback is that a differential backup will grow in size until it contains too much data to easily copy to tape. Once this happens, it is best to create a full backup, then resume differential backups. A normal pattern for this is to perform a differential backup each night from Monday through Thursday and a full backup on Friday. If you need to back up more frequently than this, then perform log file backups on a regular basis during the day, appending them to the differential backup. This means that if you need to restore, you need the full backup tape and the differential/log file tape.

You cannot combine file or filegroup backups with differential or log file backups. If all of your data is relatively static (that is, only updated by a manual process), then you might want to use filegroup backups. Otherwise, differential and log file backups would be a better choice.

## Backing Up the System Databases

Once SQL Server 7 is set up, you *must* back up each of the system databases separately. The critical databases are MASTER, MODEL, MSDB, and DISTRIBUTION (if you are using replication). The MASTER database cannot be backed up by using a differential backup or log files—you must perform a full backup. The others can be backed up with the other methods, but since these databases tend to be small, you should perform full backups of these databases, too. These databases should be backed up regularly, because having current backups will make recovery much easier. In order to make restoring easier, you can do a cold backup of the MASTER database. A *cold backup* is performed when SQL Server 7 is shut down and has unlocked the database files. This contrasts with a *hot backup*, which is done with SQL Server 7 active and providing the data to the backup system. When the server is running, access to the database files is limited to the server application itself. In order to do this, you need to stop the MSSQLServer service and then copy the MASTER.MDF and MASTER.LDF files from the \MSSQL7\DATA directory. Once you have copied them, you can place them on a network drive or back them up to tape with the Windows NT backup utility. In the event of a crash, you can restore these files first. The next big question is when the data should be backed up…ready, set, go!

# When to Back Up Your Data

"When" refers to two separate aspects—what time of day and how frequently should you back up the warehouse. First of all, we have to decide what time, but there are a number of things to consider. Any backup, whether a tape backup or a dump to disk, will consume a fair amount of resources in terms of processors, RAM, disk time, and, possibly, network bandwidth. This will definitely have an impact on the users, possibly a significant one, depending on the current load of SQL Server 7. The obvious time to back up is at night, but you need to take into consideration that data loading may be occurring or that you may have geographically scattered users that are trying to do their jobs halfway around the world.

The second part of the "when" question is how frequently should you back up. There is no easy answer to this—you have to ask yourself how much data can you afford to lose. An OLTP system may have a window that is measured in minutes. For example, if an airline loses 10 minutes of transactions, there could be millions of dollars in losses. On the other hand, a warehouse with weekly refreshes of the data doesn't need nearly the same level of backup.

With a high-volume OLTP system, you might do a complete database backup at 2:00 A.M., differential backups every hour, and log file backups every 10 minutes. If the server were to fail at 4:28 A.M., you would need to restore the 2:00 A.M. full backup, the 4:00 A.M. differential backup, and the 4:10 A.M. and 4:20 A.M. log file backups, and hopefully you could access the active log file. If not, you would lose the last 8 minutes worth of transactions.

In a warehouse, the concern lies with any ongoing data feeds from an OLTP system or via transformation tools such as Ardent's DataStage or the Data Transformation Services (DTS) included with SQL Server 7. Transformation tools allow you to bring data into the warehouse from many different systems that might use different codes to describe the same thing. For example, an accounts receivable system may indicate that a back-ordered item has a status code of "1," but the inventory system marks back orders with a "B". For more information about DTS, take a look at Chapter 8. Your backup will have to be specific to the needs of your warehouse, but using static tables, periodic full backups, and regular differential and log file backups will get you up and running again in no time. A good compromise might be a differential backup at 8:00 P.M. and log file backups every four hours from midnight to 4:00 A.M. The operator would then just have to change the tape once before going home for the cycle to continue.

With the aid of the SQL Server 7 Agent, you can (and should!) back up your database on an automated schedule. The involvement of a user on a day-to-day basis should be limited to replacing tapes and checking the logs to make sure that the backup completed successfully.

# How to Back Up the Warehouse

Microsoft has completely redone the internal backup routines in SQL Server 7 as compared to earlier versions. SQL Server 7 has the ability to dump a database to a Microsoft Windows NT Backup format tape while the database is up and running. There are a number of steps involved in successfully backing up SQL Server 7. Let's look at those steps in some detail.

## Defining a Backup Device

SQL Server 7 understands three different types of backup devices: tape, disk, and named pipes. You can create a tape or disk backup device from the Enterprise Manager. Named pipe devices are created and used by third-party backup utilities such as Computer Associates Arcserve or Seagate Backup.

To define a backup device, select Backup Devices in Enterprise Manager, right-click on it, and select New Backup Device. You must then give the device a name that refers to the tape or directory that you will be backing up to, and then select Tape or File. If you select Tape, you need to tell SQL Server 7 the physical device name for the tape, which is usually \\.\TAPE0 for the first tape device connected to the system. Only tape drives that are supported by the Windows NT backup utility and physically connected to the database server will work with SQL Server 7.

You can verify that your system has the driver loaded by opening up the Control Panel and selecting Tape Devices. If you see the name of the device and (loaded) next to it, you're ready to go. For a File backup, enter the path and filename for the backup. This may be a local drive or a network drive. In order to specify a remote drive, use the *universal naming convention* (UNC) path which describes a computer, a shared folder, and the directories under it; for example, \\AVIVA\DATABASE\BACKUP would save the backup files to a directory called BACKUP in a shared directory called DATABASE on the computer named AVIVA. You can have multiple backup devices in a single directory as long as they have separate physical files. Figure 11-3 shows how this is done using the Enterprise Manager.

Again, the same activity can be accomplished with a SQL script, as shown here:

```
use master
exec sp_addumpdevice {'tape', 'Warehouse_Tape_Backup', '\\.\TAPE0'}
```

In the case of a file or named pipe backup device, replace the **tape** keyword with **disk** or **pipe**, respectively. File backups should never be on the same physical device as the

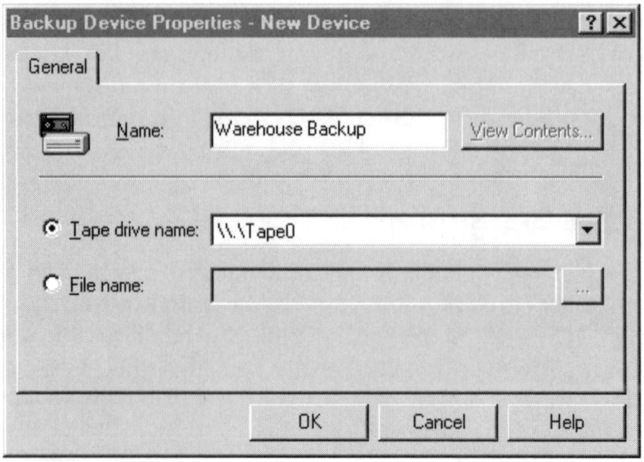

**Figure 11-3.** Creating a backup device

database, since a hard disk crash would cause you to lose both your data and your backup. If this does happen to you, assume that you are soon going to be working at the help desk again, telling people that the CD-ROM drive tray is not really a drink holder!

Strictly speaking, you do not need to create a backup device to do a backup since SQL Server 7 will allow you to explicitly back up to a specific tape or directory, but they provide an easy way to ensure that backups are done in a consistent location with standard settings. The third-party utilities will take care of the backup device themselves, relieving you of any need to use them in the case of a crash.

## Performing the Backup

From Enterprise Manager, select Tools from the menu bar and click on Backup Database. After selecting the database, you can give the backup a name and select a backup type: Database Complete, Database Differential, Transaction log, or File and Filegroup. If you select File or Filegroup, you need to select which file or filegroup you wish to back up. In the Destination section, click on Add to create a location to store the data. You can either select a predefined backup device or explicitly give a location for the backup. In order to prevent accidentally overwriting data, you should use a backup device unless this is a one-time backup. Select either Append to media (yes, this does work with a file backup!) or Overwrite existing media. If you would like this to be an automated backup, select the

Schedule checkbox and click on the ellipsis button to define the schedule. You can have SQL Server 7 run your backups at startup, during idle periods, at a single predefined time, or at regular intervals ranging from minutes to months. It's important to note that the SQLServerAgent service must be running in order for automated backups to run.

The Options tab provides features that ensure that the correct tape is inserted and that data is verified after backup, along with other advanced tape management features. Once you are satisfied with the backup settings, click OK. If you selected a scheduled backup, the backup will occur at the correct time. If you did not, the backup will begin immediately. Figure 11-4 shows you the backup screen in Enterprise Manager.

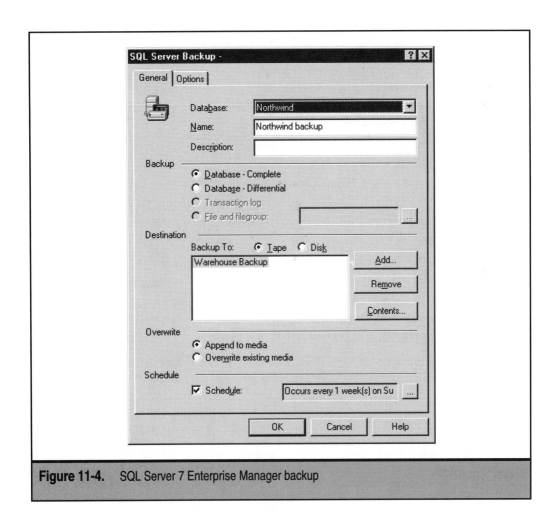

**Figure 11-4.** SQL Server 7 Enterprise Manager backup

For those of you who are curious, SQL Server 7 Executive generates the following Transact SQL code to perform the backup:

```
backup database [Warehouse]
to [Warehouse_Disk_Backup]
with  noinit ,
nounload ,
name = N'Warehouse backup',
skip ,
stats = 10,
noformat
```

In a nutshell, this tells SQL Server 7 to perform a full backup of the WAREHOUSE database to the backup device called Warehouse_Disk_Backup, with append. In addition, it should not eject the tape on completion, check the tape name or expiration date, or format the backup location (disk or tape).

SQL Server 7 also has a Backup Wizard to simplify most backup tasks. Select Tools I Wizards I Management I Backup Wizard. The wizard will ask for the following information:

▼ The database you want to back up

■ A name and description for the backup

■ The type of backup to perform (that is, a full backup, differential backup, or incremental backup—note that you cannot do a file or filegroup backup with the wizard)

■ The backup location

■ Whether you want to append or overwrite, and if you want to eject the tape when you're done (you can't eject a disk!)

▲ A media set name (for tape rotation), an expiry date (to prevent overwriting the tape prematurely), and if you want to verify after the backup is complete

Any backups performed with the wizard are done immediately—you cannot schedule the backup for later execution, which limits its functionality but makes it easy to do one-off backups.

To verify the backup, view the properties for the backup device and select View Contents. You should see your backup listed with the database name, data, and backup type. The backup log can be seen in Figure 11-5.

## Tape Rotation

When backing up a server you have to decide between cost, ease of administration, and availability of point-in-time backup issues in order to decide how many tapes you should use in order to implement your backup schedule. There are three basic strategies that we

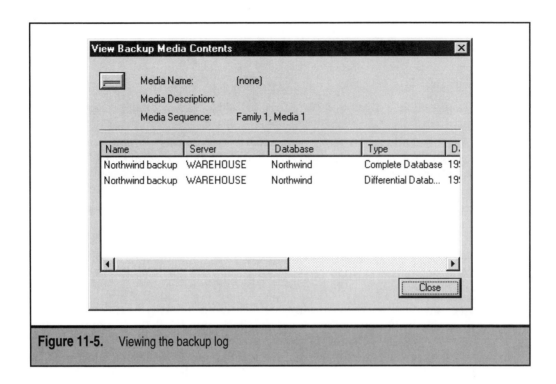

**Figure 11-5.** Viewing the backup log

will look at: son, father/son, and grandfather/father/son. In each of these, we talk about individual tapes. If your backup spans multiple tapes, think of these as tape sets with the appropriate number of tapes being used.

**SON** This is the simplest type of backup, whereby you just leave the tape in the drive and perform a full backup each night. The advantages of this are that it is cheap, because it only requires one tape, and it is easy, because the operator just needs to start the job. With a scheduled backup, this system wouldn't need any user involvement. There are a number of flaws with this system, the two biggest of which are as follows:

▼ You only have a backup from the night before, so if you find that your database is corrupt and needs to be restored to the backup from two days ago, you are out of luck.

▲ Premature tape wear, because the tape can only be used a finite number of times, and speed, because you need to perform a full backup each night.

*NOTE:* We present this son approach for completeness, but we suggest that you do not use this method.

The following table shows tape usage (actually re-usage) with the *son* implementation:

| Week | Monday | Tuesday | Wednesday | Thursday | Friday |
|------|--------|---------|-----------|----------|--------|
| 1 | Tape 1 - Full | Tape 1 - Full | Tape 1 - Full | Tape 1 - Full | Tape 1 - Full |

**FATHER/SON**   In a Father/Son setup, you need at least six tapes—four for each day Monday through Thursday, and one each Friday for a four-week period. The Father/Son scheme is highlighted here:

| Week | Monday | Tuesday | Wednesday | Thursday | Friday |
|------|--------|---------|-----------|----------|--------|
| 0 | | | | | Tape 6 - Full |
| 1 | Tape 1 - Diff | Tape 2 - Diff | Tape 3 - Diff | Tape 4 - Diff | Tape 5 - Full |
| 2 | Tape 1 - Diff | Tape 2 - Diff | Tape 3 - Diff | Tape 4 - Diff | Tape 6 - Full |

Remember that you need to perform a full backup before you do a differential backup, so we use the last tape to perform a full backup in Week 0. This tape schedule gives us the advantage of being able to go back one week in time to the specific day, and up to two weeks in time to the full backup. Tape costs are moderate since we only need six tapes, but they should be replaced regularly. Overall, this scheme provides more protection than the son rotation, but it still doesn't provide us with the robust restore capability that we like. If you do follow this scheme, it is important to rotate the Friday tapes off-site as protection in case of fire, theft, or other calamity.

**GRANDFATHER**   The Grandfather scheme is very similar to the Father/Son setup, but it allows you to keep additional backups. The following table illustrates this scheme:

| Week | Monday | Tuesday | Wednesday | Thursday | Friday |
|------|--------|---------|-----------|----------|--------|
| 0 | | | | | Tape 19 - Full |
| 1 | Tape 1 - Diff | Tape 2 - Diff | Tape 3 - Diff | Tape 4 - Diff | Tape 5 - Full |
| 2 | Tape 1 - Diff | Tape 2 – Diff | Tape 3 - Diff | Tape 4 - Diff | Tape 6 - Full |
| 3 | Tape 1 - Diff | Tape 2 – Diff | Tape 3 - Diff | Tape 4 - Diff | Tape 7 - Full |
| 4 | Tape 1 - Diff | Tape 2 – Diff | Tape 3 - Diff | Tape 4 - Diff | Tape 8 - Full |
| 5–7 | | | Same as Weeks 1–3 | | |
| 8 | Tape 1 - Diff | Tape 2 – Diff | Tape 3 - Diff | Tape 4 - Diff | Tape 9 - Full |
| 9–11 | | | Same as Weeks 1–3 | | |
| 12 | Tape 1 - Diff | Tape 2 – Diff | Tape 3 - Diff | Tape 4 - Diff | Tape 10 - Full |

This schedule is repeated, replacing the tape on every fourth Friday with a new tape. At any point in time, you can go back to any day in the previous week, any week in the previous month, and any month in the previous year. At the end of the year, you can repeat the cycle, but it is advisable that you put a new set of tapes into service as the daily tapes will be close to the end of their life expectancy. The drawback of this system is that there is a cost associated with purchasing 19 tapes a year that is close to $2,000 USD. The advantage is that the system is very straightforward to implement. Just label your tapes Monday through Thursday, Friday 1 to 3, and Month 1 to 12. As with the Father/Son system, rotate your backups off-site for disaster recovery.

**GRANDFATHER/FATHER/SON**   Two of the drawbacks of the Grandfather system are that you use a large number of tapes and that the tapes are not used evenly, contributing to the regular replacement of the tapes. The Grandfather/Father/Son system rotates the tapes themselves through each duty—Grandfather (monthly backup), Father (weekly Friday backup), and Son (daily backup). In this system, you have access to backups for each day in the previous week and each week for the last 12 weeks. The following table illustrates using the Grandfather/Father/Son system:

| Week | Monday | Tuesday | Wednesday | Thursday | Friday |
|---|---|---|---|---|---|
| 0 | | | | | Tape 10 - Full |
| 1 | Tape 1 - Diff | Tape 2 - Diff | Tape 3 - Diff | Tape 4 - Diff | Tape 5 - Full |
| 2 | Tape 1 - Diff | Tape 2 - Diff | Tape 3 - Diff | Tape 4 - Diff | Tape 6 - Full |
| 3 | Tape 1 - Diff | Tape 2 - Diff | Tape 3 - Diff | Tape 4 - Diff | Tape 7 - Full |
| 4 | Tape 1 - Diff | Tape 2 - Diff | Tape 3 - Diff | Tape 4 - Diff | Tape 8 - Full |
| 5 | Tape 2 - Diff | Tape 3 - Diff | Tape 4 - Diff | Tape 5 - Diff | Tape 6 - Full |
| 6 | Tape 2 - Diff | Tape 3 - Diff | Tape 4 - Diff | Tape 5 - Diff | Tape 7 - Full |
| 7 | Tape 2 - Diff | Tape 3 - Diff | Tape 4 - Diff | Tape 5 - Diff | Tape 8 - Full |
| 8 | Tape 2 - Diff | Tape 3 - Diff | Tape 4 - Diff | Tape 5 - Diff | Tape 9 - Full |
| 9 | Tape 3 - Diff | Tape 4 - Diff | Tape 5 - Diff | Tape 6 - Diff | Tape 10 - Full |

Before moving on, let's pick apart a few cells in this table to highlight the strengths of this system. Looking at Week 3, you can see that Tape 1 was used on Monday, Tape 2 on Tuesday, Tape 3 on Wednesday, and Tape 4 on Thursday—all for differential backups—and on Friday, we used Tape 8 for a full backup. For Week 5 we shifted forward, using Tapes 2 through 5 for the differentials and Tape 6 for the weekly. If the system crashed on Thursday in Week 7, you would need to restore the full backup from Tape 7 and the differential backup from Tape 4. If you needed to, you could go back as far as the full backup on Friday of Week 4, and you can restore the database as it was each day for the previous week.

You continue this cycle by shifting all tapes by one every four weeks. At the end of an 11-month period, each tape has been used 17 times. With an overall cost of just 10 tapes, this system balances costs with recovery and makes for a good all-around system. The drawback lies in making sure that the correct tape is being used, but third-party backup software, which you will see later in this chapter, automates the scheduling for you.

# HELP! HOW DO I RESTORE?

Well, you hope that the day will never come that you need to actually use a backup—but it will, take our word for it. During the writing of this book one of the authors had a little "accident" when someone tried to install a new hard drive in his computer. Did he have a backup? Tragically not, but he certainly wished he did! There are a number of reasons that you would need to restore your data:

1. You need to upgrade your database server to a new computer. The easiest way to do this is to install Windows NT, SQL Server 7, and any other required software, then back up the old server and restore it on the new server.

2. One of the users made a mistake. If you have ever heard someone say "Oops" just after issuing a **truncate** command, you've run into this problem. While this is a drastic situation, it does happen, as do more minor problems such as multiple data imports of the same data.

3. After playing "Let's run across the carpet in our socks and shock the DBA," you find that one of your disk drives has gone to the big recycle bin in the sky.

4. The tornado that sent Dorothy from Kansas to Oz strikes your office and sends your computer room to Johannesburg. Once you pry your knuckles off your chair and get some new hardware in place, you need to get back up and running.

Each of these problems is serious, and you need to get restored fast. Here's how to do it. Let's spend some time on restoring the SQL Server 7 database. If you can start SQL Server 7, you're halfway there. If not, you may have a corrupted MASTER, MODEL, or MSDB database. Check the server logs, which are by default located in C:\MSSQL7\LOG. If you see something that resembles the following listing, you should easily be able to find where the problem lies:

```
99/07/23 21:44:44.81 kernel    Microsoft SQL Server   7.00 -
                               7.00.517 (Intel X86)
...
99/07/23 21:44:46.23 spid1     Opening file
                               C:\MSSQL7\DATA\model.mdf.
99/07/23 21:44:46.23 kernel    udopen: Operating system error
                               (null) during the
                               creation/opening of physical
                               device C:\MSSQL7\DATA\model.mdf.
```

```
99/07/23 21:44:46.23 kernel     FCB::Open failed: Could not open
                                 device C:\MSSQL7\DATA\model.mdf
                                 for virtual device number (VDN) 1.
99/07/23 21:44:46.24 spid1      Device activation error. The physical
                                 filename 'C:\MSSQL7\DATA\model.mdf'
                                 may be incorrect.
99/07/23 21:44:46.24 spid1      Database 'model' cannot be opened
                                 because some of the
                                 files could not be activated.
```

If it is one of the system files that will not load, you need to restore it. If you created a cold backup of the system databases, restore them now. If you don't have a cold backup of these files, use the command-line utility REBUILDM.EXE, which is located in the \MSSQL7\BINN directory. Before starting the rebuild process, make sure that you have either the SQL Server 7 CD or access to the directory that SQL Server 7 was copied to for a network installation. Make sure that the SQL Server 7 services are stopped and then go to the command prompt and run the utility. You can see what this utility looks like in Figure 11-6.

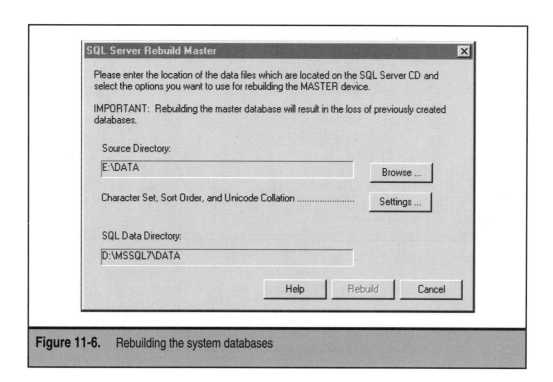

**Figure 11-6.**    Rebuilding the system databases

Since rebuilding the databases re-creates them from scratch, any databases that you have created will be inaccessible. In addition, replication and scheduled events as defined in the DISTRIBUTION and MSDB databases will not occur. In order to restore the MASTER database, you need to start up SQL Server 7 in single-user mode. To do this, make sure that the both the MSSQLServer service and the SQLServerAgent are stopped, then go to the command line and change to the \MSSQL7\BINN directory and run the command **sqlservr –m**. The SQL Server 7 startup sequence resembles the output shown here:

```
99/07/26 09:42:22.17 kernel
    Microsoft SQL Server  7.00 - 7.00.517 (Intel X86)
    Jun 19 1999 17:06:54
    Copyright (c) 1988-1998 Microsoft Corporation
    Desktop version on Windows
99/07/26 09:42:22.20 kernel
    Copyright (C) 1988-1997 Microsoft Corporation.
99/07/26 09:42:22.21 kernel   All rights reserved.
99/07/26 09:42:22.22 kernel
        Logging SQL Server messages in file
        'C:\MSSQL7\log\ERRORLOG'.
99/07/26 09:42:22.29 kernel
        initconfig: Number of user connections limited to 32767.
99/07/26 09:42:22.30 kernel
        SQL Server is starting at priority class 'normal'
                                (1 CPU detected).
99/07/26 09:42:22.33 kernel
        User Mode Scheduler configured for thread processing
99/07/26 09:42:23.45 server
        Directory Size: 3359
99/07/26 09:42:23.46 spid1
        Using dynamic lock allocation. [500] Lock Blocks,
                                [1000] Lock Owner Blocks
99/07/26 09:42:23.47 spid1
        Warning ******************
99/07/26 09:42:23.47 spid1
        SQL Server started in single user mode. Updates
                                allowed to system catalogs.
99/07/26 09:42:23.47 spid1
        Warning ******************
99/07/26 09:42:23.47 spid1
        Starting up database 'master'.99/07/26 09:42:23.48 spid1
        Opening file C:\MSSQL7\data\master.mdf.
99/07/26 09:42:23.56 spid1
        Opening file C:\MSSQL7\data\mastlog.ldf.
```

```
99/07/26 09:42:23.75 spid1
        Loading SQL Server's  Unicode collation.
99/07/26 09:42:23.83 spid1
        Loading SQL Server's  non-Unicode sort order and
        character set.
99/07/26 09:42:24.19 spid1
        5 transactions rolled forward in database 'master' (1).
99/07/26 09:42:24.20 spid1
        0 transactions rolled back in database 'master' (1).
99/07/26 09:42:24.40 spid1
        Starting up database 'model'.
99/07/26 09:42:24.41 spid1
        Opening file C:\MSSQL7\DATA\model.mdf.
99/07/26 09:42:24.51 spid1
        Opening file c:\mssql7\data\modellog.ldf.
99/07/26 09:42:26.74 spid5
        Starting up database 'msdb'.
99/07/26 09:42:26.79 spid5
        Opening file C:\MSSQL7\DATA\msdbdata.mdf.
99/07/26 09:42:26.88 spid5
        Opening file c:\mssql7\DATA\msdblog.ldf.
99/07/26 09:42:27.12 spid5
        Starting up database 'Warehouse2'.
99/07/26 09:42:27.12 spid5
        Opening file C:\MSSQL7\data\Warehouse2_Data.MDF.
99/07/26 09:42:27.13 kernel
        udopen: Operating system error (null) during the
        creation/opening of physical device
        C:\MSSQL7\data\Warehouse2_Data.MDF.
99/07/26 09:42:27.13 kernel
        FCB::Open failed: Could not open device
        C:\MSSQL7\data\Warehouse2_Data.MDF for virtual
        device number (VDN) 1.
99/07/26 09:42:27.20 spid5
        Device activation error. The physical filename
        'C:\MSSQL7\data\Warehouse2_Data.MDF' may be incorrect.
99/07/26 09:42:27.21 spid5
         Starting up database 'distribution'.
99/07/26 09:42:27.21 spid5
         Opening file C:\MSSQL7\data\distribution.MDF.
99/07/26 09:42:27.32 spid5
         Opening file C:\MSS
```

After the service is started, run Enterprise Manager, select the server, and click on Tools. Select Restore Database and choose the current backup. Click on OK and wait for it to complete.

# THE HARDWARE

Only the smallest backups can be done to disk, and then only for short-term storage. The key to a successful long-term backup strategy must involve some form of removable storage. In today's marketplace, we are now seeing recordable media ranging from 680Mb CD-ROMs to 70Gb digital linear tapes (DLTs). For the warehouse, it's safe to assume that you're not going to be backing up to Zip or even Jaz drives. We're going to be looking for a solution that is fast, has a high capacity, and is economical.

## The Solution

Tape drives currently provide the only backup option that is really practical today. Your choices mainly lie in the tape format, each of which has its advantages and disadvantages. One thing that virtually all modern tape drives have in common is a *small computer systems interface* (SCSI) interface. SCSI provides a fast, efficient interface that allows you to connect up to 14 devices (disk, tape, or CD) to a single interface card. SCSI exists in a number of different flavors, and the newest version—Ultra Fast/Wide SCSI—can handle transfer speeds in excess of 40Mb per second, which is substantially faster than any tape drive currently on the market.

### Quarter-Inch Cassette (QIC) and Travan Drives

These are the old guard drives like the Jumbo 250 that store a measly 250Mb on a single tape. Improvements to the technology, such as Travan, allow backups of up to 2Gb. There are two major drawbacks to QIC drives and tapes:

1. First of all, they are *slow*, and we mean slow. With a throughput in the range of 500Kb per second, it would take quite a while to back up the warehouse.

2. The second problem is reliability, which is nowhere near as high as the options that follow. You may find one of these drives kicking around, but we don't suggest using them for any type of production backup.

### 4mm Digital Audio Tape (DAT)

These tapes have been around for a number of years and have evolved into the current standard, DDS-3. Using a 4mm DAT cassette, these tapes have a capacity of 12Gb uncompressed, or 24Gb by employing hardware compression. With transfer rates in the range of 1Mb per second, DDS-3 backups are great for small- to medium-sized warehouses. A full backup of a 20Gb database would take about six hours with one of these tapes, making it perfect for a midnight backup. DDS-3 drives are about $1,200 and tapes are under $30 each, so this is a cheap option. If you don't have this much time available for backups or you need more capacity, take a look at some of the newer tape formats, such as DLT and AIT.

## 8mm Tape

These tapes are just digital versions of what you would use in your home video camera and grew out of the same technology. Using a helical scan system just like a VCR, 8mm tape performs the same tasks as 4mm tape but is slightly faster, with a throughput of 1.2Mb per second. These drives have lately fallen out of fashion, because 4mm drives are cheaper and provide basically the same performance. Sony has resuscitated the format with their AIT drives, which we will review in this chapter.

Before going any further, we should have a quick look at compression. *Compression* routines are used by tape hardware vendors, allowing them to place more data on their media. For example, with compression, you may fit the equivalent of 3.2Tb of information on a tape designed to only handle 2Tb. Hardware compression on 4mm and 8mm drives is often done using a proprietary compression technique, which is different for different brands or even models of drives that are otherwise interchangeable. If you need to move tapes between machines, check that each drive can read compressed tapes created on the other drives. If not, you may be out of luck if one of your units conks out on you just when you need to restore a database.

## Digital Linear Tape (DLT)

In 1994, Quantum bought the rights to a tape backup system from Digital and brought it to market as DLT. DLT is different from most other tape backup formats in that it consists of a box about 4 inches square and about 1 inch high. Inside is a single reel and 2,000 feet of magnetic tape, which is drawn into the tape back unit and loaded onto an internal reel. Instead of using a helical scan mechanism (like a VCR or 4mm tape), DLT writes eight parallel tracks during each pass across the tape. As the tape hits the other end, the read/write head moves down a notch and writes the next eight tracks. One big advantage of DLT over 4mm is that there is a read head right beside the write head, allowing the drive to verify as it goes along instead of requiring a separate verify procedure. While Quantum is the only manufacturer of the drives, they do sell the assemblies to OEM manufacturers to use in their own drives.

Quantum has licensed the manufacturing of tapes to many companies in order to ensure that the supply of blank tapes is always good. DLT drives come in various capacities ranging up to 70Gb compressed on a single $100 tape. Data transfer speeds of up to 10Mb per second are possible with data that is compressible 2:1. Quantum also sells tape changers and libraries that can handle backups in excess of 1Tb. Need more storage than this? Take a look at something like the TimberWolf 9710 from StorageTek, a tape library with up to 10 DLT drives and slots for over 500 tapes. The TimberWolf 9710 has a capacity of 41.2Tb (yes, that's correct, terabytes)!

The interesting thing about tape hardware and tape software management solutions is that while the ink is still wet on this book, the technology will be approaching, if not finishing, the next generation.

### Advanced Intelligent Tape (AIT)

AIT was built on the original 8mm tape format, similar to home video cameras, but it's come a long way in the last 10 years. Developed by Sony and introduced in 1996, AIT is the newest tape format to hit the market and competes head to head with DLT. The AIT format includes a 16Kb *memory in chip* (MIC) feature that allows the drive to quickly locate a desired spot on the tape, as well as recorded access and other information. AIT and the newest AIT 2 drives are made by vendors like Sony and Seagate, with single drives like Seagate's Sidewinder 50 providing capacities of up to 50Gb per tape (compressed) and a compressed data transfer rate of 6Mb/sec. This drive has a street price under $3,000 and blank media are in the $100 range. If you need more capacity, Seagate offers the Sidewinder 200, which packs a four-tape changer into a full-height 5 ¼-inch drive bay and handles 200Gb of data. Need even more? Spectra Logic and Qualstar have tape libraries capable of storing more than 8Tb of data on multiple tapes.

Right now there is a war going on between DLT and AIT similar to the Beta/VHS battle in the 1970s. We don't know who will win or if both will survive, but you can learn more about these formats at their Web sites. You can visit the DLT gang at http://www.dlttape.com and the AIT crew at http://www.aittape.com. Let's touch on reliability before looking at third-party solutions.

*VIP:*   After the server crashes, it is too late to find out that your backup did not work. Test your backup after you implement any new software or hardware and on a regular basis.

*VIP:*   Discard your tapes frequently—many backup programs, including the SQL Server 7 backup utility allow you to mark a tape for retirement on a certain date. Follow the manufacturers' recommendations and toss those old tapes like the leftover tuna that's been sitting at the back of your fridge for the last month.

# THE NEXT STEP—THIRD-PARTY UTILITIES

SQL Server 7 has some great new tape backup features, but it does have some limitations. One of the biggest problems is that although you can now back up to the same tape as a standard Windows NT backup, you cannot do it at the same time as an NT backup or schedule the jobs from a single console. In addition, there is no way to coordinate backups across multiple servers or platforms. The solution is third-party backup utilities. Two of the most popular packages on the market are Arcserve from Computer Associates and Backup Exec from Seagate Software.

Both of these products have many features that just don't exist in either SQL Server 7 Backup or Windows NT backup, including client machine backup and integrated solutions that can back up all of your servers and clients, including Windows NT, 95/98, 3.1, DOS, UNIX, Macintosh, and other computers. While neither of these products will make your backups better, they will make your life easier. Both products have disaster recovery add-ons that make it easy to recover a downed server from scratch. Even if your system drive with Windows NT fails, you can be up and running in a matter of minutes after replacing the defective component by booting from a floppy and restoring from tape without having to reinstall Windows NT first. Other great features include the ability to back up Microsoft Exchange Server, Oracle, and SQL Server 7 databases all in one operation and provide automatic support for tape rotation such as the Grandfather/Father/Son schemes we have discussed in this chapter. Arcserve and Backup Exec can also notify users via email, NT alerts, or pager that the backup did or did not succeed, allowing you to confirm that your warehouse is safe even though you're not there. Most vendors plan to have, if they don't already, backup agents that work with SQL Server 7. Both companies offer downloadable trial software at their Web sites, http://www.cai.com and http://www.seagate.com.

If you take one idea away from this chapter, let it be that backup is essential. Without it, anarchy reigns with dogs and cats living together in sin, as Bill Murray once said in *Stripes*. It's time to move ahead…shhhhhh! Don't say a word; whisper. Chapter 12 discusses securing the SQL Server 7 warehouse. Tiptoe through this chapter; when you find ideas and suggestions that you want to implement to make your warehouse more secure, do so. For us, security is a double-edged sword. We love it and we hate it.

# CHAPTER 12

## Securing the Warehouse

Securing the warehouse—three words that conjure up visions of the warehouse police ensuring people only see what they are allowed. This is not too far from the main security mechanisms placed in the warehouse. These mechanisms enforce a flavor of business rules native to the decision support system arena.

Operational systems implement a network of security that protects confidential information and ensures data integrity while ensuring users have access to the information needed to go about their daily business. Let's get started by looking at security policies.

# A SECURITY POLICY

There are many different ways to slice and dice a security policy. When deploying the data mart solution (special-interest pockets of data in isolated sections of the corporate infrastructure), security and access to data can prove less cumbersome than when dealing with the enterprise data warehouse. There are a number of issues related to plain common sense. As we walk you through the items, keep in mind your habits as you interact with all the electronic information you come in contact with during a normal business day.

## Workstation Security

This is the simplest, and the bottom line of a security policy. Whether you are using Windows 3.x, Windows 95, Windows 98, or Windows NT, something as simple as a screen saver password is a good place to start. As new personnel are brought into companies, they are usually briefed on the general security measures that are in place—why not ask personnel to lock their workstations when they leave their office or cubicle? The Windows NT Security dialog box, invoked by pressing CTRL-ALT-DEL, is the easiest of the three Windows platforms to use in locking the workstation. There are many inexpensive third-party products out there that engage the screen saver when the user moves the mouse cursor to a predefined spot on the screen, presses a hot key combination, or clicks on a desktop or button bar icon.

Speaking of Windows NT, many organizations are deliberately not giving users access to administrator accounts on their own personal computers to remove the ability and temptation to perform such activities as installing unauthorized software, or to restrict data access on the local machines.

## Snooping

*Snooping* involves browsing or capturing of information on someone else's computer that you have no access to on your own. This can take the form of inspecting (and in some of the worst cases, responding to) another person's email and viewing results of analysis of information to which, using your own means, you do not normally have access. There are two main ways to promote behavior that lessens the likelihood of snooping. The first is outlined in the previous section on workstation security. The other involves training users to exit their applications when they leave their work area and log off the network at the end of the business day.

# SECURITY

All businesses go through a series of exercises during operational system development. These exercises define who should be able to do what with what data. Some users, based on predefined security profiles, are allowed to **select**, **create**, **update**, and **delete** information in the database, while other users have a handful of these privileges suited to their needs. No matter how you access your data, two levels of security exist:

1.  Privileges granted via the SQL Server 7 **grant** mechanism, where users or groups of users are explicitly given permission to access the data

2.  Rights to perform certain operations on the data, based on who they are and where they sit in the company's administrative structure

As these two mechanisms are discussed, the word "user" will be used to refer both to each separate user who may access the warehouse and to a class or group of users. The first level of security for most users of the warehouse will suffice for them to go about their business. The second level only comes into play for those SQL Server 7 users who own the data sitting in the DSS repository. Let's look at these issues and highlight some suggestions specific to the warehouse environment.

## Viewing the Warehouse Data

This is the heart of the security system with most, if not all, relational databases. Because the data in a warehouse is read-only by nature, the SQL Server 7 **select** privilege is given out to warehouse users. This privilege allows specified users to view certain tales within the database. Regardless of what tool is used to access the data—Excel, Impromptu from Cognos, or any other choice—this first level of security must be in place.

## How to Manage Privileges in the Warehouse

SQL Server 7 contains a rich feature called role-based security that is ideal for operational as well as DSS environments. Let's briefly discuss role-based security, and then views.

### Role-Based Security

A *role* is a logical grouping of one or more users of the SQL Server 7 database to which privileges can be given, based on the functional responsibilities of the persons registered in that role. A role is created using the syntax shown in the next listing:

```
exec sp_addrole dss_administrator
go
```

*Enroll* describes the process of giving membership in a role to one or more users. People need a SQL Server 7 account before they can connect to the database. This is facilitated by issuing the statement shown in the next listing:

```
exec sp_addlogin 'aviva', 'snausage', 'pubs'
go
```

This command adds a login for the user using SQL Server 7 standard security. You can also use an integrated Windows NT security model with the stored procedure **sp_grantlogin**. The username component of the preceding listing is usually hooked up to a user's name. For example, suppose user Aviva Wittenberg gets the SQL Server 7 name "aviva" and the password "snausage." The username should contain only letters or the digits 0–9, begin with a letter, and contain no embedded spaces. In addition, she will be assigned a default database of "pubs." You then need to add the user to the security database to give them access. Use this command:

```
exec sp_grantdblogin 'aviva'
go
```

Once this person has the ability to connect to SQL Server 7, she is enrolled in the appropriate database role by the command shown next:

```
exec sp_addrolemember 'dss_administrator', 'aviva'
go
```

Armed with the basics, let's set up a few users and roles, then grant privileges:

```
exec sp_addlogin 'asher', 'rehsa'
exec sp_addlogin 'rachel', 'lehcar'
exec sp_addlogin 'pips', 'spip'
exec sp_grantdbaccess 'asher'
exec sp_grantdbaccess 'rachel'
exec sp_grantdbaccess 'pips'
exec sp_addrole 'finance_mgr'
exec sp_addrole 'finance_sen'
exec sp_addrole 'finance_user'
exec sp_addrolemember 'finance_mgr', 'asher'
exec sp_addrolemember 'finance_sen', 'rachel'
exec sp_addrolemember 'finance_user', 'pips'
go
```

Once the users are set up in their appropriate roles, the owner of the database objects in the warehouse grants privileges to roles, using code similar to the following:

```
grant select on employee to finance_mgr
grant select on transactions to finance_user,finance_mgr,finance_sen
go
```

The power of role-based security is that once roles have been created and they have received the appropriate database privileges, new users are simply enrolled in one or more roles, which they need to interact with the data warehouse. Even better, when a new user is given membership in a role, this new user automatically inherits the privileges that go along with the role. Membership in a role is taken away using the following code:

```
exec sp_droprolemember finance_mgr from 'bram'
go
```

and, when necessary, access to the database is taken away using the following code:

```
sp_revokedbaccess 'alyssa'
go
sp_droplogin 'alyssa'
go
```

Before discussing more issues related to keeping the warehouse safe, one of the most important things to remember can be summed up in the following tip.

> **TIP:**  Do not allow data warehouse users to see information in the warehouse that they are not allowed to view in the operational systems.

Suppose managers have decided their senior directors can interact with departmental information in their region, but not in regions that belong to other directors. In the warehouse, this same rule must be enforced. This could affect how the data is modeled in the warehouse and, after that modeling activity, how the data is moved into the DSS repository. This could mean an additional network of rollups may need to be created and stored in the mart or warehouse. A *rollup* is a level of summary containing data created by the manipulation of information at a lower level. Reporting a figure of $128,000 as the gross profit of four divisions, whose individual numbers range from $34,000 to $51,000, is an example of a rollup.

## Views

Views are the heart of many security mechanisms, not only in the data warehouse but also in many operational systems. A *view* is a logical table built as a subset of the data in one or more physical tables. *Logical* means the view itself contains no data; the data in a view is assembled from the underlying table(s) when a view is mentioned in a SQL statement. Here is a simple view definition, with the criteria in bold:

```
create view dept_south as
select *
  from dept_rllup
 where reg_cd = 'S'
```

Using this view, queries only have access to the rows in the DEPT_RLLUP table whose Reg_Cd column value is "S." Suppose you wanted to restrict viewing of rollup information for users in each region to data in their own region. The secret is to grant these users (or a role of which these users are members) the **select** privilege on the view built from their region alone. The next listing shows how this would be accomplished using a combination of role-based security and views:

```
-- Create a role for each region
exec sp_createrole southern
exec sp_createrole northern
exec sp_createrole eastern
exec sp_createrole western
go
-- Create a view of DEPT_RLLUP for each region
create view dept_north as
        select * from dept_rllup where reg_cd = 'N'
create view dept_west as
        select * from dept_rllup where reg_cd = 'W'
create view dept_east as
        select * from dept_rllup where reg_cd = 'E'
create view dept_south as
        select * from dept_rllup where reg_cd = 'S'
go
-- Grant select on each region's view to the proper role
grant select on dept_south to southern
grant select on dept_north to northern
grant select on dept_east to eastern
grant select on dept_west to western
go
```

## Where to Implement Security

Stories exist of data warehouses where the security is implemented at the tool level rather than in SQL Server 7. *Tool level* means situations where warehouse implementers use features in query and analysis tools to control the data the users are allowed to view. Even though these security mechanisms may solve a short-term problem, you are wiser using SQL Server 7 database security. The problem with tool-based security is twofold:

1. Security features embedded in certain tool vendors' products only work for that tool. If you were tempted to implement tool-based security, you would have to do so manually for each tool. It would be too easy to inadvertently allow users to view data in one area of the warehouse using tool A, whereas tool B's security restricts them from seeing the same data.

2. Each vendor's proprietary security features must be learned by all warehouse security personnel. As personnel changes (and it always does), the learning curve can get in the way of the transfer of responsibility process.

# TOOL-BASED SECURITY

In this section, we will look at implementing security using Impromptu, a SQL reporting tool from Cognos, as an example. Tool-based security, though not as fluid and portable as database engine-based security, is a matter of fact and will form some portion of your security solution. If you have been reading closely (and we are sure you have been), you know that you should implement as much security as possible within the database and avoid the potential problems of a tool-based security. With many tools, Impromptu included, you have no choice. The tool cannot be turned over to the user community before its security features have been implemented. Impromptu uses *catalogs* to collect a set of related information with a common business purpose, organized into *folders*; folders contain *items*, which are a particular category of information within a folder. Access to catalogs is where baseline security is implemented in Impromptu. Let's briefly look at the activity of giving users access to one or more of these areas.

There are two versions of Impromptu—the Administrator Edition and the User Edition. The separation of the product into these two versions controls who has access to the power of setting up and changing catalogs and who can simply work with areas to which they have been granted access. Within the Administrator version of Impromptu, the user can create catalogs and users, then grant or deny users access to both folders (logical groupings) and tables (the underlying database). If you choose to deny access to a table, a red circle with a slash appears over the folder. Cognos' Impromptu OLAP tool (discussed more in Chapter 16) is shown in Figure 12-1 to illustrate giving out access to tables using its User Profiles menu.

Once you have controlled who has access to each table, you then create folders that can contain columns from many different tables, as well as calculations based on column values. Normally, folders are defined for a logical grouping of tables such as sales, which would contain columns from the CUSTOMER, SALES HEADER, and SALES DETAIL tables. A further restriction can be set up through the Permissions drop-down list that allows users to use values as part of the **select** clause but prevents them from actually adding the column to the report. Again using Impromptu as an example, Figure 12-2 shows where folder access can be defined.

# PASSWORD SECURITY WITH SQL SERVER 7

The best way to manage security with SQL Server 7 is by using the Windows NT integrated security. This system works quite well, provided you are using a Windows NT-based network with Windows 3.x, 95, or 98 clients. Integrated security provides a single logon to SQL Server 7 while still allowing the administrator to control who has access to which databases, tables, and functions. Windows NT delivers password aging

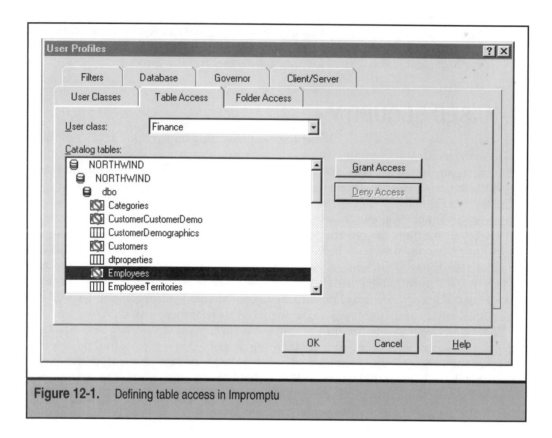

**Figure 12-1.** Defining table access in Impromptu

and a sophisticated set of password control features, yet users no longer need to worry about remembering another username and password—that will most likely be written down on a yellow sticky note on their monitor, which really ruins your security! Let's look at password selection and control features with Windows NT. Without worrying about the nitty-gritty details about syntax, let's look at two areas provided in the password management facility in Windows NT—account policies and account locking.

## Account Policies

Account policies help you enforce security on your network, including password length and the expiry. You can set these parameters by running Windows NT User Manager or User Manager for Domains and selecting Policies | Account. Suppose a user is assigned a profile with this parameter set to 60. This means that a password can be used for authentication for a period of 60 days before it has to be changed. You can also control how many passwords are remembered, preventing someone from reusing an old

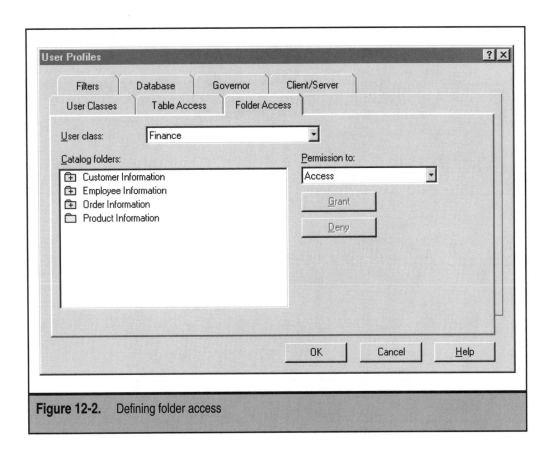

**Figure 12-2.**   Defining folder access

password until the password has been changed a specified number of times. It's also important to enforce a minimum password length. Use a value that forces users to use a password that is sufficiently long to prevent hacking, but short enough that they won't have to write down the password to remember it. In a similar vein, enforce regular password changes without forcing the users to do it so frequently that your help desk gets swamped with calls about forgotten passwords. Figure 12-3 shows you what options are available in the Account Policy screen.

# Account Locking

Account locking can serve two purposes. It assists in the prevention of deliberate or undeliberate hacking into an account by an unauthorized person, plus it detects when someone is trying to break into an account. A locked account is reset through User

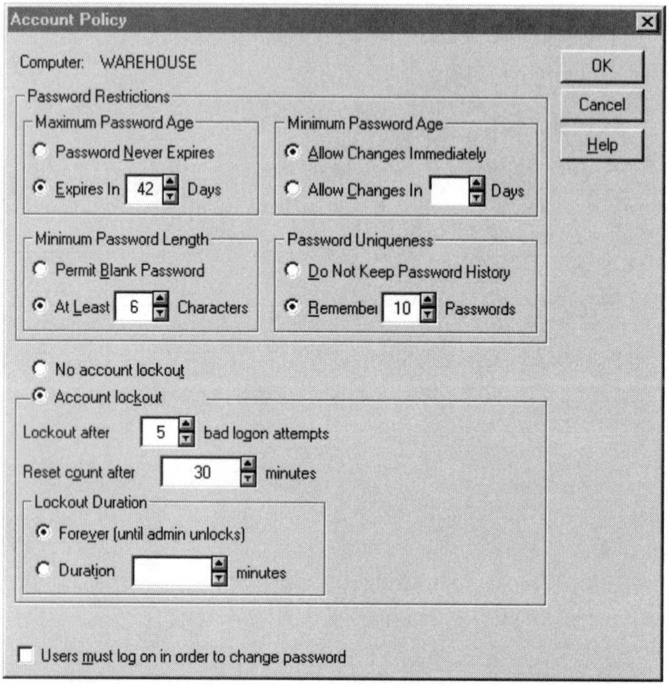

**Figure 12-3.** Windows NT Account Policy screen

Manager. You can manually lock an account by checking the Account Disabled checkbox, or it will be checked if a user trips the restrictions that you set in Account Policies. You can see this screen in Figure 12-4.

# MANAGEMENT OF DATABASE USERS

There are a number of schools of thought in this area. Some feel user management should be the responsibility of the database administrator (DBA); others feel the management should be given out to a handful of trusted users. We prescribe, most of the time, to the second approach. We are not, however, suggesting that you should give the keys to the car to people without implementing a security infrastructure first. Let's look at that infrastructure in the next few sections.

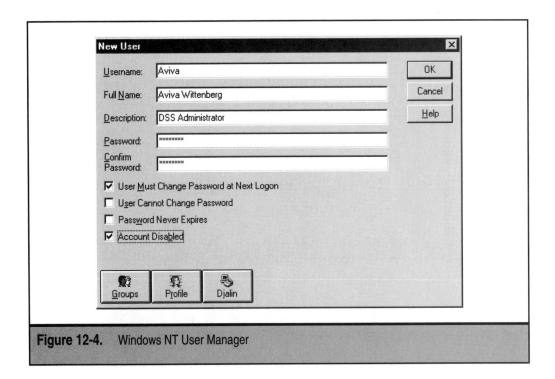

**Figure 12-4.**    Windows NT User Manager

# SQL SERVER 7 ENTERPRISE MANAGER AND SECURITY

Many prefer using the GUI interface in Enterprise Manager to perform security-related tasks with the SQL Server 7 warehouse. The SQL commands built while working with Enterprise Manager are exactly the same as those built manually using Query Analyzer, the command-line tool for accessing a SQL Server 7 database. The Enterprise Manager main console is shown in Figure 12-5.

Let's look briefly at working with two of the folders shown in Figure 12-5—Logins and Roles.

## Users

A mouse-click on the Logins folder expands the user list, and each user listing can then be opened to display the following:

▼ **Server roles**—The roles defined for the server of which the user has been made a member.

▲ **Database Access**—The privileges the user has received to access databases in SQL Server 7. In addition, on this tab you can assign database roles to the user.

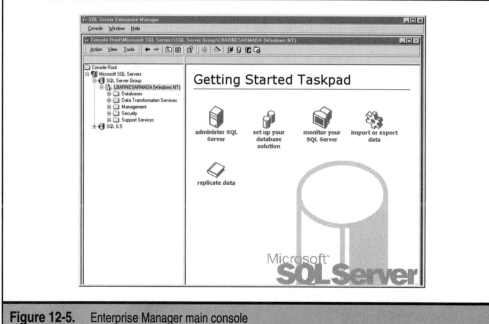

**Figure 12-5.**    Enterprise Manager main console

Figure 12-6 shows the Properties screen for user Bram. It is open on the Server Roles tab; note the General and Database Access tabs, as shown in Figure 12-6, as well.

# Roles

*Roles* are defined as a logical grouping of one or more users. SQL Server 7 has two separate roles: server and database. The difference between the two is that a server role applies to every database within a server, whereas a database role only applies to a specific database. You can use this flexibility to give a user full access to create tables in one database while preventing him or her from changing or accessing other databases.

# A Word on the Power of Enterprise Manager

To close this chapter, a word from our lawyers (so to speak). The SQL commands that can be built and passed out to users in Enterprise Manager are very powerful and can sink the efforts of the warehouse team if abused. For example, it is very easy for someone to accidentally remove a role that allows users to perform their work.

**NOTE:** Be very conservative when giving access to Enterprise Manager to power users in the user community; there is a great deal of damage that can be done inadvertently to the warehouse in the hands of the inexperienced. These people would not do anything deliberately—the power can be misused, not abused.

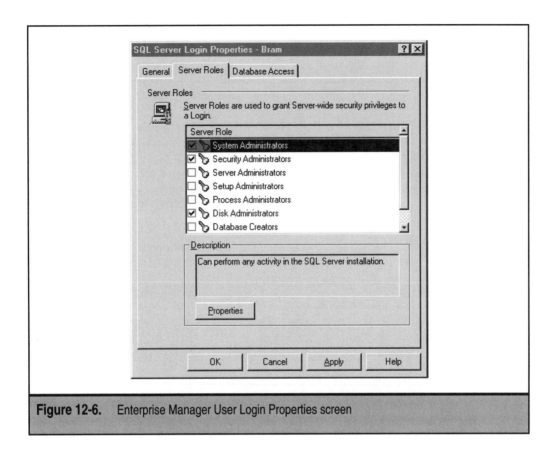

**Figure 12-6.**   Enterprise Manager User Login Properties screen

Enough said on securing the warehouse. As we alluded to earlier, security is seldom an issue until an incident comes up that compromises the data in the warehouse. The bottom line, as we state in a few spots in *SQL Server 7 Data Warehousing*, is to ensure the data is safe and users are not allowed to see something in the warehouse they do not have access to in the operational system environment. The next stop on the warehousing journey looks at RAID technology for storage of your precious data warehouse information. The RAID phenomenon has been around for quite some time, and it gets even more sophisticated as we speak. The interesting thing we have found about RAID is what the vendors would like us to think the "I" stands for in the acronym. They would lead us to believe it stands for *inexpensive*, when we know it actually stands for *independent*. Awesome is it not—the power of marketing.

# CHAPTER 13

# RAID and Mirroring

Every year, newer and faster microprocessor chips are developed. This trend of increased microprocessor speeds continues to be a constant within the high-technology industry. Based on this recurring trend, the consumers of technology now expect CPU speeds to at least double each year. This means that whenever your system is upgraded with a new CPU (a likely case), the newly tuned applications will only improve. This trend of faster microprocessor CPU chips was so consistent, even the chip name became predictable. For example, first it was the 8086, next the 80286, then the 80386 and, finally, the Pentium and Pentium II. Just as everyone became used to the standard name for the latest and greatest chip, Intel Corporation announced the Pentium chip. Whatever happened to the 80586?

What happened was Intel Corporation realized the name 80586 could not be trademarked, so they decided to change the name to a name that could be trademarked: Pentium. A *Pentium* is what would have been called an 80586 chip. What is clear from all these announcements is that chips are making the CPU faster by a substantial factor every year. CPU speed is not considered a major barrier to machine performance today.

The problem, to quote a familiar saying, is "a chain is only as strong as its weakest link." In this case, the "weakest" chain link represents your I/O throughput. The disk drives can be a major source of performance problems in a data warehouse environment, or even in a typical computing environment. Even though the I/O capabilities of disk drives have improved over the past few years, they have not kept pace with the dramatic improvements of CPU speeds. Accessing your data through disk drives is, and continues to be, one of the slowest operations a computer does, as compared to accessing data stored in memory. This issue is further intensified in a data warehouse environment due to the large volumes of data. When we are asked to tune a database, many times we learn a major source of performance problems has to do with the configuration of the disks attached to the computer upon which the database operates.

What makes this issue of choosing the "right" disk configuration even more critical is that it has one of the greatest probabilities of failure. Any point of failure within a computer system is critical, but when a disk drive fails, you not only risk the availability of the data but also the reliability of the data stored on the disk. Any system failure always puts you at risk of the user community losing trust in your ability to deliver the end-user systems that can meet their demands. They will seek out other solutions. Once lost, trust is difficult to regain. This may be your greatest risk when a system fails. Can you afford to lose face?

In a data warehouse environment, preventing failure becomes even more critical. You are probably storing historical information that if lost or destroyed will be difficult to recover. Another key problem is that a typical data warehouse has a large dataset associated with it. The larger the dataset, the longer the time to recover the data in the event of a disaster. This can quickly become a critical issue, which should be addressed early in the process. The key question here should be, "If I create a backup, do I have the time it takes to recover the data?"

With large datasets, speed of retrieval also becomes a critical issue. Retrieving a hundred records is always faster than retrieving a million records. For a particular warehouse initiative to be successful, you must turn your users' "what if?" questions around in a timely manner. You must provide the end users with the capability to sift through vast amounts of information quickly.

History has taught us that any time a vacuum is created in the marketplace, a movement will occur within the marketplace to fill that vacuum and, over time, a movement will occur to improve upon the solution. As business needs for information and the ability to ask "what if?" questions have become more acute, we have seen the trend toward building enterprise data warehouses grow. As these data warehouses grow in size and complexity, the need for disk storage solutions that improve retrieval speeds and minimize the likelihood of failure has become critical. This vacuum for improved disk I/O throughput and reliability has been a major catalyst for the development of redundant array of independent disks (RAID) technology, although the vendors often like to say "redundant array of inexpensive disks."

If you are reading this book, you and your organization must be thinking about building a data warehouse. A data warehouse will be the most complex and data-intensive system you will ever encounter—poor performance from your disk farm or a high failure rate would mean disaster.

In this chapter, RAID technology and some of its key evolution points will be explained. Then, you can make a determination if RAID is appropriate for your data warehouse, given your needs and resources. Experience has taught us that RAID is often a necessity for data warehouses.

**NOTE:** Understanding RAID technology is imperative; then, and only then, can you determine if you can live without its fault-tolerance and performance characteristics.

## WHAT LED US TO RAID?

In the beginning, you had a disk. Over time, numerous improvements have been made to this disk. A disk has become much faster at retrieving data. Many remember the "seek time" wars in favorite trade journals. *Seek time* is a measurement of the amount of time required to position a read/write head over a predetermined spot on a disk platter. Imagine yourself trying to play your favorite song on a record player. Seek time would be the amount of time it takes you to move the arm on a record player to your favorite song on the record.

The size and density each drive can contain has also steadily increased. A great example of this is the old 5 1/4-inch floppy drive compared to the 3 1/2-inch high-density drives that are standard with all personal computers sold today. The original 5 1/4-inch drive could only hold 360Kb worth of information compared to the 3 1/2-inch drive, which can hold over 1Mb worth of information. Another major trend has been the movement toward physically much smaller disk drives, which require much reduced floor space and power needs. Figure 13-1 is a quick illustration of this discussion. Just the comparison of the floppy disk to the current 3 1/2-inch disk provides an excellent

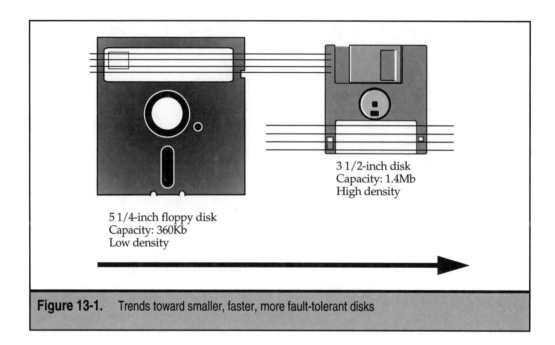

3 1/2-inch disk
Capacity: 1.4Mb
High density

5 1/4-inch floppy disk
Capacity: 360Kb
Low density

**Figure 13-1.** Trends toward smaller, faster, more fault-tolerant disks

framework for the overall industry trends in the storage industry. Remember, even though great progress has been made in the size, capacity, and speed of disks, they are a poor shadow of their cousin, the CPU.

Over time, hardware vendors have created numerous improvements to disk drive technology to meet customers' needs for faster, more reliable disk drives that are more fault tolerant. *Fault tolerant* is a computer architecture that has mechanisms in place to compensate for one or more components' failures. In the IBM world, these improvements were known as direct access storage devices (DASD); in the world of digital computers, they were known as VMS shadowing. Even though these technologies work quite well, they are still proprietary. What has been clear is the move toward open systems. *Open systems* provide a commodity-like computer system, which, in turn, brings down price points while maintaining quality. In fact, this trend toward open systems is just a reflection of the marketplace and how all products and services move through it. Figure 13-2 highlights the standard life cycle for all products and services.

If you understand the product life cycle, you can understand a major trend that affects the product and services each vendor is offering you. Through this understanding, you can better judge where the marketplace is going and when it makes sense to buy the brand name.

## The Product/Service Life Cycle

■ **Innovation:**  A unique product or service is created. Once it gains market acceptance, it enjoys no competition and very lucrative pricing and profits.

■ **Imitation:**  As a unique product gains acceptance, a number of copycat products appear. They mimic the core functionality of the original, and, in addition, they boast the inclusion of many features that should not have been forgotten by the originator. The imitators initially come in underpriced and yet overvalued compared to their functionality list.

■ **Maturation:**  At maturation, a number of brand-name products or services have established themselves. They are constantly adding features, hoping to encourage brand loyalty and achieve improved pricing. At this time, the RDBMS marketplace is between maturation and consolidation. The key vendors are constantly looking for new functionality that will encourage brand loyalty. For example, the move toward SQL Server 7 is an example of making the RDBMS data warehouse-savvy, which demands a premium in the marketplace.

■ **Consolidation:**  As the marketplace becomes saturated, there is no longer a need for so many different product or service providers. Typically during this period, vendors package multiple products together hoping to show value. The net result is that there will be fewer players in the field. The consumer will have fewer choices.

■ **Commodity:**  Eventually, all products or services become a commodity. There is no major difference between vendors, so the consumer will go for the best price. The keys to survival here are efficiencies and economies of scale. For example, when a consumer buys a laser printer today, it does not matter whose name is on the outside; there are only two or three key vendors who make the parts.

**Figure 13-2.**    Product/service life cycle

## Innovation Phase

All products/services begin at the innovation phase. The birth of the innovation phase is due to a failure or a need of a current product or service within the marketplace. Once this vacuum in the marketplace is identified, some entity builds a product or service to fill this need. In the innovation phase, a new, unique product/service is born. Because it is first, no competition exists and one of two situations occurs:

1. The marketplace quickly embraces the product/service offering, which generates immediate high demand. The problem then becomes how you meet the high demand in the marketplace. The high demand also quickly begins to raise price points due to the limited supply. This is the supply and demand curve at work.

2. The marketplace does not understand the need for new products/services. So, a market strategy must be developed to teach the marketplace the need. If this is not done, the product/service will fail. A basic strategy is developed to help the marketplace understand the need for the product/service. Pricing is a major factor for any customer, and in this scenario, it will initially be lowered to help induce the marketplace to try the new product/service. After the marketplace understands and embraces the new product/service, the need for steep discounting no longer exists and higher pricing follows.

# Imitation Phase

As the product/service gains market acceptance, it quickly enters the imitation phase. This is where a number of copycat products/services arise. If a short supply of the original product/service occurs, then these imitators quickly gain market acceptance based on the need the original product/ service created. If, on the other hand, the original product/service is meeting the demand, then the imitations begin to develop strategies to show what features they have that will cause you, the consumer, to choose them over the original product/service.

# Maturation Phase

As the imitators begin to gain market acceptance, the product/service makes the transition into the maturation phase. From all the imitators that appear, a few key brand names emerge. In addition to the brand-name products that evolve, quite a few generic products evolve. Let's review the word processor marketplace. Some key brand-name products exist: Microsoft Word, WordPerfect, AmiPro, and a series of second-tier products such as Claris Works and QuickWrite. If you choose WordPerfect over Microsoft Word, will your effort fail? No, both are excellent choices. The key is to look beyond the product/service and evaluate all other factors that affect your effectiveness with the product/service. For example, what materials and education are available to help you better use the service? The Database Professional's Library series is an advantage when you buy SQL Server: you now have a set of materials written by well-known experts to help supplement the SQL Server documentation set.

## Consolidation Phase

As these brand names become more entrenched, they move into the consolidation phase. As differences between the brand names become less apparent to the consumer, a common trend is to package many different products into one. This is done to help show added value. For example, Microsoft Office incorporates a spreadsheet (Microsoft Excel), a word processor (Microsoft Word), and some presentation software (Microsoft PowerPoint). Because each of these products is tightly integrated, each hopes to show it has a unique added value. Any time vendors can show unique added value, they can move back toward the innovation phase. Vendors can get the greatest return in the innovation phase. Yet, as one vendor announces an office suite, another brand name announces a competing product. Once again, this is the consolidation phase, where the weaker vendors will not survive or the stronger vendors will absorb them.

## Commodity Phase

Eventually, all the differences between product/service begin to fade away; then it makes no difference which service you purchase. This is where the commodity phase is entered. For example, when you look at the hamburger industry, does a major difference exist between a cheeseburger at McDonald's and a cheeseburger at Burger King? Once a business enters this stage, the name of the game is price. For example, when you buy a Sun Microsystems computer, it might contain a Seagate disk drive when you purchase it in May and a Micron disk drive when you buy it in June. This is because key vendors have the ability to maintain a consistent level of quality but use different disk drive vendors. This has given Sun Microsystems the ability to meet its supply and demand for disk drives at the best price points. You, the consumer, benefit.

In the computer industry today, consolidation is being experienced in many areas. We are reaching the point of fewer hardware vendors. In addition, many areas in this industry are already approaching commodity status. This is most evident in peripheral business. In fact, many customers are demanding commodity-like ability. Customers want to purchase a printer that will work on any computer system in-house. We are moving toward a trend where your computer peripherals will work like the electrical appliances in your home, where you have a standard electrical plug and all devices simply plug into it. Can you imagine a world where each appliance you bought required a different type plug? That kind of world would reflect many of the situations that currently exist in the computer hardware world. This is a key frustration for businesses purchasing proprietary systems, and it has begun to move us closer to open systems.

# WHY RAID?

As we move toward open systems, this need to plug and play is becoming critical, which is most apparent in the disk storage arena. For example, a customer might need to make a substantial purchase of disk storage for a legacy system, and that legacy system may be slated for replacement by an open system within a year. Business needs dictate you improve the storage capability of the disk farm on the legacy system today. To purchase a proprietary solution, which will make this investment obsolete when you migrate into open systems, would be foolish.

This is a common occurrence in today's world. Now, consumers are looking for an open system solution; they are looking for a disk farm that will work on both the legacy system and the new open system. They want disk drives to be a commodity. The disks are serving the same business purpose on both the legacy system and open system: they are storing information. This need for one solution to meet all needs has helped to fuel the need for open system solutions; hence, a RAID disk farm. The following section looks more closely at RAID and how it has evolved. This discussion of RAID and its various levels/incarnations will help you understand how to use it to your advantage in a data warehouse.

# RAID LEVEL 0—DISK STRIPING

RAID level 0 is actually a bit of a misnomer. While higher levels of RAID provide redundancy, RAID 0 only addresses performance. In this implementation of RAID, data is broken up and written to multiple physical disks and then reassembled when the data is requested by the system. The performance boost results from the fact that hard drives, while faster than ever before, are still much slower than the rest of the computer. By breaking up a 100Kb request into two or more chunks that are written to an equal number of disks simultaneously, the processor can return to its job more quickly.

The biggest drawback with RAID 0 is that if one disk drive in a set fails, you will lose the data on all drives in the stripe set, as if someone took a knife and removed a vertical piece from this page of the book. As the number of devices in an array increases, the chance of failure goes up exponentially. RAID level 3 addresses this problem and is discussed later in this chapter.

# RAID LEVEL 1—DISK MIRRORING

RAID level 1 is perhaps the simplest form for many to understand because its roots are found in DASD and VMS (a popular Digital Equipment operating system) shadowing, which contain functionality with which many readers are familiar. In RAID level 1, there are two disks and each disk contains an exact copy of the data. As the computer makes a request to write or record a block of information, the data is recorded twice, once on disk A and simultaneously on disk B.

As you can see from looking at Figure 13-3, as the data that needs to be recorded (represented by the letters and numbers going into the funnel) is passed along, it is recorded on two disks at once. RAID level 1 does provide for data redundancy because you always have a constant backup occurring on the second disk.

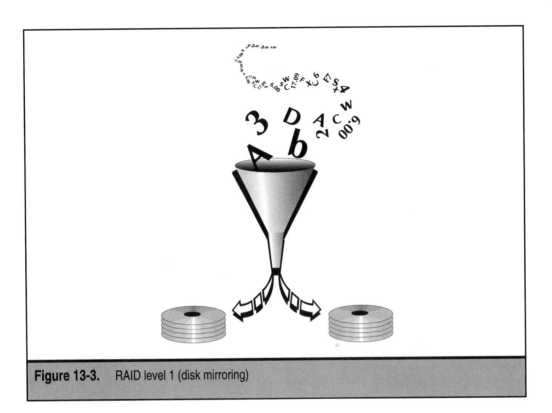

**Figure 13-3.**    RAID level 1 (disk mirroring)

Other common terms for this practice of having two disks record the same information simultaneously are *mirroring* or *shadowing*. This is a more expensive system to build because it requires twice the normal number of disk drives. Over time, this solution evolved beyond just two disks. A chain is only as strong as its weakest link. So, if the one power supply failed, the failure affected both disks. Over time, RAID level 1 evolved, as shown in Figure 13-4.

When the disk controller and the disk drives are duplicated, this is known as *disk duplexing*. Over time, all components were duplicated; for example, you would commonly see dual power supplies. This was done so no matter which component failed, your disk subsystem would continue to operate unhindered.

As the technology improved, you were even able to repair the broken disk while the system was online. This allowed you to do repairs without any downtime. As soon as a new disk was installed to replace the defective one, the RAID system was smart enough to start copying the data present on the good disk to the replacement disk.

To summarize, RAID level 1 has duplicate disks operating side by side in parallel disk mirroring. The mirroring has created greatly improved system reliability because if both disks failed, downtime would be experienced. This was, however, an unlikely situation. In terms of storage, you got only 50 percent capacity because you needed two disks to do

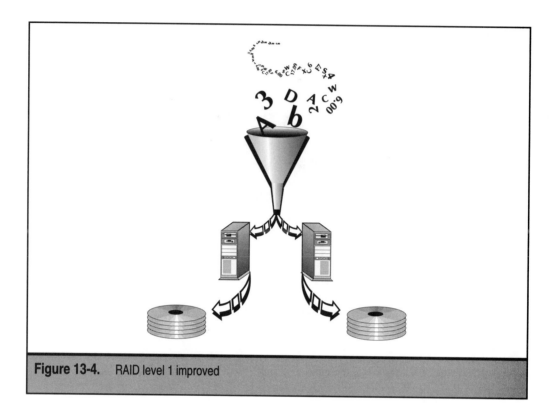

**Figure 13-4.**    RAID level 1 improved

the job normally done by one disk. This approach was considerably more expensive because you needed two disks, two controllers, and two power supplies instead of one. This level of RAID was not as successful as future levels, primarily due to price points. The marketplace sent a clear message: We want the improved retrieval speeds, we want the fault tolerance, we are willing to pay a premium, but we want better price points.

## RAID LEVEL 2—INCOMPATIBLE

RAID level 2 is not currently used due to its incompatibility with current disk drives; there is uncertainty whether this will be used anytime in the foreseeable future.

## RAID LEVEL 3—DATA STRIPING WITH PARITY

The following information was clear from RAID level 1: having the fault tolerance that mirroring provided was desirable only if a way existed to do it without doubling the costs. Once again, a vacuum was created in the marketplace and the forces at work found ways to improve upon the original solution.

The concept of a parity drive was created. A *parity drive* allowed hardware vendors to have a number of disks share an extra drive. In the event of a device failure, the parity drive would be used with the remaining functional disks to determine the contents of the defective drive. Under RAID level 1, a configuration of five drives would require five additional mirror drives, for a total of ten drives. This same configuration under RAID level 3 requires five data drives and only one parity drive, for a total of six drives. As transactions are recorded, they are striped across all drives and the parity drive. By striping the data across multiple drives and a parity driver, the data can be recovered in the event of a failure. The price points were much lower because all data drives in a set could share a single parity drive. See Figure 13-5 for an illustration of this point.

Now for a closer look at the magic of parity and how it works.

## Parity—How It Works

Parity uses basic math to accomplish its task. Each transaction is spread across each of the drives with the parity bit set on the parity drive. In the event of a failure, applying basic math can derive the contents of the missing drive. In Figure 13-6, you will see three

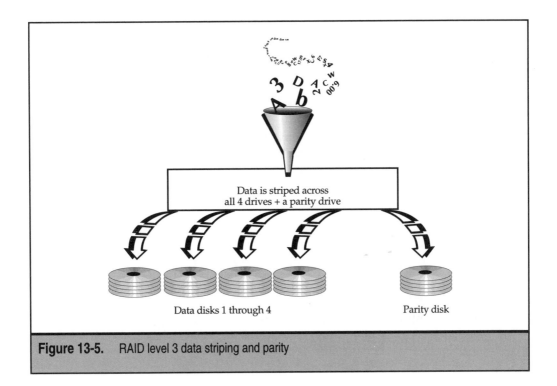

**Figure 13-5.** RAID level 3 data striping and parity

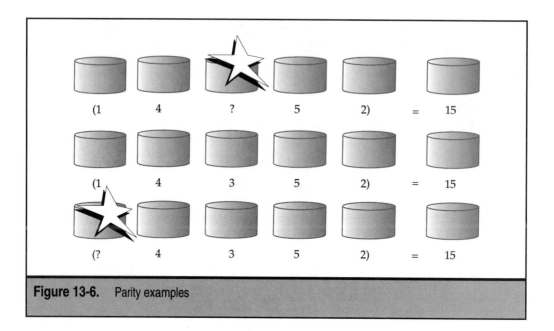

**Figure 13-6.** Parity examples

examples of parity at work. Because we know the parity is 15, the missing value can be determined by applying basic math. In example one, the missing value is 3. In example two, no defective drive exists. In example three, by applying basic math, we know the missing value is 1.

This works because the data is striped across all drives. So, when a transaction happens, the data is written to the disk array. One byte/bit is written to each disk drive, including a parity bit on the parity drive. Think of this as the logical record being interwoven across all drives. This is conceptually how parity works. By having this dedicated parity drive, the ability now exists to recover information on a defective drive. This provides good fault tolerance at a substantially reduced cost. The downside is that during a disk operation, each drive is accessed at the same time. This limits you to one I/O transaction at a time. The upside is you have high data transfer rates. This level of RAID works best for large data requests.

# RAID LEVEL 4—DATA STRIPING (BLOCK AT A TIME) WITH PARITY

In RAID 4, data is still striped across the set of drives all at once, only instead of a byte/bit of information, it is a block of information. This means you have a much higher I/O rate than in level 3.

# RAID LEVEL 5—INDEPENDENT DISK ACCESS, NO PARITY DISK BOTTLENECK

In RAID levels 3 and 4, during a read/write request, all the drives are accessed at the same time in a set. This is not the case in RAID level 5, which has the ability to access as many drives as it needs at the same time for different individual read/write requests. This gives RAID level 5 the highest I/O transfer rate of all its predecessors.

This ability to have multiple readers and writers is a powerful feature. Figure 13-7 shows two users making requests for information that resides on two different locations within the set of two disks. One request is being serviced by one disk and disk controller, while the other disk and disk controller is servicing the other request. The configuration of RAID level 5 gives you greatly improved retrieval speeds; in addition, write operations are not done together.

Unlike RAID level 3, where information was striped at a byte/bit level, in RAID level 5 it is done in a block, or even in record-striping segments. A need no longer exists for a dedicated parity disk, which was a performance bottleneck. In RAID level 5, the parity

**Figure 13-7.**   RAID level 5 (multiple readers/writers)

information is rotated. This means you no longer have the cost associated with the additional parity disk. In the event of a disk failure, you still have the needed parity information. Enough said...time for the SQL Server 7 specifics.

# IMPLEMENTING RAID WITH NT AND SQL SERVER 7

Now that we've reviewed RAID concepts, let's see how we apply this to a SQL Server 7 and NT environment. NT has supported RAID 0, 1, and 5 since Version 3.5. We'll talk more about how you implement these solutions with NT Server in this section.

Your data warehouse is key to your organization's success. You need to have a solid strategy in place for protecting this data. Keeping this in mind, we're going to turn this section upside down and start with our recommendations.

## FAT, NTFS or Raw Partitions, What Do I Use?

SQL Server 6.5 supported three underlying formats for storing data and log files, *FAT* (file allocation table), *NTFS* (NT file system) and *raw partitions* (unstructured devices). NTFS provides compression capabilities that allow you to store more information on a disk, with some sacrifice of performance.

Using FAT file formats for log information may give you a minimal performance boost. We feel that the percentage increase, 10 percent at best, is not worth sacrificing the benefits of NTFS.

**TIP:**   Use NTFS noncompressed file systems for SQL Server 7.

## RAID for Log files

SQL Server 7 log file I/O is sequential. Disks, depending on the manufacturer, process sequential I/O three to four times faster than random I/O. Instead of writing data in contiguous blocks, RAID 5 devices stripe information across a disk array. As a result, placing log files on RAID 5 devices will convert sequential I/O to random I/O. Leverage the log file's sequential I/O capabilities and place these log files on mirrored (i.e., RAID 1) devices. This strategy is also true for SQL Server 6.5, and has not changed for 7.

**TIP:**   Use RAID 1 for log files and RAID 5 for data.

## Hardware Solutions

Disk manufacturers' advances in hardware RAID 5 solutions make this choice an obvious one. The solution will be more expensive, but the additional features such as hot swapping and increased performance over the NT solution will make hardware solutions worth additional money spent.

Existing large SQL Server databases often implement a combination of NT RAID 0 plus hardware RAID 5. This is a necessary solution when the required size of the SQL Server database exceeds the underlying maximum size of the hardware RAID 5 solution. Take the example where the SQL Server database is 30Gb and the hardware RAID array is 10Gb. This is a case where you would have created an NT stripe set consisting of three to four hardware RAID 5 arrays, each with 10Gb of capacity.

The downside is that when your database grows to, let's say 50Gb, you have to break the NT stripe set, add additional disks, and regenerate the stripe set. It is for this reason that we strongly recommend that you leverage SQL Server 7's filegroup and file capabilities.

***TIP:***   Use RAID 5 hardware solutions.

## Assistance for Striping Data

Chapter 7 discussed how we use SQL Server 7 filegroups and files to create a scalable, flexible database design. SQL Server 7 will stripe information across files within a filegroup based on the available space in each separate file. The power of this solution over NT stripe sets is that you can dynamically add files to your filegroup without having to reconfigure.

This capability provides you flexibility in your database design and gives you flexibility when determining your initial database disk hardware needs.

***TIP:***   Use SQL Server 7 filegroups and files to stripe data.

After saying all this and suggesting you go this way rather than the other, let's look at NT RAID support.

# NT RAID SUPPORT

This section is an overview and not an exhaustive section on NT and its RAID support. The goal is for you to understand the basics of NT RAID support when you consider the options for your SQL Server 7 data warehouse.

NT has supported RAID 0, 1, and 5 since Version 3.5. This section will alert you to what's available directly in the NT operating system. We'll talk about the NT architecture supporting RAID and underlying features that provide reliability when storing information onto an NT disk.

Note that things can get confusing in this space. NT supports much of what is supported in underlying disk subsystems. These disk subsystems have become significantly more sophisticated since NT RAID functionality was initially released way back in Version 3.5. Vendors like EMC now have robust solutions for the NT platforms—applications that were not available when Version 3.5 was shipped. We recommend that you leverage these underlying disk subsystems where feasible. In the next section, we will have a look at *fault tolerance*. This feature is the ability of hardware systems to compensate for errors when they occur and allow the system to carry on with business as usual after alerting a human to the situation.

## Sector Sparing (Hot Fixing)

The NT operating system supports *sector sparing* (aka hot fixing). When NT encounters a bad disk sector during an I/O operation, it will attempt to move the data to a good sector from the bad sector. The bad sector is marked and will not be accessed again. The file system is not alerted of the problem when this operation succeeds. If this operation fails, the error bubbles up to the specific I/O system, which is then responsible for handling the error.

## FTDISK.SYS

The NT fault-tolerant disk subsystem, ftdisk.sys, installs itself at NT boot time, and is responsible for implementing NT RAID. It services disk I/O requests from the file system and then applies these requests to the underlying RAID system. It's transparent to the file system which level of RAID is active, if any are active at all. Figure 13-8 illustrates how this I/O is sent to two different locations, unbeknown to the application but part of the NT fault-tolerance methodology.

## NT Disk Administrator

The NT system administrator uses the Disk Administrator utility, which ships with NT and is available under the Start menu | Administrative Tools menu group. Figure 13-9 shows a sample Disk Administrator session for an NT system where RAID 5 can be enabled.

# WHAT NT RAID TO USE WHEN

The following three points sum up our experience and feelings in a nutshell. Remember, a nutshell is easily broken and many readers may desire to break our suggestions.

▼ RAID level 0 (aka disk striping) data within the disks in the stripe set is divided into 64Kb blocks and spread evenly across all disks in the stripe set. This is a viable solution when your total disk requirements are larger than the underlying disk capacity. As noted earlier, SQL Server 7 removes this as an absolute requirement for SQL Server VLDB.

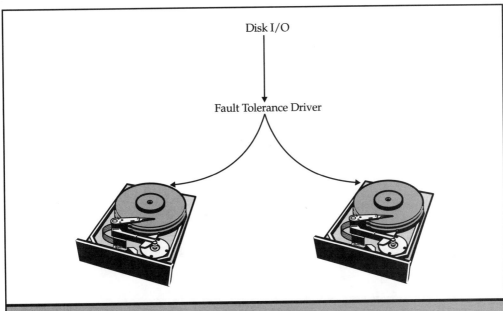

**Figure 13-8.** Fault tolerance transparent to I/O stream

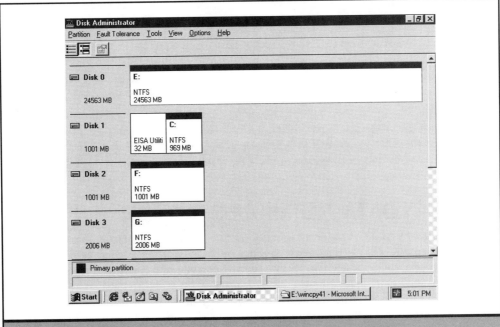

**Figure 13-9.** Disk administration with RAID 5 enabled

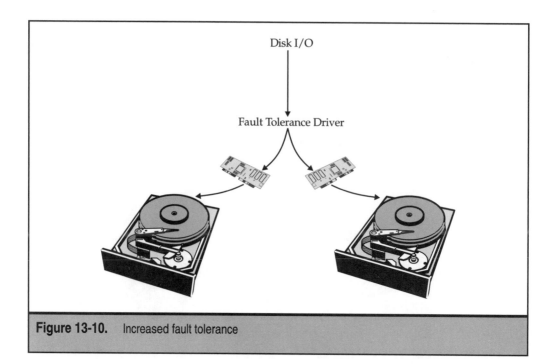

**Figure 13-10.**   Increased fault tolerance

- RAID level 1, or disk mirroring, can be implemented in the underlying disk hardware or with NT. Disk mirroring, unlike RAID 5, is a viable application of NT RAID technology. In addition to disk mirroring, disk duplexing is also a consideration for minimizing disk controller failures and making your system more fault tolerant. Figure 13-10 shows this enhancement with separate controllers for each disk pack.

▲ Given the advances in hardware RAID 5 support, we recommend that you do not use NT for your RAID 5 needs. RAID 5 (aka striping with parity) will add to your compute cycles and will significantly slow down your write performance.

## RAID—EVERY DATA WAREHOUSE NEEDS IT

Future trends in RAID clearly show the I/O barrier will continue to be broken. Getting your data from a RAID stack of many smaller disks is now faster than getting it from a larger, traditional disk. As RAID technology further develops, it continues to remove the performance constraints associated with disk retrieval speeds.

Fault tolerance continues to improve. RAID is now at the point where it is *hot swappable*, which means, in the event of a disk failure, you can fix the problem without impacting the availability of the data. RAID vendors are also reaching the point of keeping your RAID box up and running transparent to the customer. Many times when a failure happens, the box can now notify the vendor to send in a repairperson.

Bigger, improved disk caches are in the works. Bottlenecks can occur with high-performance systems due to the slower speeds of physical disk I/O. The RAID vendors are providing for bigger and bigger memory caches to remedy this problem. With these bigger caches, user requests never have to wait for a physical read or write. In the event of a read, the RAID box reads ahead of the users' requests and has the data sitting in memory, which is the fastest way to service a read request. In the event of a write request, the RAID box places the write in memory and signals the waiting process it is ready. Because the box is so fault tolerant, no fear exists that the write request might get lost due to a hardware problem.

On the horizon are numerous improvements to enhance your ability to back up the data warehouse using the RAID configuration. The RAID vendors realize a data warehouse is the most complex system a customer may ever face when working from a disk farm or a backup perspective. They are now building in tools that allow customers numerous backup options. This occurred because many of the vendors had customers who had no way to back up their large data warehouses.

Bottom line—a RAID box is the fastest, safest way to store your data. With the improved price points, increased memory caches, and new options on how to back up your data, you cannot afford to miss looking at RAID as an option for your warehouse endeavor.

Time to move on. In Chapter 14, we are going to have a look at getting the data to the users. Is that not what this whole effort focuses on in the first place? Get it out of the operational systems, scrub it, load it, make it available, and turn the user community loose.

# CHAPTER 14

# Getting Data to Users: An Introduction to Query Technologies

The data warehouse is a powerful repository of information, but it is not the total solution. As we have already discussed, the data warehouse is an integrated database that serves as a one-stop shopping center for the organization's information. The data in the warehouse can be used to better understand the business, but without access to this data, the power is meaningless. We are very aware that in organizations that do not have data warehouses, getting the information is half the battle for performing analysis on our business. How often do we find that we spend an exorbitant amount of energy going from department to department collecting information? This information can be in hardcopy reports or spreadsheets, or—if we are lucky—it is contained in a well-organized operational system. After expending all that energy, we become concerned with collating the data into a report, which may or may not be time-based, or we have a number of reports that have numbers contained within them that do not match or correspond. The problems with getting the data together and then putting it into a meaningful report can be a challenge in the best of times.

The data warehouse provides us with a great vehicle for business analysis. It has organized our business into manageable parts that are simple for end users to navigate. The overall success of your data warehouse depends upon providing simple and fast access to data. In fact, we often like to point out that to most end users the data warehouse is the access tool—they have no idea of the work and effort that went into the beautiful database behind the scenes. The selection and use of your query tools will therefore directly impact your data warehouse's success. Users must be able to easily answer the business questions that are supported by data in the warehouse. Many query tools exist today that help us gain reporting and ad hoc access to our data. Which tools you would use depend on the type of access your end users require. If you have power users who are comfortable using a tool such as Query Analyzer, this may suffice for certain requirements. Others will require more "hand holding," and will need tools that have data prepared for them, like Cognos' Impromptu or even Microsoft Excel or Access. Users work with sophisticated tools that enable them to perform business analysis—analyses that used to be difficult or impossible to achieve from the operational database. Tools that access the data warehouse are judged on the following criteria:

▼ They must allow users to view and print regular reports.

■ They must provide the ability to drill-down and investigate the "numbers" generated by the report.

■ They must allow users to easily develop their own reports and reproduce these reports as required.

▲ They must move costly personnel hours from data gathering to data analysis.

We can separate data access into three specific areas:

▼ Standard reports

■ Ad hoc queries

▲ Multidimensional analysis

Standard reports are our old friends. These are specific reports that can be distributed to users as stand-alone entities. Reports such as a listing of the current financial position would meet these criteria. The distribution of these reports can be handled by many different methods. Reports can be created and the resulting output either printed (but, how many trees need to die?), distributed electronically (email or Internet), or made available for viewing on a LAN (*local area network* in a confined area of one's business). Almost any tool can perform the creation of these reports. The factors that will help you decide what tools will be used and how these reports will be created is dependent upon the flexibility required by these reports. If a report that does not require a high degree of customization and formatting is not a big concern, then a simple query tool like Query Analyzer will meet this requirement. In cases where you need more customization of a report, then the more complete tools will be required.

# AD HOC ACCESS

Ad hoc data access presents a completely different set of output requirements. The method of extracting data from the data warehouse depends upon the expertise of the user community as well as formatting needs. If the end users are a confident group who have a relatively good grasp of SQL, then Query Analyzer can meet their needs. Many end users do not have this level of expertise in SQL and would like to be insulated from the database as much as possible. Who can blame them? Today's generation of end-user data query tools meet this requirement head-on since the users have no idea of the contents of the database in the background. These tools have been evolving at such a quick pace that it seems that every day another tool provides more functionality and better ease of use. For our discussion in this chapter, we will illustrate this with two of these tools: Microsoft Access and Cognos Impromptu. Both these tools are considered to be among the best of the breed and provide a significant amount of power to the end user, balancing ease of use and customization.

The last type of data access we need to discuss is multidimensional analysis. This is *online analytical processing* (OLAP), which you have heard so much about. OLAP provides users with the ability to view their data from many different perspectives while maintaining a sound and efficient data structure.

Whichever method you decide upon to extract data from your warehouse, just remember to evaluate each solution based on your needs. The success of your data warehouse depends on it. Your solution will be a combination of tools. One product will rarely meet all data warehouse reporting needs, so you will probably require a multiproduct solution to meet all your needs. Salespeople are very convincing, and many can sell an electric lamp to someone during a blackout. However, by following some simple guidelines, you can decide on the set of tools best suited to your data reporting requirements. When evaluating the various products, you will need to reconcile the following questions:

▼ What type of reports do you plan to create?

■ Is there a requirement for ad hoc data query?

■ Do your users have SQL knowledge?

■ Will you be performing multidimensional analysis?

■ How will you be distributing the report output?

■ Will the Internet be used for distribution?

■ How will you maintain these reports?

▲ How will you define your metadata, the layer that describes your data in the warehouse?

The choice of the right query tools will be one that will allow users to exploit the power of your data warehouse in the long term. Therefore, you must make this choice intelligently. Let's now move into some of the important characteristics of a data warehouse query tool so that you can better understand the tools and utilize them to their fullest potential.

# QUERY TOOL CHARACTERISTICS

The evaluation and selection of query tools is one of the most important decisions that you will make in the development and deployment of your data warehouse. This product will form the window through which your users will access their data. You could choose the cheapest option, that being Query Analyzer, but the long-term cost to this option is one that will become apparent. So, you then need to decide on a query tool. Will it be Sagent Data Access Tools, Microsoft Excel and Access, Cognos Impromptu, Business Objects, or some other query tool? Why is it that every question is critical when it comes to product selection? Just because! Select the wrong tool and you can handicap the success of the data warehouse mission. It's just like putting the wrong di-lithium crystals into the warp drive. This discussion does not apply to using Query Analyzer as a reporting tool for your data warehouse. If you do decide to use Query Analyzer as your only reporting tool, then you may want to think about a new career. Even though it is a robust product that can produce many of the reports that you may require, it does not meet the needs of many of today's analysts. Query Analyzer should form one part of the solution, but it does not provide all the functionality needed to leverage the work that we have done in creating the data warehouse, and usually will not provide an interface that the CEO will be willing to consider an acceptable solution.

When evaluating the various tools, what should you look for? It is just as important to evaluate your reporting requirements as it is to determine the cost to roll it out to your organization. The following are some criteria that you should evaluate during your product selection process:

▼  Ease of use

■  Performance

■  Multiple data sources

■  Centralized administration

■  Data security

■  Web-enabled

▲  Integrated analysis

This chapter will not make the decision for you as to which tool is the best, but it will help you towards making the appropriate decision for your business. Experience has shown us that many products will meet all the criteria at some level, but the final selection must be based on your own business requirements. Let's now look at each of the criteria we have defined and how each one impacts the data warehouse and the query use of our end users.

# Ease of Use

First, and probably most important, is ease of use. This factor is probably the most important to your users, and if you can make your users happy, you are halfway to a successful data warehouse. The ease of use is centered in two areas: building reports and presentation flexibility. The product must make it easy for your users to draw information from the database. Many tools provide this through a simple and intuitive graphical user interface (GUI). These tools often provide seamless installation and setup. They also possess the ability to insulate the users from the complexities that are inherent in many databases. Through ideas such as a "Catalog" or "End-User Layer," query tool administrators can prepare an environment that allows users to access the database without needing to understand how the data is linked together. By providing this simple administration and end-user layer, analysts can now focus on collecting the data they need instead of becoming intimidated by a complex data structure that requires a road map and a sextant to navigate.

The users must also have the ability to easily manipulate and change their reports to meet their needs. Whether this simply means that they can move data and change the presentation of the data or the deeper investigation of the information, this functionality needs to be present within the tools that you select.

Ease of use is a very personal matter. What may seem to be easy to one person may be cumbersome to another. During your evaluation of the tools, you should put together a cross-section of users, and together with this team determine what best suits your business' goals and user expertise.

# Performance

Performance is one item that can be the difference between users analyzing their data and users sitting around talking about what the Boston Bruins need to do to win another Stanley Cup. The level of performance is related to the whole data warehouse environment—the database, the query tool, and the SQL that is used to access your data. Together, all these items influence performance. Each of these influences affects performance. Together, they can conspire to doom your warehouse project, which will allow for some serious discussions on sports!

# Multiple Data Sources

Your data warehouse has been constructed and you need to provide the answers that your business requires to numerous questions. You start to write a new report and then discover that you need some information that is not contained in the warehouse. What should you do? Your options include the alteration of the warehouse to include this data, but this will take too long. So, you decide that you will include data from a second data source. This data source could be a flat file containing the data, or it may be another database. For example, your warehouse may contain the sales that have been completed but not contain the budget numbers—these are contained in your budgeting system. The query tool that you select must have the ability to combine data from these two sources so that the report you produce reflects the business requirement. Most query and reporting tools allow you to include data from multiple data sources, but ensure that the types of sources supported by the product will integrate well into your data warehouse and information systems.

# Centralized Administration

During your evaluation, it is important to consider centralized administration of the data that you present to your users. This is the feature that separates the men from the boys and women from the girls in query and reporting tools. A centralized administration of the tool allows knowledgeable individuals within your organization to present a simple and efficient user interface to the end users. Each query tool calls it something different. In Cognos Impromptu, for example, it is known as the Catalog. Whatever you call it, the purpose of this layer is to allow users to view their data on their own terms and to eliminate the need to understand data structures and join strategies.

The end user does not need to be concerned with this aspect of the warehouse. The user is required to simply select the data to include in the query, and the program will format the data according to the rules and formats defined during the creation of the layer.

During your appraisal of the tools, you must decide how simple and effective the administration of the tool appears, and how it will impact your reporting strategy. The administration of the end-user layer must be simple enough to use while still allowing for quick changes. These changes will be required, as the data available to the users may need to be altered to meet their quickly changing information requirements.

# Data Security

Security is an issue that could be ignored or dealt with, depending on how important you consider your data. Today, in most organizations, data security is always a concern, and we understand that completely. Any query tool that does not incorporate some additional security features is a tool that may not be one that you should consider in a data-sensitive environment. It is for this reason alone that the wide use of Query Analyzer concerns us in any data warehouse environment. Although we can define a certain degree of data security within the database, we are exposing our users to data that must be carefully managed. When it comes to Query Analyzer, we prefer to limit the use and access to the tool to only selected data warehouse users. Query tools are much more powerful in that we have the ability to define the data dictionary that the users will access by predefining what the user can see. We also can define different business views for the various groups within our organization. You can have a catalog for your human resource department that may include the salary data for all employees, whereas in the corporate directory you may have details on all employees, without any financial information.

Security should always be a concern to every organization, as the data warehouse will usually contain a plethora of information—some of which may be confidential. The security of your data from a query tool should be considered during your evaluation of tools so that you can best protect your information.

## Web-Enabled

The impact of the Internet is in turn having a profound impact on the way that we gather and distribute information. It has allowed us to make information available to many people who previously had not been able to see it. The Internet is quickly becoming our window into the world, and data warehouse information can now be distributed via the Web. Most query tools will allow you to publish your results to a page, and even to allow for drill-down capabilities provided through this interface.

Results can be formatted to meet just about any requirements. Although query tool integration with the Web is in its infancy, it is quickly developing into a required element for any tool that you may choose for your organization.

## Integrated Analysis

The power of any reporting tool is its ability to offer users the flexibility to investigate the numbers that are displayed to them. For example, if you have a summary report that displays the sales figures for your organization by region—providing the sales and profit values—you may want to "drill" into data within a specific region to see how its numbers are broken down. Therefore, you should select a product that has the ability to allow you to "slice and dice" your data. This ability to investigate your data includes the following functions:

- ▼ Drill-down into data
- ■ Transpose columns and rows (also known as pivoting)
- ■ Conditional filtering of data
- ■ Format your data
- ▲ Exclusion of columns from your display

It is advantageous for your OLAP tool to integrate with your query tool. For example, when viewing summaries within a tool like Cognos' PowerPlay, you may decide that you would like to view the detailed information that generated the summary. Cognos' Impromptu would then be invoked and a query executed that would display the detailed records. This integration can provide an extra level of functionality that will improve the flexibility of your end-user data warehouse access. Let's now look at some tools that can be used to access your data warehouse

# USING QUERY ANALYZER FOR REPORTING

Query Analyzer is one of those underappreciated tools available to end users. It can produce predefined reports with the greatest of ease, but it can also be used to create ad hoc reports. What it does not provide is the ability to investigate the numbers, since a report must be rerun to change the format and data that is being displayed. Figure 14-1 is an example of this tool.

Although it is not highly formatted (all right, the data is not formatted at all), we have generated a simple report that provides the user with a listing of all the authors in the "PUBS" database. This report, which is simple to construct, does provide users with a great deal of information. These are the types of reports that you will create using Query Analyzer. These will be static reports, which will be displayed or printed.

The downside to a tool such as Query Analyzer is its limited functionality. It will only produce static reports, and this product does not address the need for integrated analysis. The other area that should concern any data warehouse administrator is runaway SQL. So often we have heard of a user waiting two to three days for a query to return results, while at the same time the other users are complaining that the system performance is "SLOW"! This danger always exists if you include Query Analyzer in the reporting toolset in your organization. You must train your personnel to optimize their SQL and help them to understand the data warehouse database schema in order for them to build efficient reports.

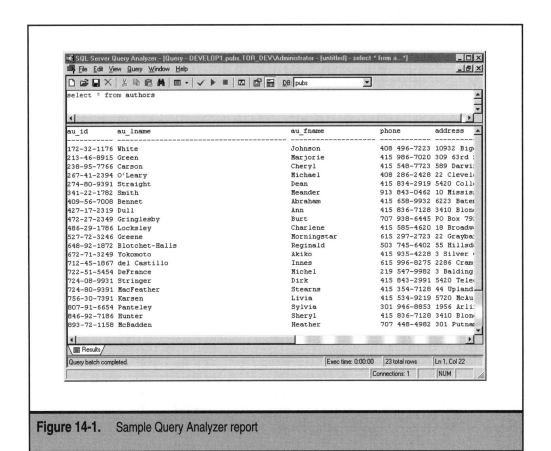

**Figure 14-1.**  Sample Query Analyzer report

# MICROSOFT EXCEL

Microsoft Excel? Yes Microsoft Excel! Believe it or not, your Microsoft Office tools can finally be used for something other than memos, financial reporting etc. Most companies invest in office productivity tools for specific reasons. One of the top, if not the most important, reasons is the second word—productivity. It is a known fact that no "office productivity" tool has actually increased productivity in an appreciable manner. One way to increase productivity is to empower the end users with information the way they want it when they want it, using a tool they are comfortable using. One of those tools is Microsoft Excel. With Microsoft Excel, you can access most any data source.

## Defining a Query

Click on the Start button, choose Programs, then Microsoft Excel. Open a new workbook. From the menu, choose Data, then Pivot Table Report. You will then be presented with the Pivot Table Wizard. A *pivot table* is an interactive table that quickly summarizes, or cross-tabulates, large amounts of data. You can rotate its rows and columns to see different summaries of the source data, filter the data by displaying, or display the details for areas of interest.

## The Pivot Table Wizard

The Pivot Table Wizard in step 1 will present you with options you wish to analyze. The choices are shown in Figure 14-2.

We have chosen an external data source. This choice will lead you to the next step—getting the data from the data sources. Click on the Get Data button, choose "Create" New Data Source, and click on OK.

### Creating a Data Source

For this step, you may need the assistance of your DBA or system administrator. They will have some of the information you will need to complete this wizard. Figure 14-3 shows you an example of what information you will need to supply.

After completing this wizard, you will find yourself back in the Pivot Table Wizard, showing your newly created data source as part of the list. Choose your data source and click OK.

You will next see a Query Wizard, and it will ask you for the names of the columns that you would like to include in your query. All this activity will be taking place in wizards other than the Pivot Table Wizard. These other wizards are setting up the infrastructure so that your pivot table can be created.

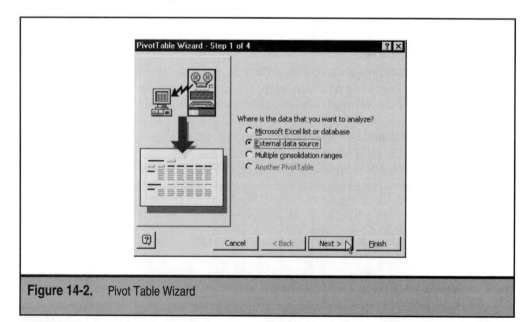

**Figure 14-2.**   Pivot Table Wizard

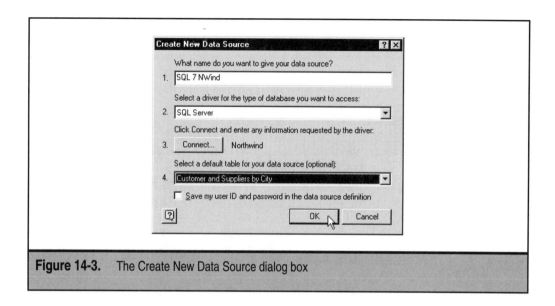

**Figure 14-3.** The Create New Data Source dialog box

## Constructing the Pivot Table

Click and drag the columns, as shown in the wizard, to their respective places on the report. If you think of rows, columns, and data, it will help you decide where to place the individual columns. Figure 14-4 shows you an example of what you will see in this step of the wizard.

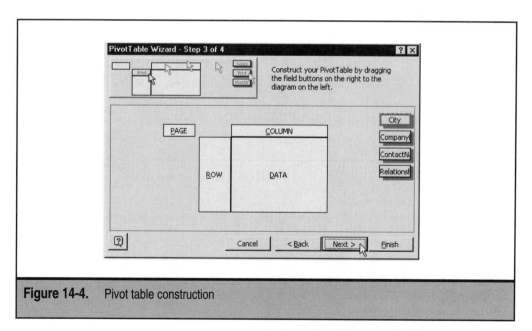

**Figure 14-4.** Pivot table construction

After completing the wizard, you will find yourself back in Excel with your new pivot table. The column names will be highlighted. You have the option of clicking on the column names and dragging them to where you would like to see them to further fine-tune them.

# MICROSOFT ACCESS

For the same reasons you would choose to use Microsoft Excel, you could choose to use Access. The reason you have a choice between Excel and Access is that you have an option. Both tools are powerful and will report to you the same data the way you want to see it. Access, however, may give you more capability to generate and customize reports

## Getting the Data

Create a new database in Access. Please refer to your documentation or help files for Microsoft Access to learn how to perform this task; after all, this is a book about SQL Server. To get to the data, choose File from the menu, then Get External Data/Link Tables. On the next screen, under the Files of Type drop-down list, choose ODBC Databases ().

This will bring you into the ODBC Data Source Wizard. You will again need the assistance of your DBA or system administrator to identify the appropriate database you should use. In the wizard, you will be presented with all the databases available to you. If you do not have a data source defined, click on New and complete the wizard. Select all the tables needed for your report and click OK. This will then form the connection to the database from which you will select your data.

## Defining the Query

When you return to Access, you will see all the tables under the Tables tab. Choose the Queries tab and click on the New button. Pick the Crosstab Query Wizard, and click on the OK button. Next, you will see a list of all the possible tables you can choose. Select the table or tables that you would like to include in your report. Figure 14-5 illustrates the performance of this task.

Complete this by choosing the columns you want to include in your report. You will be required to define the data that will form the basis of the rows and columns within your report. After you have completed the steps and saved the query, you will return to Access and see your new query. Double-click on the query to tell Access to execute it—and enjoy.

Although we know that we always get things right the first time, especially in the computer industry, it may be necessary to change the query. To make the changes that are required, you have to either go through the entire wizard again or click on design, and that is where things get complicated. So-called "power users" may revel in the complexity; however, for the rest of the users of this functionality, it may be a little too much. For most users, that is the main difference we saw between the Excel and Access options.

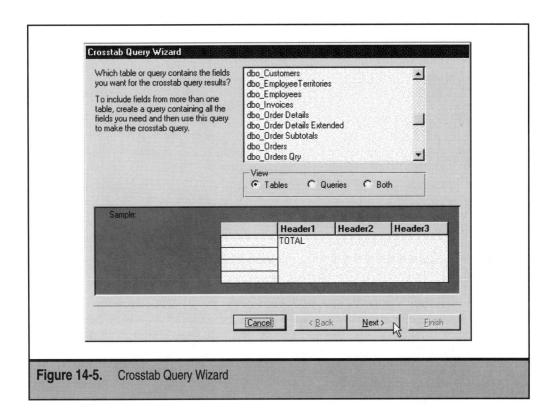

**Figure 14-5.**   Crosstab Query Wizard

Now that we have discussed a few Microsoft options, let us take a closer look at a third party product, Cognos' Impromptu.

# COGNOS IMPROMPTU

The purpose of this section is to take an in-depth look at Impromptu. Impromptu will be discussed from both the administrator and the end-user perspectives. Impromptu is available in a number of different flavors: Impromptu Server, Impromptu Web Server, and Impromptu Desktop. This book deals with Impromptu Desktop—the most common package of the three.

The heart of Impromptu is its catalog. A *catalog* contains information on how to connect to a database and acts as the end-users' interface into that database. The catalog should be designed to provide a business view of the database. Building folders, columns, calculations, and filters creates this business view. As an administrator, you will be required to perform the following tasks:

1. Define the connection to the database.
2. Create the catalog.
3. Add the required tables.
4. Define the required joins.
5. Create a folder structure.
6. Add profiles.

The following subsections will guide you through the tasks that you must complete to generate reports from Impromptu.

## Define the Connection to the Database

The first step in creating an Impromptu application is to connect to the database. This is accomplished through the database definition section. It is a good idea to have your technical support people work with you through this step. Problems at this stage are often related to infrastructure and not to the product. You simply supply the appropriate database connection string where required.

## Create the Catalog

Now that you have defined your database definition, you are ready to create your catalog. Remember, a catalog is simply a file with a ".cat" extension. The catalog definition screen is where you name your catalog, choose your catalog type, and then tell Impromptu which database to connect to (using the definition that you created in the previous step). As well, a Select Tables and an Include all Tables radio button is clicked after you decide if all tables or a subset of all tables should be made available as the catalog is set up. By default, you are choosing which tables are to be included in the database. It is a good idea to leave this option set.

**NOTE:**   If you choose Include all Tables, then unnecessary tables may enter into your catalog.

Impromptu supports four types of catalogs. The different catalog types support different needs and rollout strategies. Catalog types can be changed—for instance, you may start with a personal catalog for development purposes and then switch it to either a shared or distributed catalog. Listed next are the four catalog types and their suggested uses.

## Personal

This is a catalog that is not to be shared by any other users. This type of catalog can be used to support local applications. A good example is connecting to a local Microsoft Access application that resides on a single-user workstation.

## Shared

Designating a catalog as shared allows many people to connect simultaneously to the catalog. The deployment of this catalog is simple. Create the catalog and put it on a common networked drive where all users can see it, feel it, and touch it (especially little Tommy).

## Distributed

A distributed catalog is in many ways similar to a shared catalog. In the case of a distributed catalog, the first time the user opens the catalog, a copy of it is made onto their local PC. Subsequently, each time the catalog is opened locally, it synchronizes with the master catalog. Distributed catalogs can be used to allow users to make changes to their local catalog (add their own folders, local administration, etc.) while staying in synch with the master catalog.

## Secure

This type of catalog is used if you want a user to just be able to run reports created on their behalf. By defining the catalog's properties, we can now move into selecting the data that we will require based on our reporting requirements.

# Add Tables

Impromptu allows you to include some or all tables from a database into your catalog. If a table is not included in the catalog, then there is no way for the end user to access that table. You also have the choice of including a table but not including all the columns from that table.

Consider the purpose of your catalog carefully. Only tables that are necessary to support this purpose should be included. Many organizations struggle with the question of whether to create one multipurpose catalog or to create many purpose-driven catalogs. Do I create a sales catalog and a separate accounting catalog? Do I create one catalog for both departments and administer it with user profiles? User profiles will define the access different users will have within the model. These questions need to be answered before embarking on catalog creation.

We are seeing more organizations lean towards the purpose-driven catalogs. The rationale is that the joins are easier to administer. Based on your catalog definition, you then select the required tables that you need for this purpose. Figure 14-6 illustrates how your tables will be selected.

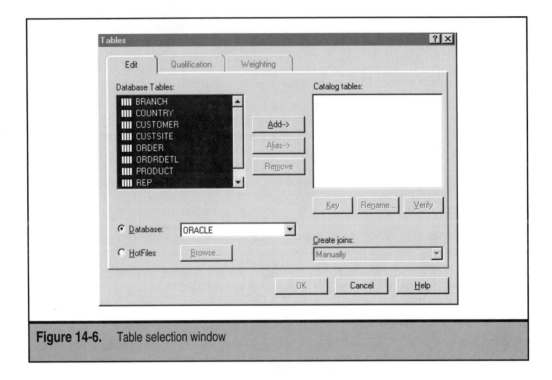

**Figure 14-6.**   Table selection window

Impromptu allows you to include SQL Server tables and/or views into your catalog. Additionally, you can add a table as an alias. This feature allows you to resolve many complex join issues in a simple manner.

Once you have selected the tables and views to include in your catalog, you must decide how you would like Impromptu to handle the joins. Impromptu can define your joins for you automatically or you can elect to define the joins yourself. We recommend that you define your joins manually. Impromptu's automatic join generation capabilities may result in a less than perfect join strategy. In particular, an automatic join strategy can create unwanted loops.

## Define the Required Joins

Impromptu allows you to put in place a join strategy for the end users. How the tables are joined should be the responsibility of the Impromptu administrator. The end user is then shielded from the management of joins, and that allows them to focus on doing their job creating reports. The end user should be able to select any columns from within a folder and Impromptu should return a correct result set. We will touch on this again when we discuss folders in the next section. Let us now look at how we define the required joins in Figure 14-7.

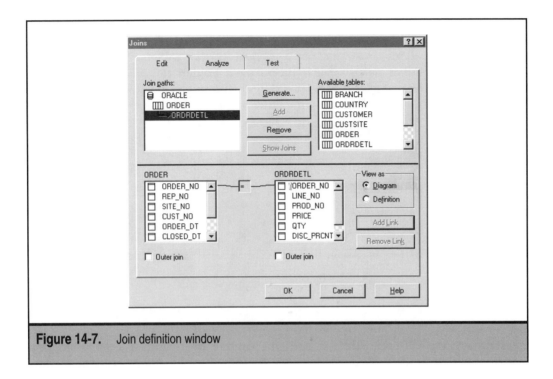

**Figure 14-7.** Join definition window

To create a join between two tables, you must first select the tables to be involved. Once the tables have been selected, you must then select the columns that are to form the join. Impromptu supports a wide array of joins, including equijoins, outer joins, complex joins, and compound joins. Remember that how tables are joined affects performance.

To assist you with your join strategy, Impromptu provides two helpful features. The Analyze tab feature checks your join strategy for possible problems such as loops and isolated tables. The Test feature allows you to choose tables to see how Impromptu resolves the join.

## Create a Folder Structure

Creating a folder is critical to the implementation of a successful catalog. The folder structure is what the end user views. This structure should reflect the business processes of an organization. It should be easy to navigate, and contain English or corporate names (Discount Percentage, not Disc Prcnt).

Impromptu, by default, creates a folder for each table that has been added to the catalog. It is a good convention to move all these tables into a folder named ADMIN. This folder is for administration purposes only and can be hidden from the common user. Organizations that do not modify the default strategy are often unsuccessful with their Impromptu rollout. We have seen implementations that have 50 root folders. These implementations offer little value to the end user.

We suggest renaming the subfolders and columns from within the ADMIN folder. These names should be proper English names that reflect terminology used within the business. This provides consistency as you create further folders. Next, organize the folders in a fashion that makes sense to the business. Folders can contain columns from any number of different tables. The key is to have columns grouped together in a manner that the user would expect. The following illustrates how to manage your folders:

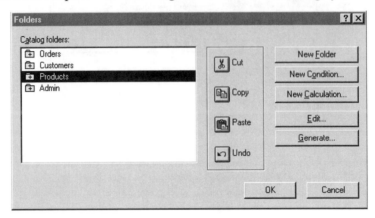

Furthermore, you can add value to the catalog by including calculations and conditions. The inclusion of calculations and conditions in the catalog ensures standard definitions are being employed throughout the organization.

We try to create major folder groups that contain all relevant subfolders underneath. This strategy causes duplication of folders but makes navigation simple for the user. Within a major folder, any combination of columns should result in a valid join. Again, this is why the ability to alias tables is so important—it permits you to use the same table in different join combinations. At the completion of the folder definition, you then move into defining profiles for your model.

# Add Profiles

Impromptu has a variety of useful administrative functions that control access and use. Impromptu allows you to add user classes, which define what a user can see and do. It is this functionality that allows you to roll out one multipurpose catalog to many users.

It is not necessary to use profiles, and some organizations don't, but it can be useful. Consider the following—you can hide certain folders, tables, or columns from an end user. Your security may require that salespeople obtain information about their sales but be restricted from seeing what margin they are achieving.

Filters can be applied based on selected values from the database. As an example, you could restrict a user from viewing a certain product type. The key is that the catalog is the central point of administration. A variety of different users can be supported through the same catalog. The folder access area, as shown in Figure 14-8, is particularly useful in ensuring the database is used in a secure manner.

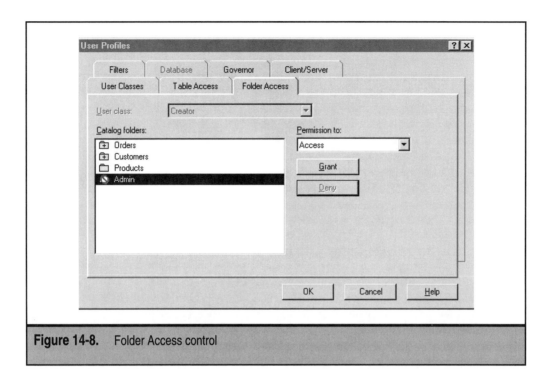

**Figure 14-8.** Folder Access control

This area allows you to grant users access to folders that would be of interest to them. The Governor tab will allow you to place restrictions on a number of different areas, which can ensure optimum performance. Consider sorting restrictions, protection against cross-product queries, limits on data retrieval, etc.

Congratulations! You have completed your catalog and are now ready to deploy it to your end users.

# IMPROMPTU FROM THE END-USER PERSPECTIVE

The purpose of this section is to discuss the functionality that Impromptu delivers to end users. Impromptu offers the same interface regardless of the database platform. The end users are not aware if they are, for example, connected to a local Dbase database through Microsoft Excel or Access.

## Getting Started

Remember that in its simplest form, a catalog is just a file. The first step in working with Impromptu is to open the catalog. Depending on how the catalog has been set up, you will have to select a user class, enter a password, and enter a database user ID and password. The login window is shown here:

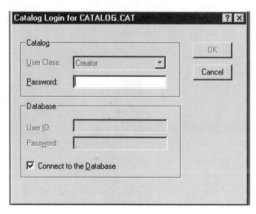

You will then connect to the required database and catalog while Impromptu handles all the administration.

Creating a report in Impromptu is a very simple process. The process is quite similar to creating a report in Word. First of all, you choose a template. The template predetermines how your data will be displayed. As an example, if you want to create a professional memorandum, Word has a template to assist you with the design. A screen listing the types of templates that you have available after an initial Impromptu installation is shown here:

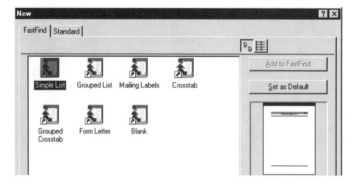

Similarly, Impromptu has templates that support most of the popular report styles. The most common template is the Simple List. The Simple List report displays each record as a row. Once you have selected a template, you will be presented with the Query dialog box where you specify items such as what data to retrieve, how to sort the output, what type of summarizing (grouping) to perform, and the conditions for data selection (referred to as filtering).

The Query dialog box is where you choose which columns you want displayed on the report. You are presented with the same folder structure that you designed in the "Administration" section. Simply navigate the folder structure to locate the columns you require for the report and then double-click it or highlight it, then press the Add->> button, or drag and drop it to the Query section. If it is easy to navigate through this section and locate the columns you require, then you probably have a good folder design in place. Remember, all the end users care about is how easy it is to create their reports.

Impromptu allows you to apply sorting, grouping, and filtering prior to displaying the report. This method is the most efficient manner of creating a report. However, these options can also be applied afterwards, which is what we will do. In many cases, to get started, users begin using the Simple List template, which presents their report in a familiar columnar and tabular format.

Impromptu now displays the report using the first 100 records, based on the selection criteria. At this stage, Impromptu allows you to apply formats, rename columns, and move columns, all without requerying the database. Next, you may want to apply a filter, group your data, and add headers. Each of these functions can be applied by simply highlighting a cell and then clicking the accompanying icon. If you don't like the result, you can simply press Undo (Impromptu allows you to apply ten Undo's by default).

To add column totals, simply highlight the column containing the values you want to sum and then click on the Total icon. Impromptu adds a footer and a total for every level of grouping that has been defined. Figure 14-8 shows you how the report might look after applying these functions.

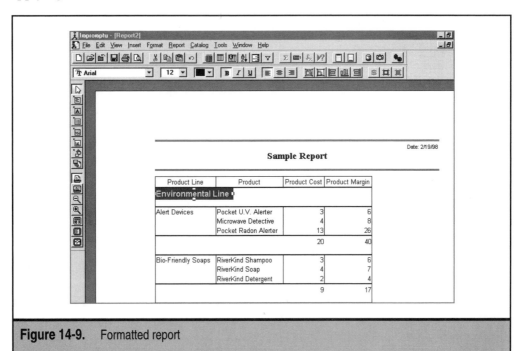

**Figure 14-9.**   Formatted report

This report can now be saved and be made available to other users. Impromptu saves all reports with an .imr extension. Remember that all Impromptu saves is the query (the formatting and the SQL), and not the data. The following listing contains the SQL that is used to create the report:

```
select c19 as c1,
       c18 as c2,
       c22 as c3,
       c21 as c4,
       rsum(c21 for c19,c18) as c5,
       rsum(c21 for c19,c18) as c6,
       rsum(c21) as c7,
       c20 as c8,
       rsum(c20 for c19,c18) as c9,
       rsum(c20 for c19,c18) as c10,
       rsum(c20) as c11
from
(select t1."PROD_LINE" as c18,
       t1."PROD_TYPE" as c19,
       (t1."PROD_PRICE" - t1."PROD_COST") as c20,
       t1."PROD_COST" as c21,
       t1."PRODUCT" as c22
from "PRODUCT" t1
where (t1."prod_line" in ('TENTS             ',
                          'BACK PACKS        ')))
order by c19 asc,c18 asc
) d1
```

The SQL generated can always be viewed from under the Report Profile tab. This is very useful in determining how Impromptu produced your result set. In particular, you can see which tables have been used in intermediate joins. Impromptu provides solutions for exporting the data to other programs. You can save your reports as HTML, Excel, Word, ASCII, and a host of other popular formats.

Query tools allow you to extract data from your warehouse on a defined or ad hoc basis. They form an important component of your data warehousing strategy. Just as you must decide on a database for your warehouse, you must complement it with the proper tools. By following our approach to selecting a product for your reporting requirements, with additional criteria based on your organization's requirements, you will select a tool that is right for you and your organization.

Time to move on.... The next chapter deals with Microsoft's new offering in the decision support server arena. This type of offering is mandatory when looking at the complete, one-stop shopping solution like SQL Server 7. Hark! Is that Plato or you, Aristotle?

# CHAPTER 15

## OLAP

Some of the previous chapters in this book established the groundwork necessary to reach the ultimate goal—decision support. That is what decision support and data warehousing is all about—supporting more informed decisions. Consider the route you drive each day to arrive at the office. If you are like us, you spend very little time contemplating the amount of work it took to construct that route. We get into our cars with the sole purpose of reaching the office. There are professionals who spend their lives planning and implementing the infrastructure required to move people in and about cities. Plan well, and you will probably live in anonymity. Plan poorly and you will certainly receive recognition (albeit the wrong sort). Shown next is the vehicle used to accomplish the mundane task of getting to and from work. This is merely the tip of the iceberg.

Quite often, a good decision support system is the result of many people toiling in anonymity. The decision support people are the glory boys (or girls). Very often, they come in towards the tail end of a project and deliver the goods. The end user has little regard for the effort expended to deliver the data to produce the end product. The decision support folks, being quite shallow in nature, typically do not spend much time enlightening the end user on the efforts endured by their peers. More than likely, they are apt to reply "*Glad I could help, just doing my job.*"

But why do we need a separate decision support tool? We have spent months (probably years) building a data warehouse; can't we use it to answer all our business questions? The answer is yes, in fact, you can answer many business questions straight from your transactional system. It is all a question of degrees. Speaking of degrees—Figure 15-1 shows the relative ease of reporting using an OLAP environment as compared to transaction-based systems.

As indicated in Figure 15-1, the simple x/y graph clearly depicts how much easier decision support becomes as we move away from transactional systems and towards an OLAP system. It's a question of purpose.

OLAP tools have a single purpose in life and that is to enable decision support. They are the "toasters" of the reporting world. Think about it. A toaster is a very practical tool. We put in our bread, depress the lever, and a little while later "presto" out comes toast. This toaster, for all its merits, will never be an oven. An oven is quite versatile and can be used to make toast. However, making toast in the oven really is a bit of overkill. So most kitchens come equipped with a toaster. Well, most data warehouses come with multidimensional analysis tools. Could we do the same sort of analysis directly against our data warehouse? Sure, but not without a great deal of effort and expertise.

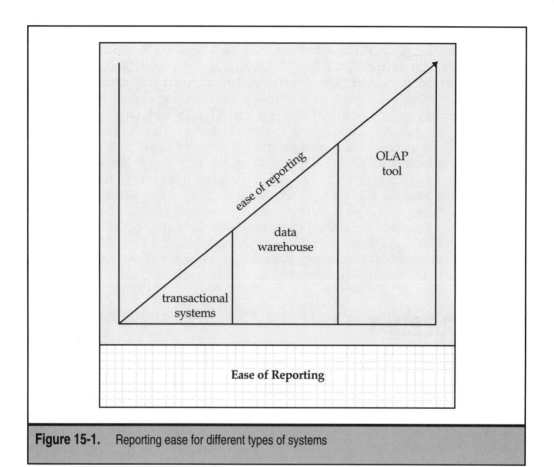

**Figure 15-1.** Reporting ease for different types of systems

Data warehouses are built to support a consistent view of the data throughout the organization. They are the result of activities such as extracting data from source systems, cleansing it, and then loading it into a target database (the warehouse). They are built for many reasons, including the desire to perform ad hoc analysis. The reality is, though, that most of the reports coming from the warehouse are not ad hoc. In fact, the queries run against the warehouse tend to be very repetitive in nature. The users of the warehouse soon gravitate toward running the same queries over and over, and the true benefits of the warehouse are not maximized. In contrast, the OLAP systems are designed to anticipate repetition (they love repetition). They provide the user with quick response time and a high degree of flexibility for those repetitive requests. Furthermore, OLAP tools are designed for ease of use and are rich in reporting capabilities.

It is extremely difficult for a data warehouse architect to anticipate all the different types of queries that will be run against the warehouse. Therefore, those users who access the warehouse natively through a query tool must have complete knowledge of the database schema, the data, and the business rules that support it. Regardless of how well the warehouse is designed, this type of user will most likely encounter what we term *Energizer Bunny queries*—queries that keep on going and going and going (and going and going and going and going and going and going and...). This occurs because the queries they develop become unnecessarily complicated, perhaps by a simple misuse of joins (the act of mixing data from different databases, tables, or schemas to satisfy a query), incorrect aggregation (the act of deliberately producing summaries), or insufficient understanding of the data. Queries and their results can scare users and decision makers away.

OLAP tools predefine how you approach the data with the principle aim to respond to queries. Naturally, this protects the users against the complexities of the warehouse, allowing them to focus on the business at hand. In light of what we have discussed so far, let's move ahead and discuss decision support.

# DECISION SUPPORT

Decision support can be simply defined as systems that allow you to make more informed decisions. Online analytical processing (OLAP) is a class of decision support tools. (Many years ago we were told that acronyms were introduced into the world of computing to deliberately create confusion. The more confusing things became, the better the job security and the demand for higher wages.) True to form, along came ROLAP, MOLAP, and HOLAP. Each technology delivers OLAP capability with a twist. Let's look at these approaches.

# OLAP

OLAP represents a class of software that allows you to perform reporting. Its most distinguishing feature is its support for multidimensional analysis. Typically, it is very user friendly and delivers key features such as slice and dice, drill-down, and multiple graphical views. Multidimensionality and many key features of OLAP are discussed next.

## Multidimensionality

Multidimensionality is best explained in the context of a business scenario. Carolyn Hu is the President of ABC Corporation, a manufacturer of synthetic seaweed. ABC Corporation has experienced terrific growth over the past several years and has been considering introducing a new line of synthetic products. Suddenly, sales drop.

Carolyn is alarmed at the sudden decline in sales and starts to search for answers. When did sales begin to drop? How are we performing this year against last year? How are we doing this month against the same month last year? Show me sales for the last six months! How did this quarter compare with last quarter?

Carolyn searches further. Where are sales declining? ABC Corporation has 3 sales divisions, 12 regions, and 72 outlets. The problem seems to be in the Western division. How are the three regions in the West performing? The problem seems to be with Evan Fitzgerald's region. We need a list of the outlets in this region showing how each is tracking to budget.

Furthermore, we must produce a report showing what products are sold in these outlets. How are these products performing against last year? What are the top 10 products sold in these outlets? Are they profitable? Should we introduce different products? Who is responsible for these outlets? All we hear is "I want answers! I want them now!"

Here comes multidimensionality to the rescue. Multidimensionality has all the answers. Multidimensionality is the boss' favorite. Multidimensionality looks at reporting from a business perspective. It translates the basic questions in life—who, what, when, and where—into dimensions. Let's look at the dimensions from the previous example; these are shown in the next listing:

```
When = time
Where = divisions, regions and outlet
What = products
Who = sales force
```

All the previous questions can be answered with combinations of the previous dimensions. Dimensions are key to OLAP and are discussed in detail later in this chapter.

## Drill-Down

Drill-down is the process of moving from summary to detailed information. Consider how Carolyn discovered where the problem with sales was. Carolyn identified a problem with the Western division, then analyzed the regions within that division, and finally isolated the poorly performing outlets within that region. Carolyn moved from summary-level information to detailed-level information.

Drill-down works for dimensions that have a hierarchy. In the earlier example, the hierarchy for outlets is division, region, and then outlet. MOLAP systems store the aggregated data for each level of a hierarchy. This is what gives MOLAP its speed. Summaries are available at the division, region, and outlet levels.

## Slice and Dice

Slice and dice sounds like something you hear on a late night infomercial. "It slices, it dices, and it can be yours for only 12 easy payments of $99 ($150 in Canada), and if you buy today we will include drill-down at no additional cost." Slice and dice is what makes OLAP systems hum. Consider traditional paper-based reports. They are made up of rows and columns. The columns typically constitute one dimension while the rows constitute another—two dimensions…how boring.

Slice and dice recognizes the world is more complicated than two dimensions can cover. Why restrict yourself? Depending on the question you have to answer, you call on the appropriate dimensions. You can view the same data set through different viewpoints or dimensions. Depending on your viewpoint, you may want to see more complicated results; for example,

▼ What was sold when

■ When items were sold and where

▲ Where items were sold and by whom

The way you can view your data is only limited to the number of dimensions you define.

## Multiple View Modes

A picture is worth a thousand words, and a thousand numbers are often better represented by a picture. Consider the chart presented in Table 15-1. "Which month had the highest sales for each product?" can now more easily be answered.

Figure 15-2 depicts the same type of product-related information presented in a more OLAP-like report.

As you can see, how the data is presented is sometimes as important as the data itself. The ability to view your data in multiple views provides great productivity gains. The example shown in Figure 15-2 illustrates this with a very limited dataset. Think about all the data in your organization.

Multidimensionality, drill-down, slice and dice, and multiple views are the foundation of any OLAP tool. These characteristics separate OLAP from other technologies. So, what about the other acronyms?

As you will see later, there are various database technologies for storing data to be accessed by your OLAP applications. In fact, certain vendors would have you believe that unless you use their technology, you are not doing real OLAP. Don't believe it! OLAP is a type of application for querying and viewing data—it exists regardless of how the data is stored. The data can be stored in a relational database, a multidimensional database, a flat file, or a Crayola-based drawing. So long as the user interface does what an OLAP interface must do, OLAP exists.

| Year | (All) | | | | | | | | | | | | |
|------|-------|--|--|--|--|--|--|--|--|--|--|--|--|
| Prod Line | Hockey | | | | | | | | | | | | |
| | | | | | | | | | | | | | |
| **Sum of Sales** | **Month** | | | | | | | | | | | | |
| **Prod** | **Jan** | **Feb** | **Mar** | **Apr** | **May** | **Jun** | **Jul** | **Aug** | **Sep** | **Oct** | **Nov** | **Dec** | **Grand Total** |
| **Mask** | 6 | 7 | 6 | 5 | 4 | 3 | 2 | 1 | 2 | 4 | 5 | 6 | 51 |
| **Puck** | 4 | 5 | 3 | 2 | 1 | 1 | 0 | 0 | 1 | 3 | 3 | 5 | 28 |
| **Stick** | 10 | 11 | 9 | 8 | 7 | 6 | 5 | 4 | 6 | 8 | 9 | 12 | 95 |
| **Grand Total** | 20 | 23 | 18 | 15 | 12 | 10 | 7 | 5 | 9 | 15 | 17 | 23 | 174 |

**Table 15-1.** Product Line Sales by Month

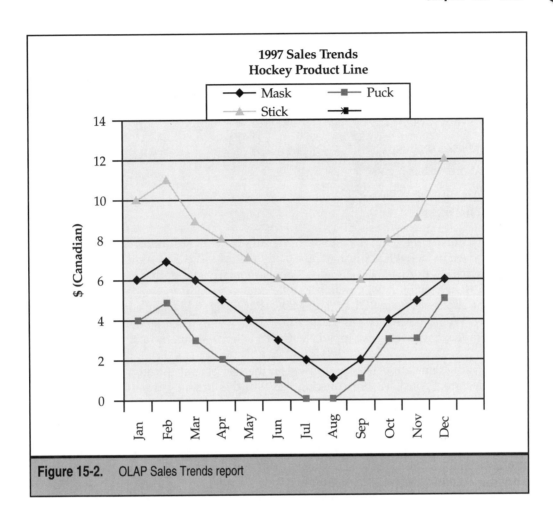

**Figure 15-2.**   OLAP Sales Trends report

Another interesting point is how whenever the users change the filter, drill-down, or rotate their data, they are really issuing a new query. Now, an OLAP user will do a lot of filtering, drilling down, and rotating. Remember also that the vast majority of these queries return summaries of thousands or millions of rows of data. Thus, whatever data structures you use to support your OLAP system, they must provide rapid response to summary-level queries.

Because such a rapid response time is required, it is not unheard of for OLAP to be performed against data marts tuned for specific subject areas rather than against enterprise-wide data warehouses. To handle their broad, diverse nature, enterprise-wide data warehouses are frequently more normalized than simple star schemas. Thus data is often extracted from the warehouse into targeted data marts to achieve the performance necessary for OLAP use. As discussed in the "ROLAP and MOLAP" section, these data marts might be contained in either relational or multidimensional structures.

# ROLAP AND MOLAP

Technology has a way of spawning fanatics. Fanatics, in turn, seem particularly adept at spawning conflict. Anyone who has tried to put a Windows PC on the desk of a Macintosh bigot knows what we mean. Perhaps you've seen other cases. Software bigots come in a variety of flavors:

▼ Macintosh bigots

■ WordPerfect bigots

■ Mainframe bigots

▲ DB2 bigots

The point is not that Macintoshes, WordPerfect, mainframes, and DB2 are bad technologies. In fact, the point may be exactly the opposite. But something about these technologies seems to make their adherents particularly stubborn.

Data warehousing has its own set of fanatics who fight major battles in their own wars. The choice between ROLAP and MOLAP is the warehousing equivalent of Greece and Troy. We have actually witnessed arguments where professionals with competing points of view have viciously ripped each other's limbs off in efforts to force their points of view.

The funny thing about these arguments is that neither side is right. At the same time, both sides are right. Let's start making sense of this mess by describing ROLAP and MOLAP.

ROLAP and MOLAP are simply terms that refer to common methods for storing data used by OLAP systems. *ROLAP* stands for relational online analytical processing, while *MOLAP* stands for multidimensional online analytical processing. In either case, the user interface is still an OLAP interface. The only difference is the database technology used to store the data that feeds the user interface.

One term that you will likely encounter when evaluating OLAP database technologies is cube. A *cube* is simply another way of referring to the dataset you wish to analyze. In attempting to make the concept of multidimensional analysis easier for novices to understand, the OLAP industry invented this 20-quid word. It is intended to imply multidimensionality, and is usually accompanied by a poorly explained picture like that shown next (which one of our ex-employees created).

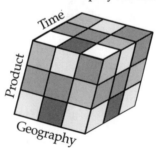

This picture is intended to show that you can locate the value for a measure based on its dimensional coordinates. For example, each cell in the cube in the illustration holds information about the measure sales. You can locate any sales figure given its product, time, and geography coordinates.

As an aside (as though we haven't already strayed enough), we've always objected to the term "cube." Cube implies three dimensions; a dimensional database is actually a space comprised of any number of dimensions. We, thus, prefer the term "dataspace" (sometimes seen with an initial capital letter, as in Dataspace Inc.) to cube.

Given the technology trends of the past few years, most of us are well versed in relational database technology; we now have a look at a sometimes scary, sometimes misunderstood, but always cheerful partner to this technology—Mr. Multidimensional database.

# MULTIDIMENSIONAL DATABASES (MDDB)

As we noted before, while OLAP is a user interface concept, there are two primary technologies for storing the data used in OLAP applications—multidimensional databases and relational databases. You probably know a bit about relational databases. The following few sections provide some background on multidimensional databases.

## Arrays

A multidimensional database is just that—a database, just like SQL Server. Data is loaded into, stored in, and queried from that database. A variety of programs can access that data. The major difference between MDDBs and RDBMSs is in how they store data. Relational databases store their data in a series of tables and columns. Multidimensional databases, on the other hand, store their data in large multidimensional arrays. For example, in an MDDB world, you might refer to a sales figure as sales with a date, product, and location component of 12-1-1999, car, and south, respectively.

## Multidimensional Database Vendors

Just like relational databases, there are a variety of tools for accessing multidimensional databases. Many users access these databases using add-ins to spreadsheets, like Excel. Other tools are intended solely as multidimensional query tools/front ends. Tools like Cognos' Aristotle can access multidimensional servers.

Finally, just like relational databases, custom programs can be written to access MDDBs. Many of these databases come with their own programming languages. Some can also be queried with other programming languages like Visual Basic.

## Is an MDDB a Data Warehouse?

For a while, there was some confusion as to whether a data warehouse could be housed in a multidimensional database. Multidimensional databases are wonderful for analyzing narrowly focused sets of data. As such, they can be strong tools for data marts. They are, on the other hand, not capable of supporting the breadth of data required to support an enterprise data warehouse. Later on in this chapter, we will compare multidimensional and relational databases for OLAP data storage. This comparison will further address some of the reasons why multidimensional databases are really data mart tools. Now that we know all there is to know about MDDB, let's back up a bit and look at relational databases.

# RELATIONAL DATABASES (RDBMs)

The other primary method for storing data for OLAP is in a relational database. The most common data structure for ROLAP data is the star schema or some variant, like the snowflake schema. In fact, many ROLAP query tools require a particular approach to schema design, such as a star schema. Understanding the schema required from the ROLAP vendor will go a long way in ensuring a successful implementation. But heed our constant droning: OLAP is a user interface, not a data storage concept. If you encounter tools that provide an OLAP user interface while querying traditional, nonstar schemas, they are still OLAP tools. So…

## What Really Defines ROLAP?

A number of query tool vendors profess to offer ROLAP tools. We don't believe that each of these offerings is actually true ROLAP. Tools that don't adhere to the definition of true ROLAP tools can be just as powerful as—in fact, can be more powerful than—true ROLAP tools. These nontrue ROLAP tools are usually some hybrid of other types of query technologies such as combinations of report writers and MOLAP tools. It is important, though, to understand true ROLAP. This understanding will help you determine the best OLAP approach for your application. This should then help you deliver a successful project. Delivering a successful project could very well save your professional dignity and, perhaps, your job—more proof of a better life through data warehousing. (As a note, if this advice does indeed save your job, please recommend this book to your associates, friends, and family—thus returning the favor by saving our jobs.)

The section in this chapter called "The Three Faces of ROLAP" addresses this issue of tools that call themselves ROLAP but don't conform to our definition of true ROLAP tools. To us, a true ROLAP tool adheres to three rules:

▼ It supports the basic OLAP concepts we've discussed

■ It stores its data in some relational database

▲ It supports some form of aggregate navigation

Let's expand on these three points.

## Adheres to Basic OLAP Concepts

True ROLAP is a form of OLAP where the data is stored in a relational database. Thus, like any OLAP application, a true ROLAP application must support multi-dimensionality, drill-down, rotation, and multiple modes of view.

## Relational Data Storage

This one should be self-explanatory. To have true ROLAP, the application's data must be stored in a relational database. Let's take this a bit further. The data in that relational database must be understandable by any program with access to that database. For example, suppose you stored data in a relational database but before you put the data into the database, you used a programming trick to translate the data into reverse Swahili notation (RSN—OK, yes, we made this one up). Another program reading that database would have to have an RSN interpreter to make your data understandable to users. Suppose, on the other hand, that your program simply stored the data in English. Then, any program that could read your database could use the data it contained.

## Aggregate Navigation

Aggregate navigation is a bit more complex. One of the things we've mentioned about data warehouses is that they frequently contain summary tables. For example, your warehouse or mart might contain a detailed, atomic-level table of sales information broken down by customer, the products purchased, and the date on which each purchase took place. Let's suppose that this table contains 400 million rows.

As users access the system, you may realize that there are frequent queries looking solely at sales broken down by customer and year, regardless of the products that were purchased or the days on which those purchases took place. As an attentive warehouse manager, you build a summary table to support these queries. The new table, being a high-level summary, contains only about one million rows.

Building the summary is pretty easy (of course, in real life, maintaining it is probably a bit harder than in the dream world of books). The query to populate the summary table, in its simplest form, probably looks something like the next listing:

```
create table year_sum_sales as
    select year, customer,sum(sales)
    from atomic_sales
    group by year,customer;
```

Now you have created not only a summary table, but also a problem. How are users going to know that the summary table exists? And even if they know that it exists, how will they know when to use it? And when not to?

Enter the aggregate navigator. *Aggregate navigators* are software components that automatically select the best table for each query. The best table is usually defined as the smallest available table that can answer the user's request. Remember that all queries could be run against the atomic-level table, but we create summary tables to speed query performance.

To perform this function, the aggregate navigator knows which summaries exist and the size of each one. Depending on the query tool, this knowledge is obtained either by the warehouse administrator telling the tool how many rows are in each table or by some automated routine that periodically checks the sizes of each table and records these size values. Imagine that you're the aggregate navigator shown next. Which way should you go? Left or right? Six of one, a half dozen of the other.

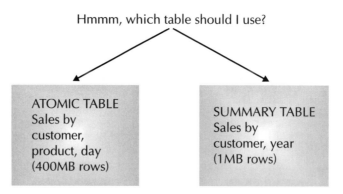

Hmmm, which table should I use?

ATOMIC TABLE
Sales by
customer,
product, day
(400MB rows)

SUMMARY TABLE
Sales by
customer, year
(1MB rows)

Let's see how you might approach three different queries.

▼ Computicus, a new clerk, just got an angry call from Mark Kerzner. It seems he thinks we charged him twice for his purchase on March 13 (of course, we couldn't possibly have done this—after all, we use computers. Right?). We need to see what we sold to Mark on March 13. Which table should we query? Well, given the fact that the summary table contains only annual data for each customer, we couldn't possibly get the answer from the summary table. Thus, we have to query the atomic-level table.

■ Spasticus, the company's vice-president of sales, calls with a request, "What were our total sales to the Everding Company in 1997?" What table do we use now? Could we answer the question from the atomic-level table? Well, yes, we could. Could we answer the question with the summary table? Well, yes, we could. Which table is smaller? The summary. Thus, our choice is clear.

▲ The company's president, Cirrhosis, calls asking for a report showing the trend in total sales for the last three years. Which table to hit here? Well, you could answer this with the atomic-level table. You could also answer it with the summary table. In either case, you will have to aggregate many rows. You therefore choose the summary table. With it, you will have to aggregate far fewer rows than you would if you used the atomic-level table. This should provide much quicker response.

Aggregate tables coupled with aggregate navigation is one tool for improving query performance. Of course, several others exist. These include things like the following:

▼   Index creation

■   Data restructuring

▲   Hardware upgrade

The concept first gained prominence in ROLAP tools such as MicroStrategy's DSS Agent and Information Advantage's Decision Suite. Tools that contain aggregate navigators are sometimes referred to as being "aggregate aware."

## Differentiating ROLAP from Online Report Writing

It's important to differentiate between ROLAP tools and report writers like Cognos's Impromptu and Crystal Reports. Report writers provide two basic functions:

▼   They allow users to point and click to generate and issue SQL calls.

▲   They allow users to format the results.

While they access relational data, report writers do not support the other basic concepts of true ROLAP. They do not, for example:

▼   Support the basic concepts of OLAP (multidimensionality, drill-down, rotation, and multiple view modes)

▲   Provide aggregate navigation

True ROLAP tools vendors—who are they? Well, the list includes companies and products like the following:

▼   Microsoft's Plato

■   Oracle Discoverer 3

■   MicroStrategy DSS Agent

■   Information Advantage Decision Suite

▲   Platinum Beacon

## Return to Troy: ROLAP Vs. MOLAP

Given that rather wordy description of the relational and multidimensional approaches to OLAP data storage, it's time to enter the fray. Which is better? Well, as is all too often the case, the answer is, it depends. Let's discuss these technologies along a few different dimensions (no pun intended). Please keep in mind that these are generalizations. They may or may not apply to any particular product or application.

## Performance

Many people evaluating reporting technologies fail to recognize that there are two key aspects of performance. The first is query time, the amount of time it takes to respond to any user's query. The second is load time, the amount of time required to populate data structures and perform those calculations necessary to prepare the system for use.

# Query Performance

Relational OLAP systems respond just like any other relational database application. Sometimes the answers come back quickly and sometimes not so quickly. Administrators can work to improve response time by building indexes and summary tables, but performance may still be hard to predict and, for certain operations, simply slow.

Multidimensional databases, on the other hand, provide a fairly predictable, and fast, response to virtually every query. This is due, in part, to the fact that multidimensional databases precalculate many, and sometimes all, possible values in their hypercubes. For example, imagine an application that reports monthly employee turnover for the past year. Also, assume that this data has only two dimensions—month and department. Assume that the company has 10 departments, as illustrated in Table 15-2. Given the traditional limitations of solar-based calendars, you can safely assume that there are 12 months in a year.

As we noted before, multidimensional databases are comprised of multidimensional arrays. Thus, the array holding the atomic-level data in this application would have 120 cells—12 months (Jan to Dec across the top) and 10 departments (1 to 10 along the side).

In addition, the multidimensional database will, when loaded with data, precalculate all combinations and summaries of that data. For example, if we had three dimensions, the database would create

▼   A three-dimensional atomic-level array

■   A two-dimensional array of data for dims 1 and 2

■   A two-dimensional array for dims 2 and 3

■   A high-level summary array broken down by dim 1

|         | Jan | Feb | Mar | Apr | May | Jun | Jul | Aug | Sep | Oct | Nov | Dec |
|---------|-----|-----|-----|-----|-----|-----|-----|-----|-----|-----|-----|-----|
| Dept 1  | -5  | -10 | 4   | -4  | 7   | 0   | -6  | -9  | 5   | -2  | 0   | -4  |
| Dept 2  | 2   | -2  | 4   | -2  | 5   | -4  | 0   | 6   | 9   | -9  | 2   | 7   |
| Dept 3  | 4   | 4   | 0   | 4   | 1   | -2  | 7   | 1   | -4  | 5   | 4   | 4   |
| Dept 4  | 6   | -8  |     |     |     |     |     |     |     |     |     |     |
| Dept 5  | 8   | -1  | 0   | -4  | -5  | 9   | -5  | 3   | 1   | 9   | 2   | -8  |
| Dept 6  | 4   | -8  | 6   | -6  | 2   | 7   | -1  | -10 | -10 | -10 | 5   | -7  |
| Dept 7  | 0   | 2   | -5  | 3   | 4   | 3   | 2   | -8  | 9   | 9   | 0   | 5   |
| Dept 8  |     |     |     |     |     |     |     |     |     |     |     | -7  |
| Dept 9  | 1   | 1   | 4   | 5   | -3  | -8  | -4  | -5  | 8   | 0   | -3  | -1  |
| Dept 10 | -6  | 5   | -4  | 0   | 2   | -9  | 9   | -7  | 6   | -7  | -5  | 5   |

**Table 15-2.**   Department Data over a 12-Month Period

- ■ A high-level summary array broken down by dim 2
- ▲ A high-level summary array broken down by dim 3

In this case, because we have just two dimensions, there are no other combinations, but there are summaries. Thus, the database will also store two one-dimensional arrays, as shown in Table 15-3. Notice how we have departmental summaries (Dept 1 through 10) as well as month summaries (Jan through Dec).

Because of all this precalculation, the response to queries at any level of summarization should be very fast. Of course, such a huge benefit does have its costs, as we shall soon see.

## Load Performance

Most multidimensional databases are not refreshed daily. In fact, a recent survey showed that the most common refresh cycle is monthly. Why is this? Wouldn't it be preferable to have more frequent updates and therefore more current data? Sadly, one of the costs of the wonderful performance you can get from a multidimensional database is long database load times.

Assume it takes 24 hours to refresh a database. In such a case, if you tried to do daily refreshes, you would always be refreshing and never reporting. This is one reason why companies have long periods of time between refreshes.

| By Dept | | By Month | |
|---|---|---|---|
| Dept 1 | -24 | Jan | 14 |
| Dept 2 | 18 | Feb | -17 |
| Dept 3 | 28 | Mar | 9 |
| Dept 4 | -2 | Apr | -4 |
| Dept 5 | 9 | May | 13 |
| Dept 6 | -28 | Jun | -4 |
| Dept 7 | 24 | Jul | 2 |
| Dept 8 | -7 | Aug | -29 |
| Dept 9 | -5 | Sep | 24 |
| Dept 10 | -11 | Oct | -5 |
| | | Nov | 5 |
| | | Dec | -6 |

**Table 15-3.**  Two Single-Dimensioned Arrays

Why does refreshing take so long? Well, precalculating data takes time. In all fairness, MDDB vendors are making progress in shortening load times. One way many are doing this is by not completely precalculating all possible values in their cubes.

Relational reporting structures, on the other hand, can often be loaded more quickly. There are a number of steps to the load process, including loading, indexing, and building summary tables. Still, because you usually don't build all possible summaries, load times are typically shorter than for multidimensional databases. In fact, it is not unusual for relational data warehouses and data marts to be refreshed on a daily basis.

## Analytic Capability

Well, what good is an analytic database if you can't analyze the data that it contains? Are there any differences in what you can do with a MOLAP vs. a ROLAP approach?

As we've already noted about 44 times, OLAP is a user interface concept, not a data storage concept. Still, given the maturity of query technologies, there are some differences in analytic rigor between MOLAP and ROLAP databases.

MOLAP database applications tend to have better support for time series and statistical analyses. ROLAP database applications, on the other hand, are sometimes hampered by the limitations of SQL.

There are a number of things that can't be easily done with a single SQL statement. For example, suppose you want to calculate the sales of each division as a percentage of your company's total sales. While you may be able to put together a complex SQL statement to answer this question, it is much simpler to run multiple SQL statements and manipulate the results.

ROLAP query tool vendors address SQL's limitations in a number of ways. They may:

▼ Ignore them, thus limiting their tools' functionality

■ Issue multiple SQL statements, putting intermediate results into temporary database tables (the MicroStrategy approach)

▲ Utilize three-tier architectures that put computers between client and server machines to manipulate intermediate results (the Information Advantage approach)

As ROLAP technologies mature, look to ROLAP vendors to close the capability gap with MOLAP vendors.

## Dataset Sizes

Multidimensional databases tend to grow in size very rapidly, particularly as more dimensions are modeled in the database. Look again at the information depicted in Table 15-2. Notice that Dept 4 was dissolved in February (i.e., it has numbers for months Jan and Feb, then nothing more for the rest of the year). Still, the database stores data for the rest of the year for this department. Even though these values are nulls, they take up space in the database. This is wasteful. If you add dimensions, even more space would be wasted. The term referring to this wasted space is *sparsity*. A sparse database wastes a good deal of space. A dense database wastes little. There are approaches for addressing sparsity, but none is perfect.

For every department that you add, you require 12 cells in the MDDB. Suppose you actually had three dimensions. For example, suppose the database also contains a gender dimension so that they can now analyze turnover by department, month, and gender. Simply by adding this dimension, your database doubles in size. Now, rather than a two-dimensional table containing 120 cells (12 months times 10 departments), the database looks like a three-dimensional cube containing 240 cells (10 departments times 12 months times 2 genders). Thus, as you add dimensions, MDDBs tend to explode in size.

Another reason why MDDBs can rapidly grow large is because of the large number of precalculated summary values that they frequently contain. Put all together, MDDBs can rapidly grow quite large. There are, on the other hand, physical limitations to how large such databases can become.

While it may vary a bit depending on how you model your relational data structures, ROLAP databases typically do not incur sparsity penalties. In addition, they support virtually unlimited growth. While it is not unheard-of to have multiterabyte-sized relational, the largest multidimensional databases are well under a terabyte.

# Dimension Handling

ROLAP databases are usually constructed as some variant of the star schema. The dimension tables in a star schema can be quite wide. For example, a customer dimension table may contain columns for things like customer name, home address, home ZIP, office address, office ZIP, area code, customer type, date of first order, etc., etc., etc. As a user, you can query, summarize, and drill-down on any of these dimension columns. For example, you could ask the database to show total sales broken down by country, then drill into state, then drill into city, then drill into ZIP, then break down by date of the customer's first order.

Multidimensional databases, on the other hand, do not provide such flexibility with dimensions. These systems are limited in the number of different dimension "levels" that they can contain. This limitation is related to the problem of database size explosions as dimensions are added.

# Maintenance Effort

MOLAP approaches are very strong in the area of maintenance. Once set up, they are fairly self-maintaining. Load it and go. To load, simply design the database and then feed it a flat file or an SQL **select** statement (if you think about it, and you really should, the result of a SQL select statement is just a flat file). The engine will accept the rows and build the database.

Relational databases, on the other hand, require more effort to populate and maintain. Population is more complex because not one, but multiple structures must be filled. In addition, indexes may need to be turned on or off during this process. Once loaded, if performance is poor, additional indexes may need to be added or summary tables created. DBAs must regularly analyze the database to keep it in working order.

## Lunch Value

In the OLAP technology selection process, it is important to consider what we refer to as *lunch value*. Lunch value is a poorly understood concept, likely because its calculation formula is deceptively complex. Lunch value (LV) is derived by the formula shown in the next listing:

```
LV = 2P + S² - 4d
where:
P = the amount the vendor paid for lunch
S = a factor representing the style of lunch
    (i.e., French = 7, Italian = 4, Delicatessen = 2,
        Company cafeteria = .043)
d = the drone factor, a value representing how much
    mindless sales pitch you had to put up with during the meal
```

Please note the inverse relationship between total lunch value and drone factor. In our experience, this category is a tie between ROLAP and MOLAP vendors. Still, we strongly recommend that you attempt to maximize total lunch value as you pursue your purchase.

## ROLAP and MOLAP Peace and Harmony

So, which technology wins? Well, as you might surmise, the answer is a resounding…"It depends." It depends on a number of factors, but primarily on the scope of your application. If you are building a large, cross-functional, enterprise data warehouse, then you probably want to use a relational database. If you are building a well-defined, highly targeted analysis-focused data mart with limited dimensionality and little need for detailed, atomic-level data, then the multidimensional approach has a lot of merit.

Earlier, we spoke about a corporate data warehousing architecture. In this architecture, a corporate data warehouse feeds smaller, narrowly focused or stand-alone data marts. Ah ha! Think about what this means to the ROLAP-MOLAP debate! It means that these technologies are not competitors, but are in many cases complementary!

Looming developments in the database industry serve to heighten this symbiosis (yes, we do get more distance out of these big fancy words). In particular, database vendors are starting to integrate ROLAP and MOLAP technologies. The first step was a technology called *drill-through*. With drill-through, the user can drill-down into an MDDB database. When the lowest level of detail in the database is reached, the user can then request that the system issue a query to a relational database that contains very detailed atomic-level data. Drill-through, though, has not been perfect. Most implementations require the system developer to custom code each drill-through query. At run time, what the user is really doing is simply filling in variables of the **where** clause for this relational query. The system then runs it and returns the result.

Depending on the vendor, drill-through is not always transparent to the user. He or she must do something different than a normal drill-down to access this relational data.

Coming soon is a more transparent drill-through—one in which the user performs a normal drill-down and the MDDB realizes that the data is not stored in the multidimensional database and therefore issues a true ROLAP query to the underlying, detailed, relational database. This ROLAP query will adhere to all the criteria of a true ROLAP query, including aggregate navigation.

In the longer term, we would like to see the industry develop fully integrated query databases. In this fully integrated model, the administrator will lay out a basic definition of the data to be contained in the system and then feed it that data. The database engine will store the data as seems appropriate, in either relational or multidimensional structures. Furthermore, the database will analyze usage patterns. Based on how the database is used, the system will adjust how each data element and summary is stored. And the best part is, this whole process will be transparent to our users. They just keep doing their work and issuing their queries. All we will have to do is feed the system our data and write the vendors our checks!

Now, let's get our hands a bit dirty in the rich soil of ROLAP land by discussing modeling data for ROLAP performance.

# Modeling Your Data for ROLAP Performance

Suppose you are developing a ROLAP application. In no other relational application will you need such rapid access to such large quantities of data. How will you achieve this performance? Well, we've already discussed some techniques. They include things like:

▼ Putting your data into a star schema

■ Indexing

■ Building summary tables

▲ Partitioning large tables into smaller tables

In fact, there are a lot of things we can do to improve performance. But, in most cases, there are trade-offs. To improve performance, we might pay a price in areas like maintainability and dataset size. For example, each of the steps just noted will have to be administered. And administration is not free. Have you seen the spiraling rates for DBAs lately?

One often-overlooked area for improving performance is security. For example, if we don't implement row-level security (i.e., security where each user can see only those rows that apply to them), we can probably improve system performance. Is the cost of these performance improvements worthwhile? Only you and your users can judge. But don't worry too much about making the wrong decision—technology jobs are a dime a dozen.

There is one other technique, a technique from the dark side of relational databases. A technique so powerful yet so monstrous that we hesitate to mention it. Use it if you must, but use it with extreme caution. And don't disclose your source for this information (unless, of course, it is to another potential purchaser of this book). Also, keep in mind that this technique will work only if your query tools can recognize this data structure. The name of this dark secret? Denormalization by a dimension.

Imagine a star schema with only two dimensions—customer and month. It contains only one fact: sales. Thus, each record in your fact table represents your sales to one customer during one month. The fact table probably looks something like the one shown in Table 15-4, with an identifier for month (Month_ID), one for customer (Cust_ID), and the sale amount (Sales). The two dimensions are month and customer.

Now, suppose that the average customer makes at least one purchase per month. How many records will that customer have in this table for a year? That's right, 12. Very good! So, to figure any customer's total sales for the year (or average monthly sales, for that matter), our program has to access 12 rows.

In Table 15-5, we denormalize by the dimension month.

Notice how we store separate values in each row for January (JAN_SALES), February (FEB_SALES), March (MAR_SALES), and so on. Now, how many rows must you access to answer the same question? That's right, 1! Thus, you hit the indexes less and the actual data tables less. Which structure will have better performance?

Keep in mind, these structures are very difficult to maintain. For one reason, while in a traditional fact table you would just insert rows for new data, in this denormalized scheme you update existing rows. For another, think about what happens at the end of the year. What do you do for the next year? Add columns to your fact table? Add a new record for each customer? Delete data from existing columns? As you get deeper into data warehousing, you will be faced with opportunities to use unconventional structures such as this. They can be powerful, but they can also be very costly.

As we noted before, true ROLAP is only one of the technologies being marketed as ROLAP. Let's take a look at some of the others.

## The Three Faces of ROLAP

One last thing you must understand about ROLAP. There are a number of different data storage approaches that call themselves ROLAP technologies. It is important to understand the difference between these before some vendor tries to convince you that theirs is the best, nay, the only way. Keep in mind, none of these is necessarily "best." Best is defined only by the demands of your particular application.

| Month_ID | Cust_ID | Sales |
|----------|---------|-------|
| 1 | 1876 | 425 |
| 2 | 1876 | 410 |
| 3 | 1876 | 430 |

**Table 15-4.** Three Rows in a Fact Table

| Cust_ID | Jan_Sales | Feb_Sales | Mar_Sales | ... |
|---------|-----------|-----------|-----------|-----|
| 1876    | 425       | 410       | 430       |     |

**Table 15-5.** Single Row Denormalized by Month

The first technology is the "true" ROLAP that we described earlier. True ROLAP systems adhere to the basic tenets of OLAP. They store their data in relational databases and every query reaccesses those relational data structures. Finally, these systems utilize aggregate navigators. The process of querying is fairly transparent to the user. He or she issues queries and the results appear on the screen.

Let's call the next technology "local cubing." Local cubes are implemented in tools like Business Objects and Cognos' Impromptu/PowerPlay combination. With this technology, the user issues a query against the relational data warehouse. The results of this query are stored in a small, local, multidimensional database. The user can then perform analysis against this local database. If the user needs data not in this database, he or she must issue another query against the relational database and rebuild, or at least modify, the local MDDB cube.

The last approach is relational storage of multidimensional cubes. Think about what a multidimensional (or a relational) database really is. In actuality, these are simply files. Database engines are simply programs that allow users to access and maintain these files. Well, perhaps "simply" is not quite correct, but you get the picture, right?

Relational storage of multidimensional cubes takes the file containing a multidimensional database and stores that file in a relational database. While it's confusing in concept, it works. You can issue queries directly against these data structures. But, you won't be able to decipher the results. To do that, you will need special application programming interfaces (APIs) sold by the vendors of these technologies. Thus, your application, or the vendor's packaged applications, will call the vendor's API. This API will translate the request into a relational query and send it to the database. The database will return its results to the API, which will translate them and return them to the requesting program.

Storing the cube in a relational database allows administrators to take advantage of typical relational tools like security and replication. Tools that use this type of technology are sold by vendors like IQ Software in their IQ Vision tool and by Cognos in an extension to their multidimensional PowerPlay product. The key points from this section can be summed up in the following points:

▼ OLAP is a user interface, not a data storage, concept.

■ OLAP systems provide four basic functions: multidimensional view of data, drill-down, rotation, and multiple view modes.

- Relational OLAP (ROLAP) is the access of data for OLAP from a relational database (RDBMS). Multidimensional OLAP (MOLAP) is the access of data for OLAP from a multidimensional database (MDDB).

▲ There is no always-best approach to OLAP. The best approach will be defined by the requirements of your application.

Now that we have spent pages and pages distinguishing between ROLAP and MOLAP, it is time to introduce a new twist, *HOLAP* (hybrid online analytical processing). HOLAP is versatile in that it allows you to store your data in either a relational database or in a cube. Microsoft's Decision Support falls in the category of HOLAP. It is discussed in more detail in Chapter 16.

# DESIGNING OLAP SYSTEMS

The key to OLAP is designing a system that allows you to manipulate your data in the way that you think about your data. OLAP delivers the goods by utilizing dimensions and facts. Dimensions are the key to OLAP. In fact, the term OLAP and multidimensional analysis are often used interchangeably. Dimensions are viewpoints into your data. They represent the *who*, *what*, *when*, and *where* of your data, as shown in Figure 15-3.

The key is translating your business requirements into dimensions. Understanding what is relevant to your business can be easily conveyed into the necessary dimensions. If you have established this fundamental point, you are making great headway towards completing the design.

## What You Need to Know About Dimensions

Dimensions are typically but not necessarily hierarchical. Each level in the hierarchy provides a level on which you can report. The movement from a higher level to a lower level is what is referred to as drill-down. For example, in the next two figures, Figure 15-4 illustrates a simple date hierarchy whereas Figure 15-5 shows a regional hierarchy.

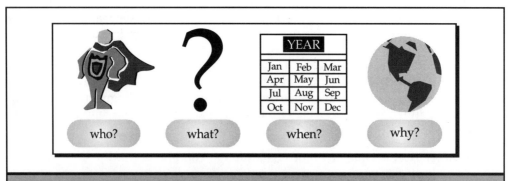

**Figure 15-3.**   The most common dimensions (that start with "W")

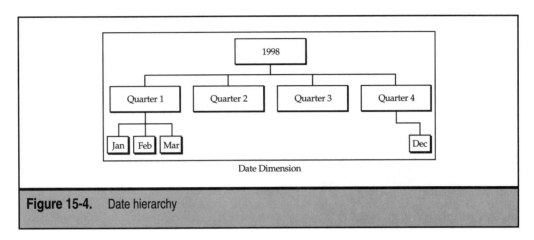

**Figure 15-4.** Date hierarchy

In this case, we can investigate our data for the entire United States, drill-down into regions, then to states, and finally to cities. The hierarchy predetermines the path we follow to move from country to city (we can only access the city Buffalo through the state New York).

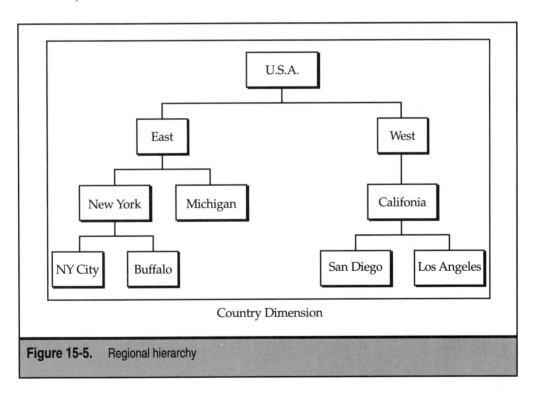

**Figure 15-5.** Regional hierarchy

Dimensions in the OLAP world differ from dimensions in the star schema world. A dimension in a star schema model will typically have many more attributes than an OLAP dimension. Figure 15-6 illustrates a typical customer dimension as found in a star schema and then illustrates how it would appear in an OLAP application.

As you can see in the customer dimension, all attributes about a customer are contained within the single dimension. On the other hand, in the OLAP world, the attributes of a customer are often best represented in more than one dimension. We usually separate the attributes of a customer into two separate dimensions, thus providing us complete flexibility in reporting. Using this technique, we can determine how much business a particular customer generates regardless of whether they have locations in more than one country or state.

A common mistake is to create what we term *restrictive hierarchies*. Restrictive hierarchies are hierarchies that limit or restrict data from being reported. Table 15-6 is an example of a restrictive hierarchy.

This hierarchy is restrictive when you have customers who have businesses in more than one country (state or city). This design makes it difficult to get a clear picture of how much business you are conducting with that customer. Remember our ex-employee from earlier in this chapter—Figure 15-7 shows another design put together by that person.

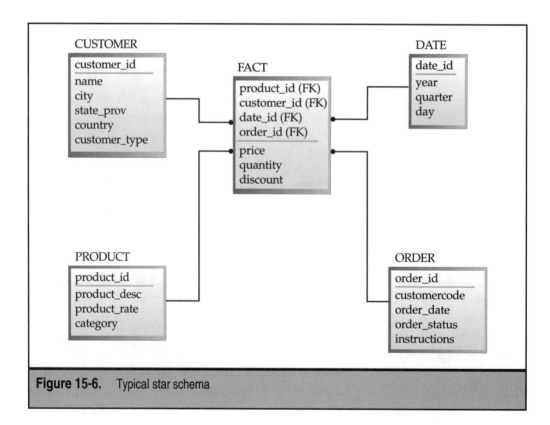

**Figure 15-6.**   Typical star schema

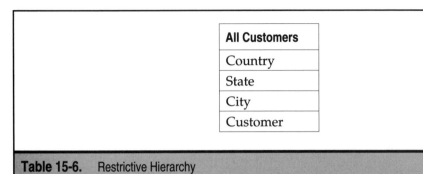

| All Customers |
| --- |
| Country |
| State |
| City |
| Customer |

**Table 15-6.**  Restrictive Hierarchy

Figure 15-7 is indicative of a poor design because it creates a restrictive hierarchy. Why? Because in the current business world, globalization has resulted in the ABC Corporation diversifying and doing business in more than one location. In the design above, the ABC Corporation has offices in several geographical locations. As a result, we would have to add each individual location to get a complete picture for the ABC Corporation. This results in a better design is created by the person who replaced our old ex-employee. Figure 15-8 illustrates the resulting improved design.

The screen shown in Figure 15-8 is indicative of a good design. The design is flexible enough to allow us to view information about the ABC Corporation in all locations. The key here is the separation of two distinct dimensions: customer and city.

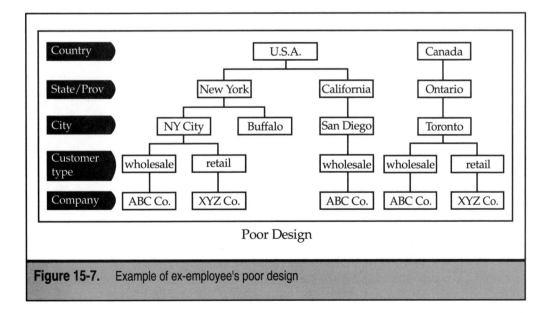

**Figure 15-7.**  Example of ex-employee's poor design

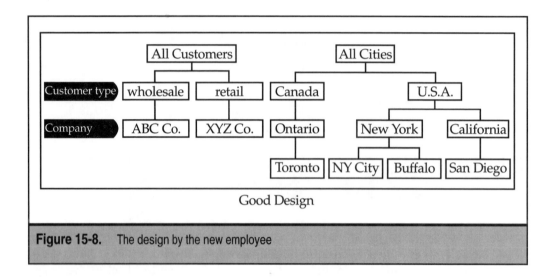

**Figure 15-8.** The design by the new employee

***NOTE:*** Never combine dimensions. A classic mistake companies make is combining dimensions such as customer and product.

The misunderstanding is that to see what products a customer has purchased, that customer and product must be in the same hierarchy. Not so. Dimensions should represent distinct viewpoints into the data. Never combine geography and sales force if a salesperson can sell into more than one geographical area. Never combine geography and customer if a customer exists in more than one location. If you do, you are limiting how the data can be reported and thus diminishing the effectiveness of the tool.

## Special Dimensions

Special dimensions are dimensions that support unique reporting requirements. OLAP systems should be designed in a way to make it easy for the end user to access and manipulate their data. The following are three examples of special dimensions that facilitate reporting.

**MONTH DIMENSION** We often include a separate dimension that contains just the month name that the transaction occurred in. The dimension would then have values ranging from January through December. This dimension when used in conjunction with your date dimension allows you to easily report month-over-month comparisons. Table 15-7 shows data that can allow this reporting to be carried out.

**THE ALPHABET DIMENSION** The model should provide easy access to the data. What happens if you have 1,000 customers but no customer hierarchy? A technique that we use is to break the customers up alphabetically. This breakdown is not meant for reporting purposes, but to simply assist the user in locating a particular customer. Figure 15-9 illustrates the advantages of utilizing an alphabet dimension.

|      | 1996 | 1997 | 1998 | 1999 |
|------|------|------|------|------|
| Jan  | 120  | 110  | 120  | 130  |
| Feb  | 200  | 200  | 100  | 300  |
| Mar  | 400  | 225  | 325  | 425  |
| Apr  | 120  | 110  | 120  | 130  |
| May  | 200  | 200  | 100  | 300  |
| Jun  | 400  | 225  | 325  | 425  |
| Jul  | 120  | 110  | 120  | 130  |
| Aug  | 200  | 200  | 100  | 300  |
| Sep  | 400  | 225  | 325  | 425  |
| Oct  | 120  | 110  | 120  | 130  |
| Nov  | 200  | 200  | 100  | 300  |
| Dec  | 400  | 225  | 325  | 425  |

**Table 15-7.**   Month Data by Year

Figure 15-9 also shows you how we forced a hierarchy by stripping the first letter from each of our customer names. Furthermore, we grouped customers whose names begin with the letters A through M together and the same for customers whose names begin with the letter N through Z. This provides an intuitive method for locating a particular customer.

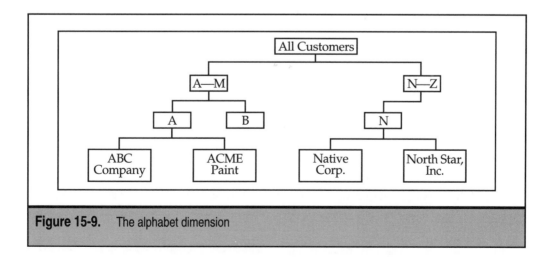

**Figure 15-9.**   The alphabet dimension

**RANGE DIMENSION**    The range dimension is useful for isolating particular ranges of data. In this case, we have created a range dimension based on price. This allows the user an extra avenue for reporting. Figure 15-10 illustrates how we can break the dimension into various ranges.

By using the price range dimension of Figure 15-10, we can easily isolate our products that fall within a particular price range. We may ask to be shown a list of customers who have purchased items in the 0–$10 price range. Again, including this as a dimension facilitates reporting. Understand how your users analyze the data and then incorporate dimensions to facilitate their analysis.

## Limit the Number of Dimensions

We must remember that we must try to limit the number of dimensions. We have often come across cases where organizations have too many dimensions on the dimension line. This tends to overcomplicate analysis. Try to stick to the relevant dimensions. The rule of thumb for most applications is five to seven dimensions. Note, however, that there will be cases where more are required.

This is an area where ROLAP has an advantage over MOLAP. This rule does not apply to the ROLAP vendors. In the case of MOLAP, you can theoretically have hundreds of dimensions. The key word in the previous sentence is "theoretically." The practical reality dictates far fewer dimensions. In a MOLAP world, the number of dimensions in a cube impacts the size of the cube. The more dimensions, the bigger the cube. Typically, the bigger the cube, the slower it becomes.

The parent-child ratio for dimensions should be limited to approximately 1 to 10. In that, I mean any parent should typically drill-down to no more than 10 children. This makes navigation easier. Figure 15-10 depicts a good and a poor design. The poor design shows all children sharing the same parent, where fruit, vegetables, meat, and dairy products are all descendants of the same parent. The good example makes navigation easier. Furthermore, the introduction of a new level allows another perspective for reporting, as illustrated in Figure 15-11.

Care must be taken when defining your dimensions, so avoid the big bang solution. Ask any end user what they want and they will usually say "everything." There is no cost to them to ask for the earth. OLAP tools work best with summarized information. Be cautious in trying to answer every business question with one model. Introducing too much detail into your model will affect performance. Poorly performing models do not get used. So remember, you must not try to satisfy all requirements at the same time—evolution is a better model in this case. Gearing your solution to a limited number of reporting levels will avoid this problem. Figure 15-12 illustrates the big bang corporate reporting levels; by focusing your reporting, you will avoid building a system that becomes obsolete before its time.

**TIP:**   Normally as you go higher up an organization, the less interested they are in the detail. Senior executives tend to look at the organization as a whole, while departmental users tend to focus on the detailed business at hand.

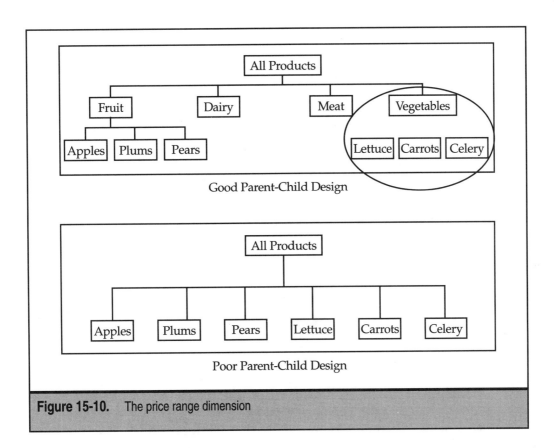

**Figure 15-10.**    The price range dimension

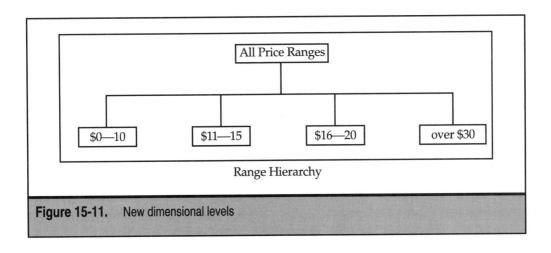

**Figure 15-11.**    New dimensional levels

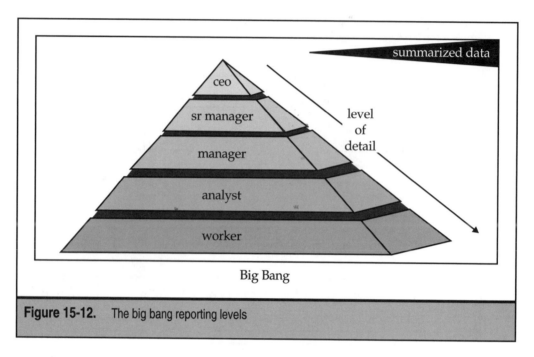

**Figure 15-12.**    The big bang reporting levels

## Facts

Facts are measurements of your business, such as revenue, cost, gross margin, gross margin percentage, quantity, and price. They are normally additive, and are directly related to the dimensions in your model. How facts are summarized is very important. Typically, if a fact is additive, it would be summarized as illustrated in Figure 15-13 in the Revenue Roll-Up. Each level is summed up to the next level above, as illustrated in Figure 15-13.

Some facts are not additive. Consider bank balances, room temperature, and price. It would be incorrect to roll up these facts in the same way we rolled up revenue. Imagine trying to evaluate temperatures in an office tower; if you added the values, you may find that the total temperature of the building was 4,000 degrees Celsius. This result is meaningless; however, by performing an average, the result may be 24 degrees Celsius. The Price Roll-Up illustrated in Figure 15-14 shows how price is averaged instead of summed at each level of the product hierarchy.

Facts are what make OLAP interesting. Consider analysis of revenue without budget or forecast to compare against. Consider analysis of revenue without gross margin and cost. Understand what the key measurements in your business are that are necessary to deliver a complete and relevant system. Now that we have learned about the various components to building an OLAP application, let's look at how we put it all together.

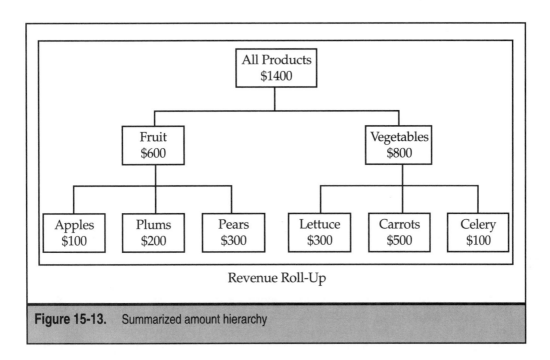

**Figure 15-13.**    Summarized amount hierarchy

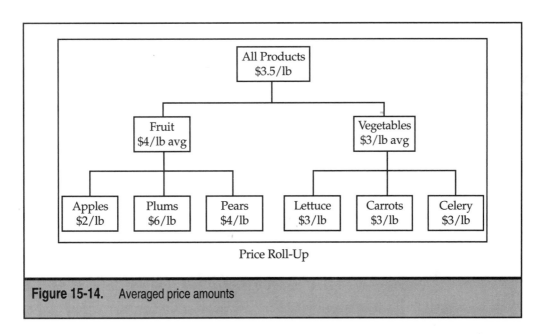

**Figure 15-14.**    Averaged price amounts

Let's take a closer look at a dimension map. A technique you can use to put a framework around an OLAP application. You don't want to hear about this stuff? Here's two words: ex and employee. So pay attention.

# DIMENSION MAP

The dimension map is a one-page requirements definition document for an OLAP project. Think of it as a scope statement for an OLAP application. The dimension map should include all the dimensions, the levels within each dimension, and counts for the approximate number of cells within the dimension. It should also include the facts for this model and detail how they are to be calculated and summarized. Table 15-8 shows a very simple dimension map and Table 15-9 shows the same scenario for the facts.

Your deliverable is neatly summarized in an easy to read, one-page scope document. This document is easily constructed and provides a basis for discussing what is expected from the project. Certainly other documentation will follow, but why expend the energy until you have reached consensus on what is to be delivered.

Once you have a consensus, you now have a means to measure the success of your project. Why are the budget numbers not in the model? They were never included in the design—have a look at the dimension map we built six months ago.

A trick we use is to build a prototype based on our initial design. This prototype can be critiqued by the end users. Remember, it is much easier to criticize than to conceptualize.

| Dimensions | | | | |
|---|---|---|---|---|
| **All Dates** | **All Products** | **All Customers** | **All Cities** | **All Price Ranges** |
| Year (3) | Group (3) | Customer type (5) | Country (3) | Range (4) |
| Quarter (12) | Line (12) | Customer (500) | State (72) | |
| Month (36) | Product (50) | | City (300) | |
| 51 | 65 | 505 | 375 | 4 |

**Table 15-8.** Dimension Map

| Fact | Summarize | Calculation |
|------|-----------|-------------|
| Revenue | Sum | |
| Cost | Sum | |
| GM | Sum | Revenue - cost |
| GM% | Sum components, then calculate | |
| Units | Sum | |
| Price | Average | |

**Table 15-9.** Fact Map

In conclusion, this chapter introduced you to the world of OLAP. The key concepts we discussed were as follows:

▼ OLAP is to empower people to make more informed decisions, but will not ensure better decisions are made. Even with good information, you can still choose poorly.

■ OLAP is a type of reporting characterized by the ability to drill-down, slice and dice, and change displays.

■ ROLAP and MOLAP refer to how data is physically stored.

■ The key to OLAP is understanding and identifying the proper dimensions.

▲ Constructing a dimension map is a great way to launch any OLAP project. It allows for a common ground of understanding.

Where do we go from here? The next chapter introduces you to Microsoft's OLAP offering; SQL Server 7 OLAP services. As you read through this next chapter, keep in mind the fundamentals from this chapter.

# CHAPTER 16

# Microsoft Decision Support Server

Now that we've reviewed OLAP, let's look at the SQL Server 7 OLAP services, the component within SQL Server 7 that provides OLAP capabilities. The goal of this chapter is for you to understand the SQL Server 7 OLAP services architecture and its main features and benefits. Most importantly, we will take you through the process of creating an OLAP database using SQL Server 7 OLAP services. This process consists of the logical design, the physical design, and the actual processing that creates the OLAP database. Hold on tight, here we go…

## SQL SERVER 7 OLAP SERVICES

SQL Server 7 OLAP services, shortened to MS OLAP for this chapter, will have a tremendous—one could say transforming—impact on the OLAP industry because of the following:

▼ **Cost**—MS OLAP ships as a component of SQL Server 7. This means that its acquisition cost is lower than existing products by a factor of 20X to 50X.

■ **Server architecture**—MS OLAP server is architected from the ground up to support ROLAP, MOLAP, and HOLAP physical formats. Most existing products in the marketplace have started as either MOLAP or ROLAP and have grafted on the other after the product's base architecture was already in place. MS OLAP is able to access all OLAP variants seamlessly.

■ **Distributed architecture**—MS OLAP provides a client-side OLAP data store in addition to the server OLAP engine. This architecture allows MS OLAP to make intelligent query decisions that minimize network traffic and processing load on the OLAP server. In addition, the client-side presence supports mobile OLAP. Users are able to retrieve the initial data from the server, disconnect, and then slice and dice the information independently from the server.

■ **Ease of management**—The MS OLAP user interface provides the OLAP database administrator with an easy to use, wizard-driven interface for creating and managing OLAP databases. State-of-the-art processing and the internal management and structure of the physical data store allow MS OLAP to seamlessly address OLAP database management issues that have traditionally made OLAP difficult to implement and maintain.

▲ **Unparalleled product support**—MS OLAP provides the OLAP for OLE DB API standard that allows popular front-end OLAP tools like Business Objects, Brio, and Cognos. More than 20 vendors in all are supporting or are in the process of supporting the OLAP for OLE DB API.

Before continuing, let's define some OLAP terms used previously and throughout this chapter.

▼ *API* **is applications programming interface**—A term used to define the interface that a programmer uses to access functionality by the provider of the functionality.

■ *ODBC* **is open database connectivity**—The industry standard API for accessing relational databases. Typically, products and programs requiring access to one or more relational databases will write once to ODBC, as opposed to once for every separate database's proprietary API.

■ *OLE DB* **is Microsoft's strategic API moving forward**—Put another way, Microsoft will continue to support ODBC; however, ODBC is a mature standard. New API features and innovations (e.g., an interface to provide fast bulk insert capabilities) will be added to OLE DB

■ A *data cube* **is the actual OLAP database**—Also referred to as *cube* for short.

■ A *measure* **is a quantitative value, or fact, that is aggregated in the OLAP cube**—An instance of a measure exists as one cell within the multidimensional cube.

■ A *dimension* **is descriptive category that describes a boundary or surface of a data cube**—Let's say we want to find the total product sales for Q2 of 2001, for the West sales region, for a particular product line. Our dimensions here are date, sales region, and product line.

▲ *Aggregation* is the intersection and summation of dimensions within your data cube.

Now that we've defined some basic OLAP terms, let's review one of the largest implementation issues today with OLAP databases—the data explosion problem.

## The Data Explosion Problem

OLAP is all about performance. Aggregate values are precalculated to save the processing time required in a traditional relational database. This is especially important for a data warehouse or data mart where the underlying fact table may contain millions, and in some cases billions, of rows. Storing these aggregations typically means that the OLAP database is larger than the source relational database by a factor of five to ten times and more. Figure 16-1 demonstrates this phenomenon.

In this example, the source sales information is aggregated by sales region. There are three fields in the relational table:

▼ Sales region

■ Hardware

▲ Software

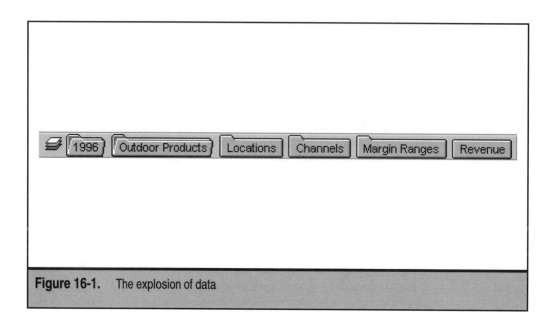

**Figure 16-1.**    The explosion of data

There is one dimension (sales region) and two measures (hardware and software), which are combined to create a derived measure named "computer products total." This one dimension contains a simple parent-child relationship. Sales districts (the children) roll into sales regions (the parent). In this example, we have four data values (two rows with two data values per row). We have five aggregated values (one value per row + three values for the parent region row). This very basic example produces a multiplier of 2.25: four data values result in nine OLAP data values.

Let's expand this. What if we're a multinational company? Now, let's roll sales regions up to territories, which then roll up into our total number. How about more dimensions? Let's take the FoodMart retail store example provided with SQL Server 7. The product dimension consists of a six-level parent-child hierarchy: product family, department, category, subcategory, brand name, and product name. As we add more calculated measures, more dimensions, and more complex dimensions, the number of OLAP elements explodes relative to the underlying data. This is a classic case of exponential growth.

## Sparse Data

We've just seen how OLAP databases store aggregated values for each intersection of the dimensions for all measures in the cube. There isn't always a value at each aggregate intersection within the cube. For our FoodMart example, Australian stores may stock vegamite, but the overwhelming majority of the other stores in the world don't. What happens when we aggregate the vegamite product and the 10 different product brands with the New York district, the Northeast region, and the United States territory? One of our favorite types of candy growing up, Goldenberg's Peanut Chews, is available in New

York, but is rarely seen even 200 miles away in Boston. This is an example of sparse data in the cube. Many OLAP databases today store a placeholder for this intersection point, and this adds to the OLAP database size.

## Addressing the Data Explosion

MS OLAP handles both data sparsity and the data explosion problem. MS OLAP does not store sparse data elements in the cube—one problem down, one to go. To solve the data explosion problem, MS OLAP has implemented leading edge technology that uses the 80/20 rule for storing aggregates. By the 80/20 rule, we mean that 20 percent of the aggregates will typically give you 80 percent of your performance boost. This is amazing technology that is unique to MS OLAP.

We are getting ahead of ourselves. We will cover these issues later in this chapter. Before drilling down into how MS OLAP creates logical and physical cubes, it's important to understand the MS OLAP architecture.

# Distributed Architecture

MS OLAP has a distributed architecture that allows it to utilize the power of the client machine and offload processing from the OLAP server. Figure 16-2 illustrates this concept; note how the traditional client to single server architecture is replaced by cubes, servers, and a handful of services.

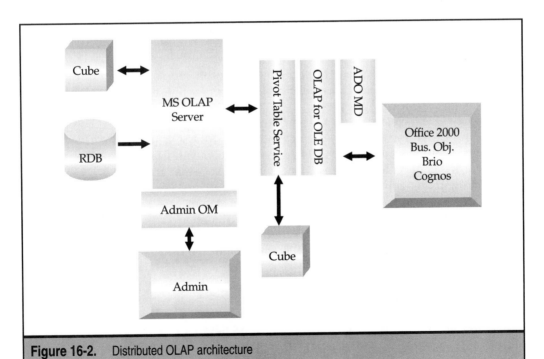

**Figure 16-2.** Distributed OLAP architecture

Moving from right to left, an end user accesses to MS OLAP through a tool like Office 2000 Excel Pivot tables or popular OLAP tools like Business Objects, Brio, and Cognos. There are several important things to note here.

First, MS OLAP supports DOLAP, or desktop OLAP. This is significant because this allows a knowledgeable worker to save their desired OLAP information on the local disk. The knowledge worker can then disconnect from the OLAP server on the corporate WAN (wide area network) and use the pivot table service to view this information offline using the same tool that initially accessed the server. This is a feature that many of today's popular OLAP engines do not provide.

Second, client-side processing capabilities provide for an efficient cache that allows MS OLAP to minimize network traffic and processing load on the MS OLAP server. This allows MS OLAP to make intelligent processing decisions; for example, if you already have January and February information and you now ask for Q1 information, MS OLAP knows that it only has to retrieve the March information from the server.

These tools interact with MS OLAP through the OLAP for OLE DB API. OLAP programming using this API is a significant topic that is worth a separate book within itself. Let's briefly review this topic so that we understand the big picture.

## Programming to MS OLAP

Experienced C++ programmers will often use the underlying OLAP for OLE DB API to access MS OLAP. Business programmers and Web developers can choose to use ADO MD, a higher-level component interface layered on OLAP for OLE DB. ADO MD supports most, but not all, of OLAP for OLE DB capabilities and is a recommended interface for business developers. Systems developers will most likely use OLAP for OLE DB for complete access to the product's functionality.

Go to Microsoft's Web site at http://www.microsoft.com/olap/ for OLAP for OLE DB and ADO MD specifications as well as white papers on these topics. Underneath this API is the pivot table service.

Now that we have an API, we need a language to pass across this API. The second part of the OLAP for OLE DB specification is the MD SQL (multidimensional SQL) language. Many of you will never have to know about this language—the front-end OLAP tools will provide you with a visual user interface that generates MD SQL. Those of you programming directly to OLAP for OLE DB will need to learn a language whose similarities with relational SQL end with the **select** statement.

Well, actually that may be an exaggeration, but remember that MD SQL's primary goal is to allow you to slice and dice your multidimensional cube. After you do this, you oftentimes need to render this onto the traditional two-dimensional relational table structure. These requirements require MD SQL to have significant language extensions to the base SQL language.

Once again, programming to MS OLAP is a separate book within itself. The bad news is that people familiar with relational databases and not familiar with OLAP have to undergo a significant learning process. The good news is that the Microsoft Web site listed earlier has a lot of good material, including the specifications for both MD SQL and

OLAP for OLE DB. SQL Server 7 also ships a sample application, the MDX sample application, a great tool for you to learn more about the MD SQL language. This sample application is a great place to start if you are a programmer interested in programmatically accessing MS OLAP.

## Pivot Table Service

The pivot table service is responsible for initiating and controlling all traffic to the MS OLAP server and interfacing to the cube stored on the client machine. The benefits to having this component running (i.e., performance and disconnected processing) have been previously listed. This service will ship with Office 2000 and provides access to both the MS OLAP server and client OLAP databases.

The pivot table service also ships with the front-end OLAP tools and provides these tools with access to databases on both the MS OLAP server and client. There is no user interface to the pivot table service. In fact, there are really only two MD SQL commands that directly address the client-side local cube: **create cube** and **insert into cube**.

The client-side processing does not have the full capabilities of the server. It is a subset of the MS OLAP server code base and provides full access to the local cube. Remember that end users will never have to know about programming to MS OLAP and the pivot table service. It is important for you to understand the basic architecture since this provides insight into MS OLAP behavior.

For example, given the local caching architecture, changes to the database on the server side will not be reflected on the client side until the next time that the client requires information from the server. MS OLAP will know on the next server access that the server information has changed and will utilize this to provide a new set of results to the client-side cache. Now that we've covered the MS OLAP client-side architecture, let's move to the server.

## MS OLAP Server

The MS OLAP server is comprised of several different components working together: The underlying multidimensional engine, the query processor, the repository, and the administrator. Note that this is a simplification but will be adequate for this discussion.

**MULTIDIMENSIONAL ENGINE**   This is the actual OLAP on disk structure. This multi-dimensional store is optimized for OLAP processing. It does not store sparse information and takes advantage of the fact that OLAP is almost exclusively a read-only database. Underlying database keys are compressed into 4- or 8-byte values to provide for efficient on-disk storage. MS OLAP doesn't need to worry about the complex issues related to transaction management. This allows it to add optimizations like storing dimension range values in underlying database extents. Given this, MS OLAP can skip an extent scan based upon information in the extent header. But I digress. The goal of this section is not to describe the MS OLAP on-disk structure; rather, it's to demonstrate that MS OLAP is well-architected, very high performance, and optimized for OLAP queries.

**QUERY PROCESSOR**   The statement execution engine may be the more appropriate term for this component. In addition, the internal architecture contains internal sub-components responsible for query optimization and the actual data access. However, at a high level, query processor will do. This component is responsible for accepting MD SQL requests and determining the optimal execution plan that satisfies the request. This component was designed from the ground level up to support MOLAP, ROLAP, and HOLAP. Compare this to many existing OLAP products that started out as either MOLAP or ROLAP and then grafted the other onto the existing architecture.

Given this architecture, the query processor can satisfy a query that references information in both ROLAP and MOLAP formats. Put another way, with MS OLAP, you define a logical cube and then decide the physical representation of that cube. Administrators will define the logical and physical cubes through the MS OLAP administrator.

**MS OLAP ADMINISTRATOR**   The administrator provides an intuitive wizard-driven interface to create and maintain cubes. The administrator stores this information into the MS OLAP repository, a separate store for OLAP metadata. The administrator interfaces with an administration object model and repository through an administration COM component.

COM is the acronym that stands for Component Object Model. COM is the underlying plumbing for Microsoft applications and provides a binary interface, which allows a COM container or consumer to request services from a COM service. All Microsoft products expose COM interfaces to their services, and the MS OLAP administration services is no exception.

If you don't understand COM, don't worry. The key takeaway here—this interface allows programmatic access to the MS OLAP administration features as well as through the user interface. Now that we've reviewed the architecture, let's see how we create and administer an MS OLAP cube.

# Creating a Cube

Creating a cube is a two-stage process. First, we create the logical structure of the cube. Second, we determine the physical structure of the logical structure.

## Creating a Logical Cube

MS OLAP, like all well-behaved NT services, provides an MMC snap-in for administration. MMC stands for Microsoft Management Console, the common administrator's interface available for NT products shipping with NT 5.0. Microsoft products shipping with the NT 4.0 Option Pack and later contain an administrator snap-in.

***TIP:***   If you're running NT 4.0 and you haven't installed the NT 4.0 Option Pack, do it. This option pack is available to existing NT license holders, either free in download from the Microsoft Web site (www.microsoft.com) or orderable by CD-ROM for a nominal charge.

Let's create our logical cube. SQL Server 7 ships with a sample FoodMart cube. Accessing an existing cube is useful; however, it doesn't give you a feel for how this cube was created. Our mission in this section is to re-create a similar cube from scratch so that you understand the process involved. Let's start by entering the MS OLAP Administrator utility.

The installation process will register your server with a name matching your NT machine name. To create a cube, you must first define a database for the cube to reside in. To create the database, follow the steps shown next, and you should get the results shown in Figure 16-3.

1. Highlight the server.

2. Right-click the mouse, then select New Database.

3. Enter the name **FoodMartTest.**

**NOTE:**  SQL Server 7's consistent user interface always allows you to right-click the mouse on a highlighted object to see the available actions on that object. All examples of initiating an action will assume this technique. Also, we will show the important screen shots only shot in the sample session, and not every screen.

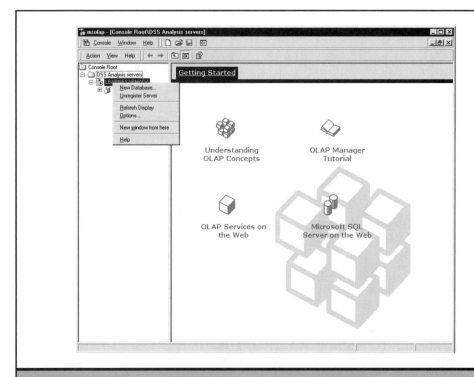

**Figure 16-3.**    Defining a new database

Now we create the test cube. Within the FOODMARTTEST database's Cube folder, select New Cube, then Wizard. Select Next to bypass the Welcome Wizard screen. Our first decision is deciding the cube's underlying fact table. Click on the New Data Source button to obtain the OLE DB and ODBC drivers available to MS OLAP. Figure 16-4 shows a list of providers to pick from.

Notice all of the available OLE DB drivers, including the Microsoft OLE DB provider for ODBC drivers. This driver provides you access to the full range of ODBC drivers. Other drivers available include the OLE DB drivers that ship with SQL Server 7, including Microsoft Access and Oracle.

For this example, select Microsoft Jet 4.0 OLE DB Provider to connect to the "foodmart.mdb" sample database shipping with SQL Server 7. Press Next and enter the full foodmart.mdb file path. Press Test Connection to ensure that you have access to this data source. Grizzled ODBC veterans will recognize that this is a great feature since 80 percent of the problems with ODBC typically occur during the initial connection to the data source. Figure 16-5 shows the Connection tab in the Data Link Properties sheet where the data source and logon information are supplied.

## Selecting the Fact Table and Measures

Now it's time to get down to business. Let's choose the fact table for this cube. For this cube, let's select the SALES_FACT_1997 table. Figure 16-6 highlights selection of this table in the data sources and table pick list.

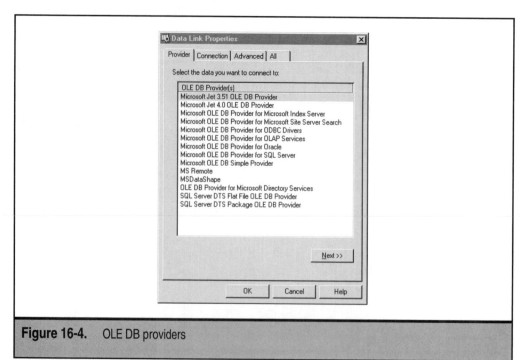

**Figure 16-4.** OLE DB providers

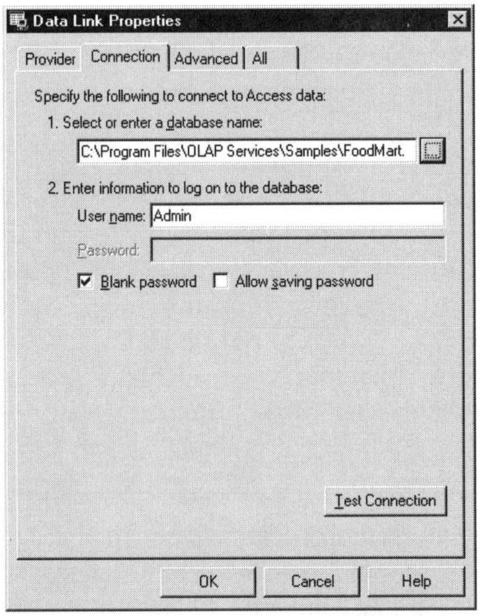

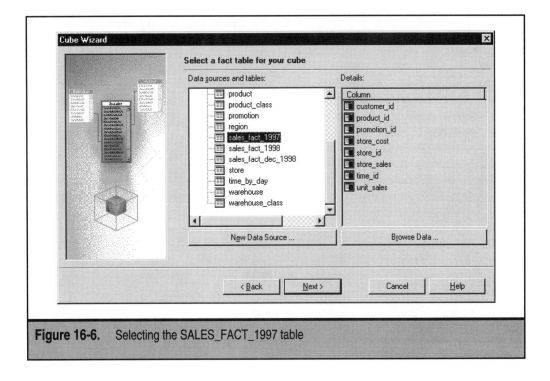

**Figure 16-5.** Filling in the Connection tab

**Figure 16-6.** Selecting the SALES_FACT_1997 table

It's important to note that we are working from an existing star schema for this example. Starting from an existing star schema dramatically simplifies the creation of your cube. We strongly recommend that you take the time to build and populate your data warehouse or data mart star schema before proceeding to the OLAP cube creation phase.

From the fact table, let's select four measures, Unit_Sales, Store_Cost, Store_Sales, and Product_ID. Note that MS OLAP removes the underscores, which creates the following: Unit Sales, Store Cost, Store Sales, and Product ID. The wizard assigns the **sum** attribute to an aggregate for a measure. An overwhelming majority of measures will be **sum**. Another useful aggregate is **count** since, combined with **sum**, it allows **average**. In this example, we'll want Product_ID to be a **count** aggregate. We'll go through the process of doing this when we modify our newly created cube later in this section. Figure 16-7 shows where a table's numeric columns are selected to define a cube's measures.

*TIP:*   MS OLAP's intelligent aggregation feature requires that all measures be derivable. **average** is not derivable and is not supported as a measure attribute. However, we'll show you later how to create **average** measures by dividing **sum** by **count**.

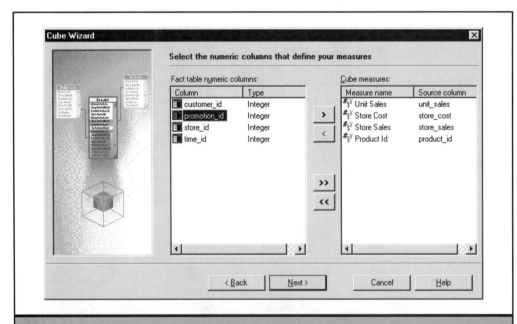

**Figure 16-7.**   Selecting numeric columns for measure definition

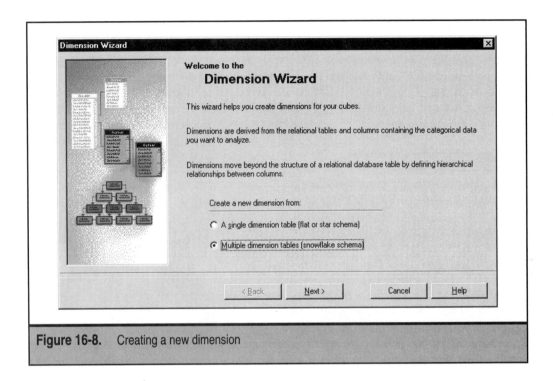

**Figure 16-8.** Creating a new dimension

## Creating Dimensions

The MS OLAP wizard moves us from selecting measures to creating dimensions. MS OLAP provides us with several options: creating dimensions from a flat table, a star schema dimension table, or from multiple dimension tables—otherwise known as a snowflake schema. Let's start with the third option. Figure 16-8 shows the screen in the Dimension Wizard after that choice has been made.

**CREATING SNOWFLAKE DIMENSIONS**    We've covered star schemas earlier in this book. A snowflake schema extends a star schema design by creating a second level of indirection from a dimension table to another table. This concept is easier to explain using a tangible example. Within the FOODMART database, we have a snowflake schema. The specific example is product table linked to the product class table. This is a classic example of a snowflake schema, where the table creating the snowflake—in this case the PRODUCT_CLASS table—describes the product hierarchy.

```
create table [dbo].[product_class] (
    [product_class_id] [int] not null ,
    [product_subcategory] [varchar] (50) not null ,
    [product_category] [varchar] (50) not null ,
    [product_department] [varchar] (50) not null ,
    [product_family] [varchar] (50) not null
) on [primary]
```

For the FOODMART source database, the product hierarchy is as follows: product family, product department, category, subcategory, brand name, and product name. The product_class table contributes all levels of this hierarchy except for the bottom two levels—the brand name and the product name—which are stored in the product table. The product_class_id is the key linking the product table to the product_class table. The Transact-SQL that creates the PRODUCT table is shown in the next listing—note that both of these table definitions are the direct output from the SQL Server 7 generate scripts feature.

```
create table [dbo].[product] (
    [product_class_id] [int] not null ,
    [product_id] [int] not null ,
    [brand_name] [varchar] (255) not null ,
    [product_name] [varchar] (255) not null ,
    [sku] [int] not null ,
    [srp] [money] not null ,
    [gross_weight] [real] not null ,
    [net_weight] [real] not null ,
    [recyclable_package] [bit] not null ,
    [low_fat] [bit] not null ,
    [units_per_case] [smallint] not null ,
    [cases_per_pallet] [smallint] not null ,
    [shelf_width] [real] not null ,
    [shelf_height] [real] not null ,
    [shelf_depth] [real] not null
) on [primary]
```

Select the Multiple Dimension Tables option and press Next; you're now at the Table Section screen. To create a dimension from a snowflake schema source, we select both the PRODUCT_CLASS table and the product tables and press Next. The wizard's next screen prompts us for the primary key/foreign key relationship between the two tables that comprises the particular instance of the snowflake schema.

MS OLAP chooses this relationship by default if a primary/foreign key relationship exists or if there is a column with the same name in both tables. In this example, both tables contain a common field name, Product_Class_ID. Let's press Next to acknowledge this relationship. We won't display these two screens; the next display will be the selecting a level screen in which you specify the dimension hierarchy.

**DEFINING A DIMENSION HIERARCHY**    All columns from the selected tables are available when deciding the different levels of the dimension hierarchy. In this example, the product dimension contains six levels. This is not an uncommon number of levels when defining a product. Given these structures, it's no surprise that you need to worry about data sparsity and data explosions in OLAP data cubes. MS OLAP contains a nice usability feature that will issue a command that retrieves the row count. It will return a warning if a level at the top of the hierarchy has more members than a member below it. Name this dimension Product. Figure 16-9 shows where levels are defined for existing dimensions.

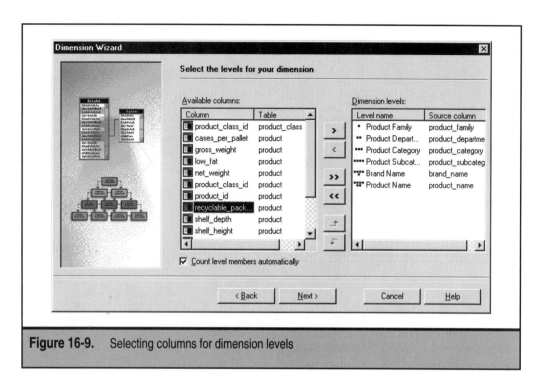

**Figure 16-9.**    Selecting columns for dimension levels

**CREATING A STANDARD DIMENSION**    Most dimensions created in the cube will be standard dimensions. Let's create a standard dimension by pressing New Dimension, selecting the STORE table, and selecting the Single Dimension option. Let's create a dimension representing the Store geography. Select the STORE table. The next screen lets us choose whether we want to create a standard dimension or a time dimension. Select the Standard Dimension option (we'll discuss the time dimension option shortly). A store rolls up into a city, which rolls up into a state or province, which rolls up into a country. Notice in the following example, as in the previous one, that we use names rather than keys to represent an entity like a store. We want our user population to search on real names, not keys. We'll name this dimension Store Location. Figure 16-10 shows the available columns, where—surprise, surprise—we have started by selecting Store_Street_Address.

**CREATING A TIME DIMENSION**    MS OLAP has a nice feature that allows the cube definer to create a dimension from a Date/Time field in the underlying fact table. However, many data warehouses already have a separate dimension representing time. The questions always arise, "Why is that necessary? Why not just store the date/time value in the fact table?" The answer is that there are many cases where an organization's fiscal calendar is different from the standard calendar. Another answer is that there is plenty of semantic information, which cannot be represented in a Date/Time field—for example, holidays and time periods where promotions are offered. This is critical information that is vital

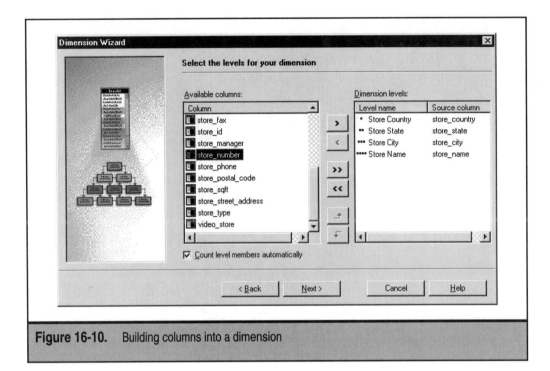

**Figure 16-10.**    Building columns into a dimension

for an organization to understand patterns in the underlying data. Retail is a perfect example. If promotions aren't represented in the time dimension, you will not be able to recognize that sales increased 50 percent for a particular product when you had a 75 percent off promotion.

Having said that, if you don't have an underlying time dimension in your relational data warehouse, MS OLAP provides a very handy feature that allows you to generate your time dimension from a date/time value. Selecting the time dimension option within the Single Dimension Wizard screen allows you to select a Date field in your fact table and then choose the type of date hierarchy that you want to build. Figure 16-11 shows where levels are built into a time dimension.

## Completing Our FoodMartTest Cube

We have to have dates and times represented. Let's add a Date dimension from the TIME_BY_DAY table. Follow the same steps for the Date dimension as you did for the Store dimension. Now we have three dimensions; Date, Product, and Store. Feel free, if you'd like, to add a fourth dimension (e.g., Customer_Location) from the CUSTOMER table and define the dimension hierarchy as Country, State/Province, and City. Note that our goal isn't to completely duplicate the existing FoodMart cube, but rather to produce a solid base for the physical design phase coming up next.

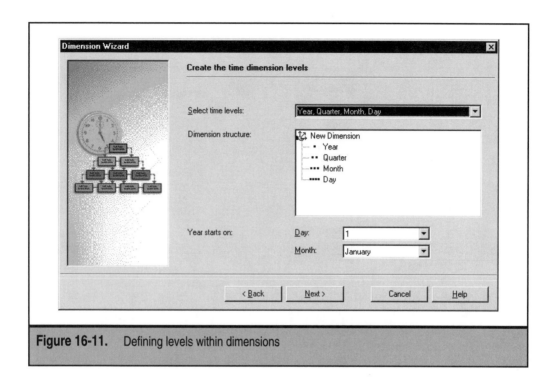

**Figure 16-11.**    Defining levels within dimensions

## What's Next?

After defining the initial Test cube's measures and dimensions, we save the cube and assign it a name. Let's look at the existing FoodMart demo, as shown in Figure 16-12, to see what the final cube looks like.

Notice that the cube has one additional measure and one calculated member. Before we get to this, let's modify the Product_id properties and convert its aggregation function attribute from **sum** to **count**. To view the Properties window, Select View | Properties from the top menu. This Properties dialog box is shown in Figure 16-13, where characteristics such as name and source columns are displayed.

How about the Food Mart Store Sales Net measure—how did it get there? MS OLAP gives you the ability to specify a formula in addition to a column when defining your measures. Select New measure and select the store_sales measure from the SALES_FACT_1997 table. Within the Source Column attribute, modify the field to represent the formula shown in the next listing:

```
sales_fact_1997.store_sales - sales_fact_1997.store_cost.
```

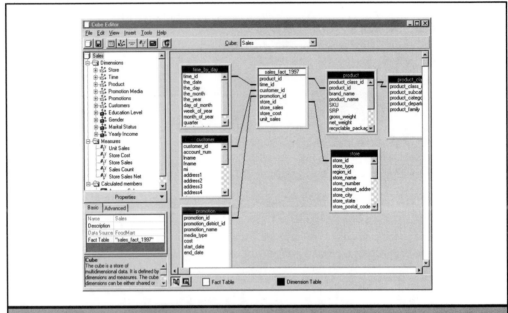

**Figure 16-12.** The finished FoodMart demo cube

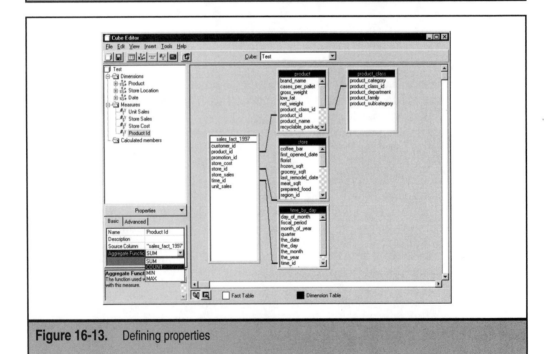

**Figure 16-13.** Defining properties

## Creating a Calculated Member

*Calculated members* provide a way for you to create calculated measures. One common use of calculated members is to use this feature to create averages. Remember from our previous discussion that MS OLAP intelligent aggregations require derivable measures. Let's create a calculated member to represent average store sales. Create a new calculated member (i.e., highlight Calculated measures, right-click the mouse, and select Create new calculated member).

You now have the option of choosing the parent dimension. This is an advanced feature, which means that you can calculate members for dimensions as well as for measures. Let's stick with the basics here and focus on creating a measure. Enter the formula into the Value field or click on the Continuation button at the rightmost corner of the text box. This brings you into the Calculated Member Builder screen, as shown in Figure 16-14. This facility provides you with a work pad to create your formula. Notice in the formula how we use the **if** function to only calculate this value if the divisor (i.e., Sales Count) is greater than 0.

OK, let's end our logical design session by closing the cube. We've completed our logical cube design, and we've created this logical cube through an intuitive wizard and user interface. It was pretty simple, right? Now you say, "Here comes the difficult part, building our physical cube." You're in for a pleasant surprise!

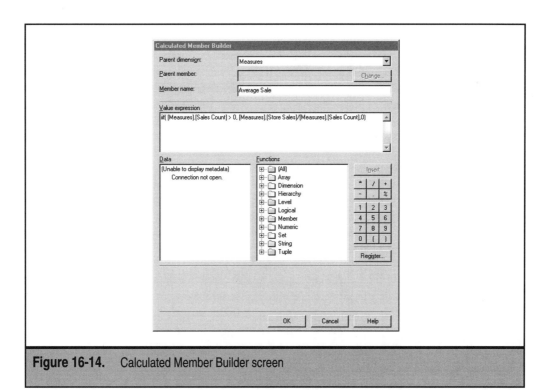

**Figure 16-14.** Calculated Member Builder screen

# Creating the Physical Data Cube

You've been very patient...pat yourself on the back and take a candy out of the container on the shelf beside the peanut butter. Just one, we said! Let's spend a bit of time on creating the cube we have spent so much time talking about.

## ROLAP, MOLAP, or HOLAP

Now that we've come to the physical design, where MS OLAP really shines in terms of ease of use and efficient disk space utilization. Select the newly created FoodMartTest cube and invoke Design Aggregations. After the initial screen, the Data Storage and Aggregation Wizard will prompt you for the specific OLAP data storage, as shown in Figure 16-15.

Your three choices are MOLAP, ROLAP, and HOLAP. MOLAP stores both the dimensions and fact table in the multidimensional database. ROLAP will leave the fact table in the relational database and will also create aggregate tables in the relational database to enable faster multidimensional access. HOLAP combines both; the fact table remains in the relational database while the dimensional tables are stored in the multi-dimensional database.

Pure MOLAP provides for the fastest, most efficient access, but results in duplicate fact tables. ROLAP is slower and consumes the most space, but uses existing databases and provides a comfort level to many IS shops. HOLAP is a nice compromise—the fact table remains in the relational database and the dimensions are moved to the multidimensional database and act as "performance boosters." HOLAP is the newest

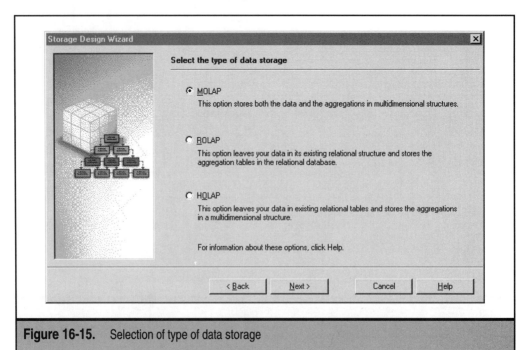

**Figure 16-15.** Selection of type of data storage

concept of the three and is currently the most popular storage mechanism for new OLAP projects.

The key takeaway from this section is that MS OLAP supports all three natively. The requestor of the information isn't exposed to this underlying structure. This structure is within the purview of the OLAP data administrator. You can even have a cube defined, which is comprised of a ROLAP partition, a HOLAP partition, and a MOLAP partition.

## The Aggregation Wizard

The Aggregation Wizard applies the 80/20 rule to determining your optimal aggregation mix. Put another way, it determines which aggregations give you the biggest bang for the buck.

The key to the technique employed by this OLAP engine is as follows. Since all measures are derivable, higher-level aggregations can be derived on the fly by lower-level aggregations. Let's say we have a Product Brand by Month aggregation. This aggregation can feed higher-level aggregations (e.g., Product Brand by Month, Product by Quarter, and Product Brand by Quarter). This ability means that now all aggregations do not have to be precalculated and stored on disk—this can happen dynamically. This one feature differentiates MS OLAP from other products in the industry. When you invoke Design Aggregations, MS OLAP presents you with the screen shown in Figure 16-16, where you can set limits on query performance or aggregation storage.

You can choose how you want to limit the total size of your cube. The first option is disk space. You choose an upper limit for the disk space that you want—or, in more cases,

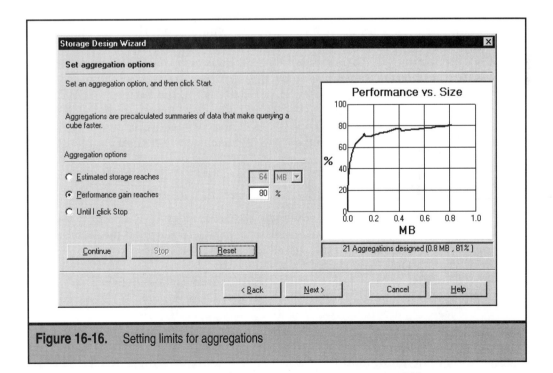

**Figure 16-16.**    Setting limits for aggregations

have to allocate to your cube—and MS OLAP will determine the number of aggregations that it can create within these space requirements.

The second option is to provide a performance boost estimate that you're looking to achieve. MS OLAP then determines the correct aggregation mix to provide you this performance boost. This feature makes your cube management with MS OLAP an order of magnitude easier than it is today with existing products. Once the wizard determines your correct aggregate mix, you can choose to save this information or you can start processing your cube immediately. For this demo, we recommend that you save your definition and do not start the actual processing of the cube.

## Building the Cube

The actual building of your cube is a CPU-intensive operation. The core information must be retrieved from the fact table and the aggregations must be calculated and then stored. If you chose ROLAP, MS OLAP will need to build summary tables in the relational database to store this information. If you chose MOLAP, MS OLAP will need to store the fact table in the multidimensional database.

The MS OLAP architecture is multithreaded, so we recommend, as with relational databases, that you host your MS OLAP databases on multiprocessor systems. The important concept here is that the CPU-intensive portion is on the build side more than on the query side.

There is still a place for existing OLAP servers; MS OLAP will not let you specify which specific aggregations to create, it will make the decision for you. Many of the existing OLAP servers give you more specific tuning options; these are primarily for administrators familiar with OLAP and the server configuration. This is an example of a high-end feature required by large OLAP installations.

MS OLAP does provide partitions, which are the mechanisms that administrators use to physically partition and separately tune large OLAP environments. In this section, we have taken you through the processes involved in designing and creating a SQL Server 7 OLAP services data cube. This process is easy and intuitive. One can see how this ease of use, along with access from popular end-user tools and the ubiquity of pivot table service (it will ship with Office 2000) will make OLAP available to the general population. Lets look at end-user access now.

# END-USER ACCESS

The first part of this chapter dealt with preparing your data for OLAP. This preparation in most organizations is an administrative function—it happens behind the scenes. As an end user, you are not really concerned about this behind-the-scenes work. What you are concerned with, though, is what gets delivered to you.

OLAP systems represent a paradigm shift in information delivery. Why not? Everything in information technology (IT) these days is a paradigm shift. The traditional method of receiving information was to get a stack of paper delivered to your office. The more important you were in the organization, the larger the stack of paper. Sometimes, you might review the reports delivered to you and even ask questions of them. These questions are what throw information technology departments into a frenzy.

The new guy in accounting wants an explanation of the Eastern sales total. Let's welcome him to the organization by placing his request 35th in the queue. Next week the report finally gets produced, only to generate another request. This is why OLAP tools are so important. The traditional reports no longer get delivered. What gets delivered is access to data. A successful delivery means that access to the data must be intuitive. Let's examine how a leading vendor delivers the goods.

# Cognos' PowerPlay

Cognos is an industry-leading provider of OLAP software. PowerPlay is their flagship product. PowerPlay 6.0 will be able to natively read MS OLAP cubes through PowerPlay Connect. Simply put, you can create your cube using MS OLAP, but your end user can use PowerPlay to perform his or her analysis. The end user is completely unaware of where the cube came from.

Going back to the previous chapter, we said that OLAP has three main characteristics—drill-down, slice and dice, and multiple displays. Let's exercise these functions within PowerPlay, starting from a simple, straightforward display as shown in Figure 16-17.

Presented with this information, an analyst may want to break down 1996 sales. In PowerPlay, to drill-down one simply moves the cursor over the data from which more detail is desired and when a plus sign "+" appears, the user simply double-clicks the mouse. The analyst would then see the 1996 data broken out to the next level of detail, which in this case is the four quarters that make up the year. Similarly, drill-down can also be performed on columns. Perhaps more detail is required on the product group "Outdoor Products." Simply move the cursor over this column and wait for the plus"+" sign to appear and then once again double-click. The resultant screen is shown in Figure 16-18, highlighting values for paraphernalia such as backpacks and the ever popular (right Ian?) cooking utensils.

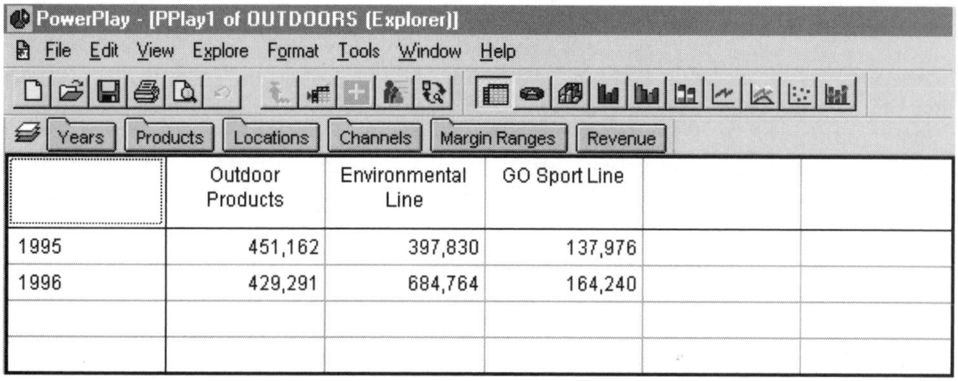

| | Outdoor Products | Environmental Line | GO Sport Line | | |
|---|---|---|---|---|---|
| 1995 | 451,162 | 397,830 | 137,976 | | |
| 1996 | 429,291 | 684,764 | 164,240 | | |
| | | | | | |
| | | | | | |

**Figure 16-17.** PowerPlay display of OUTDOORS

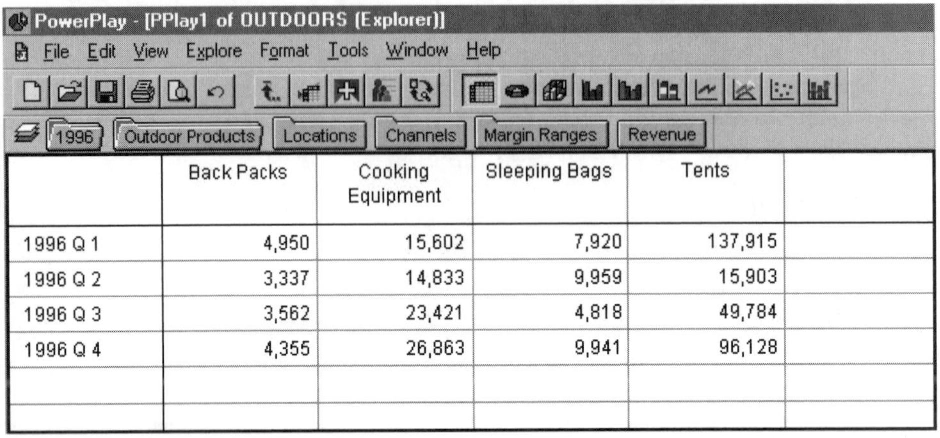

PowerPlay - [PPlay1 of OUTDOORS (Explorer)]

File  Edit  View  Explore  Format  Tools  Window  Help

[toolbar]

1996  Outdoor Products  Locations  Channels  Margin Ranges  Revenue

|  | Back Packs | Cooking Equipment | Sleeping Bags | Tents |  |
|---|---|---|---|---|---|
| 1996 Q 1 | 4,950 | 15,602 | 7,920 | 137,915 |  |
| 1996 Q 2 | 3,337 | 14,833 | 9,959 | 15,903 |  |
| 1996 Q 3 | 3,562 | 23,421 | 4,818 | 49,784 |  |
| 1996 Q 4 | 4,355 | 26,863 | 9,941 | 96,128 |  |
|  |  |  |  |  |  |
|  |  |  |  |  |  |

**Figure 16-18.**  Outdoor Products details

We can now see 1996 sales by quarter for Outdoor Products. We were able to move from summarized to detailed information by simply double-clicking. Perhaps now we would like to see where Outdoor Products sales were being made. We are now concerned with a new dimension, in this case the location dimension. PowerPlay stores its dimensions in what it refers to as a dimension line. It resembles the familiar line of tabs in a Windows dialog box, as shown here.

The dimension line contains the various dimensions that are valid for this model. In this case, Years, Products, Locations, Channels, and Margin Ranges. The rightmost tab, Revenue, contains the various measurements that the data can be viewed by. To introduce the location dimension, simply drag and drop it onto any row or column heading. The result of this is shown in Figure 16-19 where Far East, Europe, and North America are magically displayed!

Notice that the product dimension has been replaced with the location dimension. However, if you read the dimension line, you will note that we are still looking at just the Outdoor Products set of data. Next, we may want to view the information graphically. To do this, simply click on any of the graphical icons; this displays a clustered bar chart, as seen in Figure 16-20.

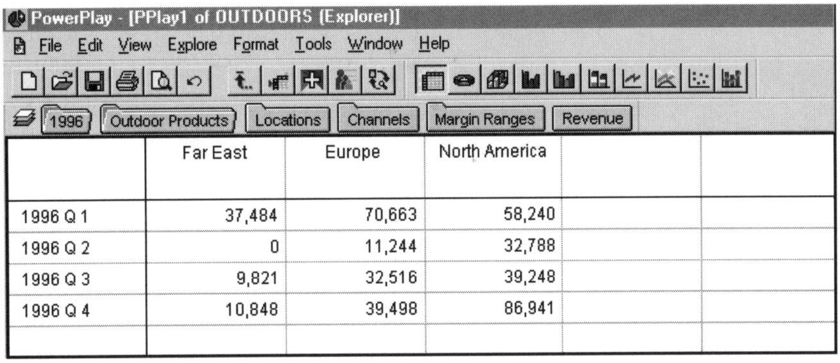

| | Far East | Europe | North America | | |
|---|---|---|---|---|---|
| 1996 Q 1 | 37,484 | 70,663 | 58,240 | | |
| 1996 Q 2 | 0 | 11,244 | 32,788 | | |
| 1996 Q 3 | 9,821 | 32,516 | 39,248 | | |
| 1996 Q 4 | 10,848 | 39,498 | 86,941 | | |

**Figure 16-19.**    Output with location dimension

A wide selection of graph types are available, and depending on the information being displayed, you will want to try different ones. No chart is perfect for displaying all data.

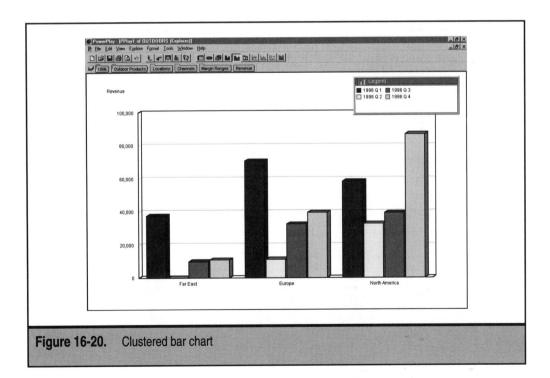

**Figure 16-20.**    Clustered bar chart

Let's move on to PowerPlay's ad hoc analysis capabilities. We are interested in calculating sales growth between 1995 and 1996. PowerPlay has two modes of operation: Explorer and Reporter. To perform calculations you must be in Reporter mode. To perform a calculation, simply highlight the components of the calculation and then choose Calculate from the File menu. A screen pops up similar to that shown in Figure 16-21, where Order, Operand, and Label are specified.

All the most popular calculations are supported. In this case, we are interested in subtracting 1995 sales from 1996 to give us growth. Figure 16-22 shows this, where the Growth label specified in Figure 16-21 appears in the rightmost column of the report.

As an analyst you may be concerned with Europe's sales. They have declined $29,672 over the previous year. Again, you can further investigate that number by simply double-clicking on it. Europe gets broken down into the countries that comprise it. The following is a simple example of how OLAP analysis is performed. To perform the analysis, we simply used mouse functions that are familiar to the most novice Windows user: double-click and drag and drop. The easier the tool is to use, the more likely it will be used. Remember, data and the tool are replacing the user's traditional report.

Now, that was a handful! The next chapter looks at a generic exercise that creeps up before and during the development and deployment of a decision support system. There is so much data out there—get on your gear…the cart is descending into the data mine as we speak. Please keep all hands inside the car and do not lean out of the vehicle until the majority of the vertical drop is complete.

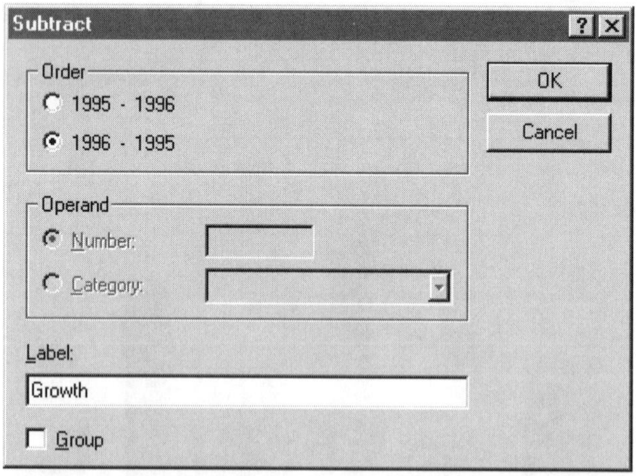

**Figure 16-21.** Selecting the calculation mechanism

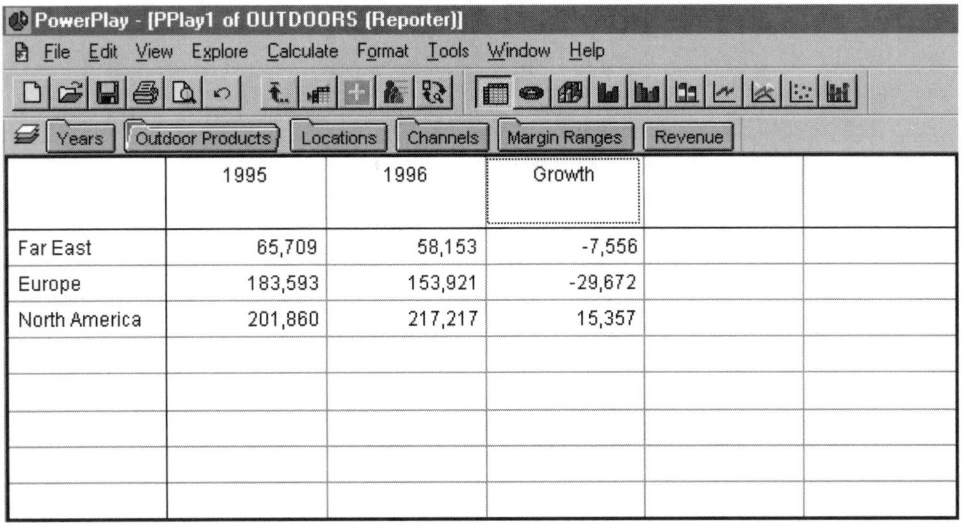

PowerPlay - [PPlay1 of OUTDOORS (Reporter)]

File   Edit   View   Explore   Calculate   Format   Tools   Window   Help

Years | Outdoor Products | Locations | Channels | Margin Ranges | Revenue

|  | 1995 | 1996 | Growth |  |  |
|---|---|---|---|---|---|
| Far East | 65,709 | 58,153 | -7,556 |  |  |
| Europe | 183,593 | 153,921 | -29,672 |  |  |
| North America | 201,860 | 217,217 | 15,357 |  |  |
|  |  |  |  |  |  |
|  |  |  |  |  |  |
|  |  |  |  |  |  |
|  |  |  |  |  |  |
|  |  |  |  |  |  |

**Figure 16-22.**   Output from the calculation specification

# CHAPTER 17

## Data Mining

This chapter is dedicated to data mining, a component of the data warehousing solution. Data mining is also called knowledge discovery in databases (KDD). There are many solutions out there, from many vendors, to assist the data mining process. Companies spend large amounts of time and money in collecting data; the data mining process helps discover what is going on with the data and with the exercise of turning data into business information.

# WHAT IS DATA MINING?

*Data mining* is a discovery process that allows users to understand the substance of, and the relationships between, their data. Data mining uncovers patterns and trends in the contents of this information. The concept is nothing new. Perhaps what has catapulted it to the forefront in some organizations are the benefits of the exercise on a short- and long-term basis. Table 17-1 shows an interesting piece we found on the Internet regarding steps in this evolution (source: www.santafe.edu/%7Ekurt/text/dmwhite/dmwhite.shtml, © Pilot Software Inc.).

Advances in the speed of the desktop computer coupled with robust software solutions have allowed companies to sift through data at speeds unheard of a few years back. With the development of faster CPUs and storage devices, the sky is the limit. Companies need not be restrained by the overwhelming amount of data they have captured since their electronic business solutions sprang to life. As early as 1996, the

| Evolutionary Step | Business Question | Enabling Technologies | Product Providers | Characteristics |
|---|---|---|---|---|
| Data collection (1960s) | "What was my total revenue in the last five years?" | Computers, tapes, disks | IBM, CDC | Retrospective, static data delivery |
| Data access (1980s) | "What were unit sales in New England last March?" | Relational databases (RDBMS), Structured Query Language (SQL), ODBC | Microsoft, Oracle, Sybase, Informix, IBM | Retrospective, dynamic data delivery at record levels |

**Table 17-1.** The Evolution of Decision Support

| Evolutionary Step | Business Question | Enabling Technologies | Product Providers | Characteristics |
|---|---|---|---|---|
| Data warehousing and decision support (1990s) | "What were unit sales in New England last March? Drill-down to Boston." | Online analytical processing (OLAP), multi-dimensional databases, data warehouses | Pilot, Comshare, Arbor, Cognos, Microstrategy | Retrospective, dynamic data delivery at multiple levels |
| Data mining (emerging today) | "What's likely to happen to Boston unit sales next month? Why?" | Advanced algorithms, multiprocessor computers, massive databases | Pilot, Lockheed, IBM, SGI, numerous startups (nascent industry) | Prospective, proactive information delivery |

**Table 17-2.** The Evolution of Decision Support (*continued*)

META Group reported that 19 percent of respondents to a survey they conducted were working on data warehouse projects in excess of 50 gigabytes; the same survey results expected that number to climb to 59 percent before the end of that calendar year alone.

Essentially, data mining provides methods and means for efficient representation and storage of large volumes of information, the extraction and transmission of that material to a disparate user community, and the means to analyze, interpret, and display that information in a useful manner. Let's move on and have a look at relationship and pattern discovery through data mining.

## Discovery

It's remarkable how relationships between data sometimes must be discovered. They are not readily evident without inspection, and they must be brought to the surface. This is an everyday occurrence evident in all areas of our lives. In the province of Ontario, for example, the last six digits (i.e., the single digit before the second hyphen coupled with the last five digits) of a person's driver's license are the year, month, and day of birth. Without this understanding, the three data elements shown in Figure 17-1 seem unrelated.

A data mining exercise could discover the relationship highlighted in Figure 17-2.

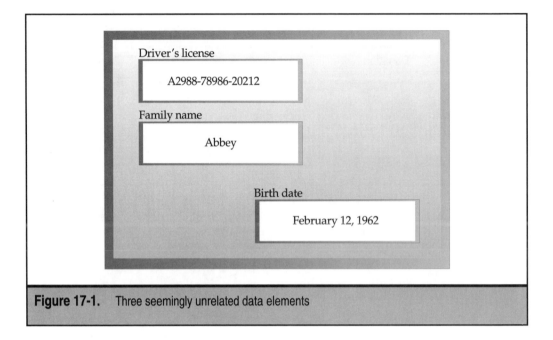

**Figure 17-1.** Three seemingly unrelated data elements

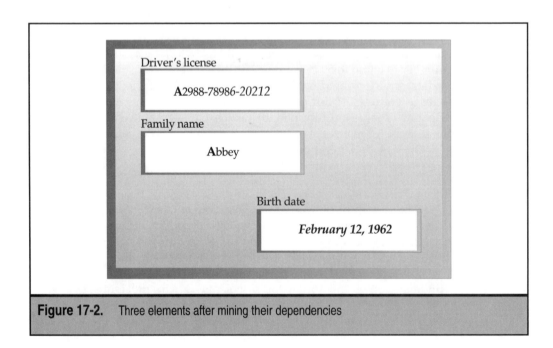

**Figure 17-2.** Three elements after mining their dependencies

Discovery deliberately goes out with no predetermined idea of what the search will find. There is no intervention in the process by the end user; the data mining discovery process wades through the source data looking for similarities and occurrences of data, which allow grouping and pattern identification. In the electronic data warehouse environment, this process must be able to do its thing in a relatively short time period. Rapid delivery of results is crucial to the adoption of a data mining product.

So much data is captured in some operational systems that the contents of seemingly unimportant data elements can easily become lost in the big picture. Suppose the customer address tracking component of a system insisted the ZIP code be entered when new customer information is recorded. This is deliberate. Until the information embedded in this code becomes useful to the analyst, the ZIP code hides itself in a network of other customer-related data, such as contact name, credit limit, and payment method. Every time an invoice is generated, the ZIP code tags along and appears on the header of the bill, as well as on the address on the envelope. The complete address record for each customer can yield invaluable geographical information of where customers are located. Knowing streets, cities, and building numbers is useful, but the ZIP code allows the pinpointing of segments of large areas within heavily populated urban areas. In this way, the substance of data becomes important, and data element values can provide an enormous payoff when absorbed by a data mining initiative.

# Relationships

Mining corporate data can throw light on a wide assortment of previously unknown relationships. How many times do you look at two or more sets of data that, on the surface at least, seem to have little resemblance to one another? Discovery of relationships can best be illustrated by looking at an everyday occurrence, such as our buying habits at the corner store.

Suppose it's early evening and you have just gone to the corner store to pick up a loaf of bread and some milk. As you grab the bread, a brightly colored bag of corn chips catches your eye. Hey, why not? At the dairy section, while you choose the milk, your wandering eyes see the red foil wrapping on a box of bite-sized cheese morsels. Guess what? These products have been deliberately placed in close proximity to one another. This chain of stores has gone about a data mining effort to study previously unknown relationships between purchases by Jack and Jill consumer. Discovering relationships is key to successful marketing. In our retail store, the parallel movement of products has been uncovered by looking for relationships between customer purchasing habits. Ever wonder why the red licorice box is placed beside the cash register? Investigation determined a direct relationship could be inferred between the amount of money spent (or wasted?) on junk food at the cash register and nonjunk food products purchased by the same customer.

In operational or data warehouse systems, the data architect and design personnel have meticulously defined entities and relationships. In this context, an *entity* is a set of information containing facts about a related set of data. The discovery process in a data mining exercise sheds light on relationships hidden deep down in many layers of corporate data.

# Patterns

The benefits of pattern discovery to a business add real value to a data mining exercise. No one can accurately predict that person X is going to perform activity Y in close proximity with activity Z. Using data mining techniques and systematic analysis on warehouse data, however, this prediction can be backed up by the detection of patterns in behavior.

A temporal component exists in pattern discovery. Parallel behavior over a two-week period can uncover a pattern that could become the reason for the implementation of a new marketing endeavor. On the other hand, detection of this behavior over a longer six-month period adds more credibility to the suggestion that a pattern has been detected. Patterns are closely related to habit; in other words, the likelihood of an activity being performed in close proximity to another activity is discovered in the midst of identifying a pattern.

You probably remember the saying, "It's like trying to compare apples and oranges." If this comparison identifies a pattern in behavior, the comparison may be valid, and it should be the basis for a discovery exercise in your warehouse data.

Data mining allows companies to see their information in ways unheard of previously. As you know, some operational systems, in the midst of satisfying daily business requirements, create vast amounts of data. The data is complex, and the relationships between elements are not easily found by the naked eye. Along comes special data mining software and pouf! It's not exactly that easy, but without sophisticated electronic data mining software, the data mining process seems insurmountable. The true nature of data mining is shown in Figure 17-3. Using data mining as a tool, data becomes information.

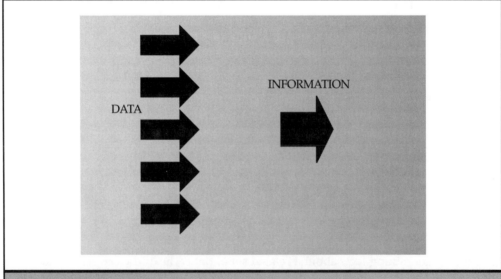

**Figure 17-3.**    Data mining in a nutshell

Data is made up of a series of characters that, on their own, mean nothing. Grouped together to form data elements, they start to take on meaning. When subjected to a data mining effort, these same data elements can yield a wealth of information.

Businesses have only a fixed amount of dollars and time to spend on knowledge discovery initiatives. When companies look at the short- and long-term benefits of data mining, all those dollars and all the time invested will pay off many times in the long run. DataMind Corp., a major player in the industry, identifies three segments in the data mining marketplace (source: www.datamindcorp.com/dmabout.html):

▼   Assisted data mining products generally require expensive, massively parallel computers and significant assistance from a vendor to "glue" together various pieces of technology. This has been a traditional approach for data mining where the vendor is contracted to perform a lengthy, on-site analysis of corporate data to try and find deeply buried information. This often results in 6–9 months worth of work to come up with one or two "chunks of gold." Engagements usually cost upwards of $300,000.

■   The desktop data mining market includes vendors whose products are oriented to a PC environment with the ability to perform mining functions on an extract of data, typically the result of a SQL query. Vendors in this space offer a "slice" of data mining functionality, often bolted on with query and report writing facilities. In this way, users can experiment with data mining on small result sets to get a feeling for how data mining might play a role in their overall analysis techniques. These products are typically priced in the $495–$2,000 range.

▲   Applied data mining is a new category of software filling a gap between easy-to-use desktop interfaces and high-end data mining complexity by focusing on specific business problems. Based on popular client/server and Web/server architectures found today in nearly all Information Technology organizations, applied data mining solutions focus on making customers self-sufficient—performing their own regular data mining activities so as to gain benefits every day, across the organization. Products to perform applied data mining hunts are priced between $50,000 and $250,000.

# BENEFITS OF DATA MINING

The primary benefit of data mining is the ability to turn *feelings* into *facts*. When meeting with coworkers, how many times do you say, "I just have a gut feeling that product X is more attractive to consumer group Y than the rest of our customer base." This feeling can become a fact when it's armed with the ability to sift through corporate data, looking for patterns of behavior and habits of customers. The fundamental benefit of data mining is twofold.

Data mining can be used to support or refute feelings people have about how business is going. It can be used to add credibility to these feelings and warrant dedication of more resources and time to the most productive areas of a company's operations.

This benefit deals with situations where a company starts the data mining process with an idea of what they are looking for. This is called *targeted* data mining. Data mining can discover unexpected patterns in behavior, patterns that were not under consideration when the mining exercise commenced. This is called *out-of-the-blue* data mining.

Let's look at a number of tangible benefits the data mining process can bring to companies, and how nicely these benefits fit into two kinds of data mining exercises.

# Fraud Detection

All too often businesses are so caught up in their daily operations that they have no time or personnel to dedicate to uncovering out of the ordinary business occurrences that require intervention. These events include fraud, employee theft, and illegal redirection of company goods and services toward the employees trusted with their management. Many companies use sophisticated surveillance equipment to ensure their workers are doing their jobs and nothing but their jobs. Examine the following types of fraud, whose evidence could be easily uncovered by a system of data mining:

▼ A group of clerks in a retail building supplies chain is systematically short-shipping orders and hiding the discrepancy between the requisition for goods and the freight bill going out with the delivery. This could be uncovered by analyzing the makeup of bona fide orders, and what is found to be a premature depletion of corresponding stock.

■ A retail clothing giant notices an unusual number of credit vouchers going out on one shift every Saturday morning in their sportswear and athletic shoes departments. By analyzing the volume and amounts of credit voucher transactions, management would be able to detect times when volume is repeatedly higher than the norm.

■ After auditing payroll at a factory, a company notices an excessive amount of overtime over a six-week period for a handful of employees. Through a data mining effort, they uncover a deliberate altering of time sheets after management signature has been obtained.

▲ Using data mining, a banking institution could analyze historical data and develop an understanding of "normal" business operations—debits, credits, transfers, etc. When a frequency is tacked onto each activity as well as size of transactions, source, and recipient information, the institution can go about the same analysis against current transactions. If behavior out of the norm is detected, they engage the services of internal, and perhaps external, auditors to resolve the problem.

Fraud detection is seen primarily as out-of-the-blue data mining. Fraud detection is usually an exploratory exercise: a data miner will dive headfirst into a data repository and sift through vast amounts of data with little or no predisposition as to what will be found.

## Return on Investment

A significant segment of the companies looking at, or already adopting, data warehouse technology spend millions of dollars on new business initiatives. The research and development costs are astronomical. An oil company can spend upwards of $35 million (U.S.) on an oil rig. Data mining historical data from within the company and any government or other external data available to the firm could help answer the big-ticket question, "Will the effort pay off?"

Everyone has struggled with time. So little seems to exist, and so much needs to be accomplished. Most workdays are supposed to last seven to nine hours. Time management has become crucial in this day and age. In a business environment, where a finite number of hours exist in a day, wading through data to discover areas that will yield the best results is a benefit of data mining. This is your return on investment. Business decision makers always try to dedicate the most time and resources to initiatives with the best return. Looking for the best way to proceed, given a finite amount of dollars and people available, is a form of targeted data mining.

## Scalability of the Electronic Solution

The major players in the data mining arena provide solutions that are robust and scalable. A *robust* data mining solution is one that performs well and can display results in an acceptable time period. The length of that acceptable time period depends on factors such as the user's past experiences and expectations. A common occurrence may be for one person to prepare a set of parameters and variables for a data mining exercise, press the ENTER key, and go off to a meeting. Two hours later, the computer screen sits full of the mining results, patiently waiting for the user's return. On the other hand, another user may sit impatiently in front of the screen, fingers drumming on the table top, waiting for what seems a light-year for results (in this situation, three to five minutes can seem an eternity). Successful mining software providers' products can ingest anything from small amounts of data all the way up to voluminous amounts. The ability to work with a wide range of input datasets is part of this phenomenon called *scalability*. Another component of scalability is the ability to deploy a data mining solution on a stand-alone personal computer, on a small group of computers tied together by a local area network, or on an enterprise-wide set of corporate computers. The transition from single to multiple users must be both transparent and seamless to the users and easy to deploy for the professionals responsible for a company-wide or workgroup-wide data mining effort.

# DATA MINING ASSISTS THE DECISION-MAKING PROCESS

As companies flatten their layers of management, they look for ways to empower employees to collect the information required to make the decisions that affect the lifeblood of their businesses. Traditional discovery methods are cumbersome. Even though the data sits somewhere in an information repository, it is hard to find. Data mining can fast-track the discovery process and allow for targeted marketing initiatives at identified segments of the population.

Decision making should be driven by knowledge of past performance, consumer behavior, and discovery of patterns and trends. Suppose a communications carrier discovered a new service offering boosted Q1 sales. The marketing effort concentrated on customers whose spending habits were between $50 and $125 per month. Through data mining, the company discovered the majority of purchases of this service were from two-income families. How did they discover this? Armed with some data mining software, they analyzed the number of phone numbers listed for their customers and found the following pattern: accounts with three different numbers listed represented over three-quarters of the new service purchases. Guess where their next targeted marketing effort concentrated?

The concept of data mining can be applied to many real-life situations with no relation to information technology. Next time you're watching a major league baseball game and the announcer tells you this batter has struck out against a left-handed pitcher with the bases empty only three of the last 102 times, think of data mining. This is the facet of data mining that looks for trends; it is the same phenomenon that stirs baseball statisticians to keep what appears to be useless information. Predicting the future is power!

A finite amount of time exists to decide what business initiatives to do next. Data mining assists the decision-making effort because it can wade through corporate data warehouse information with the click of a mouse button. As the management layer is reduced, middle- or lower-management personnel are encouraged to make inventive decisions about how much time should be spent on marketing initiatives. Data mining vast amounts of corporate data places the information required to make decisions at these people's fingertips. What once was a missing link in the data mining arena—that is, computer Windows-based solutions that fully automate the process—has been filled by the vendors highlighted in this book, coupled with an ever-growing number of others.

Data mining helps transform vast amounts of data into information. Isolated occurrences of data elements are of little or no use. When those elements are mined, relationships extracted, and patterns discovered, they become useful information. This information can be likened to the iron ore pulled from more traditional mines: the data is the raw material and the information is the commodity of business.

# DATA MINING TECHNIQUES

Remember when computers first became popular? They seemed like magic. The more you got into the ins and outs of how a computer performed operations and looked at some programming languages, the more you understood and discovered there was no magic. Data mining uses a number of techniques to discover patterns and uncover trends in data warehouse data. By looking briefly at three of these techniques, you will begin to see that data mining, as well, is not magic.

# Neural Network

Neural network-based mining is especially suited to identifying patterns or forecasting trends based on previously identified behavior. A *trend* identifies a movement in habit based on past behavior. The stock market is a perfect place for the identification of trends. When NASDAQ commodity ORCL's price over the last six months is analyzed, you may be able to predict a trend in share price over the next number of weeks. Prediction immediately springs to mind when discussing neural net mining activities—the act of delivering intelligent recommendations based on the information buried in corporate data.

The roots of this type of processing are based on what has been learned from work done on the human body's central nervous system. Knowledge can be learned from a set of widely disparate, complex, or imprecise data. There are three layers to the network: the bottom layer receives inputs, the hidden (middle) layer performs the work, and the output layer presents the analyst with outputs. In a marketing organization, the inputs could be historical information pertaining to the spending habits of clients in close proximity to the time the company undertook significant new marketing initiatives. The hidden, or middle, layer processes incoming information and passes results, in the form of patterns and trends, to the output layer. The input layer, the hidden layer, and the output layer are made up of nodes. These *nodes* are another term for processing elements, which are likened to the neurons in the brain; hence, the terminology *neural network*.

When this network is trained on the information in the input layer, it takes on an eerie human-like component as it becomes expert at ingesting seemingly unrelated elements of data and spitting out results to the output layer. The number of nodes, though unknown in the hidden layer, decreases as the results rise to the surface and are spewed out by the output layer. Figure 17-4 shows the structure of a neural network and how each node in every layer is interconnected to each node in the adjacent layer.

Suppose the network shown in Figure 17-4 weighed factors affecting the risk of loaning money to a segment of the general public. At the input layer, each node would contain information related to a single factor about the borrower, such as the following:

▼ Age

■ Checking account bank balance

■ Annual income

■ Credit rating

■ Years at current job

■ Marital status

▲ Monthly balance carried on charge card

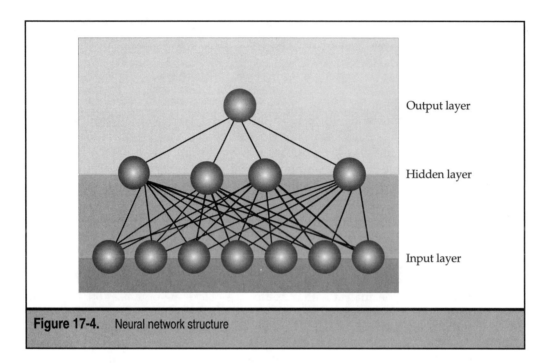

**Figure 17-4.**   Neural network structure

## Association Discovery

This technique involves studying sets of data and attempting to show associations between the occurrences of attributes within that data. Association discovery attempts to uncover similar occurrences of data values within records and produces output that can be expressed as a rule: "Eighty-six percent of the patients seen by Clinic A for hernia repairs also required intervention for a stomach-related ailment within the next six months."

A confidence factor is uncovered when mining using association discovery or association rules. The *confidence factor* is expressed as a percentage and is a measurement of the power of a prediction. Examine the following two statements:

▼ An 80 percent chance exists that consumers will purchase a coffee table when they acquire a new sofa and at least one other piece of living room seating.

▲ A 65 percent chance exists that when consumers buy a new house, they will also purchase a dishwasher.

Even outside the data mining arena, you could state that you are more confident the first purchasing habit would repeat itself than the second. By extending this type of statement, and by being able to back it up with knowledge gleaned from your data warehouse or operational system data, imagine the power this knowledge could impart to your business decision making.

When expressing data mining association rules, we speak of left-hand side (LHS) components and right-hand side (RHS) components of the association rule. When determining a confidence factor, look for the percentage that the event (in this example, purchase of a coffee table) on the RHS will occur at the same time as the two events on the LHS (in this example, the purchase of a sofa and at least one other piece of living room seating). The LHS can be one or more events, whereas the RHS tends to be a single event. Once data is mined and associations are detected, examined, and weighed, companies can decide what marketing decisions would make good business sense.

Look at one high-return item and one medium-return item at a fictitious automobile dealership called GYT Motors, which sells recreational vehicles and medium-size cars. Using association rules, it would be wise for GYT to create an environment where potential purchasers may go for a recreational vehicle. By mining client purchasing information, GYT may determine an association exists between

```
air conditioning  &  camping supplier promotion ---->> RV sales
```

with a confidence factor of 63 percent. So that sales are not lost to customers who definitely are not interested in a recreational vehicle, GYT has covered that base by uncovering the association

```
same price wagon ---->> medium-sized car sales
```

The association discovery can uncover relationships between what appear to be completely unrelated circumstances. These circumstances can have dramatic effects on how a company does business. Odd as it may seem, the associations discovered when mining data can approach the absurd! Perhaps GYT Motors may decide to move its parts department to a location between the showroom and the service department. They have discovered a high probability exists that people who need to walk past the parts counter when they have their vehicles serviced will stop and spend money on "that part they have been meaning to pick up, but never seem to have the opportunity." A popular soft ice cream vendor near where we live built a drive-through last winter. Coincidence? We think not.

# Classification

*Classification* involves grouping data together based on a set of similarities predefined by the analyst before the exercise begins. This technique examines data already classified and grouped together based on application of a membership rule. This membership rule may have a time component (for example, a calendar year, a fiscal year, a month of the year), a geographic component (for example, east or west of the Mississippi River), or a quantitative component (for example, clients with annual expenditures above or below a predetermined amount).

One of the more common applications of this technique is in the area of customer retention. Customer groups are classified and examined as almost separate entities, at which point one can decide how to retain the different groups of customers. This technique conjures up the familiar expression, "whatever the traffic will bear." Victoria's Secret discovered clientele in New York City were willing to purchase apparel regardless of the price. Why, then, would they discount this commodity to attract a loyal return customer? In line with that expression, the traffic will bear a price of $XX, so no need exists to price the good at $.8XX.

# Clustering

*Clustering* involves clumping similar sets of data together from a larger and more massive dataset. Unlike the classification technique, the clustering technique discovers the groupings as it works with the input data. Similarities are identified that lead to the segmentation of large datasets made up of members that resemble each other. Once the clusters and their members are identified, generalizations, patterns, and trends can be uncovered based on the characteristics of the members of each cluster.

Think back to your feeling the last time some edict delivered by a politician made you angry. You might have said to yourself, "Wouldn't it be nice if little insignificant me could change that edict?" Well, "little insignificant you" clustered with 10,000 other "little insignificant people" with similar opinions could bring about that change. A clustering technique could be used to assemble a set of opinions, to study the properties of those opinions, and to derive a handful of clusters that represent large numbers of voters. The bottom line of this technique is the discovery that what appeared to be entirely unrelated data values and attribute values within a given set of records actually contain information with a clear set of similarities. You run across clustered results in everyday life. Figure 17-5 illustrates how previously unrelated data shows overlap after going through the application of a data mining clustering technique.

The statement "75 percent of all pickup truck owners will always buy pickups" might have been derived using some form of clustering. Most likely, the answers from all the respondents was not a simple YES or NO, but other answers that, when clustered together, indicated an overall satisfaction with pickup trucks three times out of four; hence, the figure 75 percent.

# Sequential Discovery

*Sequential discovery* attempts to find patterns between events that occur in a progression over a period of time. To make the process meaningful in the supplier/purchaser framework—for example, retail sales—the time component of the data being analyzed is decided on beforehand. Once this decision is made, the data miner has a handle on the volume of data to be inspected and the process begins.

This mining technique can be used to search for commodity purchasing patterns that repeat themselves. If a trend or repetitive pattern is found in the nature of purchases, the

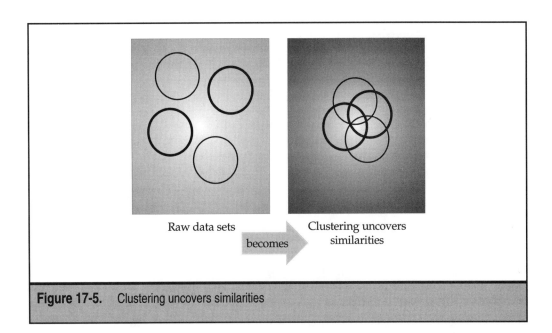

Raw data sets

becomes

Clustering uncovers
similarities

**Figure 17-5.** Clustering uncovers similarities

data mining effort concentrates on looking for more occurrences of the same habits. Data mining analyzes sets of records about purchases, looking for frequently occurring patterns over the selected time period. Suppose you uncover a specific set of purchases that precedes the purchase of a dishwasher. This information can be used to direct a marketing plan at a set of existing clients whose purchases conform to this pattern.

# DATA MINING SOLUTION CHECKLIST

What are clients looking for in a data mining solution, and how can the choice affect the integration of knowledge discovery into an existing set of decision-making resources? Some items on the checklist are mandatory; others are desirable.

## Direct Access to the SQL Server 7 Database

The total warehouse solution provided by Microsoft is the best of breed. Significant attention should be paid to the data repository where data warehouse data is stored, and this is where SQL Server 7 is an obvious choice.

*Desirable—a data mining solution should be able to provide quick, easy, and rapid access to data held in an SQL database.*

## Visual Analysis Capabilities

"A picture is worth a thousand words"—this is never more applicable than in a situation where you are mining data. The sheer volume of the data being analyzed coupled with the wide range of results being presented require visual output capabilities.

*Mandatory—a data mining solution must produce output in a graphical, visual manner.*

Coupled with this ability, because so much output is presented in columnar and matrix report format, a mining tool must support common drag-and-drop features where objects in the output can be moved to another axis on a graph. A *columnar* report is the familiar rows and columns output shown in Table 17-2. It displays descriptive information—in this case, critical quantity and manufacturer code—about a single entity.

**NOTE:** The data in the next two tables does not represent factual information and is "cooked" for the sake of illustrating matrix reports.

When the intersection points define a relationship between the column and row measurements, the report is a *matrix* report, as shown in Table 17-3.

The number 0.72 in the boldface cell in Table 17-3 means a 0.72 percent chance exists that drivers between the ages of 20 and 24 will have a fender bender in the next year (notice how the *1-year* value is selected in the time-frame column) if they drive between 31 and 60 miles per day.

A data mining product must allow the user to click on the *3-years* cell in the matrix report output and to have the output immediately transformed to a state representing the three-year time-frame results. This transformation is shown in Table 17-4.

## Ability to Ingest Large Volumes of Data

Because the volume of data fed to a data mining tool can be so large, the tool must process loads of data in short time periods. Some tools have a Microsoft Excel interface, which allows users to work with their data in a familiar environment when the amount of incoming data is small. When mining the multigigabyte data warehouse, a robust mining tool can deliver results in real time.

| Part Number | Critical Quantity | Manufacturer Code |
|---|---|---|
| ABN-2322 | 15 | TH8892A |
| ABH-2918 | 10 | HJ87662 |
| ABM-0922 | 225 | UJ8831L |

**Table 17-2.** Part Characteristics

| Time Frame | Miles | Age 16–19 | Age 20–24 | Age 25–30 |
|---|---|---|---|---|
| _1 year_ | 5–30 | 1.21 | 0.87 | 0.33 |
| _2 years_ | 31–60 | 1.26 | **0.72** | 0.35 |
| _3 years_ | 61–99 | 1.34 | 0.70 | 0.31 |

**Table 17-3.**   Age of Driver Vs. Miles Driven per Day Over a One-Year Time Frame

_Mandatory—given the common size of the data warehouse repository, the data mining tool must be able to ingest extremely large volumes of data._

## Sensitivity to the Quality of Data

When mining large datasets looking for patterns and trends, data mining software must be sensitive to the quality of the input data. When one or more attributes in that data is the source of a mining effort, you must ensure missing or incomplete data have not skewed the output and affected the outcome of the analysis. Data mining software must not only be able to compensate for that data, but it must also be able to report on the amount of bad data ingested to assist the analyst in deciding the validity of the results.

# THE FUTURE OF DATA MINING

The foundation of data mining is nothing new—the desire to conduct business based on the past behavior of customers. With the advent of larger and more powerful computers, data mining technology is primed to take off over the next few years. Not long ago, electronic data mining solutions were few. A glut of technology exists on the market now, and it's still growing.

| Time Frame | Miles | Age 16–19 | Age 20–24 | Age 25–30 |
|---|---|---|---|---|
| _1 year_ | 5–30 | 1.97 | 0.92 | 0.31 |
| _2 years_ | 31–60 | 1.32 | **0.76** | 0.37 |
| _3 years_ | 61–99 | 1.22 | 0.88 | 0.39 |

**Table 17-4.**   Age of Driver Vs. Miles Driven per Day Over a Three-Year Time Frame

The biggest reason data mining has a bright future is the computing power of today's high-end machines. One of the industry's hottest phrases is *parallel processing*. This type of processing is so well suited to data mining, it can easily be derailed by hardware not robust enough to ingest and analyze multiple gigabytes of data. It seems you cannot turn around without stumbling on yet another bigger and better parallel computing solution.

Many non-Microsoft vendors are bringing mature data mining solutions to the marketplace daily. For example, Pilot Software's Discovery Server (www.pilotsw.com) is a key piece in their decision support suite, providing analytical power and segmentation capabilities. They boast a Marketing Intelligence Library that assists the analysis process by predicting the outcome of a wide range of marketing campaigns based on the makeup of these market segments. Figure 17-6 illustrates the output that enables clientele to decide where to concentrate their energy during predictive data mining exercises.

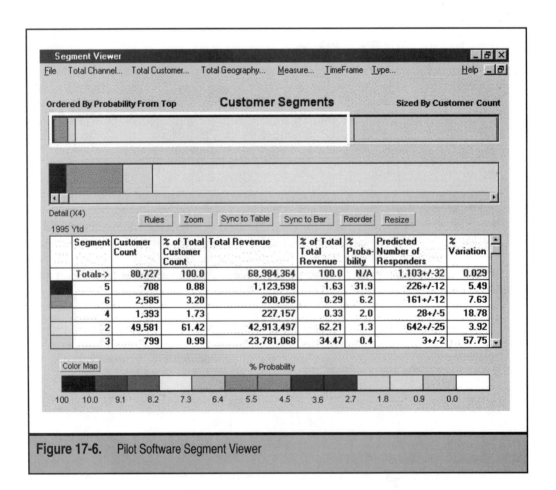

**Figure 17-6.** Pilot Software Segment Viewer

As a new breed of frontline employees contribute to the business decision-making process, arming them with data mining technology makes so much sense. These individuals live and breathe the business operations, and experience firsthand contact with consumers of the company's products and services; therefore, they are players in the selection of future business endeavors and initiatives. They may not actually make the final decision, but they are responsible for giving recommendations based on their frontline knowledge of the business. Increasingly sophisticated electronic data mining solutions enable these players to make recommendations to upper management.

The foundation of data mining has been around for some time. Machine learning and artificial intelligence are two disciplines dedicated to training machines to learn from past experiences and, based on that training, make predictions about the future. Naturally, many people have based their Ph.D. theses on machine learning, and a wealth of books, journals, and technical conferences exist worldwide dealing with the subject of data mining.

In Chapter 18, we are going to have a look at data warehousing and the Web. With the advent of the thin client, and the widespread adoption of browser-based solutions, the desire to publish OLAP and other query results to the Web is spreading like a grass fire out of control.

# CHAPTER 18

# Data Warehousing and the World Wide Web

Wake up and open your eyes—the Information Highway is upon us. Information is the key to knowledge; knowledge is the key to maintaining your organization's competitive edge. Companies that lose their competitive edge wither and die. The Internet is the world's first virtual library, with nearly unlimited information available to those who know how to unlock the secrets held within.

The Internet also represents the most efficient distribution mechanism for goods and services in the history of civilization. Every time a new way to distribute goods and services evolves, a substantial business opportunity is created. In the early days, it was the Sears Corporation's "Wish Book." It was the first firm to dominate mail order as a way to distribute goods and services. Another good example of an early adopter is the Tupperware Corporation; they distributed goods and services through a home network. They realized early on that the housewife was an untapped resource. The point is that any time a way to distribute goods and services evolves, early adopters are able to exploit a major business opportunity. Minimally, the Internet represents a very efficient way to offer goods and services—perhaps the most efficient method ever.

Think of how we can now instantly get software product updates over the Web. A company we use to develop 35mm films now offers an Internet option. We are able to download the digitized images of our pictures as soon as they are ready. By using this option, we get the best of both worlds—we can use a high-end camera and still have a digitized image; we can also get the pictures quicker. As consumers, we have choices. The Internet is about consumer choice.

As we all know, a free market is able to offer its consumers far better goods and services at much better prices than the alternatives. This is due to the effect competition has on the marketplace. The Internet represents the purest form of competition we have ever had in the history of the world. It is now having an impact on the free world that is as profound as the Industrial Revolution. How businesses transact business is being retooled as we speak today. Our children are growing up in an age where how they obtain products and services is being redefined. The paradigm is changing.

They are growing up in an age where the information of the ages is available to all, quickly and easily. The traditional barriers to knowledge acquisition are being eroded away as we speak. The problem in the future will be the filtering of information, so you do not become information-overloaded. With such drastic changes taking place, it's no wonder the evolution of your data warehouse is being altered. A data warehouse is about information and getting at it. These new Internet-enabling technologies are changing the way users harvest the information contained within the warehouse. The Internet is making it easier to obtain the information, maintain the information, and deploy the information to your stakeholders—no matter where they reside.

In this chapter, we discuss the following:

▼   What the World Wide Web is

■   What an intranet is

■   Why it is more cost effective to build and deploy applications over the Internet

- What some of the current trends taking place are
- How fast it is all happening
- What the business value of creating an intranet is
- ▲ What you can do with SQL Server 7 to deliver data to the Web by using the Web-Assistant, and various stored procedures

We will make the business case for you—that the warehouse of today and in the future will be Web-enabled. Now that we have grabbed your interest, read on.

# WHAT IS THE INTERNET?

To better understand the Internet, let's take a look at its roots. The Internet came about by research sponsored by the U.S. government. It is interesting to note that the relational database also came about due to research by the U.S. government. There was a need to sort through large amounts of information quickly. The goal with the Internet was to build a network that would provide the military with communications even in the event of a nuclear war. Isn't it funny that many people are worried that the Internet might come crashing down someday when, by design that would be near impossible. To take it down would mean you would have to disable every Internet server. By design, the Internet would automatically reroute the requests around failed servers. The Internet is designed to just keep chugging along.

The Internet, by design, is also the first truly open network standard. Since the military information infrastructure was made up of many different computers running many different operating systems, they needed a network standard that would tie them all together. Today, the Internet is all about open standards:

- ▼ Any computer
- Any network
- Any software
- ▲ Accessed by any server, worldwide

The bottom line—you get a very fault-tolerant network that is able to talk to virtually any computer, across any network, running virtually any software.

# WHAT IS THE WORLD WIDE WEB?

The World Wide Web is really the Internet with graphics. In 1993, Marc Andreessen created Mosaic, the first graphical user interface for the Internet. The creation of Mosaic brought graphics to the Internet. This made it easy to use, and what's more, Mosaic was available free of charge for any user to download. (We find it ironic that the trend is still to offer a browser free of charge for the download.)

These factors now meant anyone could navigate the Internet—yes, even you. They had taken the Internet from the once sacred realm of only the highly technical person (another name for a propeller head. A propeller head is another name for a computer geek. Many years ago the people at MIT use to wear read and white striped beanie caps, with propellers on them) to John and Susan Q. Public. We have come a long way since the creation of Mosaic in 1993. We now have many universal browsers to choose from. The two most widely used browsers are Netscape Navigator and Microsoft Internet Explorer. These browsers make it easy for the Internet to deal with all types of data, ranging from sound to video and text.

To navigate the Web, you must have a starting point. Think of a home page as the starting point. Just as Dorothy in *Wizard of Oz* had the yellow brick road, you have the home page. The home page is your key for locating information (we like to think of information as the Emerald City), which then employs Hypertext Transfer Protocol (HTTP). HTTP links you up to the information that your browser provides you with in the form of graphics, text, live audio, live video, and even live 3-D. With hypertext, your browser will be able locate and receive music and voice from the Web pages you view. Yes, you can even see and play movies from your browser. Through the use of a Virtual Reality Modeling Language (VRML) viewer, you will be able to view pages in 3-D.

Hypertext will link you to this information, no matter where it resides on the Web. So, with HTTP and a universal browser, it would be possible to have a picture of Dorothy in the *Wizard of Oz*. When you used the mouse on the computer and clicked on the image of Dorothy, the hypertext link (that's what a graphical user interface is all about, using the mouse to navigate) would take you to another location on the Web. This is another location where additional information on the *Wizard of Oz* is available. This information could be anywhere in the world; it all happens transparently to the user with a simple mouse click.

With this enhanced graphical capability, anyone can easily navigate the Internet, and millions do. Susan Q. Public has embraced the Internet in a major way. With its massive embrace by John and Susan Q. Public, you now have a very viable commercial platform to do business. This is a very important point—with the deployment of browsers like Internet Explorer from Microsoft, the Internet has become a viable commercial platform to do business on. This ability to do business on the Web is fueling a growth unlike anything the marketplace has ever seen before. In fact, no matter what trends you choose to examine, they all show you loud and clear that we are embracing the Internet at a very fast pace. It is the business tool of today, with the architecture to survive tomorrow.

# HOW FAST IS THE WORLD EMBRACING THE INTERNET?

When we think of a real fast trend that is overtaking the world, we think of the PC revolution. When we examine the facts a little closer, we learn that in the year 1997, approximately 27,000,000 PCs were sold. This is a far cry from the 250,000 that were first sold approximately 15 years ago. Yet when we think about it, this is an incredibly fast-growing trend. When we compared these numbers to the growth of the Internet, an

Internet year equals three PC years. Yes, you read it right: an Internet year equals three PC years. What has taken the personal computer 15 years to accomplish, the Internet will accomplish in less than five years.

When one looks at Internet domain name registrations, the growth rate is phenomenal! These are *URL* designations of a Web site. Simply put, a URL is an Internet address or a uniform resource locator (a yellow brick road for finding something). An example of a URL is "http://www.dbtinc.com". Think of this as your road map to any given Internet site.

A survey we found, produced by the InterNIC organization, showed that in the year 1993, when the Mosaic browser was first available for download, there were 5,946 registrations for domain names. This represented a substantial increase from the previous year when there were only 2,845—in fact, well over double-digit growth from the previous year. In the year 1997, it was estimated there would be 1,500,000 registrations. Ninety percent of these registrations were for commercial use. You can tell a commercial Web site since it will always end in ".com". For example, the Web site for Database Technologies Inc. is "http://www.dbtinc.com". Table 18-1 is a quick guide to the meaning of some various Web site designations.

The Internet explosion is happening so fast, there are already discussions about adding more designations. Just as many parts of the world outgrow their postal codes or phone area codes, don't be surprised if we quickly outgrow our Internet designations. Look at how quickly an email address has become almost as popular as a phone number.

The trend that really caught our attention was a recent rating that showed TV viewership was down due to Internet usage. According to the survey, close to 60 percent of the people who participated are watching less TV. Over 85 percent of the people are using the Internet more. Over 40 percent admitted that they are watching less TV due to the fact they are using the Internet more.

Do we think that the Internet will ever replace television? No, we don't believe it will. Think about it—we still have radio and we still have newspapers. What is clear to us is that the Internet is a very powerful communication tool. It is a very efficient way to reach

| Designation | Purpose |
|---|---|
| .com | Commercial use |
| .edu | Education |
| .org | Organization |
| .net | Network |
| .gov | Government |

**Table 18-1.** Definitions of Internet Designations

the masses. Just as television offered advantages over radio and radio offered advantages over newspapers, the Internet offers significant advantages over its predecessor. For example, would you rather watch a Stanley Cup hockey game on TV or listen to it on the radio. We would rather have the rich medium of TV. But each medium has its advantages and disadvantages.

We think this point was best illustrated by the death of Princess Diana in 1997. It was a very tragic accident. People all over the world turned to the TV to help them with this loss. The Internet was just not equipped as a medium for dealing with this tragic accident. Clearly, TV was a much better medium for dealing with emotions. After the funeral, people turned to the Internet. It was a much better medium for discussion groups and distributing the facts. Through discussion groups, people were able to better deal with the loss. It is an excellent and very efficient tool for disseminating information. This ability to effectively disseminate information is one of the major reasons it is an ideal match for your data warehouse. Later in this chapter we will discuss the advantages of building and deploying a warehouse using Internet-enabling technologies. For now, let's take a closer look at what an intranet is, keeping in mind that the two words define an approach to information dissemination—one internal to your company, the other for the general public on the outside. The words are remarkably similar and the concepts remarkably different.

# WHAT IS AN INTRANET?

An *intranet* site is where one or more applications reside, accessed using one of the universal browsers like Netscape Navigator or Microsoft Internet Explorer. Since it is an intranet site, the applications reside within the firewall and are accessed using technologies like TCP/IP, HTML, or Java. The primary purpose of intranet sites is to service internal customers.

An *Internet* site is similar to the intranet site, except the applications reside outside the firewall. They are accessed using the same technologies as the intranet site. The primary purpose of Internet sites is to service external customers. An average Internet site typically contains marketing information.

When you look at these two definitions, you realize there is not much difference. So, let's simplify the definition. An intranet is a small-scale version, inside your organization, of your Internet site. An intranet is all about communication within your business.

Up till now, if a business wanted to communicate with its employees, it would turn to traditional means, which included everything from mail to phone and email. Yet in most companies, if you surveyed the employees, the number one problem would be communication. No wonder—we are trying to solve our communication problems with very old solutions. An intranet has proven itself an excellent way to disseminate information within an organization in much the same way the Internet has proven itself an excellent way to disseminate information outside your organization.

# The Evolution of Intranet(s)

Originally, an intranet site was just a billboard of company information. For example, if someone had a human resource question, it was much easier to get on the intranet and search for the needed information. Corporations found it was easier to keep the intranet up to date than the monstrous task of keeping each employee up to date. Like a brochure or billboard, what you see is what you have. The same issues applied to sales and marketing literature on the intranet. In today's world, companies cannot wait for the literature to come back from the printers—it is always needed yesterday. Using the old methods, no matter how hard you tried, someone got missed. Face it—companies need access to information yesterday. So, intranet applications were used to supply up-to-date information on products.

Everyone knows how to use a universal browser, but try to teach your employees how to use a traditional client/server application—good luck. The fact is, with the Internet, once you publish the information, everyone knows how to access it. So, information published on the company intranet was ending up in everything from client presentations to training modules. Intranets are helping corporations be more competitive and better informed. Once established, the next step was to allow strategic customers and suppliers into the intranet. Why not provide a key supplier the information they need to work with you smarter? Why not let a customer access the information you have about them and, if they choose, update it? Why not let an employee fill out a 401k change form or a T4 short online? Table 18-2 compares the types of information classically found on a company's intranet (for internal use alone) vs. the Internet (for both internal and external use).

One of our customers does automobile fleet management for their clients. They track and approve purchases made with the fleet cards they issue. In the old days, if their

| | Internet | Intranet |
|---|---|---|
| **Information type** | Marketing, financial, investor | Proprietary, all forms of company information |
| **Audience** | Prospects, J. Q. Public | Employees, strategic partners |
| **Purpose** | Informative, only outgoing, billboard in nature | Collaborative, two-way, interactive |

**Table 18-2.** Comparison of Internet to Intranet

clients wanted to issue a new fleet card for a new employee, they would call up an operator and place the order. If clients wanted a report of their activity, they would call up and request the report. Within a few days, it would arrive in the mail. Today, their clients have the option of getting reports via an intranet application. They can literally slice and dice the data online. They also have the option of ordering additional fleet cards online. The intranet application is helping them to be more competitive and at the same time more responsive to their customers.

Another great example of an intranet at work is the Federal Express intranet site. In order to use it, you must be a customer, so by definition this is not an Internet site. It contains nonpublic information. If you want to track your package, you are empowered to do so yourself. You can get at the information when you want—this is a much better alternative for both Federal Express and the customer. For Federal Express, they get transactional efficiency. It is cheaper and faster to have the customer working the intranet site than to pay an operator to deal with the phone calls. For the customer, it means no waiting in phone queue lines, and getting the service when they want it.

These types of applications are being built in a fraction of the time and cost that it would take for a traditional client/server approach. They are allowing companies to communicate, collaborate, and transact online with their employees, customers, and key strategic partners. The marketplace is adopting Internet-enabling technologies at a feverish pace. Now let's see what some of the costs of an intranet-enabling technology might be.

## A Closer Look at an Intranet

Many times in our careers, we have heard about these wonderful technologies that would be ideal if we had a million dollars to burn and many months of effort to waste. If we were in the shoes of an individual trying to determine whether to Web-enable a data warehouse, we would ask the questions, "How much does an intranet cost?" and "What are the gotchas?" Well, the startup costs are typically very low. You probably have most of the components of the intranet in-house already. What you will get in the long run are the hidden costs.

We think the CIO of a very large cruise line put it best: "I built a Web site and now I need a team of people to maintain it." When we looked at this particular Web site, that CIO was right—he needed a team of people to maintain it. He had the largest static "billboard" site we had ever seen. They had not harnessed the power of Internet-enabling technologies at all. They had not linked the Web site up to a database, so every time there was a price change, they needed to rebuild the Web site. If it had been married to the database, every price change in the database would have automatically been reflected in the Web site by the built-in database links. The point is, watch out for the hidden costs. Technology is like any other tool—a great help when used for the right job. Use the billboard approach for the static data, and use a database link for the dynamic data.

# The Intranet and Security

Don't believe everything you read in the newspapers or hear on TV. You can make an intranet very secure. As with any security, you have to decide how much you want and how much you are willing to spend to get it, then reconcile the two. For example, on many PCs, it is possible today to buy software that will encrypt all the data so that no unauthorized eyes could ever look at every document. Yet, we have never known of any firm to use it widely, outside of a secure U.S. government installation. The reason for this is quite simple. The costs far outweigh the benefits associated with it. This same thinking process applies to your intranet site. You can have as much or as little security as you want. Just be willing to pay the price.

## An Open Society (Collaboration) Vs. a Closed Society

The other issue with security is the type of working environment you want for your team—an open society where lots of information is available for all to see or a closed society where each team member is given information on a need-to-know basis. For example, in a closed environment, the sales force might only know about their own customers and other customers within their sales region. So, when making a call on General Electric, their knowledge of that account is limited to that sales region's experience.

In an open environment, they would have access to all other regions' sales information. This means that when a salesperson in Alaska calls on General Electric, he or she would be able to collaborate with other salespeople in the firm to see what they know about General Electric. Perhaps someone in the Boston office has been working with General Electric for awhile and might be able to offer insights. The negative side to this is that when a person leaves the firm, he or she will have valuable information about the company's activities that span beyond their normal reach. This also applies to the strategic vendors you let into the intranet. Yes, they will have information about your firm that will help them to be a smarter ally; at the same time, they will have information that, placed in the wrong hands, could hurt you. It has been our experience that the benefits of allowing the free flow of information to your strategic vendors and employees far outweigh the occasional leakage of information over time. Just be smart about it. If it's confidential company information, then label it as such. It will reinforce the need to be prudent with its use. Also, choose your allies well.

# Advantages of an Intranet

Let's now take a closer look at the advantages of deploying new applications using Internet-enabling technologies. For all the reasons that it makes sense to build new applications with Internet technologies, it makes sense to build your warehouse with this technology and deploy it over an intranet.

## Single Point of Entry

How much time has been wasted in information technology organizations over the years trying to teach people how to use different applications that have been created? Each application has a different look and feel. Each application has a different keystroke sequence to invoke it. Each application has a different command sequence to use it. Each machine has a different operating system with a different set of commands associated with it. With the universal browser, you have one entrance point into your systems. Once you have learned how to use the browser, you have mastered the knowledge needed to use all applications. You don't need to be retrained with each new application that is developed. With an intranet application, you have access to all the information, applications, and data from one window.

The closest thing we have ever had to this historically is the Apple Macintosh. If you used one Macintosh program, you were well on your way to understanding them all. With the universal browser and an intranet, you have one window into all the systems. No longer do you have to launch five different applications to answer one question. You have one-stop shopping.

## Single Source for Information

It is easier to keep an intranet updated with information and have everyone go there for information than to take on the horrendous task of informing everyone. For example, if you put all the marketing information online on an intranet site, it would be much easier to keep it accurate and up to date than to go through the traditional process. Let's face it, snail mail (a term of affection for the U.S. Postal Service), company-wide meetings, newsletters, voice mail, and so forth just don't work.

By having everyone share a common knowledge base (in this example, the marketing intranet site), you are ensuring a strong, cohesive voice. Everyone sees the same message, everyone is drinking from the same well. It's in everyone's best interest to make sure the message is accurate and the well is safe. Over time, team members add their base of knowledge to the total base, making it better for themselves and everyone else in the process. What you get is a growing base of knowledge that helps everyone be more successful. By its very nature, the intranet is a collaborative technology. Over time, the application will become more and more interactive and collaborative.

## Transactional Efficiency—A Great Partnering Tool

The intranet is both a partnering tool and a customer tool. By allowing your strategic partners access to your intranet, you streamline their ability to do business with you. You are empowering them with the tool they need to get the information they need from your organization. For example, as a solution provider partner with Microsoft Corporation, we can search their intranet for competitive bulletins, white papers, and sales presentations. This type of information is critical to helping our firm close business. When we close business, it means increased product and service business for Microsoft.

Many consulting firms are joined at the hip with Microsoft, whether Microsoft and the consulting firm like it or not. Every time they close a deal, they are pulling Microsoft products and services with it. By allowing us access to the intranet site, we get/they get transactional efficiency. It is easier for Microsoft Corporation to respond to our needs, making it easier for other companies and us to do business with them. It also gives me transactional efficiency. We get the answer quicker, making us more responsive to our customers. The bottom line—this makes intranet sites a great partnering tool.

## Transactional Efficiency—A Great Customer Tool

Allowing customers access to your intranet site gives both you and them transactional efficiency. The best example of this at work is the Federal Express intranet site. When we want to track a package, we can now go online and check the status of our order. This is empowering customers with a tool to get the information they need from Federal Express quickly and easily. This gives the customers what they want, when they want it. FedEx is making it easy for the customers to do business with them. Both sides get transaction efficiency out of this. For FedEx, they are now able to meet the customers' needs in a much more cost-effective manner. This makes FedEx much more competitive, which makes the customer much happier.

## Lower Training Costs

We have discussed this in many different ways already. Once people learn how to use a browser, they then have the skillset they need to transact business over the Internet without any additional training. The training costs associated with deploying an intranet application are substantially lower.

## Lower Maintenance and Deployment Costs

An intranet is based on open standards. It is cheaper to deploy an intranet application than a traditional client/server application. The network costs are substantially reduced. The cost of the browser is next to nothing, since almost everyone is giving away the software. The cost to update the browser is practically nonexistent. In the old days, if one wanted to deploy a nationwide application, it meant sending out teams just to install the software. Today, the users can update the software without any systems personnel interaction. The browser will run on any hardware. Deploying a new application does not mean upgrading the hardware.

The icing on the cake is that it's all based on open standards. The Internet represents the purest form of competition we have ever had. You will have lots of alternative choices on every component of the application. This will bring down costs. Open standards mean lower acquisition costs and lower deployment costs, along with lower maintenance costs.

## Yes, a Square Peg Fits in a Round Hole

Yes, the universal browsers will run on any machine. No matter what the hardware, software, or operating system, anyone who has the necessary permissions can access the intranet site. You will be able to connect and communicate among all your disparate platforms. As we said, a square peg now fits in a round hole.

## Full Range of Multimedia

An intranet application allows you the full range of multimedia. You can have sounds, graphics, videos, etc. Perhaps a drawback of these large objects (i.e., sound and video stream) is they are time consuming to download using a 28.8Kb modem. In fact, we are already seeing major changes in the telecommunications industry to provide us with networks to handle these newfound capabilities. A company like L3 Communications has been founded to support these future Internet requirements. This brings application design to a new high point. When conveying information, you have a much greater toolkit of options to choose from.

## Infrastructure

Much of what you need for your intranet site you already have. This is a real advantage, since you are able to leverage investments the corporation has already made. You also do not need to build, train, and manage new project teams anymore.

## Communication

If you surveyed most employees of a corporation, they would say the number one problem today within the corporation is communication. They feel like they are getting the mushroom treatment. Unlike a mushroom, employees do not thrive in the dark. Well, an intranet site will foster and enhance communication. Your employees will feel better, your customers will feel better, and your strategic partners will feel better. You will find your organization collaborating more and coordinating much better.

## Creativity and Innovation

It seems that by the very nature of business, we tend to stifle creativity and innovation. When we want creative thinking, we typically put our bright bulbs in the boardroom and say "go at it." We also always seem to ask the same people over and over. Do you do your best thinking in a boardroom? We know we don't. An intranet site usually helps companies get back their creative and innovative spirit.

# Disadvantages of an Intranet

Let's take a closer look at some of the known disadvantages. There are always two sides to each argument, and it would be best to discuss some points on the other side of the coin.

## Do I Need Consultants?

Yes, you do. This technology is still on the bleeding edge. The skillset for this talent is in such high demand that the highest concentration of the talent is currently with consulting companies. It has been our experience that it is better to bring consultants in than to risk the time loss and mistakes if you do not. A great example of this is firewall technology. It is changing at a very rapid pace. Most organizations, unless they are very large, will find it cheaper to outsource this firewall component. Can you risk the consequences of a mistake? Does your firm really need a team of graphic artists? Our experience has shown us that a team of consultants working with employees completes the most successful intranet projects.

## What About My Competitors?

They have it, too. They are building and deploying intranet sites. They are trying to use this technology against you. It is a race, and the early adopters usually will own the playing fields. They will also be able to see what you are up to on any information you post that is not secured. It will be easier for them to learn about you, since more information about your business is in the hands of more people than ever before.

## Full Range of Multimedia

Just because you can use it, doesn't mean you should. I have seen intranet sites that are so multimedia intensive they just don't work. Everything in this world should be done with moderation. If you are not careful, you will have a Web site that is a great showcase for what technology can do, but without purpose—like an architect building a great monument to himself or herself, but you creating something that can't be lived in.

## Security

It is much easier for critical business to get outside the corporation. This is because critical information is now in the hands of more people than ever before. You must pay much closer attention to how you treat proprietary information.

## Too Much Data, I Can't Take It

With an intranet site, you are now empowering people. Some people take to power while others allow power to overtake them. If you are not careful, people will become information-overloaded.

We have discussed at great length the Internet and Web-based technologies, and you may be asking yourself how well SQL Server 7 works with the Web. SQL Server 7 has several new features and improvements that address that question. The first is the Web Assistant Wizard. Let's take a closer look at the SQL Server Web Assistant Wizard.

# SQL SERVER WEB ASSISTANT WIZARD

SQL Server 7 includes the SQL Server Web Assistant Wizard, a tool you can use to generate standard HTML files from SQL Server data. The SQL Server Web Assistant Wizard generates HTML files by using Transact-SQL queries, stored procedures, and extended stored procedures. HTML files, also known as Web pages, can be viewed by using any HTML browser. HTML files are resources for displaying information on the World Wide Web (WWW) and on internal networks.

With the SQL Server Web Assistant Wizard, you can generate an HTML file one time or as a regularly scheduled SQL Server 7 task. An HTML file can be updated whenever relevant data changes by using a trigger. A *trigger* is a special kind of stored procedure that is automatically executed when a user attempts the specified data-modification statement on the specified table.

Triggers are often used for enforcing business rules and data integrity. Referential integrity can be defined by using foreign key constraints (using the **foreign key** keywords) in the **create table** statement. If constraints exist on the trigger table, they are checked prior to trigger execution. If either primary or foreign key constraints are violated, the trigger is not executed (fired). SQL Server 7 allows the creation of multiple triggers for any given **insert**, **update**, or **delete** statement.

With this task-scheduling flexibility, and the power of Transact-SQL, you can create Web pages to do the following:

▼ Schedule a task to automatically update a Web page price list whenever a new item is added or a price is changed, thereby maintaining a dynamic inventory and price list for customers and sales staff

■ Publish and distribute management reports, including the latest sales statistics, resource allocations, or other SQL Server data

■ Publish server reports with information about who is currently accessing the server, which locks are being held, and by which users

■ Use extended stored procedures to publish information outside of SQL Server

▲ Use a table of favorite Web sites to publish server jump lists

"Show me how to use this great tool!," you say. Let us take a closer look at the SQL Server 7 Web Assistant.

## Running the SQL Server Web Assistant Wizard

The SQL Server Web Assistant Wizard is run from within SQL Server Enterprise Manager. Prior to running the wizard, you must first log into the SQL Server. The login settings are identical to those for any SQL Server login. Table 18-3 compares the steps you will end up going through to connect using the Web Assistant, using SQL Server 7 login or the Windows NT operating system authentication.

You can create a Web page with the SQL Server Web Assistant Wizard by completing these steps:

1. Start the SQL Server Web Assistant Wizard and select the database you wish to publish. Figure 18-1 shows you what the wizard could look like at this step.

| SQL Server 7 Way | NT Authentication Way |
|---|---|
| Enter a SQL Server name | Enter a SQL Server name |
| Enter a login ID | Select the Use Windows NT security to log in option instead of entering a login ID and/or a password option |
| Enter a password | Complete the steps in the wizard |
| Complete steps in wizard | |

**Table 18-3.** SQL Server 7 and NT Login Steps

2. Create a query using the Table and Columns and the Select Rows dialog boxes. Figures 18-2 and 18-3 show you what the wizard could look like at this step.

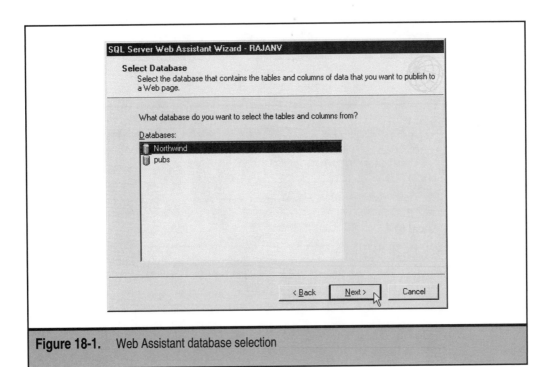

**Figure 18-1.** Web Assistant database selection

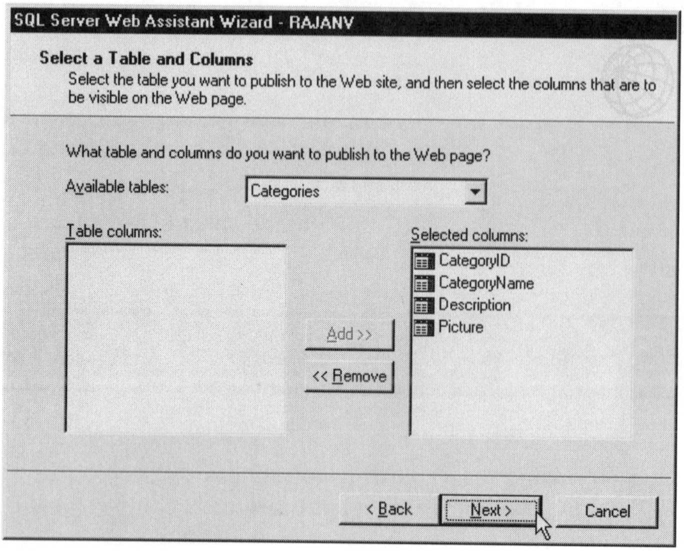

**Figure 18-2.** Web Assistant selecting tables and columns

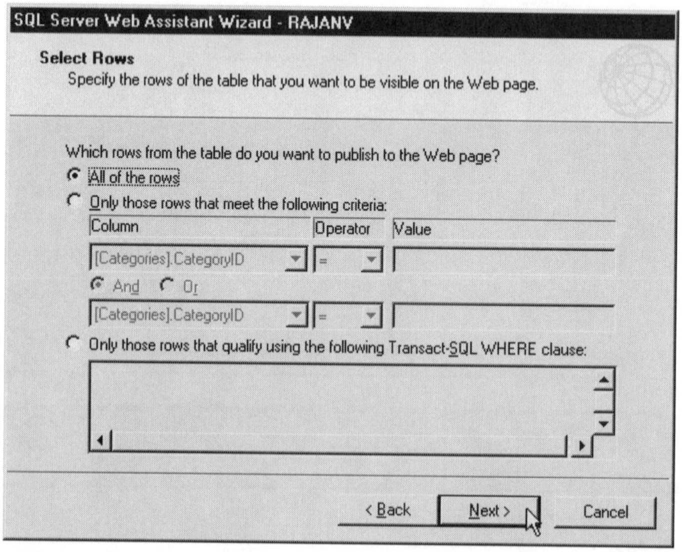

**Figure 18-3.** Web Assistant selecting rows

## Creating Queries with the SQL Server Web Assistant Wizard

The SQL Server Web Assistant Wizard first requires that each job be named. A default name is supplied based on the year, month, day, and hour (in military time). For one-time jobs, this naming convention may suffice. For jobs that will be run at a later time, or for jobs that run on a continuous basis, choose a name that will help you remember the focus of this query.

Queries that will run at a later time will appear in the right pane of the Console Root when you select the Web Assistant Jobs folder in the expanded tree view for the desired server.

The SQL Server Web Assistant Wizard offers several ways to build queries. You can build queries by:

▼   Using the tables and columns you specify

■   Using result sets of a stored procedure

▲   Selecting data using Transact-SQL statements

This can be accomplished by using the Web Assistant Wizard. Figure 18-3 shows selecting rows. The following steps then lead you through entering the Transact-SQL query:

1. From the Query dialog box in the Web Assistant Wizard, one of the steps in formulating the query is to select tables and the columns to be displayed in the query results. See Figure 18-3.

2. In the Type your query box, enter your query.

3. Complete the steps in the wizard.

You can use the free-form text option with the **execute** command to execute existing stored procedures or extended stored procedures. To execute the procedure, do the following:

1. From the Query dialog box in the Web Assistant Wizard, select the Enter a query as free-form text option and select a database.

2. Use the **execute** command with the extended stored procedure call and applicable arguments.

3. Complete the steps in the wizard.

For example, to execute a directory command in the command shell, use the xp_cmdshell stored procedure using syntax like that in the next listing:

```
EXEC xp_cmdshell dir
```

To use a query in a stored procedure, do the following:

1. From the Query dialog box in the Web Assistant Wizard, select the Use a query in a stored procedure option and select a database.

2. Select a stored procedure.

3. The procedure text is displayed and cannot be edited.

4. In the Does your stored procedure require any arguments box, enter applicable arguments for the stored procedure.

5. Complete the steps in the wizard.

Schedule the query using the Scheduling dialog box. Figure 18-4 shows you what the wizard could look like at this step, where the job details are entered.

1. From the Scheduling dialog box, select a scheduling option. Depending on your selection, you might be asked for more information, as shown in Table 18-4. Define arguments as necessary to complete your scheduling selection.

2. Complete the steps in the wizard.

You can use the SQL Server Web Assistant Wizard to execute queries on a one-time basis or as a regularly scheduled SQL Server 7 task. The Scheduling screen offers the options shown in Table 18-4.

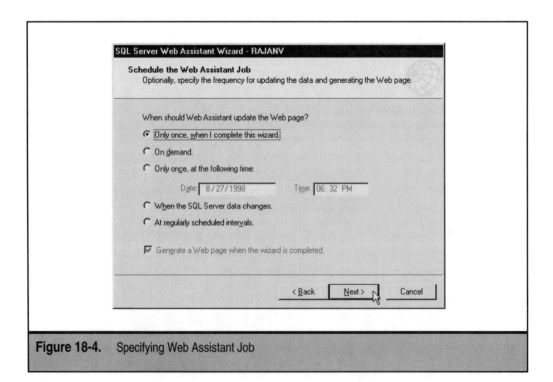

**Figure 18-4.** Specifying Web Assistant Job

| Scheduling option | Description | Arguments |
|---|---|---|
| Now | An immediate, one-time execution | None |
| Later | A scheduled, one-time execution | Date, time |
| When data changes | An automatic, triggered execution, displays alter trigger dialog box | Table(s), column(s) from expandable list |
| On certain days of the week | A scheduled execution | Days, time |
| On a regular basis | A scheduled execution | Every $n$ hours, days, or weeks |

**Table 18-4.** Scheduling Options

## HTML Template Files

To use a template file with the SQL Server Web Assistant do the following:

1. Add an <%insert_data_here%> marker to your HTML template file and save the changes. HTML tables are supported.
2. In the File Options dialog box, enter the full path and name of the HTML file to be generated.
3. Select the "A template file called" option.
4. Enter the full path and name of your HTML template file.
5. If a template file is used, formatting options do not apply.
6. Complete the steps in the wizard.

To include one URL and reference text you do the following:

1. Select the Yes, add one URL, and reference text option.
2. Enter the Internet address of the link.
3. Enter the label for the link.

To include multiple URLs and reference text:

1. Select the Yes, add a list of URLs, and reference text from a table option.
2. Enter a query that will return a two-column table containing URLs and reference text. The first column must contain the URL. The second column must contain the reference text.

## Security Considerations for the SQL Server Web Assistant

To function properly, the SQL Server Web Assistant Wizard requires the following privileges:

▼ **create procedure** privileges in the database you are accessing

■ **select** privileges on columns you want to access

▲ Adequate operating systems privileges to create files in the account in which SQL Server 7 is running

# INTRANET SUMMARY

Internet-enabling technology is here to stay. Businesses cannot afford to be like ostriches and bury their heads in the sand. This technology won't be going away. To ignore these trends just gives your competitors another edge against you. Internet technology is cheaper to deploy, faster to deploy, easier to use, and cheaper to maintain. Any application you are building today should be looking at how they can be placed on an intranet.

A data warehouse is all about information and getting people access to it. Every major data warehouse vendor has an intranet strategy. If they don't have an intranet strategy, get a new vendor because they are in trouble and won't be in business much longer. This is the way of the world. It is changing at a very fast pace. Each vendor is leapfrogging the others at every turn. What is clear is that deploying the warehouse using Internet technologies makes good sense. The goal of this chapter was to provide you with a very solid grasp of the Internet and provide you with the facts on why you should consider an intranet-enabled warehouse for your organization.

We feel that any warehouse product that does not have a strategy for dealing with the Internet is making a mistake. We also feel the future of warehousing is with Internet-enabling technologies. We feel that the combination of a SQL Server 7 data warehouse and the intranet will change your organization for the better. It will help transition your organization into a learning organization. A business will only have a sustainable competitive advantage when it becomes an organization that can learn and adapt. That's what a warehouse is all about, empowering people with the knowledge and tools they need to solve their problems. From this, the business will learn to adapt.

An organization must establish a common knowledge base. This must be a collaborative knowledge base. It must establish two-way communication into and out of the warehouse from each business unit, each strategic partner, and its customers. In this way, over time, the knowledge base feeds itself and those stakeholders around it. This knowledge base will become so vast that tools will have to be established to assist in the filtering process. Business cannot afford to let go of any scrap of information about itself that may someday hold the key to being more competitive. The combination of an intranet and the warehouse is the key to helping a business thrive and survive.

# CHAPTER 19

## Tuning the Warehouse

This chapter will disclose the SQL Server 7 secret "increase performance" knob that allows you to increase your overall system performance and targeted query or load performance by a factor of two, perhaps three—if not up to 100 times—depending upon how far you turn the knob. If only life were that easy! Unfortunately, many of us have been contacted at the end of a project when the project team is looking for exactly that. Fortunately, SQL Server 7 and NT provide us with good tools to monitor system performance and database performance. SQL Server 7 also provides tools that assist you with tuning your data warehouse workload and index configuration.

# PERFORMANCE

Good SQL Server 7 performance is dependent on many factors, the most important being a great logical database design, a great physical database design, a solid database architecture, and a robust hardware configuration. We'll start this chapter by addressing hardware configuration issues. But before we do that, let's discuss a topic on everyone's mind—SQL Server 7 scalability.

## SQL Server 7 Scalability

*Scalability* is a measurement of a system's ability to support higher-end systems, especially ones using very large databases. The question that everyone is asking today is "Does SQL Server 7 scale?" Let's start by stating that SQL Server 7's upper limit on scalability is lower than both high-end UNIX and mainframe systems. Having said that, this high-end scalability is required by less than five percent of today's database systems. In addition, SQL Server 7 has made great strides over SQL Server 6.5.

As far back as prerelease SQL Server 7, there was a SQL Server Terraserver online Web application, at http://www.terraserver.com, that allowed a Web user to drill-down on worldwide topographical image data to the granularity of one's own house. This application accessed a database that is over one terabyte in size. This database ran under SQL Server 7 beta 3 and Compaq hardware. This was a living, breathing example of SQL Server 7 scalability, even before production code was released.

Everyone's challenge moving forward is to determine their specific data warehouse requirements in order to determine if SQL Server 7 will fully support their data warehouse. SQL Server 7 will be able to support all data mart databases and a majority of VLDB data warehouse databases. SQL Server 7's ease of use, ease of management, integration with front-end tools, integration with MS OLAP services, and lower cost of acquisition make it a serious player when evaluating databases for data warehouse projects.

The last factor that everyone must consider is that Moore's law is still in effect. Moore's law states that the power of an integrated circuit will double every 18 months and the price will be reduced by 50 percent. SQL Server 7 is a case study for Moore's law—SQL Server TPC-C benchmarks have increased sixfold over the last three years.

*TPC-C benchmarks* are the prevailing standard for testing database systems today. More information can be obtained on their Web site (currently www.tpc.org). Many data warehouse projects start with limited capacity and add capacity in later phases of the data warehouse.

IS departments are confronting this issue today. Should we spend millions of dollars today for a very high end system capable of supporting multiterabyte-sized data warehouses? Or, should we buy a much less expensive system based on commodity hardware today and grow this system with the data warehouse? We can't answer this question for you; what we will submit is that SQL Server and NT should not be automatically eliminated from this equation, especially when we're talking about data warehouse projects with an 18+-month scope.

## NT Scalability

Scalable SQL Server 7 systems require a scalable NT operating system underneath it. When we talk NT scalability, we need to talk about SMP, symmetric multiprocessing, and clustering. *SMP* is an architecture mentioned in a number of places throughout this work, and is a setup involving multiple processors, each resident on its own machine, sharing each machine's resources. In addition, we need to talk about what's here today with NT 4.0 and what's on the horizon with NT 5.0.

**NT SMP**    NT 4.0 Server supports four-way SMP machines today. This is common knowledge. What many people don't realize is that NT 4.0 Server Enterprise Edition, NTS 4.0 EE, supports up to eight-way SMP configurations as well as an additional gigabyte of memory. NTS 4.0 EE first shipped in December 1997 and has been well received by the user community. This additional scalability makes NT 4.0 Server Enterprise Edition and SQL Server 7 Enterprise Edition the recommended software platform for NT-based data warehouses.

Eight-way processor systems have been common among the most popular hardware vendors since the end of 1998. Also, the new Xeon processor is a great processor for high-performance databases and have been present in most SMP systems since some time in 1998.

**NT 4.0 CLUSTERING**    NT 4.0 clustering, code name *wolfpack*, is focused more on reliability than scalability. NT 4.0 clustering consists of an *active-active* clustering environment. Two servers, each with separate I/O channels connected to disk farms, linked together by a connection monitoring a heartbeat, have the ability to assume the workload of the other server when it fails. Figure 19-1 highlights this architecture.

*Active-active* clustering allows both servers to actively process workloads, as opposed to an active-passive clustering where the secondary machine sits idle in the background waiting for the primary to fail. It's important to note that active-active clustering with SQL Server requires that one server own the database. If we want both servers to be actively processing, we will need to partition the database such that one processor is the primary and one processor is the secondary. Put another way, there can only be one active processor working on a particular database.

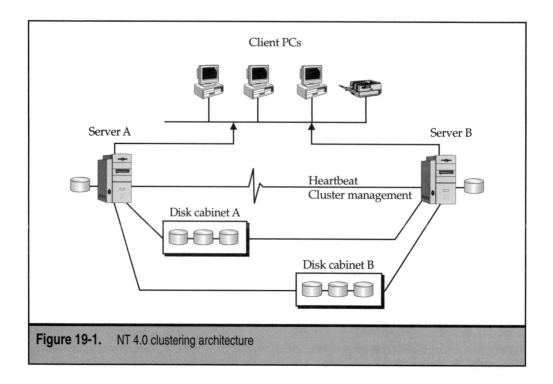

**Figure 19-1.** NT 4.0 clustering architecture

**NT 5.0 AND CLUSTERING** With the release of NT 5.0 and following releases, NT clustering will be enhanced to support clustering for scalability. Multiple servers within a cluster will be able to access common disk farms. Many people wonder what has taken Microsoft so long to implement clustering. Clustered systems have existed for many years—the DEC VAX line has had clustering for over 10 years.

Without getting into too much detail, the difference with NT clustering is that it's a *shared-nothing* architecture. This architecture is easiest understood by comparing it to other clustering architectures that rely on a cluster-wide global lock manager to arbitrate activity within the system cluster. This global lock manager becomes a bottleneck and sets an upper limit on the number of nodes in a cluster. Shared-nothing doesn't rely on a cluster-wide lock manager; this is a more scalable approach, and a more difficult approach to implement. This topic is a book of its own, so let's move on.

## Recommended Hardware Configurations

Databases like big dedicated machines, especially for VLDB data warehouses. The challenge with purchasing hardware for SQL Server 7 data warehouses is that there is an inverse relationship between the size and power of a hardware configuration and the price. The following are guidelines and not hard rules. We've only addressed SMP, disk, and memory; providing full hardware guidelines is outside the scope of this chapter.

Look for the industry "sweet spot" when purchasing SQL Server 7 hardware configurations. Today, there are some great four-way SMP machines on the market at a great price. Eight-way configurations exist today for many hardware vendors and will become the sweet spot moving into the next year.

Make sure that the machine has plenty of memory. As we all know, the key to database performance is to read the information into the database memory cache so that all succeeding references go to this cache. For large data warehouses it's important that your memory configuration has the ability to grow up to the three-gigabyte limit for Intel processors and the two-gigabyte limit for Alpha processors.

The general rule of thumb for SQL Server 7 databases is to have the database log files on a RAID 1 device and the remainder of the database spread across RAID 5 devices. RAID 5 is the most economical way to obtain hardware reliability and recoverability. See Chapter 13 for a more detailed discussion on RAID. High-end disk vendors like EMC now work with NT. You can now choose between the hardware vendor's disk architecture or go with a high-end disk subsystem for your VLDB database server.

# Database Architecture

The organization's database architecture is often the most important decision that is made for overall data warehouse performance. When we mention database architecture, we're referring to the overall data warehouse and data mart topology within an organization. For example, a division within a larger organization will typically get better query performance if users access a local data mart containing a subset of the overall data warehouse. This is especially true if the organization is linked together by a public wide area network or *WAN*. A WAN is a geographically dispersed network in which all members may not be connected at any point in time.

Of course, nothing is free in life, and your data warehouse architecture will consist of a series of trade-offs. A common trade-off is performance vs. manageability. Many data warehouses are centralized in order to reduce IS management and maintenance costs. However, the user community may feel that this centralized approach is not responsive to their needs, both for performance and flexibility. Hey, we never said that it was easy! The final answer to deploying a centralized data warehouse, deploying data marts without a data warehouse, or a combination of both is dependent upon the organization and its needs.

# Database Design

Previous chapters focused on the star schema and snowflake schemas as common data warehouse data models. These are widely accepted formats within the industry, and we won't get into the discussion of whether these formats require additional surrounding structures. We recommend that the star schema format be considered. It is the most common data warehouse structure, it optimizes your data warehouse queries, and it is supported by many front-end tools. In addition, SQL Server 7 OLAP services works seamlessly with star schemas and snowflake schemas within its Designer Wizard and related tools.

## Physical Database Design

Partitioning data warehouse information is the technique that data warehouse architects and database administrators use to reduce disk hot spots in the data warehouse. SQL Server 7 files and filegroups are the mechanisms for the database administrator to partition data across disk spindles. This section covers specific recommendations for performance. See Chapter 7 for more detail on files and filegroups.

**SEGMENTING USING FILEGROUPS**    Use filegroups to logically segment your information. SQL Server 7 tables and indexes are assigned to a filegroup. SQL Server 7 physical database design consists of determining which objects belong to which filegroups. Filegroups can be confusing when you are first introduced to SQL Server 7. The confusion revolves around the fact that objects are mapped to filegroups and not specific files. This confusion is lessened somewhat once you realize this and that the main purpose of files is to allow striping within your filegroup and flexible growth of your filegroup.

A good rule of thumb is to place each fact table in a separate filegroup. Remember that filegroups are a logical and not a physical construct. Separating key database tables and indexes into filegroups is the primary tool for your physical partitioning and provides you with control over physical disk bottlenecks.

**DISTRIBUTION OF DATA AND INDEXES**    Use files to physically distribute your data and indexes. All database objects reside in SQL Server 7 files. Files are assigned to one and only one filegroup. Database objects are assigned to data groups. SQL Server partitions tables and indexes across all files within the database object's filegroup. The physical placement of information within the multiple files is a function of the available space in each file. Files now become the mechanism for evenly distributing information across your disk farm.

SQL Server defines its internal page locator bitmaps per file and will fire off parallel disk activity on a file per file basis. Distributing your files across disks allows you to get true parallel disk I/O activity and is a recommended technique for large database tables and indexes. Defining multiple files, each on a separate disk for a large fact table's filegroup, gives the SQL Server 7 query processor the tools that it needs to speed up large queries.

The ability to add files dynamically to filegroups gives the database administrator great flexibility within the database design. Large tables will not have to be reloaded when an additional disk spindle is brought online, and data growth exceeds the current disk space allocated. SQL Server database files can auto-grow—they can be set up to automatically expand when file capacity is reached. This is a nice option to allow for unplanned activity, however, we recommend that you allocate the file to its full size to minimize file fragmentation.

## Optimizing TEMPDB

TEMPDB is the SQL Server system database used as a temporary storage and work area by SQL Server components, primarily the query processor. The SQL Server 7 query processor makes heavy use of TEMPDB, especially for VLDB queries. Because of this, we recommend that you seriously consider the following for your TEMPDB configuration for VLDB databases.

**PLACING TEMPDB**    Don't place TEMPDB on RAID devices. RAID 0 and RAID 5 exist so that the underlying database has the ability to recover given a media failure. TEMPDB is a temporary store, so there is no need to place TEMPDB on a RAID 0 or RAID 5 device. These RAID configurations will just slow all I/O to TEMPDB down. Using RAID 1 for striping TEMPDB across disks is a viable option to improve performance. However, SQL Server 7 files allow you to implement your own striping without having to worry about rebuilding the stripe set.

Place TEMPDB on its own disks; TEMPDB is created at installation time on the primary filegroup. TEMPDB cannot be moved outside of the primary filegroup. So, how do we isolate TEMPDB on its own disk or disks? SQL Server 7 provides the DBA with a mechanism to allow for the isolation of all TEMPDB I/O onto one or more disk spindles, preferably not RAID 1 or RAID 5. This is shown in the next listing:

```
alter database TEMPDB
modify file
   (name='tempdev',
    filename='c:\mssql7\data\TEMPDB_new.mdf')
```

This example above moves the TEMPDB database onto a new file. SQL Server must be stopped and restarted for this directive to take effect. For a VLDB system, we recommend that this file be placed on its own non-RAID disk. Consider striping this over multiple disks if you see the physical disk queues consistently over 2. Your next question should be, "Physical disk queues, what's that?"—which provides a nice segue way into the next section on monitoring SQL Server 7 performance.

# MONITORING SQL SERVER 7 PERFORMANCE

We must know how the data warehouse system is performing before we can really tune the system. Measuring NT performance is the responsibility of the Performance Monitor, a utility integrated into the NT product. Each well-behaved NT service provides one or more performance objects to the Performance Monitor.

## NT Performance Monitor

The NT Performance Monitor, perfmon for short, ships with NT 4 and is the primary tool for monitoring both NT and SQL Server 7 performance. The Performance Monitor utility resides within the Administration Tools folder. If you haven't activated perfmon yet, do so now; again, it is your primary tool for monitoring your machines. Perfmon gives you the ability to view performance information as a chart or report, the ability to log information into a file for future analysis, and the ability to set an alert to fire an event off on specific performance thresholds. Figure 19-2 shows where the Performance Monitor main options are set (i.e., whether you want a chart, alert, log, or report).

The system administrator enters the Performance Monitor user interface and chooses the type of session required—chart, report, log, or alert. Through the Options menu you can set the refresh interval (i.e., when perfmon queries the system structures for statistics), or you can set the refresh to manual. The shorter the refresh, the more resources consumed by Perfmon.

> **NOTE:** Activating a log with many selected objects for extended periods of time can consume hundreds of megabytes of disk space. Be aware of this for extended sessions.

The next step is to choose which objects and object attributes to monitor. Pressing the '+' toolbar button gets you the dialog box that allows you to select performance objects and their counters. You also have the ability to monitor the performance on other systems. Selecting the button to the right of the Computer field will display the Select Computer dialog box. This is a powerful implicit feature of Windows NT where most of the system utilities can be used in a client/server fashion. Figure 19-3 shows how the Processor Time counter (i.e., object) is added to the active display.

That's the perfmon basics. Let's get to the interesting topics—what should we monitor? Let's focus on the big three—processor, disk, and memory.

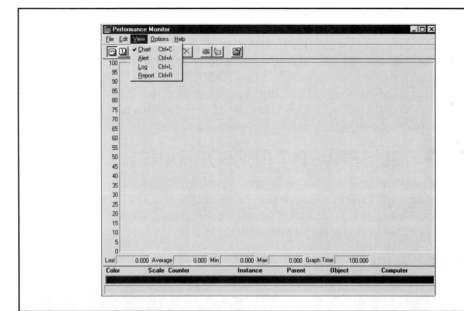

**Figure 19-2.**    Performance Monitor main options

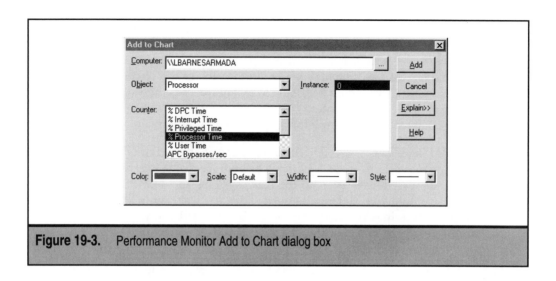

**Figure 19-3.**   Performance Monitor Add to Chart dialog box

## Monitoring CPU Utilization

We've opened a perfmon session, and have selected the '+' to add a new item to our report or chart. Let's first select the Processor object since measuring CPU utilization is key to any performance analysis. The Processor option is the default object and is displayed in the previous diagram. You have the option of choosing multiple processor counters.

The processor object, % Processor Time is sufficient in most cases. This counter will tell you if your CPU is a bottleneck for your data warehouse. The general rule of thumb is that any CPU consistently over 80 percent is considered a CPU bound system. The Instance list box lets you monitor CPU utilization for each processor of your SMP system. Each counter that you choose will be assigned a different color for your graph.

The obvious solution for a CPU-bound system is to add another processor if possible, or to get a new system. What you should also look at is the query workload mix that is causing the high CPU processor(s) utilization. Throwing processors at a poorly designed system will help performance, but will not cure your problems. We will get into how to determine the query workload mix later in this chapter.

## Monitoring Disk Utilization

Disk I/O is the area where the VLDB administrator will have the most impact on system-level performance. The previous section outlined how to use filegroups and files to spread your workload across your disk farm. The best way to determine whether you have a disk performance problem is to monitor the PhysicalDisk performance object. In order to enable the base NT physical disk counters, you need to issue the following statement at a DOS command line:

```
diskperf -y
```

These counters will be enabled the next time that you reboot your machine. Enabling the physical disk counters will result in a 5–10 percent degradation in your disk performance. However, this is a small price to pay when diagnosing the health of your system. Notice that you have the ability to monitor each of the physical disks on your system, similar to the CPUs on an SMP machine. Figure 19-4 shows how this physical disk monitoring is added as a counter.

The counters that we recommend you monitor at a minimum are as follows:

▼ **% Disk Time**—Lets you know the percentage of elapsed time the disk spends servicing requests. You can break this percentage down into read and write time. Data warehouses are read-intensive systems and TEMPDB is the only database within your data warehouse with significant write activity during normal processing. You may want to enable the read and write disk time parameters if you're monitoring your system disk performance during your data warehouse loads.

■ **Avg. Disk Queue Length**—Shows you the average I/O operations queued to a particular disk.

▲ **Current Disk Queue Length**—Measures the current queue length.

Queue lengths consistently greater than 2 mean that you have a bottleneck on a particular disk. Figure 19-5 illustrates the perfmon output after issuing an expensive query.

Note how the disk activity spikes up, followed by a processor time of 100 percent. This is typical of a large data warehouse query where information is brought into TEMPDB from disk and then processed in memory. Temporary spikes are fine; it's the consistently high behavior that is a cause for concern.

When you observe a disk bottleneck, examine the different database objects on that disk. Adding an additional file placed on a separate physical disk to these object's

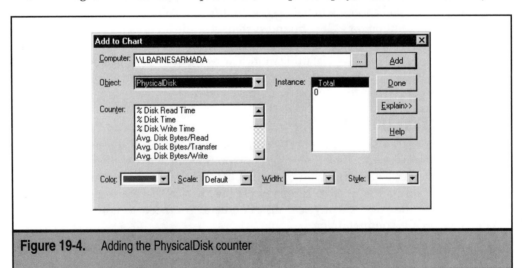

**Figure 19-4.**    Adding the PhysicalDisk counter

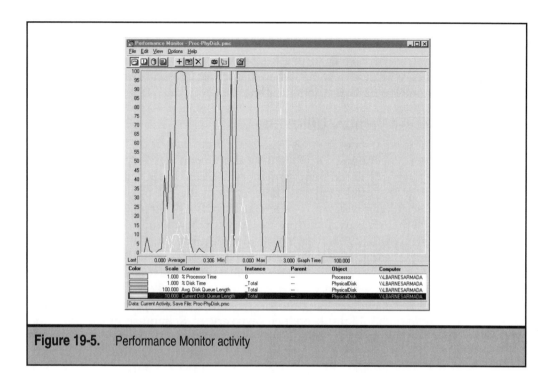

**Figure 19-5.** Performance Monitor activity

filegroup will help distribute your disk load. Of course, adding a new file to a filegroup will result in new data being distributed into this new file. To redistribute the existing information from the currently bottlenecked disk, you use a command similar to that shown in the next listing:

```
dbcc shrinkfile this_file emptyfile
```

This command will distribute all information on this file across other files within the filegroup and will invalidate further I/O to this file. This file is then dropped from the database using the following command:

```
alter database test1 remove file this_file
```

Practically speaking, you will need to add multiple files before issuing the **dbcc** command. Place each on a disk with low to medium percentage disk time values. This SQL Server 7 partitioning discussion could easily consume another 100 pages. To summarize, filegroups and files are the most powerful tool in your database performance toolkit. Activating physical database counters is fundamental to determining whether you need to do some additional tuning.

# TUNING YOUR SQL SERVER SYSTEM

SQL Server has always had fewer tuning knobs than other relational databases. This theme has continued with SQL Server 7, where the server takes care of more tuning and configuration parameters for you automatically.

## Tuning SQL Server Memory Utilization

One of the more important, if not the most important, tuning decision for the SQL Server 6.5 DBA was to determine the amount of memory allocated to SQL Server. SQL Server 6.5 required the DBA to specify the amount of memory dedicated to SQL Server. When SQL Server 6.5 started up, it would grab this memory from the NT operating system and would not relinquish it. What's worse, if underconfigured, SQL Server 6.5 would perform poorly even though there was available NT memory for the taking!

This is no longer an issue. SQL Server 7 now will take available memory from NT when it requires the memory. In addition, SQL Server monitors the NT page fault statistics and will relinquish SQL Server memory to NT when page faulting is excessive. You can also monitor page fault values through the Memory object, as shown in Figure 19-6.

The bottom line is that memory allocation is dynamic and is no longer a concern to the DBA. Data warehouses should reside on their own servers. Relinquishing memory from SQL Server to NT will occur on small-end systems running multiple applications, not a data warehouse server dedicated to serving up information efficiently. The memory tuning knobs are available to the DBA for explicitly setting memory values. The SQL Server Properties dialog box is shown in Figure 19-7, where memory can be configured dynamically to optimize performance.

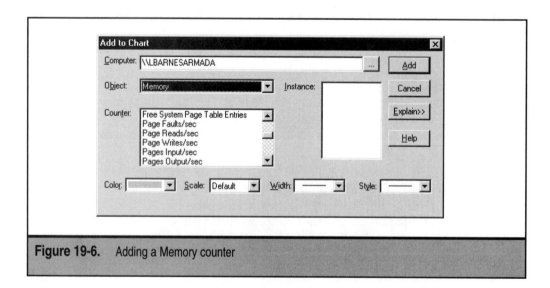

**Figure 19-6.** Adding a Memory counter

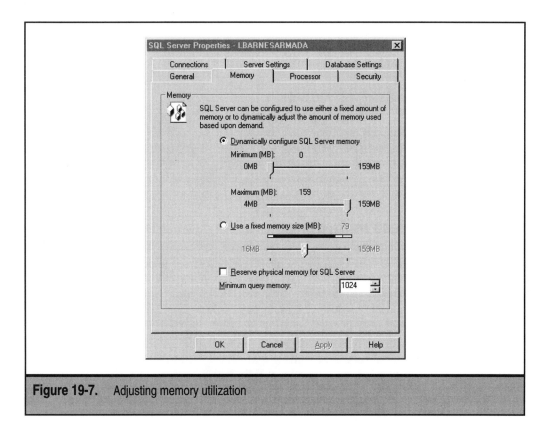

**Figure 19-7.** Adjusting memory utilization

Setting the maximum memory available to a query is perhaps the most beneficial activity. A DBA can also specify the maximum physical memory available for query.

**NOTE:** This is a server-level parameter and will apply to all queries on a selected server.

For VLDB systems, this query should be increased to a level proportional to the query mix and the available server memory. Buying new systems and optimizing existing systems will improve your overall performance issues, but many times this doesn't address the root issue, which is "Why is my data warehouse workload saturating my system?" Sometimes it's just the magnitude of the requested information, and many times it's your underlying information structure and the queries that access this information. Let's look at how to monitor and optimize your data warehouse workload.

## Monitoring SQL Server Performance

There are many SQL Server 7-specific objects and counters available to you for monitoring, a suite of which are shown in Figure 19-8.

This is an overwhelming list, where most of these apply to transactional databases. One counter that data warehouses should monitor is the SQLServer:Buffer Manager Cache Hit Ratio, which tells you the percentage of pages already in memory when a request is issued.

## Configuring the Resource Governor

SQL Server 7 also provides a system-level resource governor. A *resource governor* is a routine that allows the DBA to limit the amount of resources used by sessions running against the SQL Server 7 database. This governor will reject queries whose combined cost exceeds the value specified. This is shown in Figure 19-9 where the operator has specified a limit of 2,000,000. Chapter 9 contains more information on the query analyzer and how to view the query processor's query cost estimates.

This section has covered performance counters and settings that are applicable at the system level. These counters and settings are very useful—true data warehouse performance centers around your data warehouse query mix, the structure of your databases, and the indexes on key tables. SQL Server 7 provides a great tool for you to monitor your query workload—the SQL Server Profiler.

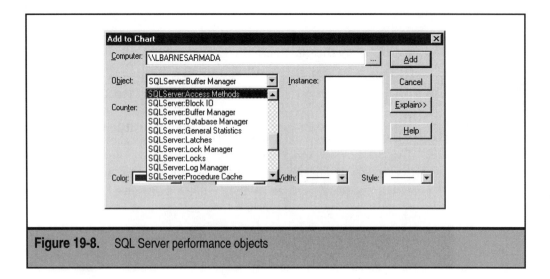

**Figure 19-8.** SQL Server performance objects

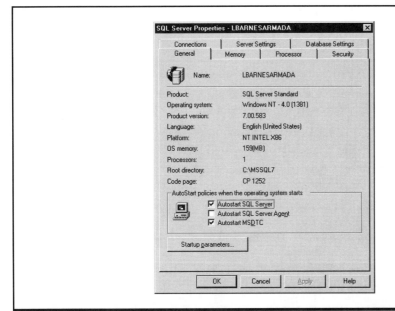

**Figure 19-9.**   Setting the query governor

# MONITORING YOUR DATA WAREHOUSE WORKLOAD

The SQL Server Profiler, profiler for short, is a tool that supports application workload monitoring. Those of you using SQL Server 6.5 will recognize profiler as the next version of SQL Trace. Those of you using SQL Server 6.5 today and not taking advantage of the SQL Trace capabilities are missing the boat. SQL Trace is a great tool, and with SQL Server 7 it's only gotten better.

The profiler consists of a utility invoked from the SQL Server 7 Program folder and hooks within SQL Server 7 that allow for the monitoring of selected SQL Server events. The profiler will take user-specified event information and send it to a profiler user interface window, a file, or a database table. We'll show you the key screens in profiler that you will care about, but first let's discuss why you should care about profiler and when you should use profiler.

## Why Care About the Profiler?

The profiler provides you with a server-side view of requests sent to the SQL Server 7 server from clients. This allows a data warehouse administrator to monitor client data warehouse activity. Profiler contains robust filtering that allows you to capture subsets of the current server activity. Combining this monitoring of client requests with system-level performance information allows you to make a positive correlation between requests and their direct impact on system performance. This information can be used in a variety of ways:

1. To understand the current client activity on your data warehouse.

2. To save a test environment execution at a later point in time for either performance testing or to reproduce a problem.

3. As a tool for analyzing applications behavior, especially a third-party data warehouse tool's behavior against your data warehouse.

4. As input into the Query Analyzer Wizard. The Query Analyzer Wizard is discussed later in this chapter.

5. As information for generating data warehouse usage analysis reports.

We recommend that you store profiler output to a file rather than a database. Storing this information to a file is faster than allowing it to be stored in the database. You will always be able to load this information from the profile output file into a database at a later point in time. This topic was covered in Chapter 10. Now that we've convinced you that you can't live without the profiler, let's review how you specify the attributes for a profiler session.

# Creating a Profiler Session

After you start the profiler utility, select the New Trace entry at the leftmost corner of the Toolbar menu. You are presented with a screen with four tabs. The first tab contains general information about the profiler session, as shown in Figure 19-10.

This dialog box determines whether you save the profiled information to a file or a database table. As we stated earlier, use a file instead of a database table. You can also choose whether other people on your system can run the profile session that you create or if you want to keep this information private. You can also choose the system that you're interested in tracing. Profiler is a true NT client/server utility, like all SQL Server utilities. Using profiler in this fashion is useful if you're running an application or queries on one system and have an adjacent system to display the profiler results on.

## Selecting Profiler Events

Choosing the Events tab allows you to select the SQL Server events that you want to monitor. Figure 19-11 shows the events specified for a sample session, with the familiar Available events in the left pane and Selected events on the right.

Your selected event mix will depend upon the goal of your profiler session. In the example presented earlier, the Selected events mix—Sessions Connect and Disconnect, TSQL: SQL Batch Started and RPC Completed—is useful for an administrator monitoring the current health of the data warehouse. This event mix is also useful for generating data warehouse usage analysis reports. Contrast this profile event mix with a

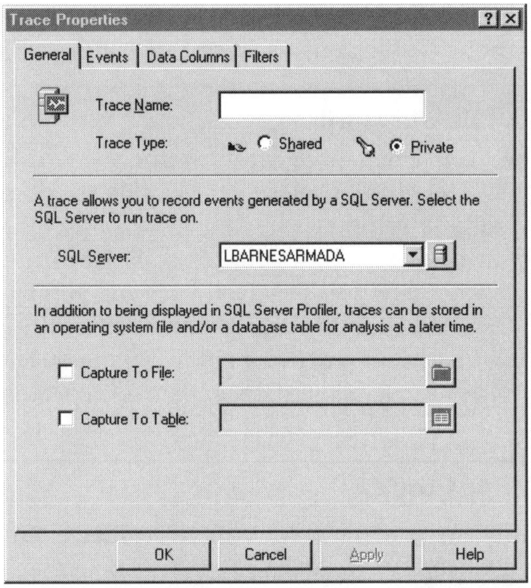

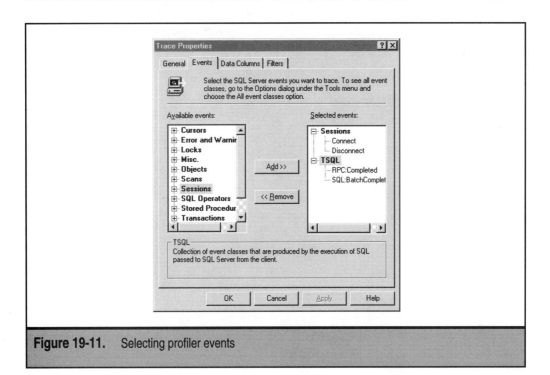

**Figure 19-10.** SQL Server 7 profiler Trace Properties

**Figure 19-11.** Selecting profiler events

server supporting a line of business applications. Additional interesting events include Locks: Deadlocks for detecting locking collisions as well as the entire stored procedure event object for applications with extensive stored procedure utilization.

## Selecting Profiler Data Columns

Now that we've selected our events, we can now specify which information we want reported for these events. The profiler selects many of these columns for you by default; Figure 19-12 shows the default settings.

The number of data columns that you select is dependent on the amount of information that you want to view on the screen vs. what you want to retrieve at a later point in time from the log. The default data columns will for the most part be relevant information and should be included in your display. What you can do is reselect the data columns in the display order that you want the information presented to you within your profiler display.

## Filtering Your Profiler Events

Last, but certainly not least, you can filter which profiler events you want displayed and/or persisted into your log file. Enabling all events on a machine will in many cases provide you with more information than you are interested in. This is especially true if the SQL Agent is driving tasks such as replication, backup and restore, and scheduled maintenance tasks.

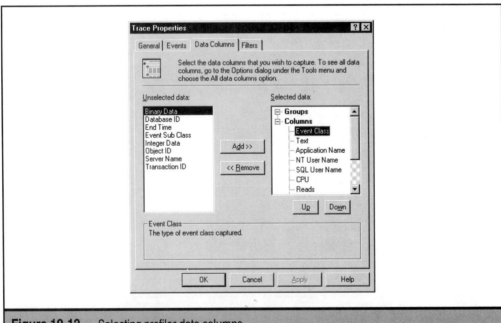

**Figure 19-12.** Selecting profiler data columns

Selecting the Filter tab allows you to filter with a robust set of criteria including server name, username, database ID, and application name. Database ID is a very useful filter mechanism if your data warehouse contains more than one database. Note that this is even useful for systems with only one data warehouse database since this allows you to filter out SQL Server queries to system databases like MSDB. You can issue the following query to obtain a database ID for a particular database:

```
select name, dbid from sysdatabases
```

Filtering out by application name is another powerful mechanism to separate out all events from the ones relevant to you. Figure 19-13 illustrates how to exclude all events from the profiler utility and the SQL Agent processes.

Note that the SQL LIKE syntax is used within a name and the names are delimited by the semicolon (";").

## Using the Filter Group Capability

The profiler provides you with grouping capabilities that allow you to group the profile output into a format that is conducive to your analysis. This gives you the capability of postfiltering an existing log file and saving this key information for future reporting and playback purposes.

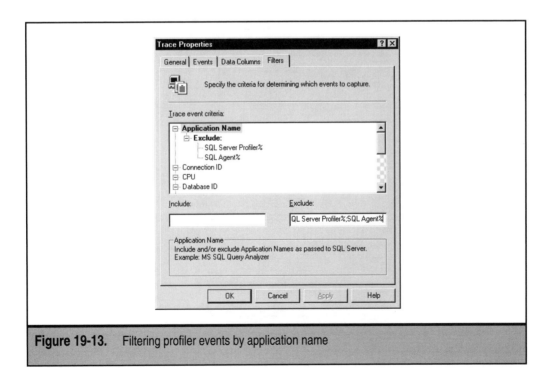

**Figure 19-13.**    Filtering profiler events by application name

You choose your grouping by first highlighting a Data field in the Data Columns screen. You then use the Up button to move the data column to the Groups folder. The Down button will move a data column out of the Groups folder. Figure 19-14 shows the output screen with the application name and server name in the Groups folder.

These settings will produce the output shown in Figure 19-15; the window provides a wealth of information that can prove helpful to the administrator's job of keeping the database performing well.

What's important to note here is that you can move through multiple iterations of the profiler output. Given the previous log, we may decide to further filter by only keeping SQL statements containing a **select**. We further modify the filter by adding the entry **%select%** into the Filters Include text box.

**NOTE:**   The profiler will perform a case-insensitive search, so you don't have to worry about the case when defining a profiler text filters.

## The Power of the Profiler

The profiler is a powerful tool for you to monitor, record, and play back your data warehouse workload. So, now that we have this information, how can we use it to tune our data warehouse? The answers, McDuff, lie in yon next section!

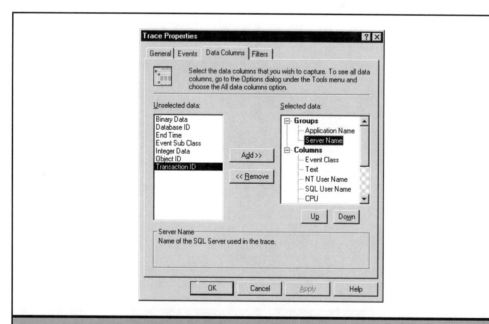

**Figure 19-14.**    Profiler group by report

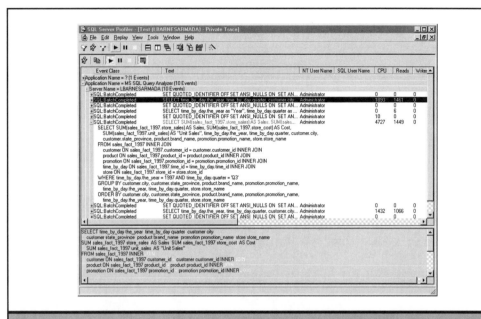

**Figure 19-15.** Profiler report grouped by application name and server name

# TUNING YOUR DATA WAREHOUSE

The profiler has the ability to replay an existing log file. This is a great feature for building test suites for both regression testing and for data warehouse performance testing. The following is one example of how to use this capability. First, open an existing log file. Then, filter on CPU with a minimum value of 6,000 and text with a value of **%select%**, which will give you a list of all select queries that took over a minute of CPU time to execute. Next, start a Performance Monitor session and monitor the parameters highlighted earlier in this chapter. Finally, select Replay to run these queries against a test system.

Expand this simple performance test by running a mix of these profile sessions from several profile test drivers. Note that this is an inexpensive way to test your data warehouse system performance. More sophisticated data warehouse systems will most likely want to have this process automated.

## Query Analyzer

The Query Analyzer, first discussed in Chapter 9, is a superb tool for analyzing SQL Server 7's query processor's plan for a particular query. One area that we want to point out about the Query Analyzer's visual execution plan is that performance problems for the query will be highlighted in red. The query plan displayed in Figure 19-16 is from a sample FOODMART database; this is an unoptimized query whose results end up more promising once SQL statement tuning exercises have been completed.

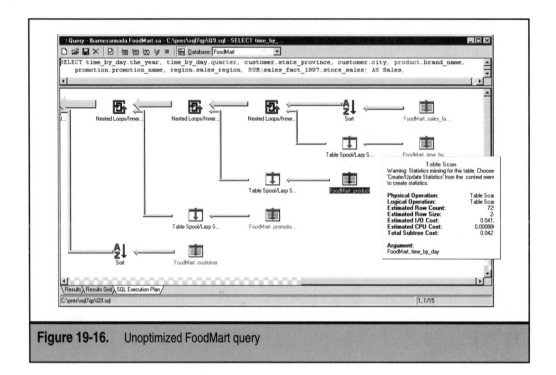

**Figure 19-16.**    Unoptimized FoodMart query

You'll note that the query optimizer will tell you that it's using a table scan because there's no statistics available for the table. When you see a portion of the query analyzer plan in red, you want to right-click the mouse on the entry to either create an index or to create or update statistics using the dialog box shown in Figure 19-17.

## Creating and Updating Statistics

SQL Server 7 allows you to create a statistics page for columns that are not indexed. This is a nice feature because it provides the query processor with as much information as possible. The query processor is very sophisticated—the more good information in, the better the resulting query plan. The Statistics dialog box allows you to specify how you want to sample your data when creating the index or column statistics page. You can choose the number of rows, the entire table, or a percentage of the table. The default chooses a percentage of the table and makes its decision based upon table size.

Note that you can choose to not automatically recompute statistics. That's right, the default SQL Server 7 setting is to automatically regenerate the statistics information based upon an internal algorithm that factors in the changes to the underlying information. This is an incredibly useful feature when you consider that a majority of poorly performing data warehouse workloads are due to outdated statistics information.

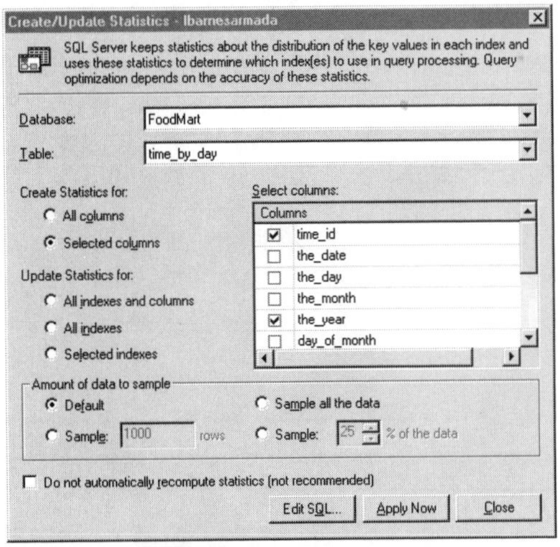

**Figure 19-17.** Create/Update Statistics dialog box

You can choose not to automatically update statistics if you have robust processes that update the statistics when required. However, we recommend that you leave this option on. The incremental performance penalty that you pay when statistics are recalculated pales in comparison to the damage that out-of-date statistics can do to your data warehouse performance.

## Index Analyzer

Last, but certainly not least, SQL Server 7 ships a great utility that analyzes either a query or a workload and recommends selected indexes to increase performance. This utility comes out of Microsoft research and utilizes an underlying API into the query processor, which returns the plan and estimated cost for the input query. This API allows the Index Analyzer to deterministically determine the optimal indexes for a particular query. Contrast this to other expert tools that use a set of heuristics to determine the optimal indexes for a particular design and query mix.

The Index Analyzer can be invoked from the Query Analyzer for a particular query. Select the Index Analyzer toolbar entry—it's the tenth entry from the left and looks like a lightning bolt—and you will be rewarded with the output of this analysis with appropriate recommendations, as shown in Figure 19-18.

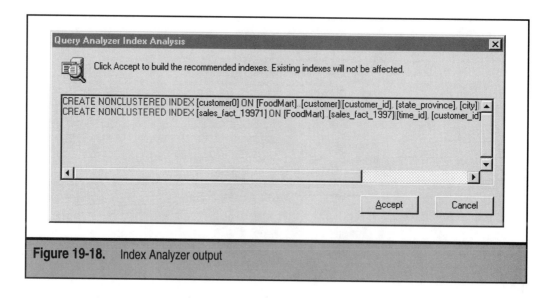

**Figure 19-18.**  Index Analyzer output

You can either accept the recommendations to build the indexes or not. That's just for one query. What's more useful is to run the Index Analyzer Wizard against a selected profile workload. Remember the profile that we traced and then filtered down to the most expensive data warehouse queries? Let's use this workload to determine whether we have missed a potentially important index. You invoke the Index Tuning Wizard from the Management group within the Select Wizard dialog box.

This wizard sends you through dialog boxes prompting you for the system and database, and whether you have a saved workload file or if you want to create a new workload file. For this example, let's select the workload that we've already saved and filtered to only include our expensive queries. The Index Tuning Wizard is highlighted in Figure 19-19, where a workload file is being specified.

You can then specify the tables that the Index Analyzer should include in its analysis. You may want to eliminate some tables because, let's face it, in order to accurately determine what indexes you need, the Index Analyzer will have to run through many test queries to determine the best index mix. When determining the Index Analyzer input profiler workload trace, consider the completeness vs. time to execute factor. For our limited example, the Index Analyzer returned the recommendation shown in Figure 19-20; notice how it has decided that there would be a 0 percent improvement in performance if the suggested index recommendation were followed.

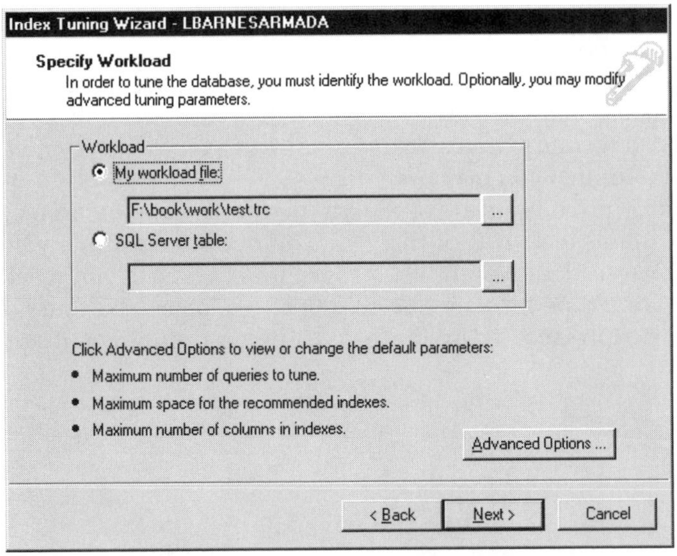

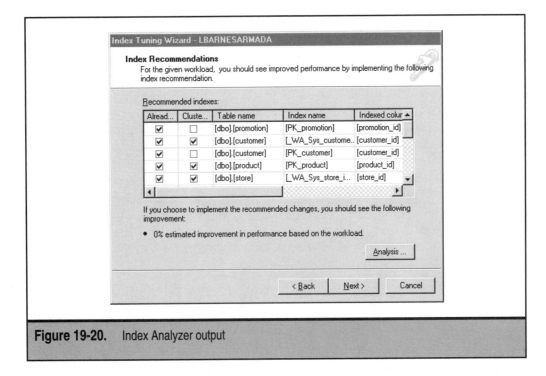

**Figure 19-19.** Specifying a workload file

**Figure 19-20.** Index Analyzer output

The Index Analyzer will even tell you the estimated workload performance improvement that you will see. Note that this sample is extremely limited—don't take the 5 percent performance boost as a base metric for what performance boost you will receive. We don't recommend that you use the Index Analyzer exclusively to determine your data warehouse indexes. However, we highly recommend that you run the Index Analyzer against a workload of expensive queries in a typical query mix to see if there's any index or indexes that you may have missed.

SQL Server 7 provides state-of-the-art performance measurement, along with profiling and tuning tools out of the box. The query analyzer's visual query plan alone will save your data warehouse programmers days if not weeks of time. Not only is SQL Server 7's performance vastly improved, data warehouse developers' and administrators' performance is also improved. The saga continues; it's time to move on.

# CHAPTER 20

## Maintaining the Warehouse

After 19 chapters of blah, blah, blah (or as they say on the television show *Seinfeld*, "Yada, Yada, Yada"), what are you going to do with all this newfound knowledge? You obviously have staying power; you have survived the preceding 19 chapters. In spite of possessing this knowledge, you will be faced by yet another daunting task, that of maintaining your warehouse. We are sure it does not come as a surprise to you that the true cost of owning and operating a warehouse is not unlike any other software application. What we mean is that approximately 80 percent of the total cost of owning and operating the warehouse can be directly attributed to costs associated with its maintenance. The care and feeding of your warehouse will require a significant time and financial investment.

You might ask yourself, "What can I do to minimize this obvious expense?" Microsoft in all its infinite wisdom has already thought about your question, and provided an excellent answer to help minimize the true costs of ownership. (Imagine—20 chapters and you are just now hearing the term TCO—true cost of ownership.)

Yes it's true with the use of the SQL Server Agent, you can actually maintain the warehouse in a cost-efficient manner. These wizard-driven tools make maintaining your warehouse easy, efficient, flexible, scalable, and automatic. In other mords (don't you hate it when you wix your mords), this deals with the administrative tasks associated with the warehouse. Let's now take a closer look at SQL Server Agent and all its components

# AUTOMATING ADMINISTRATIVE TASKS

Automating an administrative task means to have a programmed response to a predictable set of conditions or events. In other words, these tasks can be happening while you are out playing a round of golf or attending IOUG-A Live! Tasks that are typically very repetitive by nature are ideal candidates for automation. A good example of this might be to write a procedure that examines a disk to see how much free space is available. When it approaches 90 percent, the NT administrator is notified. By automating these recurring administrative tasks, you free up time to perform more critical tasks. Let's take a look at a very real life administrative task that could easily be solved by automation.

## Automatic Administration

Consider backing up of your warehouse and show how you could automate it. Suppose you have a SQL Server administrator, Java-the-Hut. One of his responsibilities is to back up all the company servers every weekday after normal business hours. Java-the-Hut wants to be sure that the backups run smoothly. If there is a problem, he must correct it before work begins the next day. In this example, all the company servers are networked. To automate daily backups, Java-the-Hut does the following:

▼ Defines himself and his manager, Leia, as operators, and defines Leia as the fail-safe operator. Think of a *fail-safe operator* as a backup to the primary operator.

■ Sets up a nonproduction server as a master server. Think of a *master server* as the primary server. Then, he enlists the other company servers as targets or subordinates in this master server.

■ Creates a backup job with Transact-SQL job steps. A *job* is a particular function within the SQL Server Agent. This is discussed in greater detail later in this chapter.

■ Schedules the job to begin every evening at 8 P.M.

■ Defines the job to notify Java-the-Hut by pager and to write an event to the Microsoft Windows NT application event log if the backup job fails.

▲ Starts the SQL Server Agent service, which must be running before administration tasks can be automated.

Java-the-Hut can leave work at 5 P.M., confident that his servers are backed up on schedule. If the backup job encounters a problem, SQL Server Agent pages him and records the event. If Java-the-Hut is unavailable because he is on vacation or has forgotten to turn on his pager, SQL Server Agent pages Leia to resolve the problem. If SQL Server Agent encounters no problem with the backup job, Java-the-Hut and Leia can return to work the next day confident the servers are backed up.

Administrators, application developers, and analysts can all benefit from task automation within the warehouse. Let's take a look at the steps involved in automation:

▼ Establish which administrative responsibilities or server events occur regularly and can be administered programmatically.

■ Define a set of jobs and appropriate alerts. An *alert* is what action you want to happen when certain conditions happen.

▲ Run the SQL Server Agent service. You do this through the Services control panel.

Let's take a closer look at the various components to automatic administration.

# Automatic Administration Components

There are three main components to administration in SQL Server 7—jobs, operators, and alerts. In addition to discussing these three pieces, we are going to spend a bit of time on some related issues.

## Jobs

You can use jobs to define an administrative task once so it can be executed one or more times and monitored for success or failure each time it executes. For you mainframe programmers out there, think of a job as a JCL (job control language) stream. For the UNIX programmers (soon to be NT programmers), think of a job as a CRON sequence. Jobs can be

▼   Executed on one local server or on multiple remote servers

■   Executed according to one or more schedules

■   Executed by one or more alerts

▲   Made up of one or more job steps

Job steps can be executable programs, Windows NT commands, Transact-SQL statements, ActiveScript, or replication agents. Scheduling your administrative jobs is a way to automate administrative tasks. You can schedule local jobs or multiserver jobs. You can define a job to run:

▼   Whenever SQL Server Agent starts

■   Whenever CPU utilization is at a level you have defined as idle

■   Once, at a specific date and time

■   On a recurring schedule

▲   In response to an alert

Figure 20-1 shows you what you can expect to see when setting up a new job.

You can also execute a job manually; scheduling jobs is always optional, though we recommend taking the time to set them up to run unattended (want to retire at 10 P.M. or 4:30 A.M.?).

**VIP:**   Only one instance of a particular job can be run at a time. If you execute a job manually while it is running as scheduled, SQL Server Agent refuses to initiate the manual request.

All jobs are enabled by default. To prevent a job from running according to its schedule, you must disable the schedule. The job can still execute in response to an alert or when a user issues the start command.

SQL Server Agent automatically disables schedules that are no longer current. If you edit the schedule after SQL Server Agent has disabled it, you must reenable it manually. Schedules are disabled if:

▼   They are defined to run once, at a specific date and time, and that time has passed

▲   They are defined to run on a recurring schedule and the end date has passed

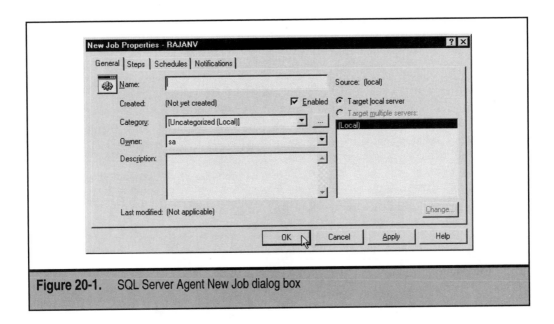

**Figure 20-1.**   SQL Server Agent New Job dialog box

**SCHEDULING BASED ON CPU USAGE**   To maximize CPU resources, you can define a CPU idle condition for SQL Server Agent. SQL Server Agent uses the CPU idle condition setting to determine the most advantageous time to execute jobs. For example, you can schedule a daily backup job to occur during CPU idle time and slow production periods.

Before you define jobs to execute during CPU idle time, determine how much CPU the job requires. You can use SQL Server Profiler or SQL Server Performance Monitor to monitor server traffic and collect statistics. You can use the information you gather to set the CPU idle time percentage.

Define the CPU idle condition as a percentage below which the average CPU usage must remain for a specified time. Next, set the amount of time. When this time has been exceeded, SQL Server Agent starts all jobs that have a CPU idle time schedule.

**IMPLEMENTING JOBS**   You can automate administrative tasks using SQL Server Agent jobs. You can only define the job one time, yet you can run it many times. You can run a job manually or schedule it to run in response to schedules and alerts. This topic explains the tasks you complete to implement a job.

Figure 20-2 shows the job execution and job-step processing that occurs when a job is run in SQL Server.

Jobs can be written to run on the local server or on multiple servers. To run jobs on multiple servers, you must set up at least one master server and one or more target servers.

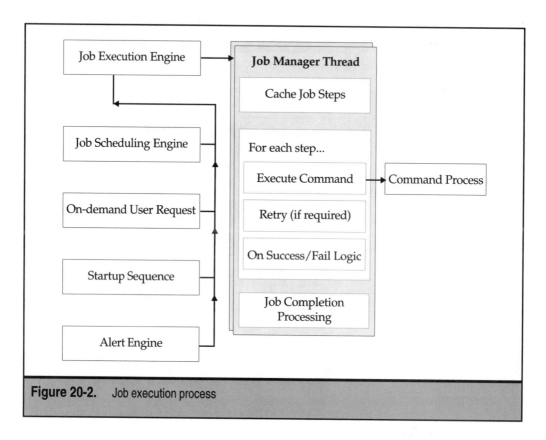

**Figure 20-2.**    Job execution process

## Operators

An *operator* is an individual responsible for the maintenance of one or more SQL Servers. In some enterprises, operator responsibilities are assigned to one individual. In larger enterprises with multiple servers, many individuals share operator responsibilities. Operators are notified in one or more ways:

▼ Email

■ Pager (through email)

▲ Net send (Windows NT-based messenger service)

You may choose to define an operator's email alias as an alias assigned to a group of individuals. In this way, all members of that alias can be notified at once.

**ALERTING OPERATORS**    You can define operators to be notified in response to an alert. You can assign rotating responsibilities for operator notification by using pagers. For example, if one or more defined alerts occur on Monday, Wednesday, or Friday, Mary is notified. If those alerts occur on Tuesday, Thursday, or Saturday, Joe is notified. If Mary or Joe cannot be notified on the respective day, or if the alert occurs on Sunday, the fail-safe operator is notified.

SQL Server Agent establishes its own mail session independent of SQL Mail. SQL Server Agent uses its own mail session to notify operators using email or pager notification. If you have defined SQL Server Agent to notify operators by net send only, you need not configure SQL Mail.

**SQL SERVER AGENT**   SQL Executive is now called SQL Server Agent. SQL Server Agent manages jobs, alerts, operators, and notifications, as well as replication jobs. SQL Server Agent allows multitasking, multischeduling, and multiserver and idle-time jobs.

**DEFINING OPERATORS**   The primary attributes of an operator are name and contact information. It is recommended that you define operators before you define alerts. You must set up one or more of these to notify an operator:

▼ A MAPI-1-compliant email client. SQL Server Agent requires a valid mail profile in order to send email. Examples of MAPI-1 clients include Microsoft Outlook and Microsoft Exchange clients.

■ Third-party paging software and hardware with SQL Mail.

■ You need these to use the electronic paging features.

▲ Microsoft Windows NT is required for you to use net send notifications.

**NAME AND CONTACT INFORMATION**   Every operator must have a name. Operator names must be unique and can be no longer than 128 characters. An operator's contact information defines how the operator is notified. Paging is implemented using email. To set up pager notification, you must install on the mail server software that processes inbound mail and converts it to a pager message. The software can take one of several approaches, including the following:

▼ Forwarding the mail to a remote mail server at the pager provider's site. The pager provider must offer this service, although the software required is generally available as part of the local mail system. For more information, see your pager documentation.

■ Routing the mail by way of the Internet to a mail server at the pager provider's site. This is a variation on the first approach.

■ Processing the inbound mail and dial using an attached modem. This software is proprietary to pager service providers. The software acts as a mail client that periodically processes its inbox either by interpreting all or part of the email address information as a pager number or by matching the email name to a pager number in a translation table. If all of the operators share a pager provider, you can use SQL Server Enterprise Manager to specify any special email formatting required by the pager-to-email system. The special formatting can be a prefix or a suffix. If you are using a low-capacity alphanumeric paging system (for example, limited to 64 characters per page), you can shorten the text sent by excluding the error text from the pager notification.

▲   Net send. The Net send notification method specifies the recipient (computer or user) of a network message. This method is not supported on Microsoft Windows 95 or later. Figure 20-3 shows you an example of how to set up an operator.

**DESIGNATING A FAIL-SAFE OPERATOR**   The fail-safe operator is notified about an alert after all pager notifications to the designated operators have failed. For example, if you have defined three operators for pager notifications and none of the designated operators can be paged, the fail-safe operator is notified. The fail-safe operator is notified when:

▼   The operator(s) responsible for the alert could not be paged. Reasons for this typically include incorrect pager addresses and off-duty operators.

■   SQL Server Agent cannot access system tables in MSDB database; in other words, the database is down—when the database is down, the SYSNOTIFICATIONS system table is unavailable.

▲   Because the fail-safe operator is a safety feature, you cannot delete the operator assigned to fail-safe duty. To get around this, you must reassign fail-safe duty to another operator or delete the fail-safe assignment before you can delete the account of the operator assigned to fail-safe duty.

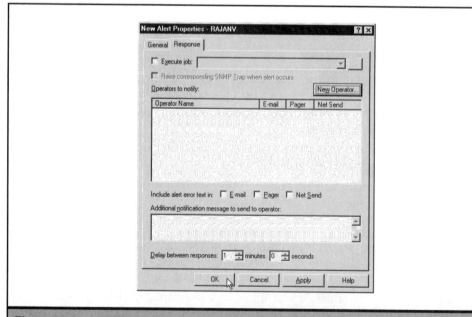

**Figure 20-3.**   SQL Server Agent New Alert Properties dialog box

## Alerts

An alert is a definition that matches one or more SQL Server events and contains the appropriate responses should those events occur. In general, an administrator cannot control the occurrence of events, but can control the response to those events with alerts. Alerts can be defined to respond to SQL Server events by the following:

▼ Notifying one or more operators

■ Raising an SNMP trap

■ Forwarding the event to another server

▲ Executing a job

**DEFINING ALERTS**    When errors, messages, or events are generated by SQL Server 7, they are entered into the Microsoft Windows NT application log. We find it useful to review this log from time to time. The SQL Server Agent works its magic by reading the application event log and comparing events to alerts that you have defined. When a match is found, an SQL Server 7 Agent fires off an alert. Figures 20-4 and 20-5 show examples of what you will need to complete when defining alerts.

Our experience has taught us that you should monitor the size of the Windows NT application event log to ensure it is of a sufficient size to house important SQL Server event information. Alerts must be defined before notifications can be sent. The primary attributes of an alert are name and event specification. Every alert must have a name. Alert names are governed by the same rules as names for jobs.

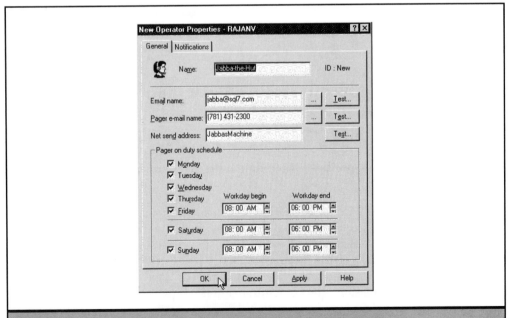

**Figure 20-4.**    New Alert Properties—Response

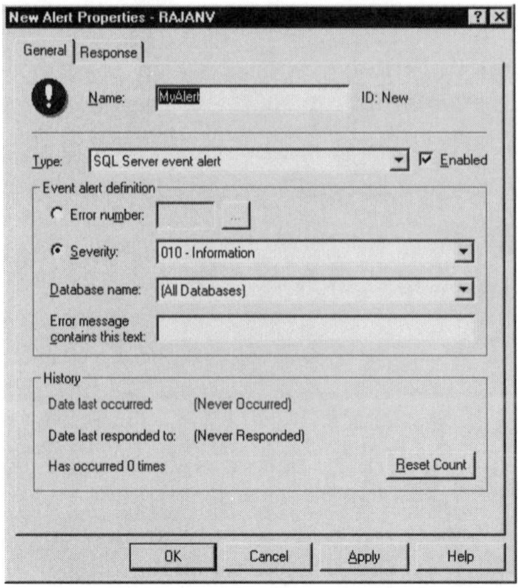

**Figure 20-5.** New Operator Properties—General

**SELECTING AN EVENT** You can specify an alert to occur in response to one or more events. You specify the set of events to trigger an alert according to the following:

▼ **A specific error number**—SQL Server Agent fires an alert when a specific error occurs.

■ **Severity level**—SQL Server Agent fires an alert when a certain category of event occurs.

■ **Database**—This specifies a database in which the event occurred if you want to restrict the alert to a specific database.

▲ **Event text**—This specifies a text string in the event message if you want to restrict the alert.

**CREATING A USER-DEFINED EVENT MESSAGE** You can create user-defined event messages if you have special event tracking needs that are not addressed by standard SQL Server event messages. User-defined event messages generate error numbers greater than 50,000. Additionally, you can then assign them a severity level. Then, a class of alerts can be written to fire when that severity level is raised. User-defined event messages must be unique and have a unique error number and unique language.

When using SQL Server Enterprise Manager, you should select the Always write to Windows NT eventlog option. By default, user-defined messages with a severity less than 19 are not sent to the Windows NT application event log when they occur, and therefore do not trigger SQL Server Agent alerts.

If you administer a multiple-language SQL Server environment, you should create user-defined messages in each of the languages that you support. For example, if you are creating a new event message that will be used on both an English and a French server (e.g., "Houston, we have a problem" or "M. Houston, nous avons une problème"), use the same event number for both but assign a different language for each.

### Defining Jobs, Operators, and Alerts

To define jobs, operators, and alerts you can use the following:

▼ SQL Server Enterprise Manager

■ Transact-SQL scripts

▲ SQL-DMO objects

Regardless of what method you use to define your administrative tasks, they do not run automatically until the SQL Server Agent service has been started.

# RESPONDING TO EVENTS

Microsoft SQL Server 7 events are written to the Microsoft Windows NT application event log. You can define an alert on one or more events to specify how SQL Server Agent should respond. SQL Server Agent monitors the Windows NT application event log for SQL Server events. When events that you have defined for action occur, SQL Server Agent automatically responds according to your specifications. For example, if an event of severity 17 occurs, you can specify that an operator be notified immediately.

Automated event response is called *alerting*. When an event occurs, SQL Server Agent compares the event details against the alerts defined by the SQL Server administrator. If it finds a match, SQL Server Agent performs the defined response.

You can define alerts to do the following:

▼ Notify operators

■ Raise an SNMP trap

■ Execute a job

▲ Forward the event to the Windows NT application event log on another server

The Microsoft Windows 95 version of SQL Server Agent uses a SQL Server Profiler trace to support alerting. Alert forwarding and SNMP traps are not available in Windows 95.

# Forwarding Events

You can forward all Microsoft SQL Server 7 event messages that meet or exceed a specific error severity level to one server running SQL Server. You can use event forwarding to enable centralized alert management for a group of servers by selecting a server with less traffic to be the alerts management server. In this way, you can reduce the workload on heavily used servers. In a multiserver environment, it is recommended that you designate the master server as the alerts management server. Advantages of setting up an alerts-forwarding server include the following:

▼ **Centralization**—Centralized control and a consolidated view of the events of several SQL Servers is possible from a single server.

■ **Scalability**—Many physical servers can be administered as one logical server. You can add or remove servers to this physical server group as needed.

▲ **Efficiency**—Configuration time is reduced because you need to define alerts and operators only once at one server.

## Disadvantages

Disadvantages of setting up an alerts management server include the following:

▼ **Increased traffic**—Forwarding events to an alerts management server can increase network traffic, although this can be moderated by restricting event forwarding to severity events only above a designated level.

■ **Single point of failure**—If there is a problem with the management server, the delivery of the alerts will be interrupted.

▲ **Server load**—Handling alerts for the forwarded events causes an increased processing load at the alerts-forwarding server.

## Guidelines

When configuring event forwarding, follow these guidelines:

▼ Avoid running critical or heavily used applications on the alerts-forwarding server.

■ Avoid configuring many servers to share the same forwarding server. If congestion results, reduce the number of servers that use a particular alerts management server.

■ The servers that are registered within a server's SQL Server Enterprise Manager constitute the list of servers available to be chosen by that server as the alerts-forwarding server.

■ Define alerts that require a server-specific response on the local server instead of forwarding them.

- The alerts-forwarding server views all the servers forwarding to it as a logical whole. For example, an alerts-forwarding server responds in the same way to a 605 event from server A and a 605 event from server B.

- After configuring your alert system, periodically check the Microsoft Windows NT application event log for SQL Server Agent events.

▲ Failure conditions encountered by the alerts engine are written to the local Windows NT application event log with a source name of SQL Server Agent. For example, if SQL Server Agent cannot send an email notification as it has been defined, an event is logged in the application event log.

If a locally defined alert is disabled and an event occurs that would have caused the alert to fire, the event is forwarded to the alerts-forwarding server. This allows local overrides (alerts defined locally that are also defined at the alerts-forwarding server) to be turned off and on as needed by the user at the local site. You can also request that events always be forwarded, even if they are handled by local alerts.

# MULTISERVER ADMINISTRATION

Wow! This, in our experience, should really get the juices flowing. In most organizations today, databases and their respective servers are spread across the entire enterprise. What this means is that you need someone there for the care and feeding of these machines and the databases that live on them. You are probably saying, "So what, this is something I have gotten used to." With SQL Server 7, you don't have to settle for that. You can centrally control and administer any server or database from a central location. This has a tremendous impact on the cost involved in maintaining your data mart, not to mention the integrity of the data and database. Multiserver administration is the process of automating administration across multiple servers in a network. You can benefit from multiserver administration if you:

▼ Manage three or more servers

▲ Schedule information flows between enterprise servers for data warehousing

A multiserver administration configuration consists of at least one master server and at least one target server. A master server distributes jobs to and receives events from networked target servers. A master server stores the central copy of job definitions for jobs run on target servers. Target servers periodically connect to their master server to update their list of jobs to perform. If a new job exists, the target server downloads the job and disconnects from the master server. Once the target server completes the job, it reconnects to the master server and reports the job status. Figure 20-6 is a simple example of multiserver administration with more than one target and one master server.

For example, if you administer departmental servers across a large corporation, you can define one backup job (complete with job steps), operators to notify in case of failure, and an execution schedule. You can write this backup job one time on the master server,

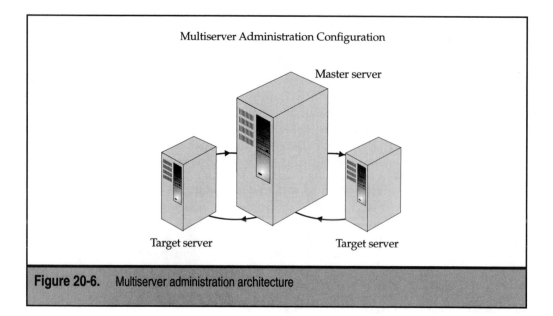

**Figure 20-6.** Multiserver administration architecture

then enlist each departmental server as a target server in the master server. In this way, all the departmental servers can run the same backup job even though you defined it only one time.

Multiserver administration features are intended for members of the sysadmin role. However, a member of the sysadmin role on the target server cannot edit the operations performed on the target server by the master server. This security measure prevents accidental deletion of job steps and interruption of operations on the target server.

## Defining Multiserver Jobs

The Make Master Server Wizard assists you in designating your system as multiserver. It takes you through the steps to:

▼ Check the security settings for the SQL Server Agent service and the Microsoft SQL Server service on all servers that will become target servers (TSX). Both services must be running in Microsoft Windows NT domain accounts.

■ Check that all servers in the multiserver configuration are running SQL Server 7.

▲ Define a job and select one or more target servers.

You can define a Windows NT server running SQL Server Agent to be the master server. You can enlist other servers running SQL Server Agent to be the target servers. Each target server reports only to one master server, which must be running Windows NT Server. The target server can be running any of the platforms supported by SQL Server. Figures 20-7 and 20-8 highlight the Welcome screen for the Make Master Wizard and allows you to specify the destination for notifications.

# Multiserver Administration Components

You must define the components of multiserver administration to create multiserver jobs. Let's look at these pieces individually.

## Master Server

We suggest that you define your master server on a nonproduction server so production is not slowed down by target server traffic. This is very important; otherwise, you will create a performance bottleneck. If you forward events to this nonproduction master server, you can centralize administration on one server. To set up a master server, you must define a master server operator (MSXOperator) on the master server. If you want to dismantle a multiserver configuration, you must defect all the target servers from the MSX master server.

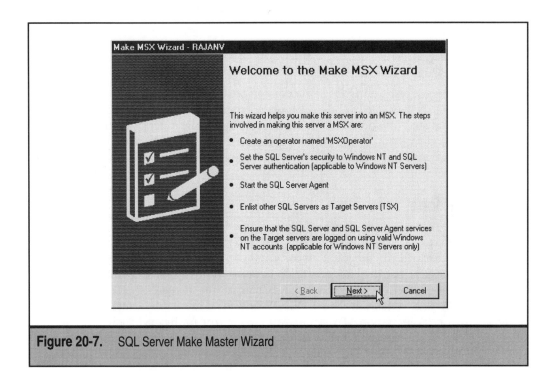

**Figure 20-7.**    SQL Server Make Master Wizard

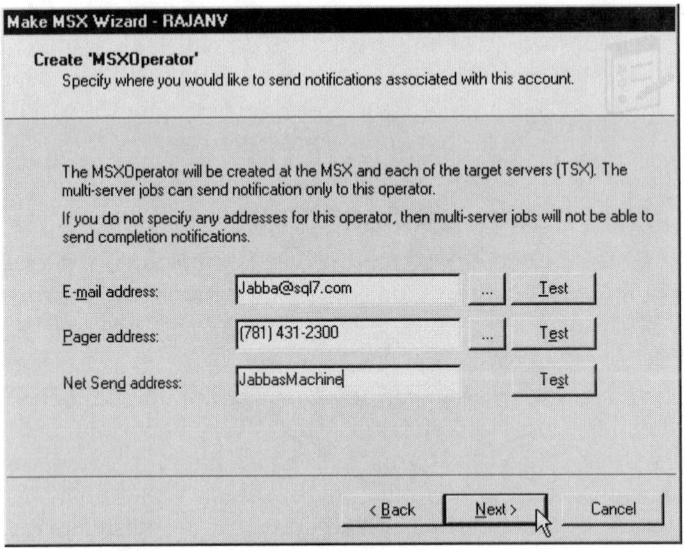

**Figure 20-8.** Specifying where to send notifications

## Target Server

A target server must be running the same version of SQL Server as the master server. You can enlist target servers into and defect target servers from the master server. A target server can be enlisted into only one master server. You must defect a target server from one master before you can enlist it into a different one. If you change a target server's computer name, you must defect it before changing the name and reenlist it after the change.

## Multiserver Jobs

You create jobs for multiple servers in much the same way that you create jobs for stand-alone servers. For a multiserver job, you must also specify one or more nonlocal target servers that will run the job. You can create a job from the Multi Server Jobs node on the master server. You then assign the job to one or more target servers. When a target server polls (periodically connects to) the master server, it reads the sysdownloadlist table in the MSDB database. The SYSDOWNLOADLIST table contains operations assigned to the target server. These operations control multiserver jobs and various aspects of the target server's behavior. Examples of operations are deleting a job, inserting a job, starting a job, and updating the target server's polling interval.

Operations are posted to the SYSDOWNLOADLIST table in one of two ways:

▼ Explicitly, by using **sp_post_msx_operation**.

▲ Implicitly, by using other job stored procedures.

If you use job stored procedures to modify multiserver job schedules or job steps, or SQL-DMO objects to control multiserver jobs, issue the commands shown in the next listing after modifying a multiserver job's steps or schedules to keep the target servers synchronized with the current job definition:

```
execute msdb.dbo.sp_post_msx_operation 'DELETE', 'JOB', '<job id>'
execute msdb.dbo.sp_post_msx_operation 'INSERT', 'JOB', '<job id>'
```

You do not have to post operations explicitly if you use

▼ SQL Server Enterprise Manager to control multiserver jobs

▲ Job stored procedures that do not modify job schedules or job steps

The bottom line—SQL Server 7 is more highly automated than earlier versions of SQL Server and does a better job of automatically configuring itself to meet processing demands. These features lower the potential for exception conditions that would trigger alerts. Scheduled jobs remain a good feature for implementing recurring tasks such as backup procedures. This chapter has given you a flavor of the power of jobs and alerts, and what they can do in SQL Server 7. Naturally, we have simply touched the tip of the iceberg.

Speaking of the iceberg…remember what we all found out that fateful night in the North Atlantic (most of us, of course, were not there, but we sure have found out a lot about it anyway!). It was a night to remember, a Titanic adventure. The morsel of ice that the starboard side of the ship hit was only the tip of a huge submerged mountain of ice. Data warehousing has many pitfalls and menaces looming below the surface as well. It is a reorientation for many of the team's players. Plan the technology; plan the team; plan the outcome; plan the tools! Get the finished product to the desktop in a reasonable time frame before your hungry user community loses interest. The SQL Server 7 journey is now complete. Please take all your belongings as you leave the warehouse. As this is the termination of this trip, we wish you all a pleasant stay in wherever your data warehouse/decision support journey ends up taking you…and to all a good night!

# Index

**S**

## U

## V

**WARNING: BEFORE OPENING THE DISC PACKAGE, CAREFULLY READ THE TERMS AND CONDITIONS OF THE FOLLOWING COPYRIGHT STATEMENT AND LIMITED CD-ROM WARRANTY.**

### Copyright Statement

This software is protected by both United States copyright law and international copyright treaty provision. Except as noted in the contents of the CD-ROM, you must treat this software just like a book. However, you may copy it into a computer to be used and you may make archival copies of the software for the sole purpose of backing up the software and protecting your investment from loss. By saying, "just like a book," The McGraw-Hill Companies, Inc. ("Osborne/McGraw-Hill") means, for example, that this software may be used by any number of people and may be freely moved from one computer location to another, so long as there is no possibility of its being used at one location or on one computer while it is being used at another. Just as a book cannot be read by two different people in two different places at the same time, neither can the software be used by two different people in two different places at the same time.

### Limited Warranty

Osborne/McGraw-Hill warrants the physical compact disc enclosed herein to be free of defects in materials and workmanship for a period of sixty days from the purchase date. If the CD included in your book has defects in materials or workmanship, please call McGraw-Hill at 1-800-217-0059, 9am to 5pm, Monday through Friday, Eastern Standard Time, and McGraw-Hill will replace the defective disc.

The entire and exclusive liability and remedy for breach of this Limited Warranty shall be limited to replacement of the defective disc, and shall not include or extend to any claim for or right to cover any other damages, including but not limited to, loss of profit, data, or use of the software, or special incidental, or consequential damages or other similar claims, even if Osborne/McGraw-Hill has been specifically advised of the possibility of such damages. In no event will Osborne/McGraw-Hill's liability for any damages to you or any other person ever exceed the lower of the suggested list price or actual price paid for the license to use the software, regardless of any form of the claim.

OSBORNE/McGRAW-HILL SPECIFICALLY DISCLAIMS ALL OTHER WARRANTIES, EXPRESS OR IMPLIED, INCLUDING BUT NOT LIMITED TO, ANY IMPLIED WARRANTY OF MERCHANTABILITY OR FITNESS FOR A PARTICULAR PURPOSE. Specifically, Osborne/McGraw-Hill makes no representation or warranty that the software is fit for any particular purpose, and any implied warranty of merchantability is limited to the sixty-day duration of the Limited Warranty covering the physical disc only (and not the software), and is otherwise expressly and specifically disclaimed.

This limited warranty gives you specific legal rights; you may have others which may vary from state to state. Some states do not allow the exclusion of incidental or consequential damages, or the limitation on how long an implied warranty lasts, so some of the above may not apply to you.

This agreement constitutes the entire agreement between the parties relating to use of the Product. The terms of any purchase order shall have no effect on the terms of this Agreement. Failure of Osborne/McGraw-Hill to insist at any time on strict compliance with this Agreement shall not constitute a waiver of any rights under this Agreement. This Agreement shall be construed and governed in accordance with the laws of New York. If any provision of this Agreement is held to be contrary to law, that provision will be enforced to the maximum extent permissible, and the remaining provisions will remain in force and effect.

NO TECHNICAL SUPPORT IS PROVIDED WITH THIS CD-ROM.

# About the CD

The enclosed CD-ROM includes SQL Server 7 Evaluation Edition, which expires 120 days after installation.

## SYSTEM REQUIREMENTS

▼ PC with Pentium or Alpha processor (166 MHz or higher)

■ Microsoft Windows 95, Windows 98, or Windows NT Workstation 4.0, Windows NT Server 4.0, or Windows NT Server Enterprise Edition (Service Pack 4 or higher is required for all Windows NT versions)

■ 32MB RAM

■ Microsoft Internet Explorer 4.01 with Service Pack 1 or later

■ Hard-disk space required:

    ■ Typical installation: 185MB for a typical installation (plus an additional 20MB for English Query)

    ■ Minimum installation: 80MB

■ Takes advantage of up to two processors

■ CD-ROM drive

■ VGA or higher resolution monitor; Super VGA recommended

▲ Microsoft Mouse or compatible pointing device

This program was reproduced by Osborne/McGraw-Hill under a special arrangement with Microsoft Corporation. For this reason, Osborne/McGraw-Hill is responsible for the product warranty and for support. If your CD is defective, please return it to Osborne/McGraw-Hill, which will arrange for its replacement. PLEASE DO NOT RETURN IT TO MICROSOFT CORPORATION for product support. End users of this Microsoft program shall not be considered "registered owners" of a Microsoft product and therefore shall not be eligible for upgrades, promotions or other benefits available to "registered owners" of Microsoft products.